AS Business Studies

SECOND EDITION

AS Business Studies
SECOND EDITION

MALCOLM SURRIDGE & ANDREW GILLESPIE

Hodder Arnold

A MEMBER OF THE HODDER HEADLINE GROUP

Orders: please contact Bookpoint Ltd, 130 Milton Park, Abingdon,
Oxon OX14 4SB. Telephone: (44) 01235 827720, Fax: (44) 01235
400454. Lines are open from 9.00 – 6.00, Monday to Saturday, with a
24 hour message answering service. You can also order through our
website www.hoddereducation.co.uk.

British Library Cataloguing in Publication Data
A catalogue record for this title is available from the British Library

ISBN-10: 0 340 88541 6
ISBN-13: 978 0 340 88541 3

First published 2004
Impression number   10 9 8 7 6 5 4 3 2
Year   2008 2007 2006 2005

Artwork on page 102 by Tom Cross.
Cover image by Fusako Akimoto.
Typeset by Fakenham Photosetting Limited, Fakenham, Norfolk.
Printed in Dubai for Hodder Education, a division of
Hodder Headline, 338 Euston Road, London NW1 3BH.

Contents

Acknowledgements		**vi**
1	**Introduction**	**1**
2	**Objectives and strategies**	**5**
	Setting up in business	5
	Types of business	21
	Business objectives	30
	Stakeholders	39
	Business strategy	44
3	**Marketing**	**57**
	What is marketing?	57
	Market research	62
	Market analysis	68
	Marketing objectives, strategy and tactics	74
	The product life cycle and portfolio analysis	80
	Marketing mix	91
	Elasticity of demand	104
4	**Accounting and finance**	**114**
	Profits, costs and revenues	114
	Break-even analysis	121
	Cash flow forecasting and management	131
	Sources of finance	141
	Budgets	149
	Cost centres and profit centres	158
5	**People and organisations**	**169**
	Organisational structures	169
	Theories of motivation	180
	Motivation in practice	191
	Planning and developing the workforce	202
	Leadership and management styles	211
6	**Operations management**	**226**
	What is operations management?	226
	Types of production	231
	The scale of production	236
	Stock control	243
	Productivity	253
	Quality	258
	Lean production	265
7	**External influences**	**277**
	Markets, competition and the business cycle	277
	Interest rates and exchange rates	289
	Inflation and unemployment	298
	Business and the law	306
	Ethics and social responsibility	317
	Technological change	325
	Index	**337**

Acknowledgements

Many people contributed to the creation of this book. We are grateful to the team at Hodder & Stoughton for their patience, good humour and attention to detail. David Linnell offered numerous suggestions regarding the text, improving the final version in many ways. This process was continued by Anna Clark without whom the book would have contained numerous errors and would have been much longer! Thanks also to Alexia Chan and Tessa Heath for their work on this latest edition.

Thanks to Ali for her smiles and inspirational ideas, and to his beautiful baby daughter Clemency, from Andrew Gillespie. Thanks also to Jamie, Jonathon, Eleanor, Connie, Joss and Alexander.

The authors and publishers would like to thank the following for permission to reproduce copyright illustrative material:

© Anna Clopet/CORBIS p. 236; © Assignments Photographers/CORBIS p. 17; © BDI Images pp. 136, 286; © Bettmann/CORBIS p. 77; © Bo Zaunders/CORBIS p. 161; © Catherine Karnow/ CORBIS p. 261; © Christopher Farina/CORBIS p. 214; © CORBIS p. 182; © Elder Neville/Corbis Sygma p. 91 (image b); Fiat p. 71 (3 images); © George Hall/CORBIS p. 327; © Kamal Kishore/ Reuters/CORBIS p. 278; © Najlah Feanny/ CORBIS p. 248; Nick Nicholson p. 85; PA Photos/ Barry Batchelor p. 188; © Patrik Giardino/ CORBIS p. 254; © Peter Aprahamian/CORBIS p. 91 (image a); © Rex Features 2004 p. 47; © Rex Features 2004/Alex Segre p. 300; © Rex Features 2004/Jonathan Banks p. 58; © Robert Maass/ CORBIS p. 49; © Tim Graham/CORBIS p. 135;

and the following for permission to reproduce text material:

BPI p. 63; Cadbury Schweppes plc pp. 70, 222–223; Dyson p. 17; Financial Times pp. 27, 228, 246; IFPI p. 68; In-Stat/MDR p. 81; Innocent Ltd p. 9; Lands' End, Inc. p. 97; Nexus Technology Limited p. 176; Ovenu p. 8; Philip Allan Updates p. 17; Pilkington plc p. 78; Professional Researcher p. 177; Telegraph Group Limited pp. 125, 178, 213, 222-223; Tesco plc pp. 46, 265; © 2003 Time Inc./Fortune pp 7, 34; Walkers Snack Foods Limited p. 78; World Markets Research Centre p. 254; Sunday Times pp. 34, 75, 270; © The Guardian/Nick Pandya p. 196; © The Guardian/ Patrick Butler p. 207; © The Guardian/David Gow p. 319; © The Guardian/David Gow & Geoff Gibbs p. 332; © The Guardian/Paul Brown p. 334; © The Observer/Oliver Morgan p. 326.

© Crown copyright material on pp. 13, 145, 284, 298, 299 and 300 is reproduced with the permission of the controller of HMSO and the Queen's Printer for Scotland.

Every effort has been made to obtain necessary permission with reference to copyright material. The publishers apologise if inadvertently and sources remain unacknowledged and will be glad to make the necessary arrangements at the earliest opportunity.

Introduction

Aim and organisation

This textbook provides a comprehensive coverage of the Business Studies specification material of all the major examination boards at AS level. It is written by two senior examiners who have been closely involved in the development and examination of the subject at this level. Because of this, the book provides a clear insight into the knowledge and skills required to achieve the highest grades in this new examination.

The book is divided into seven main chapters:

- Introduction
- Objectives and strategies
- Marketing
- Accounting and finance
- People and organisations
- Operations management
- External influences

Within each of these chapters, the book is divided into relevant units which cover a particular aspect of the specification. For example, within Marketing (Chapter 3) we examine areas such as market research, marketing strategy and the marketing mix.

Each individual unit contains various features to prepare you fully for your exams. These features include the following:

- **Business in focus** – these are excellent examples of business activity to highlight points covered in the text and provide you with greater understanding of key topics. They present some good examples to use in your exams.
- **People in business** – these are features on some of the most important figures in business, such as Richard Branson of Virgin, Charles Dunstone of The Carphone Warehouse and Bill Gates of Microsoft. If you have ever wondered how to make a million, read these!
- **Points to ponder** – these are specific points or stories to make you think a bit more about certain business issues.
- **Key issues** – this feature highlights some of the current issues in business and, hopefully, will keep you ahead of the competition in terms of your knowledge of business. For example, we look at recent developments in technology and the development of the Single European Currency, and examine the implications of these for UK firms.
- **Examiner's advice** – we hope you will find this feature absolutely invaluable. Throughout the book we highlight common mistakes that students make in exams and show you how to avoid them! We also give advice on how to answer questions, different ways of approaching topics and try to help you to use your knowledge to maximise your grade.
- **Maths moments** – where appropriate, we give you advice on how to carry out relevant calculations and prepare for the mathematical parts of the specification. This is an aspect of business studies that many students find difficult. We have tried to show you how easy it can be and how you can use calculations to support your answers.
- **Application in action** – in these features we show you how to apply your understanding to different business scenarios and industries – a vital skill at AS level.

At the end of each unit, we provide a series of questions designed to review the material in that section; we also provide several data response or case study questions to help you to apply the information you have learnt. After each chapter, there are also several typical exam questions for you to practise. All the answers to these questions are provided in the *AS Business Studies Second Edition Teacher's Resource CD-ROM* (ISBN 0340 885 408).

We hope you will find the book useful in your studies and that it proves a valuable course companion.

Researching in business studies

Your understanding of this subject will benefit from reading as much as you can about what is happening in the business world. Although you will not be tested directly on your knowledge of actual business events, the more you can find out about what firms are doing the better, as this will help you to apply your understanding. Try to follow recent stories in the press and read the business section of one of the main newspapers at least once a week. Also, look out for programmes on the television: a variety of programmes are broadcast covering different aspects of business activity. These are well worth watching because they help to integrate your understanding of the subject by pulling together all the different elements.

The Internet is also a superb place to look for information on organisations. You might want to look at sites such as *www.Biz-ed.ac.uk* which offers a number of different resources or any of the major newspaper sites (such as *www.guardianunlimited.co.uk*) where you can search for relevant articles under key words.

Skills and exams

To do well in your exams, it is important to demonstrate different examination skills. A good exam performance is based on a sound knowledge of the subject and the ability to relate this information to the particular question and situation. Success in AS Level Business Studies requires knowledge plus skills!

There are four main skills you will need to demonstrate to succeed at AS:

1 First, you will need to **demonstrate knowledge** of the particular topic.
2 You will also have to **apply this information** to the particular situation or industry and explain your ideas.
3 An important skill is that of **analysis**. Writing

analytically means you have to develop your ideas by following a line of argument. Think '*why?*' and consider the causes and consequences of any of the ideas you put forward.
4 **Evaluation** is sometimes called the key to high marks. This skill requires you to weigh up different ideas and come to a conclusion about their relative importance.

Skills and questions

It is important to recognise the skills required by different types of question. For example, if the question asks you to *explain* your ideas, you simply have to state what they are and what they mean. If it asks you to *discuss*, you must develop your ideas in some depth and consider how important they are. As a rough guide the more marks a question has, the more likely it is you will need to *analyse* and *evaluate*. Also, you will see that the command words (or verbs) used in a question provide a good indication of what the examiner is looking for. Words such as *state* or *list* simply require basic information, whilst phrases like '*To what extent . . . ?* mean you need to write a longer answer containing analysis and evaluation.

Do try and look at recent exam papers and mark schemes to get an understanding of what the examiners are looking for. You should also try and get hold of the Chief Examiner's report which reviews candidates' performances in a particular exam and highlights good and bad practice. Remember, examination skills are like any other skill: they cannot be gained in a few hours or even a few days. You need to practise past papers regularly to acquire these skills.

Mark schemes

Your exams will be marked using a 'levels of response' mark scheme. This means that the examiner will read your script and look for the level of skills you have demonstrated. If you have explained something well, this is a higher level than if you have explained it rather weakly, for example. To achieve the highest grades, you have to demonstrate the different skills at the highest level. However, remember that all your skills are based upon your subject knowledge. Without this you cannot make progress.

Table 1.1 shows a typical mark scheme for a 10 mark question. You can see from this mark scheme that all the skills are being assessed. This means it is in response to a question that asked candidates to evaluate. Each skill is assessed separately and within each skill a level of response approach is used. If you were to show limited analysis, for example, you could only get a maximum of 1 mark for this skill.

You can see the importance of making your points, developing them and then weighing them up. If you were to simply apply your ideas but do nothing more with them, you could only get the marks for content and application (4 marks out of 10).

One of the most common mistakes made by students in examinations is to spend too much time on the lower skills and not enough on analysis and evaluation. Whilst a sound knowledge of topics is essential, for the higher marks you must do something with these ideas and show why they matter and why they are important. For the high mark questions, you need to develop a line of argument and not just have lots of undeveloped points. A few points developed fully is much better than a list of ideas – no matter how long the list is.

It is important to do exactly what the question asks of you. If the question simply asks you to explain two ideas, this is precisely what you should do. Do not waste valuable time explaining more than two or analysing your ideas if the question does not require it.

Higher level skills

The higher level skills are the ability to analyse and to evaluate. When analysing a point you are trying to demonstrate a detailed understanding of what it is, why it matters and/or what factors might affect its importance. For example, the idea that a higher price may lead to a fall in sales is relatively straightforward. To analyse this you might want to consider issues such as the nature of the good, the sensitivity of demand to price and the degree of customer loyalty. To evaluate you must demonstrate judgement. You have to think about the points you have made and comment on what determines their significance. For example, having outlined a series of actions a firm could take, you should suggest which one is most likely and why. Or having suggested the different ways in which a firm might be affected by a change in its circumstances, you should suggest and explain which outcome is most probable.

Essentially, evaluation is based around the idea that any decision depends on the nature of the situation. There are thousands of organisations in the world operating with different technologies, different customers and different resources. The way in which one firm reacts to a situation or is affected by change will vary and you must demonstrate that you understand this. Try to think what will make one outcome more likely than another. And you must explain your reasoning. When you evaluate, you have to develop two sides of an argument, weigh up the different factors on each side and come to a conclusion about their importance. You might use phrases like these: '*This factor might be particularly important when . . .*' or '*In these circumstances the firm is likely to do X rather than Y because . . .*'.

Content 2 marks	Application 2 marks	Analysis 3 marks	Evaluation 3 marks
2 marks: candidate identifies two relevant factors	2 marks: good application	3–2 marks: good analysis	3–2 marks: good evaluation
1 mark: candidate identifies one relevant factor	1 mark: limited application	1 mark: limited analysis	1 mark: limited evaluation
0 marks: no relevant content	0 marks: no application present	0 marks: no analysis present	0 marks: no evaluation present

Table 1.1 *A sample mark scheme*

Remember that it is better to develop a few ideas in depth rather than just list points: you don't need 10 points for a 10 mark question – you only need two or three. It is also important to write in full sentences. It is almost impossible to analyse or evaluate using bullet points, so make sure you write in prose.

Examination advice
Timing

One of the main challenges of all examinations is timing. Whatever you do, make sure you actually finish the exam and answer all the questions. If you have not written it, the examiner cannot mark it! This means that you need to know in advance how long each examination lasts and how many questions you will be expected to answer in that time. It is helpful to practise as many past paper questions as you can, and to complete many of them working under timed conditions.

Once you are actually in the exam room, you need to allocate your time appropriately. This means that you have to make sure that you have enough time for the higher mark questions (i.e. do not spend too long on the small mark ones!) and that you do not get stuck on one question – leave enough time to complete all the questions.

Read the question!

Make sure you read the questions thoroughly. Unfortunately, some candidates know quite a lot about a particular topic but do not use their information effectively because they do not answer the actual question set. In some cases, they answer the question they wish they had been asked rather than the one they were actually asked!

Here are two important tips:

1 Look at the command word of the question to see which skills you have to demonstrate. For example, is it asking you to explain, analyse or evaluate?
2 Read each word of the question and look for any words that should be referred to specifically in the answer. Does the question refer to a 'small' firm? a 'rapid' change? a 'new' policy? This helps with higher level skills.

Preparation

To prepare thoroughly for your exams, read each of the units in this book carefully and make sure you have good notes on them. Also, look at all the different features, because they will help build on the basic text. For example, the **Business in focus** features will allow you to support your ideas with relevant, modern examples of these concepts in practice. Complete all the review questions at the end of each section to ensure you have a good grasp of the material. Revise in an organised and methodical way. Preparation is the key to exam success.

We hope this book will give you knowledge, skills and added confidence – good luck!

Objectives and strategies   2

Introduction

- An introduction to business
- How can businesses be classified?
- How and why do people set up in business?
- What are the different forms of organisation?
- Why do aims and objectives differ from one firm to another?
- How do firms achieve their objectives?

>> Setting up in business

What is business?

The word 'business' is actually derived from the idea of 'busy-ness'. This idea of 'busy-ness' quite accurately describes most organisations: they are busy organising resources, producing, selling, managing people and keeping track of the finances. The people running the business have to organise people, money, materials and machines to produce a good or service (a product) to sell or exchange with their customers.

> ### Key terms
>
> A **good** is a physical product such as a car.
> A **service** is an intangible item such as education and financial advice.
> A **product** is a more general term covering goods and services.

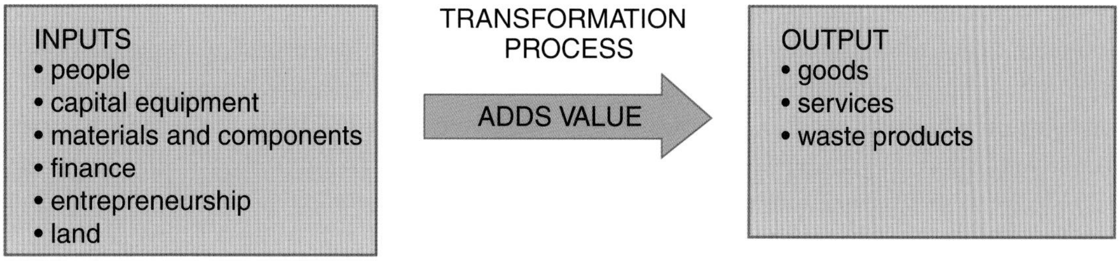

Figure 2.1 *The transformation from inputs to output adds value*

Types of business

There are, of course, hundreds of thousands of types of firms producing goods and services in the economy. Businesses can be classified in several ways.

Classifying businesses by sector

- The primary sector comprises firms involved in extractive industries, such as mining, fishing and forestry.
- The secondary sector comprises businesses involved in manufacturing, such as the car industry and firms producing personal computers.
- The tertiary sector consists of organisations in the service sector, such as universities, banks and the travel industry.

In the UK, the tertiary sector has been growing in importance whilst the secondary sector has been declining. The primary sector is very small indeed in the UK.

Classifying firms according to size

Firms are often classified according to their size. The size of a firm can be measured in terms of:

- the value of its sales revenue
- the share of the market it has (e.g. Ford sells 30% of all the cars sold in the UK)
- the number of workers employed
- the value of the things it owns (the items owned by a firm are called its assets).

The most appropriate way of measuring the size of a firm depends on the industry you are considering. For taxi firms or haulage firms, it may make sense to measure the number of vehicles; in the retail sector (shops) you may want to measure the number of outlets a firm has. In some cases, a firm will be big using one measure of size but small using other measures! If you look at the National Health Service, for example, it has thousands of employees but does not generate sales revenue.

Inputs, outputs and transformation

The process of business involves turning inputs into outputs. Firms take resources and transform these in some way to produce a product. Thus, a brewery uses hops, malt and water, as well as labour services, the brewery buildings and machinery, as inputs. The outputs are beer or lager. To be successful, the value of the outputs needs to be greater than the value of the inputs. In other words, the selling price of the beer must exceed the cost of the inputs. In this way, the organisation 'adds value'.

Over time the nature of the goods and services produced and the way we produce them has changed considerably. New technology, new markets, changes in customer tastes and employee needs have all led to revolutions in the various aspects of business activity. You only need to look at the incredible growth of the Internet and the thousands of new products launched in our shops each year to help you appreciate how rapid the rate of change is in the business world. DVDs, computer games, flat-screen televisions and Internet shopping from supermarkets are all relatively new products or services. The business world is always changing, with new firms developing and others ending. This is what makes business so fascinating to watch and study, and why those involved in business have to monitor their markets very closely all the time.

However, despite the incredible amount of change occurring in the business world the basic elements of all businesses remain the same:

- resources
- a transformation process to add value
- output
- managers to plan, organise, coordinate and control the whole process.

The most successful organisations are those which can manage this transformation process most effectively. This means that they use their resources efficiently and do not waste them, and that they produce goods and services which their customers value highly. The 'best' firms offer customers excellent products and, at the same time, add a great deal of value for their owners.

At the moment, organisations such as Microsoft, Tesco and Ryanair are thought of as highly successful. However, even they cannot guarantee success in the future. Markets change, new competitors emerge, customers' tastes change, managers and employees leave. These developments can turn organisations from being winners into losers very rapidly. Marks & Spencer was regarded as an excellent British business in the 1980s and early 1990s; by the year 2000 it was attacked for poor management and disappointing financial performance.

Some firms, such as Cadbury, have existed for over 100 years. By comparison, some of the biggest businesses in the world, such as Microsoft and AOL, are relatively new. As the business world changes, re-shapes and develops organisations must look for the new opportunities this creates and, also, be aware of the possible dangers.

To see how Marks & Spencer, AOL and Microsoft are doing now, visit: *www.marksandspencer.com/thecompany*, *www.aoltimewarner.com* and *www.microsoft.com*.

POINTS TO PONDER

As of January 2004, the five largest companies on the UK Stock Exchange were as follows:

Rank	Company	Market value £m
1	BP	100 589
2	HSBC	97 309
3	Vodafone	95 109
4	Glaxo Smith Kline	77 306
5	Royal Bank of Scotland	48 675

Table 2.1 *The UK's five largest companies*

POINTS TO PONDER

In 2003 the ten most admired companies in the world were as follows:

Rank	Company	Business activity
1	Wal-Mart Stores	retailer
2	General Electric	conglomerate, including jet engines, power generation, financial services and plastics
3	Microsoft	computing
4	Dell Computer	PC manufacturer and retailer
5	Johnson & Johnson	healthcare and hygiene products
6	Berkshire Hathaway	investment business
7	Procter & Gamble	manufacturer of family, household and personal care products
8	IBM	computing
9	Coca-Cola	soft drinks
10	FedEx	delivery service

Table 2.2 *The world's ten most admired companies*

The process of managing a business is, therefore, a tremendously challenging one. It involves ensuring the right mix of inputs, the development of an efficient transformation process and the production of goods and services that customers want.

Customers' needs change (think of the decline in tea consumption in the UK), the goods and services available change, and the possible inputs change (e.g. new technology) – all of which makes management an ever-changing challenge.

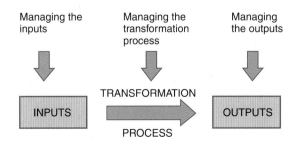

Figure 2.2 *Managing a business*

Business in focus

Rik Hellewell owns Ovenu, an oven cleaning service in the UK. Hellewell left school at 16 and became an apprentice with a local engineering firm; he soon left and joined a carpet and upholstery business. He knew he did not like working in factories and that he wanted to be 'master of his own destiny', but it took ten years to make the final decision to leave. He spent £500 designing and building a portable cleaning tank that could be used to clean ovens; he also developed his own cleaning substances. Then he registered his ideas at the Patent Office. His business idea is simple: he visits your home and cleans your ovens, hobs and microwaves. It appeals to busy people whose time is at a premium, or people who would rather restore their appliance than buy a new one. In Hellewell's first year he cleaned 368 ovens. Five years later he started selling the idea, the cleaning products he had developed and the Ovenu name. He now has 85 people with their own Ovenu businesses who pay him an initial £7250 and then a monthly fee of £145. Between them they clean over 50 000 ovens a year.

Source: Adapted from www.ovenu.co.uk

1 What do you think are the main factors that will determine the success of Ovenu in the future?

- Is it cheaper?
- Is it easier to buy?
- Is it better designed?

Yet another matter to consider is the cost of running the business. Will you be able to make any money from your idea? Or is it likely to cost you more than it earns you?

In some ways, having the idea for a business is relatively easy. Most of us have had an idea for a new product or service at some point in our lives; what matters is whether it is possible to turn the idea into a reality that people want, and whether it is profitable.

So, when considering a business idea you need to think about a number of factors:

- Is there likely to be any demand? If so, how much? How many units do you think you will be able to sell over the next few years?
- Is the idea profitable? Will the income (or revenue) cover the costs? If so, will the business make enough profit for it to be worthwhile? Imagine you are in a job paying £30,000 a year at the moment. You may be unwilling to leave this and start your own business if you only expect to earn £15,000. How much would you need to earn for you to be willing to take the risk of starting out on your own?
- Will you be able to provide the product or service? How difficult is the product to produce? Do you have the skills to develop the idea?
- Would people buy the product or service from you rather than from other firms? Can you offer a better price? Or a better service?

The idea is the easy bit!

The first thing to do if you are thinking of setting up in business is to identify a business opportunity and decide exactly what product or service you want to offer. You will need to be sure that there is a market for your product or service, and that people will be prepared to pay for it.

You must also be confident that people will be willing to buy the product or service from you, rather than from someone else. Ask yourself what makes your product better than other firms':

Doing research

To answer these questions you will need to find out about the market and about customers' needs and wants. What do your potential customers like and what don't they like? How much are they prepared to pay for the product? What are your competitors' prices? This information can be discovered through market research.

It may seem obvious to say that you need to research the market before actually setting up in business, but many individuals are short of money at this stage. Because of this, they prefer to use the

Business in focus

Innocent Drinks was set up in 1998 by three friends, Adam Balon, Richard Reed and Jonathan Wright. The first smoothies went on sale in May 1999. **innocent** smoothies can now be found throughout the UK in over 4000 stockists, including selected Sainsbury's, Waitrose and Safeways, as well as Harrods, Harvey Nichols and the Met Hotel, Park Lane. The three founders talked about setting up a business throughout their student days, but it took a few years working in management consultancy and advertising before they came up with the idea. The idea of making pure, unadulterated drinks was prompted by a holiday when the three friends realised that they hadn't eaten anything fresh or nutritious for weeks. From this kernel of an idea, the **innocent** brand and its range of 100% pure fresh smoothies were born.

With £500 worth of fruit turned into smoothies, the three of them considered that 'Jazz On The Green', a charitable jazz festival they had set up three years previously and attended by 20 000 people, would be an excellent opportunity to test the product. Two recycling bins, one labelled YES, one labelled NO, were set up alongside their makeshift stall with a poster that read 'Do you think we should give up our day jobs to make smoothies?' Richard says: 'At the end of the day, the YES bin was just about full and the NO bin was practically empty. It gave us the confidence needed and so we went in the next day and resigned from our jobs.'

The creation of a detailed business plan followed, as did the raising of capital (helped by an email to their friends, asking if they knew anyone rich). A private investor provided enough investment to put them in business, enabling **innocent** to continue without having to cut corners or compromise the quality of the product in any way.

innocent takes a very firm stance on developing its foodstuffs. Richard says: 'The first products we launched under the **innocent** brand, a range of fresh fruit smoothies, kick against the mass of adulterated products. Always made from fruit, they are the only 100% fruit smoothies on the market that do not use concentrates, and are made with fresh juices. They contain absolutely no added water, sugar, preservatives or flavourings.'

The company now commands a 40% slice of a market with a retail value of about £50m, according to market researchers AC Nielsen. The market itself has grown sharply in the last two years alone. In 2001, it was estimated **innocent** had 21% of a market worth £20m. The company is known for its somewhat offbeat approach to business. Its offices in London's Shepherd's Bush is known as Fruit Towers and is as trendy as the product. The aim of the company is simple: 'We want to make the best fresh drinks in the whole world ever.' They say 'Just think of **innocent** drinks as your one healthy habit – like going to the gym but without the communal showers afterwards.'

innocent employs 43 people and has been voted 'Best small to medium sized business' at the National Business Awards 2003. It also continues to win industry awards such as the Great Taste Awards (four gold medals in as many years). The product range now includes thickies (yoghurt-based fruit drinks), orange juice, and each season a new seasonal smoothie recipe is launched.

Source: Adapted from www.innocentdrinks.co.uk

1 To what extent was the market research undertaken by the friends at the jazz festival useful?
2 In what ways might creating a business plan have been useful in the development of the business?
3 What problems do you think the business is likely to face in the future?

money that they do have to develop the product rather than finding out what customers actually want. However foolish this may seem, people who have had a business idea are often so eager to get on with starting up that they think market research is a waste of valuable time and money.

Given that the amount of money you have available to spend, research is likely to be limited, you will probably have to carry out most of it yourself rather than use specialist companies to do it for you. The cheapest and quickest way of doing this is to see what information about the market *already* exists. What data has been collected and published in the past? There is a tremendous amount of information already available on the Internet, in libraries and in newspapers, for example. If you visit *www.statistics.gov.uk*, for example, you will find the Office of National Statistics online, with lots of government data on the economy, the labour market, transport and UK society; if you visit *www.guardianunlimited.co.uk* you will be able to look through past copies of the *Guardian* newspaper.

However, in some cases you may have to gather information for the first time (this is called **primary research**). For example, you may want to discover what people in your local area think of your idea, whether they are likely to use your service or what they think of your business name. This sort of information will not exist already, so you will need to undertake new research.

Primary research can be tailored precisely to your own needs but can be quite expensive and time consuming, compared with using information already collected.

What makes an idea successful?

If you want your business to be successful, you must be sure that there will be enough demand for your product or service. You must also be sure that your sales will be high enough to cover your costs in the long run. Although it is common for firms to make a loss when they first start out, obviously you cannot afford to carry on making losses for long periods. If you do, your business may be forced to close. So before you start, you have to try and make sure demand is going to be high enough.

Pricing

How much you actually earn from your business will depend, not only on how many items you expect to sell, but also on how much you charge for each one. If you multiply the number of units sold by the average price you charge, this gives the **total revenue**. Getting the price right is crucial. Charge too much and you may not sell enough. Charge too little and you may sell a lot but not make enough revenue to cover the costs.

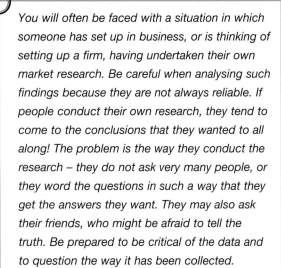

We can calculate revenue by multiplying sales by the price at which the products are sold. Thus, if a car dealer sells 100 cars a year at an average price of £15 000 the revenue earned will be (100 × £15 000) = £1 500 000.

1 If a bookshop sells 2500 books a week at an average price of £2, what is the total revenue per week?
2 What is the revenue of the bookshop per year?
3 What assumption have you made, to answer question 2?

The product

The level of demand for a product will also depend on the good or service itself. Is it something people really want? Does it meet a need and what else is available? Are there competitors offering a similar or better product at a better price? If so, you may struggle to survive. A successful product is one offering good value for money. This does not necessarily mean that it is cheap, but that it provides a high level of benefits compared with the price charged.

A product or service is more likely to be successful if it has a **Unique Selling Proposition or point (USP)**. This is something which makes it different from the competition. For example, you may decide to keep your shop open later than the competition, to deliver to the door or to tailor-make the product to the customers' orders. Burger King's USP is its flamed-grilled burgers, for example.

It is difficult to measure the actual number of business start-ups because sole traders do not have to register their business. The most commonly used measure uses the number of businesses registering for Value Added Tax. In the UK, around 170 000 to 180 000 businesses start up a year using this indicator.

People in business

Trevor Bayliss OBE was born in Kilburn, London, in 1937 and brought up in Southall. At the age of 15 he was swimming for Britain and at age 16 he joined the Southall Mechanics Laboratory. He studied mechanical and structural engineering at the local technical college.

Later on in life, he had a variety of jobs including being a salesman, running his own swimming pool company and working as a stuntman on various TV shows. In 1991 he started to develop a wind-up radio. His first working prototype ran for 14 minutes and in 1994 this was featured on *Tomorrow's World*. Eventually, the product's potential was spotted by corporate finance expert Christopher Staines and South African entrepreneur Rory Stear, who raised the funding to set up BayGen Power Industries in Cape Town. The company employs disabled workers to manufacture what came to be known as Freeplay radios. In June 1996 the Freeplay Radio was awarded the BBC design award for Best Product and Best Design.

According to Trevor Bayliss, 'The hardest thing when you have an idea is bringing it to the market place . . . I believe there is an invention in all of us. It's also very difficult for a person who has got a good idea to get it to the market place. When I first went to British industry everybody turned me down. They were probably looking at me because I wasn't wearing a tie and not looking at the invention . . . I got rejection letter after rejection letter.'

Visit *www.tbf.websfor.org/thetbf/home/home.asp* for details of the Trevor Bayliss Foundation, which has been set up to encourage and support inventors and engineers.

Business in focus

Mandy Haberman is the inventor of the Anywayup Cup, a beaker for babies that does not spill its contents no matter what they do with it. She came up with the idea when she saw a baby spill Ribena on a white carpet. She went home and worked on numerous prototypes. However, despite her confidence she could not get anyone else interested in producing her product and had to get it produced herself.

When the Anywayup Cup – produced by a partner company – went on sale it was an amazing success, with half a million sales in its first year. However, a UK company, Jackel International, soon brought out a similar product under the Tommy Tippee brand and sales of the Anywayup Cup fell dramatically. Mandy had to sue for patent infringement, which led to an agreement in which she was paid damages and costs. Sales of the Anywayup Cup are now over £10 million worldwide. Her company still has an average annual spend of around £100 000 in legal fees alone in order to protect her product. Originally Mandy found it difficult to get her product distributed – it was only when she sent a full cup of Ribena in the post to the buyer at Tesco's that she could get him to pay attention. The cup was surrounded by tissues and a note saying that if the tissue was covered in Ribena he shouldn't bother contacting her, but it if wasn't he should telephone her. He did, and the product is now widely distributed.

For more information on Mandy Haberman, visit *www.mandyhaberman.com*.

1 To what extent is having a good idea enough to ensure the success of a new business?

Protecting the idea

One of the problems of having a good idea is that other people may copy it! To some extent this is inevitable. Other people and companies can see what you have done and replicate it. A few years ago a book called *The Little Book of Calm* was published. This was a small book of advice on how to keep calm, which was displayed next to the tills in book shops and sold hundreds of thousands of copies; within months there was the *Little Book of Joy*, *The Little Book of Happiness* and so on. It is possible to gain some protection by taking out a **patent** or through **copyright** legislation.

Key terms

A **patent** gives inventors the rights to an invention of a new product or process under the Copyright, Designs and Patents Act (1988). This right lasts for 20 years.

A **copyright** provides legal protection for authors, composers and artists under the Copyright, Designs and Patents Act (1988).

A patent is a means of protecting a new invention. You can take out a patent by registering your product or production process at the Patents Office. This means that other people or firms cannot copy your invention unless you agree to licence it to them. You can charge them for the licence. However, to really protect your idea you need to take out patents all around the world to prevent it being copied elsewhere. This can be expensive. Also, if someone does copy your patented idea, you have to pay to take them to court. To find out more about patents, visit the UK Patent Office at *www.patent.gov.uk*.

Patents are absolutely vital to the success of firms in industries such as pharmaceuticals. Firms need to protect their inventions to recover the enormous costs of developing new products. Without such protection, they would be unlikely to invest in research into new products. Even so, other firms may take the basic idea and adapt it to try and avoid patent legislation. And, even if they are using your idea, it is up to you to take them to court – which can involve very high costs.

Firms can also protect their products by registering a trademark. A trademark is any sign that can distinguish the goods and services of one firm from those of another. It may be words (e.g. the Coca-Cola script), logos (e.g. the apple on Apple computers), pictures (e.g. the lion of MGM) or a combination of these. Other firms cannot use signs which infringe on a trademark.

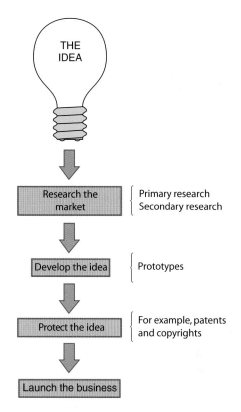

Figure 2.3 *First research the market, then protect your idea before setting up the business*

POINTS TO PONDER

In a typical year the UK Patent Office receives 30 000 applications for patents, of which about 8000 are granted.

At any one time, around 295 000 granted patents are in force on the UK patent register, these being patents either granted in the UK by the Patent Office, or granted in Munich by the European Patent Office.

In a typical year, 80 000 trademark applications are received by the Patent Office, with the majority being registered.

Source: The Patent Office

A copyright provides protection for written work, music or plays. Any of these are automatically protected as soon as they are created. You do not need to register your work for it to be copyrighted and if anyone wants to copy it they must pay a fee. The fees paid are known as **royalties**. However, you may have to prove that you were the first person to come up with a particular story or piece of music.

Business in focus

Mike Batt, who composed the music for the television programme *The Wombles*, had to pay an undisclosed six-figure sum over a legal battle over a piece of music that consists of nothing but one minute's silence. Mr Batt was accused of stealing the 'music', which appears on his album, from the American composer John Cage, whose 1952 composition was silent. Mr Batt called his piece 'A One Minute Silence' and this was allegedly infringing John Cage's copyright.

Every now and again you will read of disputes between people who are arguing over who wrote a song first. Some musicians always send a copy of any new music they have written to their solicitors to ensure they can prove when they wrote it.

Financing a start up

Once you have researched the market and, assuming it still looks like you have got a good idea, you will need to raise some money to actually start the business. If you are lucky, you may have some savings. However, this may not be very much and you may be worried about risking all your savings in a new venture. So, where else can you get money?

Borrowing from family and friends

In many cases, people setting up in business have to borrow from family and friends. This has its advantages – the people who have lent you money may be willing to wait for some time to be repaid. On the other hand, you may feel worried about borrowing money from friends or family in case you cannot pay them back. You may also find that they want to become more involved in the business than you would like and this can put a strain on your relationship with them.

The bank

Another alternative is to borrow money from a bank. This has the advantage of being a formal arrangement (sometimes borrowing from friends and family can cause problems because the arrangement is not clearly set out). However, banks will charge interest on any money they lend. This means you have to pay them a fee in return for them lending you the money. Banks will usually leave you to run the business for yourself, but they will insist on being paid, whereas you may be able to delay payment to friends.

Raising money may be particularly difficult for a new firm especially if the person involved has no previous experience of running a business. Banks may be wary of lending to them. Also, the business may only have a few assets to use as a guarantee for a loan – this is called collateral. The interest charges on any loans may be high because of the risk that the business will fail.

Investment

Yet another way of raising finance is to bring in outside investors. In return for putting money into the business, they gain some control over it. You may not want to raise money this way if you want to remain totally in charge.

The decision on how to raise business finance will depend on a combination of factors:

● Where can you get money from?
● What will it cost?
● When and how will you have to repay?

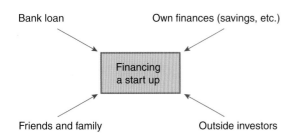

Figure 2.4 *Sources of finance*

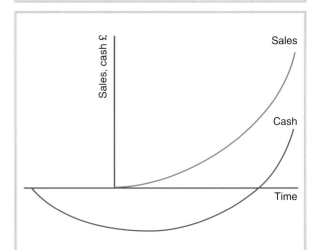

1 With reference to the above sales and cash data for a new business start up:
   a) Explain why cash flow may be negative in the early period.
   b) Explain the possible significance of the negative cashflow for the entrepreneur.

Siting a business

The location of a business can be crucial to its survival. The location of a hotel, a restaurant or a new shop can make all the difference between success and failure. It is important that the business is in a suitable place for employees and suppliers, and especially customers. Even in the case of a manufacturer, the location can be important because it can affect the costs of production and the ease of getting the product to the market.

However, small firms often lack the money to afford the best location. For example, someone setting up a new shop may not be able to pay high street rents and so may end up in a side street, away from most of the customers. Also, the best locations may already have been taken, meaning that the new business is immediately at a disadvantage compared with existing firms.

Business in focus

One of the most successful entrepreneurs in the UK is Reuben Singh, who was listed as the youngest self-made millionaire in the UK in 1998 when he was just 22! His newest company, Alldaypa, is attracting a great deal of attention. It is a 24-hour, seven-day-a-week personal assistant, which performs all the tasks you would expect a secretary to fulfil but via the phone or the Internet. It enables small firms to compete more effectively.

On signing up with Alldaypa you are given a personal website (www.yourcompanyname.alldaypa.com), email addresses and phone number. The number will put a caller in touch with one of the Alldaypa team who will have information about your company. 'And we're not just a message-taking service,' Singh is keen to emphasise. 'We can check and send out emails and faxes, access your diary and check your meetings for the next day. And each client that rings up will have music in his ear, thinking you're a professional office. So you have a professional office with no office costs, no secretary costs, no rents, rates or service charges.'

Singh started his first business in 1995. 'The day I was 17 I got the keys to a £40 000 BMW, I really had no need to start any business. But because I had a belief that I could do it and everyone around me said I couldn't, I did it. If they'd said I could, I wouldn't have started – that's the kind of person I am.'

The growth and successful sale of his chain of jewellery and accessories shops, Miss Attitude, earned him his European Entrepreneur of the year 1999 award, as well as a place in the *Sunday Times*' 'Most powerful individuals under 30'.

'There's a difference between a businessman and an entrepreneur. The businessman is the astute and practical character; the entrepreneur is the dreamer, the one with the vision. Together they are the accelerator and the brake, so you need both.'

'The only limit I have is the limit of my ambition.'

1 What do you think are the skills needed to be a successful entrepreneur?

The first few years

New businesses are particularly likely to fail early on – over 50% do so in the first five years. If a business can survive this period, it will usually continue for many more years afterwards. One reason why firms often fail in their early years is because it takes time to build up a base of regular customers.

For your first few months or even years, customers may be unaware that your business exists. Even if they do know you are there, they may be uncertain about using your business because you are relatively new. Over time, providing you offer good value for money, you are likely to build up a reputation and attract more people by word of mouth. You should also be building up **customer loyalty**, meaning that the same people come back again and again. This should mean that you have a more steady flow of income and that you can predict what you will be earning more easily. In the early stages of the business, however, income may be slow to come in, even though costs may be relatively high!

This leads us on to the problem of **cash flow**. Cash flow refers to the timing of receipts of money from customers and money paid out. If a business's customers are slow to pay, it may have cash flow problems and be unable to pay its suppliers. In the early days, a business's suppliers may expect to be paid promptly, making it more difficult to manage cash flow. Small firms usually lack power in the market. To win contracts they may have to give customers a long time to pay, while suppliers may insist on being paid quickly because they are afraid the business may not be around for long! This puts pressure on a new firm's cash flow.

Only around 64% of businesses are still trading three years after they are set up.

A business plan

If you are thinking of starting up a business, one of the things you should always do is produce a **business plan**. This sets out *what* you are hoping to achieve over the coming few years and *how* you will achieve these targets.

A **business plan** is a report setting out the objectives, financial projections and market analysis of an organisation.

The plan should include:

1 Your objectives – what do you hope to achieve with this business? How much money do you expect to make? How much time do you want to spend working?
2 Information on the market and competitors – how big is the market? Is it growing? Who will be your main competitors?
3 Sales estimates.
4 Estimates of costs, revenues and profits.
5 Research on customer needs and how you think your business will meet these needs.
6 Information on what makes your business different from the competition, e.g. your Unique Selling Proposition.

Producing a business plan is a very useful exercise for anyone who is setting up in business because it makes them think carefully about what they are doing. Too many people rush into it without thinking through their idea. Planning makes you look in some detail at the different aspects of the idea and consider some of the potential problems.

A business plan is also a useful document if you are hoping to raise money. Banks nearly always insist on seeing a business plan. If you have no idea where you want the business to go, it is unlikely you are going to succeed – and so the bank is unlikely to lend to you. In comparison, someone who produces a well-thought-out and well-researched plan of what they want to achieve, and how they intend to achieve it is more likely to be successful. As a result, the bank is more likely to lend money. Banks often provide individuals who want to start up in business with a pack of information to help them formulate a plan. Visit your local bank and ask for one.

Research by Professor David Storey of Warwick University suggests that there is a 70% survival rate for business start-ups in the UK where the owner is over 55 years old when it started. This compared with an average survival rate for all start-ups of just 19%.

The most causes of commercial insolvency (i.e. business failure) include:

- loss of market
- tax liabilities
- poor management
- lack of working capital/cashflow
- personal extravagance
- legal disputes
- fraud

Source: Society of Practitioners of Insolvency

Key issues

New businesses help to create a dynamic economy in which there is choice for the consumer and in which competition ensures an efficient service. Governments are very keen, therefore, to encourage people to set up in business. This involves making the process of setting up easier and making it easier for firms to survive (for example, through easier access to finance). The UK government is eager to create a climate in which survival is easier, and to simplify the process of establishing and running a business. However, success is difficult for several reasons:

- individuals are often trying to do everything themselves
- competition can be stiff – even if you do have a new idea, someone may imitate it fairly quickly
- managing the finances can be difficult and money can be slow to come in.

People in business

Figure 2.5 *James Dyson*

James Dyson, designer of the Dyson vacuum cleaner, likes to describe himself as a 'vacuum cleaner junkie'. Based in Wiltshire, his company Dyson Appliances has a turnover of over £275m.

Success has come rapidly since Dyson's distinctive yellow and grey vacuum cleaner was first marketed in the UK in 1993, but it only came after years of hard work and struggle. Dyson studied interior and product design at the Royal College of Art in the late 1960s. His first job was working on the development of a high-speed landing craft. He then worked on the Ball Barrow wheelbarrow which was his first success. The Dyson cleaners not only looked distinctive but also incorporated totally new technology. Whereas all other vacuum cleaners use motor suction, the Dyson cleaner is based on a dual and root cyclone. This was the first real breakthrough in vacuum cleaner technology since H.C. Booth patented an electronically-powered suction machine with a filter bag in 1901.

In the Dyson, dirty air enters the outer cyclone chamber and spins at 200mph. The air then passes into the inner cyclone chamber where the dust is accelerated to 924mph. Tremendous centrifugal forces are exerted on the dust particles driving them out of the air. The air then passes through two filters whilst the dirt accumulates in a clear plastic tank rather than a bag.

Despite his own enthusiasm, Dyson's partners at the Ball Barrow company were not impressed by the first model of his revolutionary vacuum cleaner. So in 1979, he decided to develop the product on his own. For the next four years he earned almost nothing as he worked on his design, which took over 5000 prototypes to perfect. The first finished vacuum was completed in 1983. For the next two years he tried to find someone to license the product. The major companies were very wary, not least because his design would mean the end of the bag refill market, which is worth more than £100m a year. Unable to find a licensing deal in the UK, he went to the USA but his design was copied by the company which had bought the license and which then brought out its own version! Dyson eventually won a court case against the company and was awarded £4m in costs.

Following this Dyson decided to go it alone and set up his own company. However, he struggled to raise the finance needed because potential lenders felt he did not have enough experience of manufacturing. Nevertheless, he persevered and now produces over 5000 cleaners a day!

Dyson has continued to innovate since producing his first vacuum cleaner. Following the Dual Cyclone he developed the Root8Cyclone, which had greater suction power. He then moved on to producing a vacuum robot that cleaned a room automatically, without you having to push it – the robot has three on-board computers, 50 sensory devices, and took 60 000 hours of research to develop. Dyson then moved on to washing machines, developing Contrarotator – the world's first ever two-drum washing machine.

1 Why do you think new inventors have so many problems getting their ideas developed?
2 Do you think the government should intervene to help inventors? What could the government do?

Source: Gillespie A., 'Filling a vacuum', Business Review, November 1997, Volume 4, No. 2 and www.dyson.com

APPLICATION IN ACTION

- Think carefully about what starting up actually requires when examining a particular business. A retailer needs to be near customers, so the physical location is very important. With other services such as design, computer programming or consultancy the actual location may not be so important. In manufacturing, access to inputs may be the key.

- When trying to build up a customer base, think what will be most important – your qualifications (e.g. if you want to be a financial adviser), a licence (to set up a taxi firm) or equipment (to be a website designer).

QUICK CHECK QUESTIONS

1   Services are part of the ………….. sector of the economy.

2   Manufacturing firms are part of the………. sector of the economy.

3   State three ways of measuring the size of a business.

4   Finding out what customers want is called …………….. …………….

5   What is a USP?
a)   a unique sentimental proposal
b)   an underlying sales pitch
c)   a unique selling proposition
d)   an undervalued sales part.

6   State two reasons why people might set up in business for themselves.

7   Legal protection for a new invention is called a ………………

8   State two possible sources of finance for a new business.

9   A business plan:
a)   guarantees success
b)   is needed by the government to set up a business
c)   may help to attract investors
d)   is required for a business to have limited liability.

10 If you write a book, your work is automatically protected by:
a)   competency
b)   copyright
c)   patent
    d) trademark.

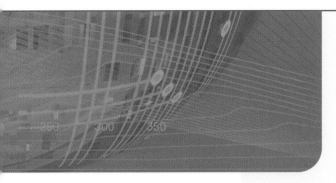

Progress questions

1 Explain two reasons why people might want to set up in business for themselves. *(6 marks)*

2 Eva Herzagobova wants to set up her own restaurant. She has already been to visit the bank but was told that she needed to produce a business plan.
   a) What is meant by a business plan? *(2 marks)*
   b) Outline the possible elements of Eva's business plan. *(6 marks)*
   c) Explain the possible advantages for Eva of producing a business plan. *(6 marks)*

3 Imagine you are considering setting up a hairdressing salon.
   a) Identify four costs you might have to pay. *(4 marks)*
   b) Outline the information you might want to gather about the market and competition. *(6 marks)*
   c) Explain how you might set the price for a haircut. *(5 marks)*
   d) Outline two ways in which you might promote the business. *(6 marks)*

4 Explain two ways in which a coffee shop can build up customer loyalty. *(6 marks)*

5 After a career working for Ford, Tommi Makinen has recently left the company to set up his own shop selling car parts and car accessories. At the moment, he is looking for new premises. Explain two factors that might influence exactly where he opens up the new shop. *(6 marks)*

6 After five years trying to make a career on his own as an accountant, Kevin Cook accepted defeat and went back to work for one of the large accounting firms.
   a) Explain two difficulties facing people who set up a small business. *(6 marks)*
   b) Explain two advantages of working for a large firm rather than for yourself. *(6 marks)*

7 Dmitri Smirnov curses the day he decided not to patent his new computer programming software. Weeks after announcing his breakthrough, other companies were using his ideas in their own projects. At the time, he had been trying to save money and had not realised how important a patent was.
   a) Explain what is meant by a 'patent'. *(2 marks)*
   b) Explain the possible benefits to an inventor of having a patent. *(4 marks)*

8 Jon Doe recently took Wamadamadingdong, a band, to court for using his music and not paying him royalties. The band was accused of breaking his copyright.
   a) What is meant by a 'copyright'? *(2 marks)*
   b) What is meant by the term 'royalties'? *(2 marks)*

9 Henrietta Farrar wanted to set up her own riding stables but needed to raise £200 000 to buy the premises she needed. Explain two ways in which she might raise the necessary finance. *(6 marks)*

10 Many new businesses in the UK only survive a few years. Explain three possible reasons why new businesses might fail. *(9 marks)*

Analytical and evaluative questions

11 After five years working at the Tate Gallery, Emma Jones has decided to take the plunge and set up her own art gallery with her husband, in London, specialising in modern art.

   a) Examine the possible reasons why she has taken this decision.   *(8 marks)*

b) Discuss the ways Emma might finance her new business.   *(15 marks)*

12 After several years running a pub, Alfie Blackburn is setting up his own café. To what extent would drawing up a business plan guarantee his success?   *(15 marks)*

Case study   **25 marks**

Amanda Cardenet is thinking of setting up her own business producing handmade greetings cards, although she will need to raise the finance necessary to do it. She has undertaken some research into the market and is about to produce a business plan. Her idea is to produce cards based on the local area; she thinks these will have tremendous appeal but is worried that others might copy her idea. She is not sure if she can protect her ideas with a patent or not.

1 Explain whether it is possible for Amanda to protect her business idea with a patent. *(3 marks)*

2 Explain factors Amanda should include in her business plan.   *(6 marks)*

3 Analyse the ways in which Amanda might raise the finance necessary to set up in business.   *(7 marks)*

4 Discuss the factors which might determine whether Amanda's business is successful or not.   *(9 marks)*

>> Types of business

There are several different types of business format. Each one has advantages and disadvantages. In this unit we consider three of the most common forms of business: sole traders, private limited companies and public limited companies.

Sole traders

When individuals set up in business on their own they are known as 'sole traders'. Plumbers, decorators, window cleaners and hairdressers are nearly all sole traders. The people running these businesses work for themselves. In some cases, sole traders do hire other people to help them out but they remain responsible for the overall business and are actively involved in the running of it on a daily business.

What does it take to be a successful sole trader?

Although all sorts of people can succeed as sole traders, there are certain qualities which most of them have in common.

First, you need to be someone who is willing to work on your own, who has the confidence to take your own decisions and who can turn your hand to almost anything. After all, as a sole trader you may have to serve customers, decide what equipment to buy, deal with suppliers and keep accurate and up-to-date business records. This requires a wide range of skills and an enormous degree of flexibility.

Second, sole traders have to be used to working hard: running your own business is no easy task. You must also be prepared for stress! All the decisions of the business are yours alone, so if you do get it wrong there is no one else to blame. On the other hand, if it is successful the sense of achievement and the rewards are yours as well!

Third, becoming a sole trader requires a high level of self-discipline because you are your own boss; there is no one to tell you what to do. This can be very exciting, because you decide what is going to happen. It also means you have to motivate yourself to get things done. For example, you have to organise your day properly and to use your time effectively.

What are the advantages of being a sole trader?

One of the main advantages of being a sole trader is that it is so easy to start up in business. Unlike starting other types of organisation, you do not need to register with anyone or fill in any special forms; you can just start trading. If you suddenly decide you want to be a gardner, an artist, an interior decorator or cleaner, you could start up in business tomorrow! It may be wise, however, to get some training first!

Many people also enjoy being their own boss rather than having to take orders from other people. They like the freedom to make their own decisions, to decide when and where to work, what to do and how to do it. Being a sole trader can, therefore, be very enjoyable. You can also make decisions quickly. You do not have to check with any one to get permission to do something. This can be incredibly motivating: you are the boss!

What are the problems of being a sole trader?

Whilst being a sole trader can be very fulfilling, it also brings with it many challenges. Making all the decisions can be exciting, but you carry all the responsibility. If you work for someone else and there is a real problem, you can always pass it over to them to solve. Being a sole trader can, therefore, be quite lonely; some people find it difficult to cope with the pressure. Some people also find the hours quite demanding as well. This is particularly likely to be an issue in the early years when you are trying hard to build up enough business. As a sole trader you may be working very long hours each week and you may not be able to take much holiday because you cannot afford to close the business and risk losing customers.

Another difficulty is raising finance to set up and

expand. You generally have to rely on your own money or money from friends and family (plus the money from the business itself, once it is up and running). Of course it is possible to borrow from the banks or other financial institutions but they often charge smaller businesses quite high interest rates because they are worried about the risk of failure and want to cover their losses.

Being a sole trader is also quite risky if anything goes wrong. This is because sole traders have **unlimited liability**. The sole trader keeps any rewards the business makes, but is also personally responsible for any losses. If their businesses have problems, sole traders can lose their personal possessions.

> ### Key terms
>
> *Unlimited liability means that the owners are personally responsible for the debts of the business and there is no limit to this responsibility; this means they may have to sell their personal possessions to pay off any debts.*

In many ways, working for other people in a large organisation is much easier because:

- you have other people to share ideas with
- you may receive a more regular income
- you may be able to call on experts to help you solve problems.

Advantages	Disadvantages
A sole trader: makes his or her own decisions which can be motivating	A sole trader: has limited sources of finance
can make decisions quickly and respond raidly to changes in the market	relies heavily on his or her own ability to make decisions
has direct contact with the market	may work long hours and have limited holidays, leading to stress
setting up is easy	has unlimited liability

Table 2.3 *Advantages and disadvantages of being a sole trader*

On the other hand, there is not the same sense of achievement and satisfaction of having created something for yourself.

Companies

To avoid some of the problems of a being a sole trader, you may decide to establish a **company** instead. A company is a type of business owned by **shareholders**. Each share that is owned represents a part of the company. The more shares someone owns the more of the company belongs to them.

THE COMPANY

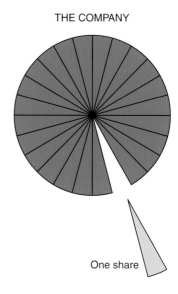

One share

Figure 2.5 *Each share represents a part of the company. A shareholder owns part of the business*

To set up a company, individuals have to complete various documents and register the business at **Companies House**. This process is known as **incorporation**.

> ### Key terms
>
> *A company is a separate legal entity which can own assets and is liable for its own debts. Owners of a company have limited liability.*

Once it is incorporated, a business has its own legal identity, separate from its owners. The company can own property, equipment and other goods in its own right and is responsible for its own debts. If the company fails, the shareholders can lose the money that they invested in the business when they bought shares but they cannot lose more than this. This is because a company has limited liability. This means that a company is responsible for the money it owes but that the personal possessions of its owners are safe, because there is a limit to the amount for which they are liable. This is different from a sole trader, who has unlimited liability and could lose everything if the business had financial problems.

Having limited liability is essential for companies to raise moeny by selling shares. Without it investors would be far less likely to buy shares because of the risk to their possessions. It would mean giving money to others and risking everything you had ever earned. With limited liability, you know what the maximum amount is that you could lose.

One problem with setting up a company is that the business must pay to have its accounts checked annually by independent accountants (called auditors). These accounts must be made public, so that outsiders can see the revenue and profits of the business, as well as what it owns.

Advantages	Disadvantages
A company: ● has limited liability	A company: ● must pay the costs of registering
● can raise finance from selling shares	● has to make its financial accounts public
● is often perceived as being more established than sole traders	● has to pay for its accounts to be audited each year
	● has to disclose information, e.g. this year's profit, what the business owns
	● is subject to company law, i.e. greater regulation than a sole trader

Table 2.4 *Advantages and disadvantages of setting up as a company*

Why become a shareholder?

By investing in a company, shareholders become the owners of the business. This means that, if the business is successful, the value of their shares should increase. Shareholders should also receive some of the profits that the company makes each year. The part of the profits paid out to shareholders is called the dividends. The more profit a firm makes, the bigger the dividends are likely to be. Each year the firm will announce the dividend payment per share: the more shares a person has, the more dividends they receive in total.

Key terms

A **shareholder** is an owner of an organisation. There are different types of shares but an 'ordinary' shareholder has one vote per share and receives a dividend if it is paid each year.

A **dividend** is a reward paid by the company to its shareholders.

Shareholders can also influence the policy of the business. Most types of shares grant their owners voting rights. Each share is worth one vote. So, by buying more shares, people can get more votes and have a greater influence over what the firm actually does. If someone owns more than 51% of the shares they control the business and, therefore, can decide company policy.

In the UK, financial institutions such as banks, pension funds and insurance companies own most company shares. These organisations buy shares to make a profit through the dividends they receive and by selling the shares at a higher price later on. They can then pass their profits on to their own investors.

EXAMINER'S ADVICE

It is quite common to get a question which asks you whether someone should set up as a company or operate as a sole trader. To answer this successfully you need to weigh up the advantages and disadvantages of each form of business. Does the business need to raise money by selling shares? Is limited liability an important issue? Is the person willing to disclose financial information about the business or do they prefer more secrecy? There is no definite answer. It depends on the type of the business, the need for finance, the financial risks involved and the aims of the people involved.

Private and public companies
Private companies

Private limited companies have 'ltd' after their names. They are owned by shareholders and the owners can place restrictions on who the shares are sold to in the future. For example, many private limited companies are owned by families who limit the sale of shares to other members of the family, making sure that 'outsiders' do not become involved. Owners of shares in private limited companies cannot advertise their shares for sale; they have to sell them privately.

Business in focus

Mars is one of the world's largest private family-owned companies, worth around $14bn. It all started with Frank Mars back in 1911, when he and his wife Ethel started making and selling a variety of butter-cream sweets. Its businesses include:

- snackfoods, such as Mars, Twix and M&M's
- petfoods, such as Pedigree and Whiskas
- drinks, through vending machines such as Klix and Flavia
- foods, such as Dolmio sauces and Uncle Ben's rice.

For more information, visit www.mars.com.

1 Discuss the possible advantages and disadvantages to Mars of being a private family business.

Public companies

Public limited companies have 'plc' after their names. Once again, they are owned by shareholders but unlike private companies restrictions cannot be placed on the sale of these shares. Shareholders in public companies can sell their shares to whoever they like. This can cause problems if another firm starts to buy up shares in the business in an attempt to gain control of it. Some of the shareholders may want to resist this takeover, but they cannot stop fellow shareholders from selling their shares.

Key terms

A **takeover** occurs when one firm buys up the majority of shares in another company.
A **private limited company (ltd)** has shareholders but its shares cannot be advertised or sold on the Stock Exchange.
A **public limited company (plc)** can advertise its shares and its shares can be sold on the Stock Exchange.

Trading shares in plcs

Another difference between plcs and 'ltd' companies is that shares in plcs can be advertised in the media. This is why you can see the share prices of public companies listed in the newspapers, but not those of private companies.

Because there are no restrictions on the sale of plc shares, thousands of shares are traded every day. The purchase and sale of shares is usually organised through a stockbroker who acts as an intermediary between the buyers and sellers. The price at which the shares were bought and sold on the previous day can be found in most newspapers; the current price can be found on the Internet or from a stockbroker.

The value of a company at any moment can be calculated by multiplying the price of each share by the number of shares available. The result of this calculation is known as the market capitalisation of the business and shows what it would cost to buy up all the firm's shares. The market capitalisation will change when the share price changes.

Key terms

The **market capitalisation** of a company is its current market value.

What determines the price of a share?

The price of a share depends on how much people want to buy it. The greater the demand the higher the price is likely to be. The demand for shares will depend on what people think will happen to the business in the future. If they think the company is going to do well (perhaps because it is about to launch a new product or because the market for that product is growing fast) they are likely to want to buy shares now.

INTERPRETING DATA

Company ABC plc		
	2004	**2005**
Number of shares	10m	10m
Market capitalisation	£20m	£22m

1 Comment on the data above.

Business in focus

In 2003 Google, the world's most famous search engine and one of the most powerful brands on the Internet, started preparations for its flotation. The valuation of the business is around £15bn, and one proposal was for an online auction of its shares. The flotation would allow the company to raise capital and motivate staff with share options.

Some worry that the flotation could significantly change the business culture. Google still cherishes the dot.com business culture of the late 1990s, proclaiming, 'you can be serious without a suit', employing a former chef to the Grateful Dead rock group, and equipping its office with roller-hockey equipment and lava lamps. A flotation would bring fortunes to Larry Page and Sergey Brin, the Stanford University computer science students who founded the site in 1998, and the two venture capital firms that invested in them.

According to the *Financial Times*, Google achieves annual profits of about $150m from $500m of revenues.

Google facts:
- 200 million searches a day
- 3.1 billion web pages indexed
- more than 1000 employees
- the name Google is based on the word googol, which refers to the number represented by 1 followed by 100 zeros.

1 What might determine the value of the shares of Google when it floats?

Becoming a public company

When a private limited company becomes a public limited company this is known as a flotation. This involves selling shares to the general public via the Stock Exchange. To do this, the firm needs specialist advice about the best time to sell, the price the shares should be sold at and who to sell the shares to; they will also need to provide information about the company to prospective investors. A flotation, therefore, involves specialists such as accountants, stockbrokers and merchant banks; not surprisingly it can be an expensive process.

Key terms

*A **flotation** occurs when a private limited company sells its shares on the Stock Exchange and becomes a public limited company.*

Why become a public limited company?

Becoming a public limited company gives many advantages:

- It is possible to advertise shares, which means they should be easier to sell. As a result, a plc should be able to raise more money than a private limited company
- Because public companies' share prices are quoted in newspapers, people tend to be much

POINTS TO PONDER

The number of UK companies quoted on the UK Stock Exchange is around 1700. At the end of 2002 these companies had a market value of over £1 147bn. Three years previously, the stock market value had been over £1 800bn. The number of new companies joining each year can vary quite considerably: it was 172 in 2000, but only 59 in 2002.

On the Stock Exchange over 706 billion shares were traded in 2002 (an average of 148 000 trades each day). These shares had a value of over £1 800bn In 2002 there were 23 rights issues (this occurs when a firm issues more shares to its shareholders to raise finance), raising over £6.4bn.

more interested in them than they are in private companies. Because of this, public companies get more press coverage.

- People believe public companies are always bigger and more successful than private companies, even though this is not necessarily the case. Becoming a public company is good for a firm's image.

What are the disadvantages of being a plc?

There are various disadvantages of being a plc, including the following:

- The shares of public companies are traded regularly (every few minutes in some cases!). This means the share price is constantly changing. Managers must always be aware of the share price because, if it falls too low, a competitor may try to buy shares and gain control of the business. In a private company it is possible to control the sale of shares. This is not possible in a public company and so managers are much more concerned about what is happening to the share price. If the business is taken over they may lose their jobs.
- In some cases, entrepreneurs who have turned their businesses into public companies to raise more finance have found it difficult to adjust to the fact that they answer to new 'outside' owners. Fed up with having to justify their actions to 'outsiders', both Richard Branson and Andrew Lloyd Weber bought back control of their companies and turned them into private limited companies.

It is important to remember that not all attempted flotations are successful. If the company sets the price of its shares too high, it may not be able to find buyers.

POINTS TO PONDER

Not all private companies are small and not all public companies are large. Littlewoods and Mars are both private companies owned by family members, for example.

Advantages	Disadvantages
Public limited companies: • can sell shares to the general public, so have more access to finance	Public limited companies: • are subject to greater regulation than a private limited company, e.g. they have to include more information in their accounts
• tend to receive more media attention, which is free publicity	• are more liable to have activities investigated by the media and they may have to behave more ethically because of this
• the public tend to assume plcs are bigger and more successful than ltds	• cannot control who shares are sold to and so are more vulnerable to takeover

Table 2.5 *Advantages and disadvantages of operating as a plc*

INTERPRETING DATA

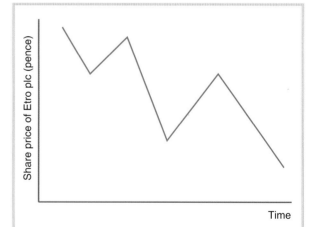

1 Examine the possible significance of the above data for Etro plc.

Business in focus

JCB, the UK manufacturer of construction equipment, has annual sales of £750m of which more than 70% is exported. Its headquarters are in Rochester in the Midlands and the company is owned by the Bamford family. In terms of units sold, JCB is the world's fifth biggest maker of construction machines, such as excavators. Its competitors in the global, $70bn (£43bn) a year, construction-equipment industry include big, publicly-quoted US groups, such as Caterpillar, Case and Deere, as well as Komatsu of Japan. Joe Bamford, father of Sir Anthony, the present chairman, set up JCB in 1945 and the family has refused to sell any of the company to outsiders. Sir Anthony says the lack of external shareholders means he can 'concentrate on running the company', rather than spending time briefing analysts and other outsiders.

The company is particularly proud of its powers of innovation – as a result of which its product line has mushroomed in recent years to include lift trucks, tractors and earth movers. 'What we have achieved so far has come almost entirely through internal growth. We're happy ploughing our own furrow,' Sir Anthony adds.

Financial Times, 16 March 1999
For more information on JCB, visit www.jcb.com.

1 Why might Sir Anthony Bamford believe it is important to keep the company a private limited company?

The divorce between ownership and control

A company is owned by its shareholders. In the case of a public company, there are likely to be thousands of different owners. Many of these are likely to be private individuals, although the biggest share owners tend to be financial institutions such as banks or pension funds. Obviously, all these owners cannot run the company at the same time and so they leave

this to the managers. The shareholders elect a Board of Directors (usually about 12 people) to represent them and make sure the business is being run in their best interests. Although on a daily basis the managers make the decisions, the overall objectives and strategy will be determined (or at least approved) by the Board of Directors. Any major decisions are agreed by the owners. If the company wanted to carry out a takeover, for example, all the shareholders would have to be consulted and would be asked to vote on it.

EXAMINER'S ADVICE

The decision about whether to float a company and turn it into a plc is a very important one. Whilst it brings many advantages, such as the ability to raise more finance, you need to consider whether it actually fits with the desires and ambitions of the people involved. If the business is owned by family members, for example, do they really want to release control? Similarly, if the business is mainly owned by a dominant entrepreneur who has built up the business from scratch, will he or she be able to cope with the demands of outsiders who will want a say in how the business is run?

It is also worth thinking about the actual process of a flotation. What price will the shares be sold at? Will there be enough demand for the shares at this price? What about the fees for the various advisers? What will the owners do with the money raised by flotation?

The shareholders must also approve the amount that the Board of Directors suggests is paid out as dividends each year. All companies must also have an Annual General Meeting (AGM) to which the shareholders are invited and every shareholder must receive a copy of the company's Annual Report. At the AGM, the directors and managers give an overview of the company's position and respond to any questions that shareholders might have. The larger shareholders will also be in fairly regular contact with the company throughout the year to make sure they are up to date on what is happening. If any unusual event occurs needing shareholders' approval (such as a major investment), the directors may organise an Extraordinary General Meeting

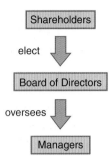

Figure 2.6 *How shareholders influence the business*

(EGM). In reality, the majority of private shareholders do not attend the AGM (or the EGM) – provided the dividends and share price are acceptable they are often happy to leave the decisions to the directors and managers.

In many ways, this relationship between owners and managers explains why the format of plcs has been so successful. The people who are good at running a business do not have to have the funds to own it, whilst the people or institutions with money do not need to be expert managers. Both groups can benefit from the arrangement.

However, there is a 'divorce between ownership and control' – that is, the owners and managers are generally different people and this can cause problems. What the managers want to do may differ from what the owners want them to do. For example, the managers may believe it is best for the firm to develop a new range of products, whilst the owners may prefer to have the profits paid out to them as dividends. Similarly, the managers may believe the best thing for the business in the long term is to invest in training or overseas expansion; this may cost money in the short term but will have long-term benefits. However, the owners may not want to take the risk of long-term investment.

In some cases, this 'divorce between ownership and control' can mean that managers decide to go ahead with certain plans without fully consulting the owners in case they disagree. Shareholders should, therefore, keep a close eye on the business to make sure they know what is happening.

The problem of a divorce between ownership and control only exists in companies (a sole trader is the owner *and* manager!), and is most likely to occur in public companies. It is usually less of a problem with private limited companies as the owners are

often involved with the management of the business as well.

QUICK CHECK QUESTIONS

1   A sole trader:
a)   has limited liability
b)   can sell shares
c)   can make all the decisions for him or herself
d)   is owned by the government.
2   If a business has limited liability, investors:
a)   can lose all their personal possessions
b)   can lose the amount they have invested in the business and no more
c)   can only lose £500.
3   A company:
a)   has its own legal identity
b)   is owned by employees
c)   is owned by suppliers
d)   has unlimited liability.
4   A public company:
a)   is owned by employees
b)   is owned by the government
c)   can sell shares on the Stock Exchange
d)   cannot make a loss.
5   State two advantages of being a sole trader compared with setting up as a company.
6   The amount paid to shareholders out of profits is called a ....
7   When one company buys control over another this is called a ....
8   When a private limited company becomes a public limited company this is called a:
a)   sell out
b)   flotation
c)   buy out
d)   share fest.
9   All public limited companies are bigger than private limited companies. True or false?
10   The shareholders interests are represented by the ....of ....

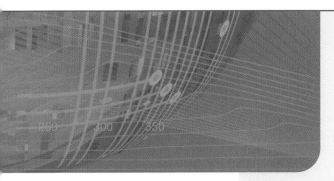

Progress questions

1 Julia Carraher is an interior designer based in London. She set up her own business last year and is a sole trader. She has unlimited liability.
   a) What is meant by 'unlimited liability'?
       (2 marks)
   b) Explain two advantages to Julia of setting up as a sole trader as opposed to setting up a company.
       (6 marks)

2 John Stravinsky has been running his own business as an architect for three years. The business has done well and has grown quite rapidly. John is considering turning the business into a private limited company. Explain two advantages to John of establishing a private limited company rather than operating as a sole trader.
   (6 marks)

3 Which of the following statements are true?
   ● A company is always owned by its managers.
   ● A private limited company is always owned by family members.
   ● A private limited company is always smaller than a public limited company.
   ● A public limited company has plc after its name.
   ● A company is owned by shareholders.
   ● Ordinary shareholders have one vote each.
   ● Ordinary shareholders have one vote per share.
       (1 mark each)

4 Explain two differences between a private limited company and a public limited company.
   (6 marks)

5 Jon Andrews is considering buying some shares. Explain two reasons why people buy shares in companies.
   (6 marks)

6 BookEnds Ltd is a highly successful publishing company which has had at least one of its books in the top ten bestseller lists for the last three years. The owners are eager to expand the business and are considering turning the company into a public limited company. Discuss the factors the firm might take into account when deciding whether to become a public limited company.
   (9 marks)

7 The Managing Director of Xanadu Films plc, a film production company, is concerned about the firm's share price, which has been falling recently. Explain two reasons why the share price may have fallen.
   (6 marks)

8 Which of the following statements are true?
   ● A public limited company is owned by the government.
   ● Public limited companies can advertise their shares.
   ● Shareholders in private limited companies cannot sell their shares.
   ● The shares of public limited companies are quoted on the Stock Exchange.
   ● Share prices can only increase.
   ● A dividend is the money a company pays to its shareholders.
       (1 mark each)

9 At a recent meeting for shareholders Mr Alan Willoughby stood up and accused the management of following their own policies at the expense of the shareholders. 'You pay yourselves too much, you waste our money on unncessary projects and you are failing to keep costs down.' Some commentators said these problems had occurred due to a divorce between ownership and control. What is meant by a 'divorce between ownership and control'?
   (3 marks)

10 What is meant by the term 'limited liability'?
    (2 marks)

Analytical and evaluative questions

11 Jenni Foster worked in the travel business for many years before setting up her own business putting together tailor-made holidays for wealthy clients. After a few successful years she now employs one other person and is considering expanding. She is thinking about making the business a private limited company. Analyse the possible advantages to Jenni of changing her business from being a sole trader to becoming a private company. *(8 marks)*

12 In 2002 Malcolm Manto took his hotel business public, becoming a multimillionaire in the process. From the very first few weeks of being a plc Malcolm has thought of taking the business private again. Discuss the factors he might consider before doing so. *(15 marks)*

13 Farnam Hotels Ltd has been owned by the Farnam family for three generations. Madge Farnam is the Managing Director, but several other family members have shares in the company. Madge is urging the other shareholders to make the business a public limited company. Discuss the factors the shareholders may take into account before making this decision. *(15 marks)*

>> Business objectives

Corporate aims and goals

The corporate aim is the overall purpose of the business. Imagine you have set up your own business. What is it that you really want to achieve? Do you want to become the biggest business in the world? Or the best-known? Do you want it to be the business making the largest profits? Or is the most important thing that you have fun and enjoy the work, regardless of how much you earn? Would you be happy if it made you just enough money to live on?

The answers to these questions are all business aims. We tend to assume that the aim of all firms is simply to make a profit. In fact, the aims are likely to be far more complex than this. Profit may be one of the aims. However, those involved in the business also may be looking for a range of other things, such as a good quality of life, a motivating job or the chance to contribute to society.

Key terms

A **profit** occurs when the value of a firm's sales is greater than the costs.

The mission statement

Organisations often produce their aims in the form of a mission statement. Mission statements set out in writing what the firm wants to achieve, and often include information on the markets it wants to compete in and the values of the business, i.e. what it believes in and how it wants to act. Mission statements make the corporate aims of the organisation clear for everyone to see.

Key terms

A **mission statement** is a written statement of a firm's aims.

Aims can vary greatly between organisations. Just look at the examples below:

'Our purpose in the UK is to meet the everyday needs of people everywhere to anticipate the aspirations of our consumers and customers and to respond creatively and competitively with branded products and services which raise the quality of life.' **Unilever**

'McDonald's vision is to be the world's best quick-service restaurant experience. Being the best means providing outstanding quality, service, cleanliness and value, so that we make every customer in every restaurant smile.' **McDonald's**

Tesco's Core Purpose is 'Creating value for customers, to earn their lifetime loyalty.' **Tesco**

'To bring inspiration and innovation to every athlete* in the world (*if you have a body you are an athlete).' **Nike**

'Our mission is to serve customers the best quality and choice to meet their everyday shopping needs.' **J Sainsbury plc**

'Though we make toys, we are not just a toy company. Though we make money, we are not driven by profit. Though we are famous for our product, we are defined by our philosophy. Our name comes from the combination of the Danish 'leg godt', which means to 'play well'. It is both our name and our nature. We believe that play is the essential ingredient in a child's growth and development. It grows the human spirit. It encourages imagination, conceptual thinking and creation.' **Lego**

'Our strategic intent is to help people find better ways to do great work – by constantly leading in document technologies, products and services that improve our customers' work processes and business results.' **Xerox**

'Oxfam works with others to overcome poverty and suffering.' **Oxfam**

POINTS TO PONDER

NASA's mission statement reads:

'To understand and protect our home planet
To explore the Universe and search for life
To inspire the next generation of explorers
. . . as only NASA can.'

What determines a firm's aims?

The aims of a firm will be determined by its owners and its managers. The owners will have certain aims of their own, such as a desire for the business to grow, a desire to establish the firm as the leading provider of a particular type of product or service or even to keep the business within the family. However, their aims might be influenced by what the managers think is realistic given the existing state of the firm and the market conditions.

The aims of a firm may well change over time. When people first set up in business they sometimes think it will be their path to fame and fortune (and for some it is!). However, as the years go by, people often find they have other aims in life: they want more time to bring up their families, to travel, to take part in a sport or hobby; they are often prepared to accept less profits from their business provided they can fulfill these other ambitions.

The aims of a firm will also vary with changes in the state of the business environment. If the economy is in a recession, for example, a firm's main aim may be to survive! In a more prosperous period, it may aim to increase its share of the market.

POINTS TO PONDER

Mission statements are not fixed forever – they can be changed as the business develops. In October 2002, for example, Microsoft changed its mission statement from 'To empower people through great software – any time, any place, and on any device' to 'To enable people and businesses throughout the world to realize their full potential'. As the company has developed into new areas, such as the Internet, games and mobile phones, it has had to change its mission statement to reflect new circumstances.

Business in focus

The mission statement of J Sainsbury plc is: 'Our mission is to serve customers the best quality and choice to meet their everyday shopping needs.

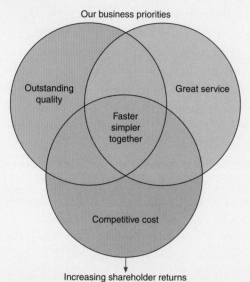

Our business priorities

Outstanding quality

Great service

Faster simpler together

Competitive cost

Increasing shareholder returns

Figure 2.7 *Sainsbury's three bubbles*

To deliver our mission, and restore profitable growth, we are focusing on our three bubbles:

- **outstanding quality** and choice in food and then, importantly, in other general merchandise products and customer services that make the weekly shop more convenient
- **delivering great service,** serving customers consistently well in all our contact with them, but especially at checkouts and in shop floor availability
- having **competitive costs,** implementing our transformation programme to create an efficient business, so we can pass the benefits of lower costs onto our customers in competitive prices
- doing all of this 'faster, simpler, together', working as a team to meet the needs of customers and our stores who serve the customers.'

www.j-sainsbury.co.uk

1 Despite the above mission statement Sainsbury's has been losing market share to Tesco. Why might this be?

Objectives

The corporate aim or mission sets out the overall vision of where the company wants to be. For example it may want to be 'the market leader' or 'the world's largest provider'. To fulfill its mission, a firm must set specific objectives. Objectives are targets that need to be achieved to reach the overall aim.

Imagine an organisation which sets out to be 'the leading provider of soft drinks in the UK'. This highlights what the organisation is trying to achieve but lacks detail. The detail is in the objectives. To become the leading provider of soft drinks, for example, the firm may set an objective of 'increasing sales by 20% over the next five years'. If the organisation can achieve its various objectives, it will have achieved its aim.

SMART objectives

So, the objectives provide more specific targets for managers. To be effective objectives need to be SMART:

- Specific – they must set out exactly what the firm is trying to do (such as increase sales or profits by a certain percentage).
- Measurable – it must be possible to measure whether the objective has been achieved.
- Agreed – there is no point simply telling someone that they have to achieve something. The other person has to be involved in setting the objective so that they feel part of the process. They must agree it is an appropriate target.
- Realistic – the target has to be achievable. If you set an objective which is not attainable people will be less likely to work towards it because they know it is not realistic.
- Time specific – it is important to specify how long people have to complete the objective rather than leaving it open ended

Typically, businesses set objectives that relate to:

- profit
- growth
- social considerations
- employee welfare.

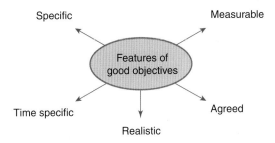

Figure 2.8 *Good objectives are SMART objectives*

Profit

Most organisations set out to make a profit. This profit can be used to reward owners and invest into the firm. Profit is vital for growth and to increase the wealth and income of the owners. To achieve its profit targets, the firm may set further objectives such as 'to increase revenue by …' or 'to decrease costs by …'.

However, there are some organisations, such as hospitals, schools, museums and the police force, that do not set out to make profits; these are owned by the government and are not profit-making organisations. Similarly, many clubs, sports teams and societies are non-profit making. These organisations set different objectives, such as to reduce waiting lists (hospitals) and to win the local league (a cricket club).

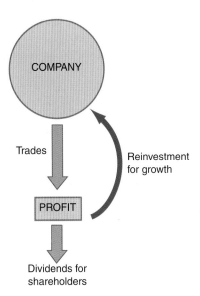

Figure 2.9 *Profits are needed for investment and dividends*

Growth

Some firms set growth or increasing market share as their main target. In the short run at least, this may mean they have to sacrifice profits to gain more of the market. For example, they may cut the price to sell more, and this might reduce their overall profits. Profits may also fall if the firm buys new equipment or facilities to allow it to produce on a bigger scale. In the long term, growth may lead to more profits. In the 1980s, many Japanese firms were successful in a range of markets such as motorbikes, cameras, watches and videos by entering with a low price to gain market share. The long-run objective was to destroy European producers and to gain control of the market.

MATHS MOMENT

$1+1=2$

Dave's Doughnuts sells 10 000 bagels a year in its home town; other shops in the town sell 20 000 in total.

1 What is Dave's Doughnuts share of the local market?
2 Dave's Doughnuts has set the objective of 50% market share by the end of next year. Assuming the market as a whole does not grow, how many bagels would the company have to sell to achieve this objective?

The top ten global companies in 2003 were as follows:

Rank	Company	Revenues ($ millions)
1	Wal-Mart Stores	246 525.0
2	General Motors	186 763.0
3	Exxon Mobil	182 466.0
4	Royal Dutch/Shell Group	179 431.0
5	BP	178 721.0
6	Ford Motor	163 871.0
7	DaimlerChrysler	141 421.1
8	Toyota Motor	131 754.2
9	General Electric	131 698.0
10	Mitsubishi	109 386.1

Table 2.6 *2003 top ten global companies*

Source: www.fortune.com, © 2003 Time Inc. All rights reserved.

Social considerations

Many organisations have social objectives. These set out what they hope to do for society in general, or for their local community. Targets may include recruiting more women or people from different ethnic groups, creating more jobs in the local area, reducing pollution levels or ensuring the fair treatment of disadvantaged groups.

Employee welfare

Many organisations appreciate the importance of people to their success and their responsibilities to their employees. After all, an employee spends much of his or her day working for the organisation. In return, the organisation may consider the type of work it provides, how it treats people and the career and social opportunities available within the firm.

The ten best companies to work for in the UK in 2003 were as follows:

Ranking	Company	Business description	UK headquarters	Staff	Sites	Sales £m	Pre-tax profits £m	Founded	Web address
1	Microsoft	Computer software	Reading	1595	3	17 622	7145	1975	microsoft.com/uk
2	Richer Sounds	Hi-fi retailer	London	455	50	94	5	1978	richersounds.com
3	Flight Centre	Travel agency	London	352	80	100	1	1995	flightcentre.com
4	People Soft	Computer software	Reading	257	1	2100	288	1993	peoplesoft.co.uk
5	Bromford Housing Group	Housing agency	Wolver-hampton	418	51	37	3	1963	bromford.co.uk
6	Timpson	Shoe repair and key cutting	Manchester	979	336	55	5	1865	timpson.com
7	Asda	Super-markets	Leeds	136 499	276	135 437	6710	1965	asda.co.uk
8	Bacardi-Martini	Drinks manufacturer	Southampton	530	1	349	N/A	1862	bacardimartini.co.uk
9	Electronic Arts	Computer and video games developer	Chertsey	494	3	131	6	1982	uk.ea.com
10	Hiscox	Specialist insurer	London	303	4	500	−34	1901	hiscox.com

Table 2.7 *The ten best companies to work for in the UK*

Source: Adapted from Sunday Times (100 Best Companies supplement), 2 March 2003

It is always important to try to identify a firm's overall aim and its objectives. After all, if you do not know what it is trying to achieve, you cannot tell whether it is doing well or not! Imagine that a football team sets out to achieve a draw in a match because this will give enough points to win the league. If you did not know this was the aim, you might criticise its performance and the result.

Whenever you are asked to comment on a firm's policies, try to work out what it is trying to achieve. If the objectives are not very clear, it is worth writing about this as well. If the firm does not seem to know where it is going, it is less likely to succeed.

Business in focus

'Oxfam's culture reflects a passionate commitment to overcoming the injustice of poverty and suffering. We seek to be:

- making a difference
- innovative
- collaborative
- accountable
- cost-effective.

Oxfam's beliefs: the lives of all human beings are of equal value. In a world rich in resources, poverty is an injustice which must be overcome ... Working together, we can build a just and safer world, in which people take control over their own lives and enjoy their basic rights. To overcome poverty and suffering involves changing unjust policies and practices, nationally and internationally, as well as working closely with people in poverty.'

1 What types of specific objective might Oxfam set itself? Remember that good objectives are SMART objectives.

Short-term and long-term objectives

When deciding what they want to achieve, firms can set both short-term and long-term objectives. If firms are aiming to grow in the long term, they may want to invest in training their staff, building up their brands, expanding into new markets and putting money into developing new products. All these activities may prove effective in the long run but cost money; in the short term profits may fall.

By comparison, a firm which wanted to maximise its rewards in the short run and was not concerned about the long term might cut back on all these activities. Imagine, for example, that you took over a business and were determined to make as much profit as you could in the next year. What could you do to achieve this objective? You could stop most of the repairs to the buildings and facilities, you could stop all research into new products, you could stop training people, you could end most of your advertising. In the short run profits may increase, but in the long run your business may be in a much weaker position.

UK firms are often criticised for setting objectives which are 'short-termist' and do not involve long-term planning. Critics say that UK businesses fail to invest enough to ensure they are strong enough in the long term. Instead, they often go for short-term rewards. In their defence, UK managers often blame their investors for insisting on short-term rewards. Many shareholders in the UK are companies such as pension funds and banks. These companies need to make money for their own investors and often want these earnings quickly; if a firm cannot deliver, they simply move their investment elsewhere. By comparison, in some other countries, such as Japan, investors are often other firms involved in the same industry (e.g. suppliers and distributors); these firms are more willing to wait for long-term gains and have an interest in the long-term survival and success of the company.

Why have objectives?

By agreeing objectives with other members of the organisation, managers can ensure that everyone is working towards the same overall goal. Without clear objectives, people will tend to do their own thing.

Objectives can also be very **motivating** for employees because they set out exactly what the firm wants them to achieve. If you are set a clear target, you know precisely what you have to do. Without a target, you may not be sure whether you are doing the right thing. Having a target also means you can measure your progress: you can see how you are getting on and whether or not you are likely to make your goal.

Objectives are also used to **review** plans. Managers can measure how much has been achieved compared with the target that was set. If the objective has not been reached, managers and employees can discuss why this has happened and what they can do differently to achieve the target next time. They can learn from their findings.

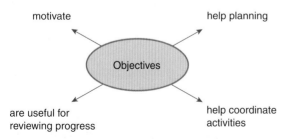

Figure 2.10 *The reasons for objectives*

Key issues

In the past, it was often assumed that the only real objective of all private sector organisations was to make a profit. In recent years, we have tended to take a much broader view of business activity, the reasons why organisations exist and what they set out to achieve. Prompted possibly by changes in society, many firms now set a wide range of objectives. Whilst profit remains important to the survival and expansion of firms, the need to meet social objectives is increasingly recognised. It will be interesting to see how the role of business within society and the public's perception of this role changes in the future.

QUICK CHECK QUESTIONS

1 Which of the following is the best example of an objective?
a) to enter new markets
b) to increase profits by 8% this year
c) to launch new products
d) to improve employee morale.

2 To achieve an objective a firm will develop a ....

3 A statement of a firm's overall purpose is called a .... statement.

4   Good objectives should be SMART. The S refers to:

a) solid
b) sensible
c) supreme
d) specific.

5   Good objectives should be SMART. The M refers to:

a) manageable
b) massive
c) measurable
d) mundane.

6   Good objectives should be SMART. The A refers to:

a) agreed
b) actual
c) anonymous
d) appealing.

7   Good objectives should be SMART. The R refers to:

a) random
b) radical
c) realistic
d) rancid.

8   Good objectives should be SMART. The T refers to:

a) typical
b) time specific
c) tense
d) totally real

9   Profit is a common objective of a business. This is measured by .... Less ....

10 Short-termism occurs when:

a) firms only accept short-term contracts
b) managers are only hired for short periods
c) managers focus on short-term, not long-term, gains
d) customers do not stay long with the business.

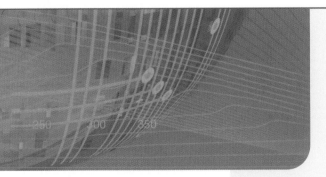

Progress questions

1 What is meant by a 'corporate aim'?   *(2 marks)*

2 What is meant by an 'objective'?   *(2 marks)*

3 What are the features of a good objective?
                                                  (2 marks)

4 The managers of the Pricedown, a discount clothes retail chain, are in the process of setting the firm's objectives for the next five years. State and explain two objectives the firm might set.
                                                  (6 marks)

5 For many years the Frantic Greetings Card company, which has 30 shops across the UK, operated without any clear, corporate objective. Explain the possible benefits to the company of introducing a corporate objective.   *(6 marks)*

6 Outline the possible objectives of the organisations below:
   ● a school
   ● a library
   ● a small, family printing company. *(3 marks each)*

7 Increasing profit is a very important objective for most firms. Explain why a business might want to make a profit.   *(6 marks)*

8 Explain why a supermarket chain might set growth as a main objective.   *(5 marks)*

9 Every year, the senior managers of Moretti plc, a large multinational oil company, leave their offices and go to a hotel to spend one week discussing their objectives for the coming year. Explain two factors which might affect the objectives the firm sets.   *(6 marks)*

10 Many UK firms are criticised for setting short-term rather than long-term objectives.
   a) Explain why UK firms might set short-term objectives.   *(4 marks)*
   b) Explain the possible consequences for UK firms of setting short-term rather than long-term objectives.   *(6 marks)*

Analytical and evaluative questions

11 Andy Buckle, the programmes director of a television company, set a target of an average of 10 million viewers for evening programmes, but failed to achieve it. Analyse the possible reasons why this target may not have been met. *(8 marks)*

12 Ekorette Ewane had built up a small computer repair business almost by accident. He had taught himself how his own computer worked, then his friends had asked him for help and it developed from there. Over the last few years his business had grown from just him to three other staff, and a turnover of several thousand pounds. His business advisers said it was time to take stock and think carefully about where the business was headed next. Discuss the possible benefits of establishing objectives for the business for the next five years. *(15 marks)*

13 To what extent should profit be the main objective of private sector business? *(15 marks)*

Case study   50 marks

Fulton's Ltd is a family firm which operates in the pottery industry. It is based in Stoke. The company is over 150 years old and has always been owned by the Fulton family. The present Managing Director is Alfred Fulton. He is tremendously proud of the family business but believes that it may be the time to turn the company into a plc. The business has struggled in recent years against much bigger, lower cost, overseas producers. For the last two years the company has actually made a loss and it looks unlikely that it will make a profit this year either.

Alfred has plans for a major modernisation of the organisation and even diversification into newer areas. At present, the company produces mainly for the trade – hotels and restaurants – but Alfred thinks there is still room in the market for well-designed crockery, bought directly by householders. This will require significant investment, however. Alfred always wants to make major changes to the way in which the firm produces. This will involve a substantial upheaval for staff but may ensure the survival of the firm. He also intends to review the company's suppliers and see if he can get better value for money.

However, he must first convince other members of the family to agree to a flotation of the company.

Some of them are very concerned that, if the company becomes a plc, the whole way in which the business is run is likely to change. 'If we become a plc you can bet that the firm will be forced to focus more on the short term rather than the long term,' said Alfred's brother. Alfred's response was, 'On the other hand, can we survive as we are?'

1 Distinguish between a private limited company and a public limited company. *(4 marks)*

2 Explain why it is important for companies such as Fulton's to make a profit. *(6 marks)*

3 Discuss the possible implications of the proposed flotation for the company's suppliers. *(10 marks)*

4 If Fulton's focused more on the short term than the long term, examine the possible implications for the business. *(8 marks)*

5 Would you advise the owners of Fulton's to turn the company into a plc? Justify your answer. *(12 marks)*

6 Discuss the possible implications for Fulton's employees if it becomes a plc. *(10 marks)*

>> Stakeholders

Business in focus

Shell companies recognise five areas of responsibility:

1 **To shareholders:** to protect shareholders' investment, and provide an acceptable return.
2 **To customers:** to win and maintain customers by developing and providing products and services which offer value in terms of price, quality, safety and environmental impact.
3 **To employees:** to respect the human rights of employees, to provide them with good and safe conditions of work, and good and competitive terms and conditions of service, to promote their development and best use of human talents.
4 **To those with whom they do business:** to seek mutually beneficial relationships.
5 **To society:** to conduct business as responsible corporate members of society, to observe the laws of the countries in which they operate and to express support for fundamental human rights.

According to the firm, 'Profitability is essential to discharging these responsibilities and staying in business. It is a measure both of efficiency and of the value that customers place on Shell's products and services. It is essential to the allocation of the necessary corporate resources and to support the continuing investment required to develop and produce future energy supplies to meet consumer needs . . .'

1 Why does Shell believe profits are important?

Who are the stakeholders?

All business activity affects many groups in society. For example, a decision to expand a company may affect:

● the employees, in terms of changes to their jobs
● the local community, in terms of increased traffic and noise levels, and the jobs created
● the local shops (new jobs may be created and more people may have greater spending power)
● suppliers may receive more orders
● retailers may have more products to sell.

All of these different groups are called stakeholders. A stakeholder is an individual or group which is affected by the actions of a business. A key issue for managers is the extent to which they should take the views of these stakeholders into account. Should managers only be concerned about what their owners think? Or should they also take their employees' needs into account? What about their suppliers? Or people who live in the area? Obviously, firms have to behave within the law and this means they automatically have some legal obligations to these groups. The question is, should they do more than this and, if so, how much?

Stakeholders and business success

Some managers believe that stakeholders are very important to the success of their business. They think that if a firm pays attention to the needs of different stakeholder groups, this will help the firm to succeed. For example:

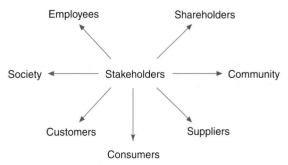

Figure 2.11 *Stakeholders in a business*

Business in focus

'The John Lewis Partnership is owned in trust for the benefit of its employees. The Partnership's founder, John Spedan Lewis, defined as the supreme purpose of the organisation 'the happiness of its members.'

All profits are either reinvested in the business or distributed to Partners as Bonus and other benefits. A proportion of each year's profits is retained for reinvestment in the business to ensure that it remains healthy and successful. And each year, the Partnership's Board decides the annual Bonus rate. Bonus is paid as a simple percentage of the Partner's pay, the same rate for everyone in the organisation, on the basis that pay is the best measure of each individual's contribution to the total result. In addition to Bonus, Partners receive a package of other benefits, most notably the Pension, a non-contributory scheme for which all qualify after five years service. Other benefits include subsidies on theatre and cinema tickets, a chain of four Partnership holiday centres and the Partnership Sailing Club which maintains five yachts.

Source: John Lewis Partnership
For more information on the John Lewis Partnership, visit
www.johnlewis.com and www.john-lewis-partnership.co.uk.

1 What is the supreme purpose of the John Lewis Partnership?
2 How do you think this might affect the way the business is run?

- If employees are treated well, they are likely to be more motivated and work more effectively for the business.
- If suppliers are paid on time and kept well informed, they will provide good quality products for the firm and make sure they supply their products on time and in the right quantities.
- If the firm tries to help the community (for example, by providing jobs or by investing in local schemes) this provides a better environment for employees to work in and helps to recruit and retain employees.
- If the firm tries to reduce any negative impact it has on the environment, this leads to a better quality of life for everyone.

By taking account of its stakeholders a firm:

- may attract more **investors**. Investors are increasingly looking at how firms behave, as well as what they actually produce. Firms that exploit child labour, produce guns or harm the environment, for example, may find it more difficult to raise finance.
- may find it easier to **recruit staff**. Employees are often interested in a company's treatment of stakeholders and take this into account when deciding whether to accept a job.
- may find that the government (at both local and national level) is more co-operative because of a good track record. This may make it easier to get permission for certain activities or in preventing unfavourable legislation from being introduced.

The stakeholder approach takes the view that it is much better to work *with* these different groups, rather than to take a more selfish approach, focusing purely on owners' and managers' needs.

Firms take many decisions which affect their stakeholders. For example, whether or not to expand production in the UK. A firm may decide to produce in this country even if it is more expensive than locating elsewhere because it keeps jobs in the UK. Some companies have to decide whether or not to provide employees in developing countries with similar rights to employees in the UK. It may be cheaper and legal to employ child labour in some countries or to avoid some of the UK's safety procedures, but should they treat their stakeholderes better than this?

'You can't get better than a Kwik Fit fitter'

This slogan accurately reflects the views of the founder of Kwik Fit, Sir Tom Farmer. Sir Tom built the business up over 20 years and, at the very centre of its success, was his employees. 'We at Kwik Fit recognise that our people in our centres are the all important contact with the customers and they are the key to the success of the Kwik Fit Group.' The company provides extensive training, allows employees to become shareholders and respects their input. 'Customer delight is vital, but without the people at Kwik Fit there would be no product,' says Sir Tom.

Stakeholders v Shareholders

Some managers believe that the needs of stakeholders should not be considered. These managers believe they should only pay attention to their owners – the shareholders – and that the needs of stakeholders are irrelevant and often expensive to address. For example:

- Improving the quality of life of employees is not the firm's responsibility and is likely to involve unnecessary spending on training and better conditions.
- Managers should try to force suppliers to cut their prices to save money for the firm; the company should also try and pay as late as possible, to keep its own money in the bank as long as possible.
- A firm should not worry about the environment or the community unless the law says it has to; any changes in its production process are likely to be expensive.

The extent to which a firm pays attention to its stakeholders depends on what the owners and managers believe is important. It also depends on the power of the stakeholder groups themselves. If suppliers are particularly strong or employees are well organised, the firm is more likely to pay attention to their needs and interests.

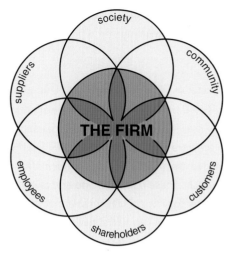

Figure 2.12 *The stakeholder approach believes that the interests of different groups overlap*

Welway plc is a manufacturer of lights and lamps. Below is some data on the company.

	Compared with last year
Number of employees	−12%
Profits	+29%
Number of suppliers used	−20%
Average price of goods	+8%

Based on the data, would you say the firm was stakeholder friendly or not? What other data might help you to decide?

Interest in the environment has grown rapidly in the last decade. In 1981 there were around 30 000 members of Greenpeace; there are now over 200 000. In 1981 there were 18 000 members of Friends of the Earth; now there are over 100 000. This interest in environmental issues puts more pressure on firms to be environmentally friendly.

Whilst some firms are more responsive to stakeholder needs than others, this does not mean they can meet all of their stakeholders' needs. There is almost inevitably some trade-off between the requirements of different groups. Perhaps the key is the willingness of firms to listen and take stakeholders into account when planning; this does not mean they can always do what stakeholders want.

EXAMINER'S ADVICE

The stakeholder concept is an important one for many businesses and, as a result, questions on this area are quite popular. Typically, you will be asked to identify the benefits of such an approach. These might include employee and customer loyalty, and favourable media coverage. However, whilst the stakeholder approach may seem appealing, do remember that it is rarely possible to please all of the people all of the time. No matter how much firms may want to meet stakeholders' needs, some trade-off is almost inevitable. It is also important to remember that not all firms believe such an approach is appropriate: some managers will stress their responsibility to the firm's owners above all else.

Key issues

Our view of the responsibilities of organisations is continually developing. Many customers, investors and employees now believe firms have a much greater responsibility to society in general than they did in the past. Increasingly, we not only expect firms to take responsibility for their own actions but also for others in the supply chain – firms may well be held responsible for the actions of their suppliers, for example. This means that organisations must take more care when planning and include a wider range of views and interests than would have been the case in the past. It also means the definition of a 'successful' business is now likely to include several indicators, apart from just profit; for example, we may want to examine the social impact of a firm's activities as well as its profitability.

APPLICATION IN ACTION

There are many different stakeholders, and the way firms react to them will differ. John Lewis prides itself on its treatment of its staff (called Partners), who in fact own the business. Ben and Jerry's Ice Cream paid great attention to its suppliers as well as its employees, particularly its local suppliers in Vermont where the business was established. The Co-Operative Bank asks its customers what they regard as the most pressing issues. Firms may not be able to serve all stakeholder groups equally, so may focus on some particular groups.

QUICK CHECK QUESTIONS

1   A stakeholder:
a)   owns the business
b)   is owned by the government
c)   is affected by a firm's decisions
d)   has legal control over the business.
2   State two possible obligations a firm might have to its employees.
3   State two possible obligations a firm might have to its suppliers.
4   State two possible obligations a firm might have to its community.
5   State two possible obligations a firm might have to its shareholders.
6   Which of the following statements is true?
a)   all shareholders are stakeholders
b)   all stakeholders are shareholders
c)   dividends must be paid every year
d)   companies' profits belong to the government.
7   Give an example of how shareholder and employee interests may conflict.
8   Give an example of how shareholder and supplier interests may conflict.
9   Give an example of how shareholder and supplier interests may work together.
10 Give an example of how shareholder and customer interests may work together.

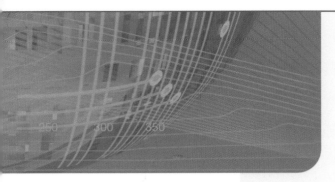

Progress questions

1 What is meant by the term 'stakeholder'?

(2 marks)

2 Explain two reasons why a manufacturing business might take account of its stakeholders' views. *(6 marks)*

3 Some managers believe that they do not need to take account of their stakeholders' views. Explain the arguments against taking account of stakeholders' views. *(6 marks)*

4 Bultman plc is a mass producer of nuts and bolts. It has been based in Birmingham for 30 years but is considering closing the UK factory and producing in Eastern Europe to reduce costs. Examine the ways in which this move might affect different stakeholder groups.

(8 marks)

5 'We believe that our stakeholders are absolutely crucial to our success.' Explain how stakeholders can affect the success of a firm.

(6 marks)

6 Distinguish between shareholders and stakeholders. *(3 marks)*

7 Explain two possible obligations a firm has to its employees. *(6 marks)*

8 Explain two possible obligations a firm might have to its suppliers. *(6 marks)*

9 Explain two possible obligations a firm might have to the local community. *(6 marks)*

10 Explain two possible problems of meeting the needs of different stakeholder groups. *(6 marks)*

Analytical and evaluative questions

11 Analyse the possible obligations of a school to its stakeholders. *(8 marks)*

12 To what extent do the objectives of the stakeholders of an oil company necessarily conflict? *(15 marks)*

13 Discuss whether a leading chain of sandwich shops should switch to organic ingredients.

(15 marks)

Case study   **50 marks**

Cerutos owns a chain of high street stores. It is one of the major buyers of UK-produced clothes and has a significant impact on the success of this industry. In recent years, Cerutos has been criticised for providing a poor and uninspiring range of products which are overpriced. Following numerous complaints from its shareholders, the Chairman and Managing Director were forced to resign. In an effort to improve its performance, it has made drastic cuts in the number of staff it employs. It has also decided to switch from UK suppliers to cheaper suppliers from abroad. The UK Clothing Industry Association has criticised Cerutos for its sudden decision to change suppliers and has highlighted the damage this will do to their industry. 'Cerutos has a responsibility to its suppliers which is as important as its reponsibility to its shareholders. This will damage its business in the long term.' The media has also criticised the firm for sacking so many of its own staff, 'A firm's employees are its most important stakeholder group – without them you have no business. A firm must honour its responsibilities to its employees', said one business analyst.

1 *What is meant by a stakeholder?* (2 marks)

2 *Examine how switching to cheaper overseas suppliers might damage Cerutos' business in the long term.* (8 marks)

3 *Explain two possible responsibilities Cerutos might have to its customers.* (6 marks)

4 *Examine the possible responsibilities Cerutos might have to its employees.* (8 marks)

5 *Discuss the ways in which Cerutos might react to the criticism from the media.* (11 marks)

6 *'Cerutos has a responsibility to its suppliers which is as important as its responsibility to its shareholders.' Evaluate this view.* (15 marks)

>> Business strategy

Objectives and strategies

A strategy is a long-term plan showing how a firm will achieve its objectives. So, the objective is the desired destination and the strategy is the means of getting there. For example, the objective may to be to increase profits; the strategy may be to reduce costs or increase revenue. If the objective is to boost sales, the strategy may be to launch more products or to sell more of the existing products overseas.

Key terms

A **strategy** is a long-term plan and a means of achieving the company's objectives.
Diversification occurs when a firm moves into different markets.

The strategy a firm chooses is absolutely critical to its success. If a firm chooses the wrong route, it will struggle to be successful. Imagine you wanted to visit somewhere you had never been before but set off in the wrong direction with the wrong map – the chances are, you would never get there. If, on the other hand, you chose the right route and planned your journey carefully, you would have a much better chance of succeeding. The same is true in business. If you know where you want to go and choose the right route, success is more likely.

The choice of strategy depends on the objectives and the firm's resources. It will also change as the market conditions change just as the best route to a destination can also change over time.

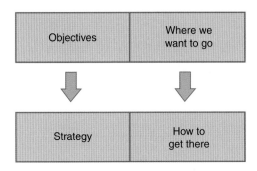

Figure 2.13 *Objectives and strategies*

Devising a strategy

The following are examples of strategic decisions:

- In 1999, Somerfield supermarkets suffered because of the price war waged by Tesco and Asda (now owned by Wal-Mart). From January to November, the fall in its share price knocked £1.8 bn off its market value. In response to its decline, the company changed its strategy and exited from large-scale supermarkets and retreated into local convenience stores. The recovery plan involved the sale of 140 large Somerfield stores and 300 Kwik Save shops. The local stores were positioned as convenience stores where consumers could do top-up shopping. They stocked more local produce and store managers were given greater responsibility.

- In the 1990s, British Airways pursued a strategy of globalisation. This involved developing links with other airlines so its own passengers could have access to the world via partner companies. It also changed the designs of its planes to reflect a more international image (rather than being very clearly a British company). In the late 1990s, the company's performance was rather disappointing and it had to change its strategy, focusing more on reducing costs with the objective of restoring profits.

- Virgin has actively pursued a strategy of diversification; this means it has moved into several different markets. The firm operates in any areas where it believes its brand can add value and its managers can offer a good service which is both profitable and fun. This has led them into running railways, airlines, motorbike taxis, a mobile phone company, making wedding clothes and many other different kinds of

businesses. The company has also ensured that each business is kept separate from the other ones; although they carry the Virgin name and make use of the 'Virgin' approach, they are managed separately.

- In 1996, Unilever, producer of brands such as Dove, Clavin Klein and Knorr, set out its Path to Growth Strategy. This had three key financial benchmarks:
  - underlying sales growth of 5–6% a year
  - an operating profit margin of more than 16%
  - double-digit growth each year in the earnings per share (essentially the profits of the company per share).

  To achieve this the company sold off or ended production of many of its lesser known brands and focused on its core (or 'power' brands) such as Dove, which it extended into numerous different markets.

- In recent years, Boots the Chemist has struggled to find a coherent strategy. In an attempt to revive its fortunes after the attacks from supermarkets in product areas such as soaps and shampoos, it adopted a 'wellbeing' strategy focusing on high-value services such as dentistry, opticians, aromatherapy and health and beauty services. This strategy proved unsuccessful and the company is now trying to focus once again on its core high street business.

INTERPRETING DATA

Brian Connelly was hired by Madisons Supermarkets two years ago to turn the business around.

Using the data below, comment on his success.

	This year	Two years ago
Turnover	£200m	£160
Profit	£10m	£9m
Number of stores	20	15

Business in focus

Over the past few years, Tesco's the retailer has been hugely successful not only in the UK but also abroad.

According to the company, its strategy is 'for long-term growth, and focuses on four elements:

Core UK business

The UK business remains our core market. Our focused strategy of providing exceptional value and choice for customers ensures that we continue to increase our market share. We have four store types: Extra, our hypermarket destination shopping offer; Superstores; Metro, our town centre and city centre stores; and Express, our convenience offer.

Non-food business

We now have a 5% market share. Our goal is to be as strong in non-food as in food. Our non-food offer encompasses electrical, home entertainment, clothing, homeshop, cookshop and, in our largest stores, white goods.

Retailing services

As customers' shopping habits change, we change and respond by providing new products and services. Our e-commerce business has grown rapidly. We are the world's largest grocery e-tailer and operate our system in the international markets. Both tesco.com and Tesco Personal Finance demonstrate our ability to extend the Tesco brand. We have also moved into Telecoms, launching a fixed-line phone service and a directory enquiry service.

International

Tesco has successfully opened up new growth markets in Central Europe and Asia. The proportion of total Group space outside of the UK was 47% at the half year 2003/2004. We now operate in Hungary, Poland, the Czech Republic, the Slovak Republic, Thailand, South Korea, Taiwan, Malaysia and the Republic of Ireland. In 2003/2004 we acquired the C Two-Network, a price-leading retailer in Japan.'

Source: www.tesco.com, 2003

1 Why do you think Tesco has moved away from just its core strategy?

Different kinds of strategy

When deciding on its strategy, a firm has to consider the scope of its activities:

- How many markets will it compete in?
- Will it offer products just in the UK or in other countries?
- What range of products and services will it offer?

Niche strategy

One option is to choose a niche strategy; this focuses on one small segment of the market. Mills and Boon only produce romantic novels, for example, and Umbro produce only football clothing. When competing in a niche, a firm specialises on one area of the market; this could be a way of avoiding the major producers who may not be interested in a relatively small segment.

Mass market strategy

A mass market strategy, on the other hand, aims at the market as a whole; products such as Ariel washing powder are mass market products. The Morgan car company clearly pursues a niche strategy producing a traditional, hand-built sports car; the Ford Mondeo is a mass market car aimed at a much larger number of drivers.

Which strategy?

The strategy a firm chooses depends on a range of factors.

- The skills and assets of the firm – a strategy should build on a firm's strengths – and minimise the impact of its weaknesses.

Figure 2.14 *Strategy depends on . . .*

- The market itself – an effective strategy will aim to exploit market opportunities – and to avoid or tackle market threats.
- The competition – the best strategy will depend on what competitors are doing and will aim to outperform them.

SWOT analysis

To decide on the best strategy to follow, firms usually undertake a SWOT analysis. This means, that a firm examines its Strengths, Weaknesses, Opportunities and Threats.

People in business

Figure 2.15 *Karan Bilimoria, the founder of Cobra Beer*

Cobra Beer was set up by Karan Bilimoria in 1989. Karan is the son of an Indian general and a graduate of Cambridge University. Rather than pursue a more traditional career path he decided to become an entrepreneur after university.

He started out by importing polo sticks from India to sell to Harrods. He then moved into beer, specifically targeting Indian restaurants in the UK. Sales of Cobra Beer are now worth over £50m a year. The success of the business has been partly due to its highly focused niche strategy of selling through Indian restaurants and therefore not attacking more established

brewers head on. Amazingly the beer that is perceived as being from India is actually produced in Bedfordshire. However Karan is now considering producing in India because of the enormous potential in this market. In 2002 beer consumption in India grew by 10% (although at an annual 0.6 litres per person per year consumption remains low).

Karan is also keen to enter the mass market in the UK and distribute Cobra Beer more widely to supermarkets, pubs, bars and clubs. This will mean that Cobra will now directly challenge brands such as Stella Artois, Carling, and Heineken.

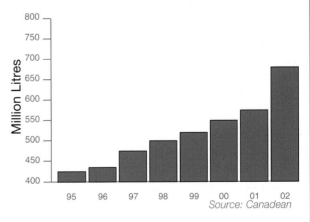

Figure 2.16 *Growth of beer consumption in India*

Common strengths

A firm's strengths and weaknesses are internal factors. Strengths work in its favour and weaknesses leave it vulnerable to competitors. For example, a business could have a number of strengths:

- Brand name – a firm may have a well-known name which could make it easier to launch new products or could mean it has brand loyalty. This would help protect it against actions by competitors. The brand names of Sony, Marlboro, Rolex and IBM are extremely powerful assets for the companies involved.
- Distribution network – a widespread and effective network can make it easier to get products to the market. Coca Cola has an incredible distribution network, which is one reason for its large market share.
- Employees – a firm may have well-trained employees who are more productive than their colleagues in competing firms. Microsoft's staff has huge creative and technical expertise which have enabled the company to stay ahead of the competition.

Common weaknesses

For many businesses, their strengths are balanced by their weaknesses. Some common weaknesses are set out below.

- A lack of new products – a firm may be relying on relatively old products for its sales. This may make it vulnerable in the long run. In the 1990s, Marks and Spencer was heavily criticised for having a very poor product range and failing to anticipate market requirements.
- High costs – many of the UK banks have a large number of high street outlets. Although you might think this is a strength, they are very expensive to run and may not be needed as more and more people turn to telephone and Internet banking. In the short run at least, the high costs

of these outlets make it difficult for the banks to compete with new competitors, such as Egg and Virgin who have lower costs.
- A high level of borrowing – if interest rates are high or rising and the firm has a high level of borrowing, this may mean it has to repay relatively large sums on its loans.

The strengths and weaknesses of a firm can change over time. For example, Japanese firms used to be associated with poor quality and unreliable products. This changed in the 1980s and 1990s to such an extent that UK companies adopted Japanese sounding names because consumers would assume they made high quality products (for example, Matsui)!

Common opportunities

Opportunities and threats are external factors. Opportunities create areas where the firm can develop and threats are factors that may weaken a firm's position.

For example, opportunities could include:

- New markets due to economic or political change – the opening up of Eastern Europe in the 1990s has created all kinds of opportunities for UK firms. For some it offers the chance of a cheaper production base; for others it offers cheaper suppliers or a new market.
- New technology – the rapid growth of the Internet in recent years has created incredible opportunities for firms. E-commerce is a particularly good example of this – more and more firms are now offering their products and services through the Internet. The amazing rise of companies such as Amazon.com and Lastminute.com show the potential opportunities of new technology.

An opportunity is only an opportunity if a firm can actually take advantage of it, i.e. if it has the resources necessary to exploit it.

Common threats

Firms may face a variety of threats:

- Economic change – in the late 1990s the UK exchange rate was very strong. This made UK

Figure 2.17 *Jack Welch*

Jack Welch is one of the most respected business leaders in the world. From the time he took over General Electric in 1981 until 1999, he increased the value of the company from $14bn to more than $400bn, nearly quadrupled sales to over $1000bn and has grown profits almost six times to $9.3bn.

At the beginning of the 1980s, GE was a giant of a company, full of rules and traditions. Jack Welch brought about a revolution, introducing a culture which allowed the company to react quickly and expand rapidly. One of Jack Welch's last initiatives before he retired was to make sure the company was exploiting the potential of e-commerce. To prepare for e-business he urged his staff to throw out their preconceptions. The initiative was called 'destroyyourbusiness.com' because the senior managers believe that only 'by imagining the end of the old business can you create something new'.

goods expensive in terms of foreign currencies and made it difficult for UK firms to sell abroad. It also made imported goods cheaper.

- New competitors – in 1999 Wal Mart took over Asda supermarkets. Wal Mart is a huge American supermarket that has successfully pursued a strategy of low prices. Its large size means it can bargain with suppliers for good deals and pass this on to the consumer. The entrance of Wal Mart into the UK posed a real threat to existing UK supermarkets.
- Changes in legislation – these can force firms to change their policies. The increased interest in the protection of the environment means that companies may be forced to change their production process even more in the future to reduce pollution emissions. The car industry is well aware that the government and customers are concerned about the damage that cars do to the environment and are looking for alternatives. Unless the car companies can react by changing their products to become more environmentally friendly, customers may use public transport much more. This is why car companies are spending millions of pounds each year developing electric cars.

Factors that may threaten some firms do not necessarily threaten all firms – it depends on whether they are protected, e.g. by having a patent.

Why undertake SWOT analysis?

The purpose of SWOT analyses is to identify the *existing position* of the firm and to flag up possible future *external changes* in its environment. This is an important part of the planning process. A firm will seek to build on its strengths and protect itself against its weaknesses. It will also aim to exploit market opportunities whilst trying to reduce the impact of any threats. By undertaking a SWOT analysis, a firm examines the nature of its market in depth. This is a very valuable exercise because it forces managers to think about the present situation of the firm and what might happen in the future. It is very easy for managers to let things continue as they are without thinking about what could be different; many managers wait until a crisis occurs before they really examine the firm's position. SWOT analysis may help to prevent such a crisis; by identifying its weaknesses and possible threats, a firm may be able to take steps which prevent these becoming a danger in the future.

Business in focus

In the 1980s LEGO, the Danish toy maker, undertook a SWOT analysis to help to formulate its strategy.

This analysis might have included the following factors:

Strengths
- a globally recognised brand
- a high level of technological expertise and quality production
- a family-owned business enabling it to plan long term without the short-term pressures from outsiders
- financially independent – the company had very few borrowings

Weaknesses
- over-reliance on one product: the Lego bricks
- an inward-looking management style
- a conservative culture

Opportunities
- extend the brand
- license the brand
- form alliances with other firms
- open more theme parks

Threats
- danger of imitations and new entrants to the market
- greater competition for childrens' spending, e.g. mobile phones
- children maturing younger and growing out of Lego at an earlier age (called 'age compression')

Following this SWOT analysis, Lego:
- started to open more theme parks worldwide to reduce its reliance on Lego bricks
- launched products for different age groups, e.g. Mindstorm, which were robot models for teenagers
- formed various alliances with film companies to feature characters in the Lego range
- worked with Microsoft to develop the Mindstorm characters
- recruited more outsiders to the firm to increase its diversity.

For more information on Lego, visit www.lego.com.

Although techniques like SWOT analysis can help a firm in its planning, they do not guarantee that the right plan is actually chosen. All SWOT analysis can do is highlight the present situation of a firm and the future possibilities within its markets. It is up to management to interpret this information correctly and decide exactly what the firm has to do. Even if the right plan is chosen, it still has to be implemented correctly! Implementation is one of the most difficult stages in the whole planning process: people resist change, perhaps the required finance cannot be raised or certain activities take longer than expected.

A problem with SWOT analysis is that managers are often reluctant to identify the firm's weaknesses or possible threats (or are not capable of doing this). There is a tendency within any organisation to overemphasise its strengths without realising the true significance of threats which exist and sometimes without fully appreciating the opportunities which exist. Companies such as IBM, Xerox (who make photocopiers), Ever Ready (who made batteries) and British Airways have all lost major shares in their markets because they failed to anticipate threats.

APPLICATION IN ACTION

- One of the big issues facing firms in recent years has been the rise of the Internet. This has posed many strategic questions for manufacturers and retailers – whether to sell via the Internet and how to use the Internet to promote the business.
- Another strategic issue is the European Union – firms have to consider whether to trade within the Union and, if so, how much. These decisions have to be continually reviewed – for example, with more countries joining the Union and with so many countries joining the single currency, the euro.

QUICK CHECK QUESTIONS

1 The strategy is the plan of how to achieve the objectives. True or false?

2 If a firm moves into a completely new market, this is known as:
a) dilution
b) dimunition
c) diversification
d) deregulation.

3 A small part of a market is called a ......

4 SWOT analysis involves an examination of:
a) strengths, weaknesses, opportunities and threats
b) strengths, waste, outsiders and threats
c) sudden weaknesses, outstanding threats
d) social ways of overcoming threats.

5 In SWOT analysis, what might be an 'S'?
a) new markets opening
b) high levels of cash
c) limited distribution
d) poor brand image.

6 In SWOT analysis, what might be a 'W'?
a) customer loyalty
b) new competitors entering the market
c) poor quality goods
d) market growth.

7 In SWOT analysis, what might be an 'O'?
a) negative cashflow
b) unique selling proposition
c) opening of new markets
d) high borrowing.

8 In SWOT analysis, what might be a 'T'?
a) potential takeover by another firm
b) low borrowing
c) growing sales
d) high profit margins.

9 SWOT analysis:
a) guarantees a firm's success
b) helps a firm's planning
c) looks only at the internal functions of the business
d) looks only at the external environment in which a firm operates.

10 A firm may protect a new invention by taking out a ....

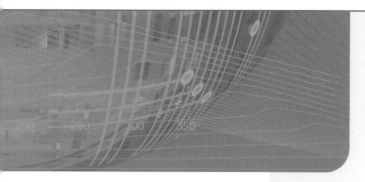

Progress questions

1   What is meant by a 'strategy?'   *(2 marks)*

2   What factors should a firm take into account when deciding on a new strategy?   *(6 marks)*

3   Explain the relationship between a firm's objectives and its strategy.   *(4 marks).*

4   Explain the difference between a 'differentiation' strategy and a 'low-cost strategy'.   *(4 marks)*

5   David Jason is the founder of Jason Engineering, a company which produces engine parts for the motor industry. Rather than compete head on with other manufacturers, David has adopted a niche strategy focusing on less common and higher-priced items. Explain the possible advantages and disadvantages to Jason Engineering of adopting a niche strategy.   *(4 marks)*

6   Eva Poloni decided to set up a health club in her local area. Rather than target wealthy households, she decided to target the mass market. Explain what is meant by a mass market strategy in this case.   *(4 marks)*

7   Freefall is a company which provides training for people who want to learn how to parachute. The company has had a few bad years recently and has called in management consultants to decide what to do next. The consultants have advised the company to produce a SWOT analysis. What is meant by a SWOT analysis?   *(4 marks)*

8   Research and analyse the strategy of one of the organisations listed below (or one of your own choice):
The Body Shop
Nike
McDonald's
Sainsbury's
IBM
Virgin   *(8 marks)*

9   Outline two possible opportunities and two possible threats facing the car industry in the future.   *(8 marks)*

10   Explain how economic change can provide both opportunities and threats for hotels.   *(8 marks)*

Analytical and evaluative questions

11   Produce a SWOT analysis for British Airways or a business that you know.   *(8 marks)*

12   To what extent can undertaking a SWOT analysis benefit a sole trader running his own plumbing business?   *(15 marks)*

13   Helmut Reiner is the chief executive of a business that has specialised in producing different varieties of tea. He is considering moving the business into the herbal drinks market. Discuss the possible advantages and disadvantages of this strategy.   *(15 marks)*

End of chapter questions

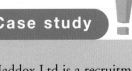

Jav Faruq left school after his A Levels. Although he had done well at school and many people had expected him to go on to university, Jav had known for many years that what he really wanted to do was to set up his own business. His main passion in life was fishing and for years his burning desire was to set up an angling shop in his home town. He was absolutely sure there was a gap in the market and when he asked his friends what they thought, they assured him it was a good idea. He had a vision of a shop with all the latest equipment, attracting people from miles away. According to Jav, all he had to do was raise the money to set up the shop in the right location and the customers would arrive in their hundreds.

Although he has had a part-time job for the last couple of years at a local supermarket, Jav has no savings of his own to put into the business. He asked his mum whether she could help him out, but she did not have any money to spare either. The

only possibility, she said, was Jav's uncle, Imran, but Jav and he had never got on very well and he did not have much interest in fishing. On the other hand, Imran did have an eye for a good deal!

Jav decided to visit the bank. Having studied Business Studies at school, he knew he would need a business plan.

1 *Explain two factors which might be important when Jav is choosing a location for his shop.*
(5 marks)

2 *Outline two factors which Jav should include in his business plan.* (6 marks)

3 *Analyse the ways in which Jav might raise the finance necessary to set up his business.*
(8 marks)

4 *Discuss the factors the bank might take into account when deciding whether to lend Jav any money.* (11 marks)

Maddox Ltd is a recruitment agency based in Birmingham. It is owned by Jim and Sophia Maddox who set the business up in 1974. Their son, Paul, also works in the business. The company specialises in finding temporary office staff to cover for illness, maternity leave or sudden increases in workload at other firms. Although there have been a couple of years when profits have dipped, the business has generally gone from strength to strength and it now has offices in 12 cities in the UK. Jim feels the time is right to pass the business over to Paul and is ready to enjoy early retirement. Sophia, however, believes that now is the time to push for real growth. 'Everyone is looking for a flexible labour force at the moment and we can help provide the staff they need as and when they need

them. Why not seize the opportunity and expand on a major scale to really push the business forward? Let's float the business now and become a plc. This will allow us to raise the finance we need for expansion and to improve our IT facilities. We can grow the firm for the next ten years or so and then sell up. Get this right and we'll be multi-millionaires!' Jim is less keen. 'We have built this business up by taking the long-term view, being willing to take things slowly and carefully. If we go public, the investors will want us to deliver short-term rewards rather than think long term. If we don't, the share price will collapse and we will be vulnerable to take-over. Best to stay as we are and keep it in the family.'

Continued

1 *Maddox Ltd is a private limited company. Explain what is meant by the term 'private limited company'.* (4 marks)

2 *Jim is worried about what will happen to the company's share price if the business is floated. Explain two factors which might determine the share price of Maddox.* (6 marks)

3 *Analyse the factors which might influence whether or not Maddox Ltd becomes a public limited company.* (9 marks)

4 *Jim feels that if the company becomes a plc 'the investors will want us to deliver short-term rewards rather than think long term'. Discuss the possible consequences of switching to a more short-term approach for a company such as Maddox.* (11 marks)

Case study   **50 marks**

Hayfield Entertainments plc runs three theme parks in the UK. The parks consist of a variety of rides, shops, fast-food stalls, bars and play areas. The parks have targeted mainly young people aged 16 to 25, looking for a good day out. Attendance figures grew steadily through the 1990s. With higher average incomes, more leisure time and better facilities, the parks proved very popular.

Increasingly, the company has been feeling under attack from other theme park operators who have been expanding rapidly and have been cutting their prices. Hayfield's managers were particularly worried when they read that Edge, a leading US theme-park operator, was going to open a series of parks in the UK, targeting exactly the same market segment. Edge is a huge operator in the United States and, with its vast resources, could cause major problems for Hayfield.

Hayfield has also found that its target age group wants more and more thrills, and ever more dramatic and frightening rides. This requires increasing investment and there is less time to earn back the money before customers become bored once again.

In response to the changing environment, the Hayfield management team has decided it is important to think carefully about what to do next. They have undertaken a SWOT analysis of the business as part of the planning process. Their findings included the following:

Strengths
● We own several excellent sites within the UK, including large areas of undeveloped land.

Weaknesses
● We have relatively high levels of borrowing.

Opportunites
● Growing numbers of families are going to theme parks.

Threats
● An aggressive marketing policy from Edge and other operators.
● A possible downturn in the economy.

Following its review, the company has decided to change its strategy and focus more on family business. The aim is to target families and develop theme parks where people can come and stay for a whole weekend, rather than a few hours. This would require heavy investment in hotels and a much broader range of entertainment, but the firm feels this is an unexploited market opportunity.

1 a) *Hayfield Entertainments is a public limited company. What is meant by a 'public limited company'?* (3 marks)

   b) *Discuss the possible advantages and disadvantages to Hayfield Entertainments of being a plc rather than a limited company.* (9 marks)

Continued

2 a) *What is meant by 'SWOT analysis'?* (3 marks)
  b) *Examine the ways in which SWOT analysis might benefit a firm like Hayfield Entertainments plc.* (7 marks)

3 *Examine two possible reasons why Hayfield decided to change its strategy.* (8 marks)

4 *Discuss the ways in which a downturn in the economy might affect Hayfield Entertainments.* (10 marks)

5 *Discuss the factors which might influence whether or not the new strategy is successful or not for Hayfield.* (10 marks)

Case study

65 marks

'The Body Shop mission statement is:

- To dedicate our business to the pursuit of social and environmental change
- To creatively balance the financial and human needs of our stakeholders' employees, franchisees, customers, suppliers and shareholders
- To courageously ensure that our business is ecologically sustainable, meeting the needs of the present without compromising the future
- To meaningfully contribute to local, national and international communities in which we trade by adopting a code of conduct which ensures care, honesty, fairness and respect
- To passionately campaign for the protection of the environment, human and civil rights and against animal testing within the cosmetics and toiletries industry
- To tirelessly narrow the gap between principle and practice, whilst making fun, passion and care part of our daily lives.

The Body Shop believes it should be open and honest in its business dealing and, in 1991, committed itself to an active programme of assessment on the impact of its activities. This 'stakeholder audit' includes:

- a social audit
- an environmental audit
- an animal protection audit.

Senior managers must run the organisation in such a way as to satisfy the different groups of stakeholders. This may not be easy and conflicts of interest may develop. Priorities may have to be

agreed and compromises made. The managers' jobs may be made much harder as the different stakeholders' objectives change over time, according to how the firm is performing.

The stakeholder audit involves a mix of focus groups, market research-style questionnaires, face-to-face interviews and data collection. The information is collected from each stakeholder group. The findings are published and lead to further action by the firm. The overriding objective is to make the Body Shop more efficient, accountable and more effective.'

Source: Times 100 Case Studies 1999

1 *The Body Shop has a very distinctive mission statement.*
  a) *What is meant by a 'mission statement'?* (2 marks)
  b) *Examine two reasons why a firm might produce a mission statement.* (8 marks)

2 a) *Identify four possible stakeholder groups of The Body Shop.* (2 marks)
  b) *Examine two possible responsibilities the firm might have to each of these groups.* (8 marks)

3 *Discuss the possible reasons why The Body Shop might have decided to undertake a 'stakeholder audit'.* (15 marks)

4 *Senior managers at The Body Shop must run the organisation in such a way as to satisfy the different groups of stakeholders. However, the firm recognises that possible conflicts may occur between different stakeholder groups. Discuss the possible areas in which a conflict of*

objectives between stakeholder groups of The
Body Shop might occur.   (15 marks)

5 'The success of The Body Shop is mainly due to
its social and environmental objectives.' Discuss
this view.   (15 marks)

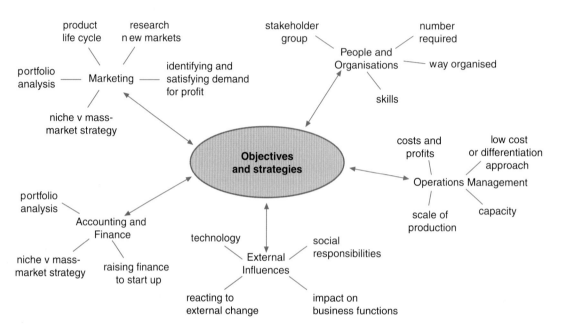

Figure 2.18 *Relationships between Objectives and Strategies and other topics in the AS specification*

Marketing

Introduction

- What is marketing?
- What does the customer need? What do customers want?
- What is the right product? The right place to buy it? The right price? The right way to promote it?

>> What is marketing?

Introduction

A formal definition of marketing should include the following features:

- It is an exchange process – that is, it is two way. The firm offers the customer something (normally a good or service) and in return receives something, usually payment.
- It is mutually beneficial because both sides should gain from the exchange. Customers should be satisfied and firms should make a profit (assuming the firm is a profit-making organisation). Firms are unlikely to give away products for nothing.
- It aims to identify and anticipate customer needs. It is not always enough to just *identify* customers' needs: the customers may not know themselves what they want. In some markets, such as fashion and film, firms have to anticipate what customers will want in the future. They have to predict trends even before most customers know what these trends will be.
- It aims to delight customers. Nowadays satisfying customers may not be enough, many other firms are doing this as well! Much better is to *delight* the customer.

The purpose of marketing is to match the abilities and strengths of the firm to the needs of the market. A business aims to supply goods and services that customers want and which will generate suitable rewards for the organisation.

Marketing involves:

- market research – this involves gathering and analysing information to make better marketing decisions.
- market analysis – this is an examination of market conditions to identify new opportunities.
- marketing strategy – this involves developing a plan detailing how and where to compete.
- The marketing mix – this covers the decisions all businesses have to make regarding selling prices, how and where the product is sold, the image of the product and the precise nature of the product itself.

Effective marketing means that the organisation understands its customers and provides them with what they want, when they want. At the same time, it ensures the firm itself benefits from this transaction. Marketing involves a whole range of activities, including finding out what customers want, developing new products, packaging and

Figure 3.1 *The marketing process*

promoting the products, and setting the price. All these activities are aimed at providing goods and services which will satisfy the customer (so he or she will buy it), and at making a profit for the firm. The better the marketing, the better the product or service which is provided for the customer and the more money the business should be able to make.

Markets

All businesses trade in markets. A market occurs when buyers and sellers come together to trade. The buyers demand products, while the sellers supply them. Markets can be small, local markets with a

Figure 3.2 *Markets come in many forms*

specified location. Other markets are national or international with no single location. For example, the world market for oil is a global market in which buyers and sellers are linked by telephones, faxes and the Internet, and trading takes place in many locations.

> ### Key terms
>
> *Marketing* anticipates, satisfies and delights customer needs and wants in a mutually beneficial exchange process.

> ### EXAMINER'S ADVICE
>
> *Many students assume that marketing is just about making customers happy. In fact, the organisation needs to fulfill its own objectives as well. There is no point making the customer happy if you cannot make a profit, for example. It is important to remember that a firm must cover its costs in the long run when undertaking marketing activities.*

Company orientation
Market orientation

A market-oriented (or market-led) firm is one that bases its decisions on the customers' needs. It continually monitors its environment to find out what customers want, what competitors are offering and what changes are occurring in the market. By being market-oriented, a firm should be able to ensure that the product or service it provides matches its customers' needs.

Product orientation

By comparison, a product-oriented (or product-led) firm focuses more on what it *can* produce and hopes that this will fit with customer requirements. This is a very risky approach because the firm may end up producing something the customer does not want.

Although being production oriented is less likely to succeed than being market oriented, it can work if the customer has limited choice (for example, in the past in Eastern Europe the government only allowed a few firms to produce particular products).

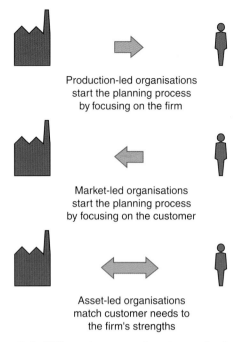

Production-led organisations
start the planning process
by focusing on the firm

Market-led organisations
start the planning process
by focusing on the customer

Asset-led organisations
match customer needs to
the firm's strengths

Figure 3.3 *Different approaches to marketing*

If it is lucky, the firm may happen to produce a product that people want.

Asset-led marketing

A wise firm may adopt an approach which looks for market opportunities and matches these to the firm's own strengths. This is known as 'asset-led marketing'. Rather than basing its activities just on what the market wants, this approach focuses on the most *appropriate* opportunities, given the firm's assets. These assets might include the firm's brand name, its access to markets, its marketing expertise or its product range. For example, IBM used the knowledge and expertise it gained from selling computers to move into the consultancy business.

> **Key terms**
>
> A **product-oriented** firm bases its planning on its own requirements.
> A **market-oriented** firm bases its planning on customer needs and wants.
> An **asset-led** firm bases its planning on customer needs and wants and its own strengths.

POINTS TO PONDER

- In 2003, *The Independent* newspaper launched a tabloid version in London. It was particularly aimed at commuters who use the London Underground and find a broadsheet paper difficult to open in such cramped conditions. Young readers are also said to be much more enthusiastic about reading tabloids. *The Independent* said the tabloid has increased its net sales by 20 000 copies a day.
- In 2003, Frank Bruno, a very popular British ex-heavyweight boxing champion, went into a psychiatric hospital. An early edition of the *Sun* newspaper had the front page headline 'Bonkers Bruno Locked Up'. This generated an outcry from the general public and the *Sun* reacted quickly, changing the headline to 'Sad Bruno in Mental Home'.

Adding value

The value of something depends on the benefits it offers, compared with the price. The more benefits something offers in relation to the price, the better value it is. This means a product does not have to be cheap to be good value. It has to be cheap in relation to the benefits it provides. You may spend quite a lot of money on a pair of trainers, for example, but if they are just what you wanted, you may think they are good value for money.

> **Key terms**
>
> The **value** of something depends on its price in relation to its benefits. If the price is low compared with the benefits, it is good value.

To be competitive, a firm must at least match the value offered by its competitors. Wherever possible, it must offer better value to keep its own customers and win some from the competition.

To summarise, the aim of a firm is to provide benefits which customers are willing to pay for. To do this, it will need a detailed insight into customer needs. It will also have to monitor these needs, because they will change over time and because competitors are also trying to offer new, attractive products and services. The first bank to offer telephone banking provided its customers with an additional benefit; it was not long before others followed and the first bank had to think about what else it could do to offer more benefits than the competition. Internet banking followed swiftly.

Business in focus

In 2002, Microsoft made a major shift in its marketing approach. Instead of just telling people how good the new features in its products were, it would concentrate on explaining why these features help the buyer to save time and/or money. For example, it wants to show businesses that by paying to upgrade they can actually save money, because the new system will be more reliable and crash less. About 75% of the world's businesses are running their PCs with operating systems that are more than ten years old so the market for people upgrading is huge if Microsoft can convince the customer of the benefits of doing so.

1 Why do you think Microsoft changed its approach?

Key issues

'Everyone is involved in marketing.' In the past people have tended to think of marketing as something which is carried out by specialists.

Nowadays, firms stress that everyone in the organisation is involved in marketing. This is because every member of the organisation contributes in some way to the success of the firm. The person answering the phone, the person filling out the order form and the person packing the goods into the box for despatch all contribute to the customer's satisfaction.

Firms are also stressing the need to think of **internal customers**, as well as external customers. This means that it is not just the person who buys the final product who matters, it is anyone you do work for. Whenever you complete a piece of work for anyone (including your teachers and examiners!), you should think of them as customers. For businesses, this focus on customers *within* the firm, as well as outside, should lead to an improvement in the quality of the product or service.

APPLICATION IN ACTION

Generally, most firms are now more market aware than they used to be – they have to be to survive, given increasing levels of competition. However, some still seem very inward looking. This is often true in technical and specialised firms, which focus so much on what they are doing that they may lose sight of what customers want. On the other hand, in some cases the customers would not even know what they want until the product is developed, and if a breakthrough is made this can be successful provided it taps into a need.

QUICK CHECK QUESTIONS

1 The best definition of marketing is that it involves:
a) selling products
b) making customers buy products even if they don't want them
c) meeting customer needs and wants profitably.
2 A product-led business is inward rather than outward looking. True or false? Why?

3　Marketing is one function of a business. Name three others.

4　Finding out what customers want is called
………….. ………………..

5　A market involves demand and ……….

6　The process of transforming inputs into outputs that are worth more is called
……………….. …………………

7　State three factors that might influence demand for a product.

8　Which of the following is a marketing activity?
a)　recruiting staff
b)　raising finance
c)　producing goods
d)　understanding customer needs.

9　Which of the following is a marketing objective?
a)　recruiting two new staff
b)　increasing sales by 10%
c)　reducing costs by 5%
d)　increasing cash holdings by £20 000.

10　Which of the following is a marketing strategy?
a)　developing new products
b)　increasing sales of brand X by 5%
c)　reducing the number of defects by 3%
d)　cutting levels of borrowing.

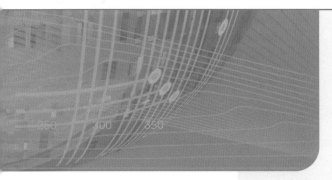

Progress questions

1　What is meant by 'marketing'?　(2 marks)

2　Marketing is said to be 'a mutually beneficial exchange process'. Explain what this means.
(3 marks)

3　Explain the importance of delighting customers.
(4 marks)

4　Explain two ways a music shop might increase customer satisfaction.　(4 marks)

5　What is meant by 'market-led marketing'?
(2 marks)

6　What is meant by 'product-led marketing'?
(2 marks)

7　What is meant by 'asset-led marketing'?
(2 marks)

8　Explain two benefits of asset-led marketing to an organisation.　(6 marks)

9　What is meant by 'good value'?　(2 marks)

10　Explain two reasons why marketing may be becoming more important to organisations.
(6 marks)

Analytical and evaluative questions

11　Analyse the benefits to a retail business such as PC World of becoming more market oriented.　(8 marks)

12　To what extent should universities be market oriented?　(15 marks)

13　Discuss the factors that might influence demand for holidays.　(15 marks)

Many shoe shops in the UK remain in the dark ages and only offer customers what their factories want to produce, rather than what they want to wear, according a new report from retail consultants Verdict.

It argues that shoe shops fail to provide a quick response to fashion trends, disappointing customers who are increasingly aware of what international designers, such as Gucci and Prada, are producing. The market, Verdict claims, is wide open for specialised shoe shops which are more market-led. Commentators have said that the existing UK shoe shops are doomed to failure because of their product-oriented approach. 'Their profits tend to be extremely poor because they do not seem to understand the fundamental principle of marketing, which is to add value. If you look at the manufacturers abroad they clearly adopt an asset-led approach to marketing and generate high returns. Some of the UK firms seem to actively resent their customers and see them as a necessary evil.'

The majority just rely on the same factories and merely serve as outlets to sell what the factories want to produce. Many shoe shops are reducing the number of suppliers that they do business with, but have yet to tackle design. Verdict believes that the strongest footwear retailers are Nine West and Pied a Terre, which offer different products and a range of clothing.

The UK footwear sector is dominated by C&J Clark, which has increased its market share from 7.9% in 1994 to 10.1% last year – partly as a result of a witty advertising campaign.

Source: Adapted from the Daily Telegraph, *14 June 1999*

1 *What is meant by 'market-led'?* (2 marks)

2 *Explain two possible advantages to a retailer of an asset-led approach to marketing.* (5 marks)

3 *Analyse the possible ways in which UK shoe shops could add more value for their customers.* (8 marks)

4 *'The existing UK shoe shops are doomed to failure because of their product-oriented approach.' To what extent would you agree with this view?* (10 marks)

>> Market research

What is market research?

The aim of market research is to gather information that may be useful to the firm when marketing its products. This could be information about sales, competitors, market size, new developments in the market or a wide range of other things. By gathering information, the firm should be able to make better decisions about what to do next.

Market research *involves the gathering, analysing and presenting of information relevant to the marketing process.*

Market research can be used to help firms in a number of different situations:

- When considering the launch of a new product, a firm may want to know the size of the market.
- If a firm is changing the brand name of a product, it may want to find out how customers might respond.
- Information on customers' reactions to different product prices may be invaluable.
- Researching consumers' views on an advertisement before launching can help to make sure that the 'right' advertisements are used.
- To assess how a product is doing, a firm may want to measure its sales.

Perhaps one of the most crucial questions market research can address is whether it is worthwhile competing in a particular market. How large is the market? Is it growing or shrinking? What profits could be made in the industry? What competitors exist? The firm will also be interested in the future of the market and whether it is it likely to grow or shrink.

POINTS TO PONDER

Album sales by type of music (2003):

Pop	31.2%
Rock	29.2%
R&B	8.4%
Dance	7.2%
Middle of the road	6.4%
Hip-hop/Rap	5.5%
Classical	3.8%
Jazz	2.6%
Country	1.8%
Folk	1.2%
Other	1.3%

Source: BPI

Research can also be used to determine possible changes in marketing policies. Should the firm change the price? Should it change the promotional campaign? Which brand name should the firm choose?

Essentially then, market research can be used in three main areas:

1 to identify market opportunities
2 to assess the relative worth of different plans

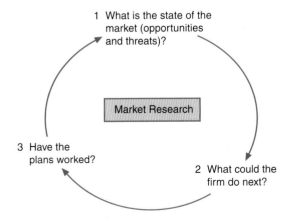

Figure 3.4 *Three main uses of market research*

3 to review the success of the plans once implemented.

So, research provides a firm with information. If it is undertaken effectively, it can help to provide firms with a competitive advantage by enabling them to make better decisions.

Types of research

There are two types of market research; primary and secondary. Primary research involves gathering information for the first time. Secondary research uses information already gathered. If you were thinking of launching a new type of shampoo and gave it to a group of people to try first, this would be primary research. If you read some information about the shampoo market in a newspaper, this would be secondary data. Primary research is also called field research; secondary research is also called desk research.

Key terms

Primary research involves gathering and analysing data which has been collected for the first time.
Secondary research involves gathering and analysing data which has already been gathered.

Primary and secondary research have advantages and disadvantages and each is appropriate in certain situations. If a business is trying to assess the response of viewers to a new advertisement, primary

Primary research	Secondary research
● up to date	● may be out of date or in an inappropriate format
● specific to the firm's needs (and could be kept confidential)	● available to other firms; may be very general
● may be expensive to collect	● normally cheaper than primary research
● not available immediately as it takes time to collect.	● quicker to gather than primary research.

Table 3.1 *A comparison of primary and secondary research*

research will be essential – secondary data would not exist. However, if the firm was interested in population trends or the state of the economy, it should be relatively easy to find this information from secondary sources.

Primary research

Primary data can be gathered in a variety of ways.

- By observation – shops record customers on video tape to see how they wander around the store and what attracts their attention.
- By experiment – stores sometimes change their displays or their promotional offers and then monitor the results. Companies often launch a product in a test market first to see how it sells. Then, if it succeeds, they sell it nationally. The problem with test marketing is that competitors get to see your product before it is fully launched and they may try to get to the market first.
- Through surveys – you may have been stopped in the street and asked your opinion of something: this is a face-to-face survey. Firms also use telephone and mail surveys to find out what their customers think.

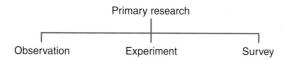

Figure 3.5 *Types of primary research*

Sampling

A firm may want to gather information using a survey. Usually, it is not possible to interview all of the people the firm is interested in: this group is called the population. It may be too expensive or would take too long to talk to everyone in the target population. For example, imagine a firm was thinking of launching a magazine aimed at 16 to 18-year-olds; it could take months to interview everyone of this age in the country. Instead of doing this, the firm might decide to take a sample. A sample is a group which is intended to represent the overall population. By interviewing, say, 1000 16 to 18-year-olds, the firm would hope to get an impression of what all people of this age group think.

Obviously, the results are not totally reliable because the firm has not actually asked everyone in the population, it has only asked some of them. This means that the firm cannot be totally confident of the results. This is why, when firms produce market research results, they also state a confidence level. If the confidence level is 95%, this means the firm thinks that 95% of the time the results from the sample will represent the overall population. If the confidence level is 98%, it believes the sample results will represent the overall population 98% of the time. The degree of confidence depends on the size of the sample – the bigger the sample the more likely it is that the findings will represent the population and the higher the degree of confidence. Managers must take account of the confidence level when using information to make a decision.

> ### Key terms
>
> *A **sample*** is a small number of people or items which is meant to represent the target population. *A **confidence level*** is a measure of the reliability of the findings of primary research.

Types of sample

So, a sample is used to represent the population as a whole. There are different ways of selecting a sample:

- A random sample is when all the members of the population have an equal chance of selection. If you wanted a random sample of students at your school you could take a list of names of all the students then randomly pick a certain number.
- Quota samples occur when the interviewers select people within the population who meet set criteria, e.g. 300 males and 200 females, aged 20 – 24 years. The interviewers can choose whoever they want, provided these criteria are met. They could interview people on the street. A quota sample is easier and quicker to complete than a random sample (as you do not need to know all the members of the population), but it is not random because members of the population do not have an equal chance of selection.

Quantitative and qualitative research

Quantitative research is based on relatively large samples and is statistically valid. It is used to show what has happened in a market, and its findings can be expressed in numerical terms; for example, sales of Brand X have increased by 45%, 12 million people watched Eastenders last week or the market for soft drinks is worth over £4 billion.

Qualitative research, by comparison, is based on the opinions of a small focus group or in-depth one-to-one interviews, and aims to understand why customers behave in certain ways or what they think of a product. Rather than focusing on *what* happened, it examines *why* customers do what they do. For example, a focus group might be used to discuss consumers' views of a brand to understand shopping habits.

Secondary research

This form of research uses data that has already been collected for another purpose. Secondary data can be gathered from a variety of sources:

- Newspapers – papers such as the *Financial Times* and the *Times* are good sources of business information.
- Magazines – trade magazines such as *Marketing Week* and *The Grocer* are valuable sources of data specific to an industry.
- Government publications – these provide information on matters such as consumer spending and imports, for example.
- The Internet – this carries an astonishing amount of data.

Whilst secondary data is usually quicker and cheaper to get hold of than primary information, it is not always in the right format or up to date. The research may have been undertaken in the previous year when what you want is this year's figure.

Alternatively, it may organise sales data within a market according to the sales per region, and what you need is more local data.

 ## Key issues

Rapid advances in information technology are making it easier and cheaper for organisations to gather information on their customers. More information can be processed more quickly and more cheaply than in the past. The growth of store cards and loyalty schemes, for example, mean that firms can now match your spending patterns to the area you live in, your income and your marital status every time you use the card. This gives retailers a tremendously detailed insight into what we are buying.

Which is best – primary or secondary research?

The most suitable type of research depends on the firm itself and the nature of the information it needs. If a firm is investigating a problem which is very specific to its own products or services (such as the impact of an advertising campaign) it will need to use primary research. If it is studying more general trends, secondary research will be acceptable. The resources of the firm have an impact, as will the speed at which the information is required. If data is needed quickly and the firm has limited resources, secondary research is more likely to be used.

How useful is market research?

The value of market research can be judged in terms of the quality of the information it provides relative to the cost and time taken to gather it. If the information is good quality, is gathered relatively quickly and cheaply, the firm will no doubt be satisfied with the research. If, however, the information arrives too late to be of use, then it will be of limited value.

POINTS TO PONDER

Not all market research gets it right. The estimates of the number of visitors to the Millenium Dome were way out. Some analysts seem to have been overly optimistic because they wanted the project to succeed. The research was based on what the number of visitors would be if the Dome was full of the best attractions in the world rather than the attractions it actually had.

EXAMINER'S ADVICE

If you are faced with market research information in a question, make sure you do not take it at face value. Ask yourself:

- *How recent is the data?*
- *How large was the sample size?*
- *How was the data collected? Are the findings likely to be reliable?*

Sometimes primary data is collected by people who are not professionals and who want particular answers (for example, they are trying to prove their idea for a new product is a world beater). This can influence the reliability of the data!

APPLICATION IN ACTION

- Film companies often use focus groups to see how audiences react. They sometimes change the editing and ending as a result. Consumer goods producers often use focus groups for ideas for new products or an initial reaction to a product idea.
- Most firms do not have the resources to do anything other than the most basic primary research themselves – they usually need to use outside experts.

QUICK CHECK QUESTIONS

1   Gathering data first hand is called .... market research.

2   A small section of the whole population is called a ....

3   A 95% confidence level means:
a)   there is a 95% chance the product will succeed
b)   95% of people will buy the product
c)   if the research was repeated, 95% of the time the results would be the same.

4   Focus groups provide .... data rather than quantitative data.

5   Which of the following statements is true?
a)   In a random sample, every member of the population has an equal chance of selection.
b)   In a random sample, everyone in the UK has an equal chance of selection.
c)   Standing on the street corner and asking people questions is an example of a random sample.

6   Using government statistics is an example of secondary research. True or false?

7   Which of the following statements about primary market research is NOT true?
a)   It can provide tailor-made information for the organisation.
b)   It can be gathered using surveys.
c)   It has already been gathered.

8   A quota is a random sample. True or false? Explain.

9   Market research can be used to estimate the size of a market. This may be measured in terms of v.......... or v...............

10   '75% of the target market would try the product' is an example of quantitative data. True or false?

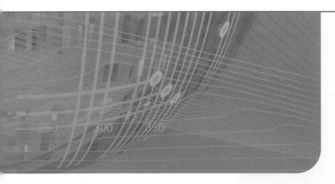

Progress questions

1   What is meant by 'marketing research'? *(2 marks)*

2   Explain two possible advantages to a chocolate manufacturer of primary market research.
(6 marks)

3   Explain two possible advantages to a chain of health and fitness clubs of secondary market research.
(6 marks)

4   Explain two possible disadvantages to a sportswear manufacturer of secondary research.
(6 marks)

5   What is meant by a 'sample'?
(2 marks)

6   What is meant by a 'quota sample'?
(2 marks)

7   What is meant by a 'random sample'?
(2 marks)

8   What is meant by a '95% confidence level'?
(2 marks)

9   Explain the possible reasons why firms use samples as part of their market research.
(6 marks)

10 Explain two reasons why a manager might prefer to make a decision based on experience rather than use market research?
(6 marks)

Analytical and evaluative questions

11 Marco Ferini is thinking of leaving his job working for a travel agent to set up his own business specialising in skiing holidays. Examine the ways in which Marco might research his idea.
(8 marks)

12 Sally would like to set up a shop selling cosmetics and offering beauty treatments. Discuss the ways in which market research might help Sally set up her new business.
(8 marks)

13 Fulsoms produces a successful range of smoothie drinks in a variety of fruit flavours. It is in the process of developing a new one. To what extent would market research guarantee the success of a new drink from the company?
(15 marks)

>> Market Analysis

What is market analysis?

As its name suggests, market analysis involves a detailed examination of market conditions. Such analysis has a number of features which are discussed below.

The size of the market

An estimate of the size of the market can be made, either in terms of the total volume of sales or the value of sales. For example, the market for computer games could be measured in terms of the number of games sold or the value in pounds of the sales.

Firms will be interested both in the existing size of the market and its future size. A market may be big at present but could decline (e.g. What will demand for DVDs be in ten years' time? Will a new product have replaced this technology?). Alternatively, a market may be small at the moment but may be likely to grow fast in the future (e.g. 3G mobile phone technology is still new, but may grow fast in the future). If a market is shrinking, a firm may have to decide whether to carry on competing in it or not; it may have to look for alternative markets. Competition is likely to be fierce in a shrinking market because there are less and less customers available. By comparison, in a growing market all firms can expand without having to take sales from each other.

INTERPRETING DATA

Company A

	This year	Last year
Number of units sold	20 000	15 000
Sales revenue	£80 000	£90 000

1 Comment on the significance of the data above for company A.

POINTS TO PONDER

Music format sales 2002:

- sales of CD albums were down 6%
- sales of singles were down 16%
- sales of cassettes were down 36%
- sales of VHS were down 42%
- sales of DVD were up 58%.

Source: IFPI

Market share

It is helpful to know the market shares of all existing firms within the market. The market share of a firm or a brand is the percentage that it has of the market sales. For example, if brand X has a 20% market share, this means either that 1 in 5 products bought is brand X (if the market size is measured in terms of units sold) or that £1 out of every £5 spent in this market is on brand X (if the market is measured in terms of value). Firms with large market shares (e.g. Microsoft, Gillette, Walkers and Coca-Cola) have great power over suppliers and distributors. They are likely to be able to demand preferential treatment and better rates.

INTERPRETING DATA

Company A

	This year	Last year
Market share	20%	10%
Total market	£5m	£12m

1 Comment on the significance of the figures above for company A.

Segments within the market

A segment is a part of a market made up of consumers with similar needs and characteristics. If firms can identify particular segments, they can target these and adjust their marketing accordingly.

MATHS MOMENT

$1+1=2$

Market share =

$$\frac{\text{sales of the product}}{\text{total market size}} \times 100 = \%$$

If the product has sales of £20 000 in a market worth £400 000,

Market share $= \dfrac{£20\,000}{£400\,000} \times 100 = 5\%$

1 A manufacturer makes products worth £300 000 each year. Sales within the entire market are valued at £9 000 000. What share of the market does the manufacturer have?

POINTS TO PONDER

Between 1999 and 2003 Gillette saw its world market share of disposable razors fall from nearly 55% to less than 45%. To make matters worse, its rival Schick launched the Quattro in 2003 to attack Gillette's Mach 3. The Mach 3 stressed the benefits of three blades – each one slightly closer to the skin than the one before – to 'shave you closer'. The Quattro had four blades! Gillette had previously decided to launch new products less frequently because the new products were taking sales away from the old ones. With falling market share and the arrival of the Quattro it saw the need to invest more in developing new products.

Key terms

Market analysis is a detailed examination of market conditions. This is useful for marketing planning.

The *size of a market* can be measured in terms of the number of items sold (volume) or the amount of sales in terms of pounds spent (value).

A *market segment* is an identifiable group with similar needs and wants within a market.

Segmentation

As we have seen, segmentation is a means of dividing up a market (into segments) to identify consumers with similar needs. If you look at the market for magazines, for example, publishers produce different publications for different groups: some focus on particular sports, some are based on hobbies or interests, others are targeted at particular lifestyles. By identifying the needs of different groups, the publishers can produce an appropriate range of magazines.

Segmentation happens in most markets:

INTERPRETING DATA

Malvolio Ltd produces a range of cereals. It has collected data on its existing sales and likely market trends. It is considering which age group to target with new products in the near future.

What would your advice be and why?

How might this affect the marketing of the company's products?

Age	Percentage of sales of existing products	Expected growth of sales in the market as a whole from this segment over next three years
Under 15s	5%	+4%
15–24	40%	+1.2%
25–39	25%	+2.8%
40–60	20%	+4%
Over 60s	10%	+19%

Business in focus

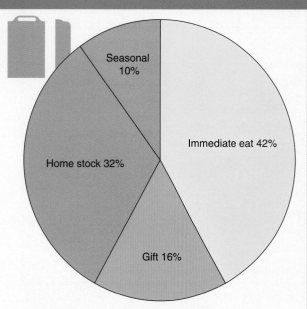

Figure 3.6

The chocolate confectionery market can be divided into four segments:

Immediate eat:
- bought by someone for themselves or for others to eat that day
- usually bought by children
- bought as a snack, treat or pick-me-up
- bars or bags of chocolate, sweets or chewing gum.

Gift:
- bought to give to someone else
- amount spent relates to the relationship with that person
- bought for birthdays, as a romantic gesture or a thank you.

Homestock:
- mainly bought by mothers for the family
- aken home to last the week
- used in lunchboxes, as a treat for the children in the evening, watching TV
- multipack, large blocks of chocolate and large bags of sweets.

Seasonal:
- mainly for Christmas and Easter
- easter eggs, selection boxes and giftpacks.

Source: Cadbury Schweppes plc

1 Discuss how identifying segments like this may help a firm such as Cadbury in its marketing.

- In the toothpaste market there are toothpastes aimed at small children, smokers and people with sensitive teeth. Each of these products targets a specific group and tries to meet their particular requirements.
- The washing powder market has powders for hand-washing, for automatic washing machines, biological powders, powders with and without softener. Each of these is aimed at customers with specific needs.
- Firms in the car market have identified and developed a number of segments. Different models of car target different groups. Car manufacturers produce vehicles for city drivers, family car drivers, young professionals and safety-conscious drivers.

Ways of segmenting markets

There are many different ways of segmenting markets.

- **Age** – many products are aimed at particular age groups in society. SAGA organises holidays for the over-50s, whilst Club 18–30 offers a very different type of holiday aimed at a younger age group.
- **Gender (male or female)** – products such as clothes obviously differ for men and women, but other types of producers also target men and women in different ways. Certain alcoholic drinks (for example, the liqueur Baileys) are aimed at women.
- **Income** – businesses produce goods and services for groups with particular levels of income. Thus, products like Rolex and Porsche focus on higher income groups, whilst supermarkets such as Aldi and Netto target those with lower incomes.
- **Socio-economic groupings** – this is a method of segmenting people based on their income and jobs. The different categories include A, B, C1, C2, D and E. Group A are senior managers and professionals; group E are low-income and unemployed. Newspapers often target different socio-economic groups. For example, the *Financial Times* tends to be read by social groups A and B.
- **Usage rate** – some firms, such as BT and tobacco companies, distinguish between heavy users of

their product and light users, because this may affect the services offered and the promotional techniques used (e.g. light users may be targeted to turn them into heavy users!).

- Purchase occasions – when do people buy flowers or a greeting card, for example? In both of these markets, the producers have tried to increase the number of purchase occasions, to provide more situations when we would send someone a card or flowers.

Key issues

Segmentation typically focuses on aspects such as income, age, gender or the location of different groups. That is, it is related to the *characteristics* of the buyers.

More modern methods of segmentation focus on the *motives* people have when they buy products. Why do people buy chocolate, for example? To reward themselves? Because they feel unhappy? To give as a present? Why do

Business in focus

Manufacturers and analysts often segment the market in terms of the different products being sold. For example:

- The UK Baby Products market can be segmented in terms of baby toiletries, nursery products, infant and nursery toys, baby clothing and disposable nappies.
- The oral hygiene market can be divided into mouthwash, denture care, dental floss, electric toothbrushes and toothpaste.
- The greeting card market can be split into Christmas and New Year cards, spring cards (for Mother's day, Father's day, St Valentine's day and Easter) and everyday cards (for birthdays, weddings, engagements, good luck and get well).

1 Choose a particular type of product and identify different segments which exist in this segmentation.
2 How does this affect the way the products are marketed?

Figure 3.7 *Fiat and Alfa Romeo manufacture a range of vehicles for different segments of the market.*

people buy chewing gum? Because they want fresh breath? To relieve stress? To help them stop smoking? If a firm understands why someone buys their products this may influence the way they are promoted.

Is segmentation worth it?

If a firm can identify different groups in a market, it can offer products that precisely match their requirements. Instead of producing one version of their product or service for everyone, firms can adjust what they do according to the different needs of each segment. This should lead to more sales and profits. However, it is more difficult and more expensive to produce and market several different products, rather than just one. A firm must weigh up the potential benefits with the possible costs. Some products, such as the multi-purpose lubricant WD40, are not adapted for different markets; this product is marketed as having hundreds of uses but the basic product and promotion of it are the same.

What makes a market segment attractive?

Not all identified market segments are necessarily attractive. There may well be a market for a magazine called *Scrabble Weekly*, for example, but this is unlikely to attract the major publishers

because the market segment is fairly small. A market segment must, therefore, be big enough to be worth competing in. For an asset-led approach, it must also fit with the firm's own strengths. The firm must take into account whether the segment will continue to be sufficiently big in the future. If the firm was worried about future competition or a change in consumer trends, for example, it may not enter, even if the market looks attractive in the short term.

APPLICATION IN ACTION

- It is important for students to appreciate the many different markets that exist in terms of size and growth. The market for cars, for example, is huge. Even if the market in general is not growing very fast at present, it still generates millions of pounds of sales. Of course it is also important to remember that some segments of the car market, such as overseas markets or types of vehicle, may still be growing fast. The growth of voice recognition software or fingerprint-activated door locks, by comparison, is quite fast but at the moment the markets remain quite small.
- Fast growth markets at the moment include cosmetic surgery, male cosmetics, DVDs and digital radios. Mature markets include toothpaste, washing machines and watches. Declining markets include fast food and cabbage.
- Firms can create markets (e.g. the Sony iPod), but at the same time are likely to be affected by market trends, e.g. high sales in the UK typewriter market are unlikely, whereas a new fruit drink business may find a more receptive market.

EXAMINER'S ADVICE

It is important to consider how the marketing of the product will change according to the needs of different groups. Imagine you are writing a travel book for example.

- *How might a travel book vary according to the age of the target market?*
- *How would a guide book aimed at single people differ from one aimed at families?*
- *How would it differ for people going on holiday compared with people going on business trips?*

Remember, you need to examine the impact of selling to different market segments in terms of the price charged, the image of the product, where it is sold and the way it is promoted.

QUICK CHECK QUESTIONS

1 State two ways of measuring the size of a market.
2 Give the equation for market share.
3 If the sales of a brand are £200 000 and the total market sales are £500 000, what is the market share of the brand?
4 If a market was worth £5m and then grows by 20%, what is it now worth?
5 If a firm's sales are increasing, so is its market share. True or false?
6 Give two examples of markets in decline.
7 Give two examples of growing markets.
8 Give an example of a small market and a large market.
9 Identify two segments that exist within the banking sector.
10 To maximise profits firms should target all the available segments in a market. True or false?

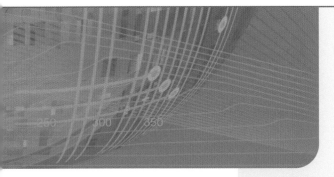

Progress questions

1 What is meant by the term 'market analysis'? (2 marks)

2 Explain the possible impact on a firm of operating in a shrinking market. (6 marks)

3 What is meant by the term 'market share'? (2 marks)

4 How might the size of the mobile phone market be measured? (2 marks)

5 Explain two possible benefits to a car manufacturer analysing a market. (6 marks)

6 What is meant by 'market segmentation'? (2 marks)

7 What makes a market segment attractive to a firm? (6 marks)

8 Explain two possible benefits of segmentation to a publisher. (6 marks)

9 Explain two possible problems of segmentation for a firm. (6 marks)

10 Explain how the market for toys and games could be segmented. (8 marks)

Analysis and evaluation

11 Examine the possible advantages to a cosmetics company such as L'Oreal of gaining a larger market share.

12 The market for household cleaning products is increasingly segmented. To what extent is greater segmentation within this market desirable?

13 After many years working for Microsoft as a computer programmer Francesca Delores wants to set up a business producing her own computer games software. To what extent will an analysis of this market help her to succeed in her business?

Marketing objectives, strategy >> and tactics

SMART marketing objectives

A marketing objective is a target set by the marketing function. It sets out what the firm wants to achieve in terms of its marketing activities.

Like any good objective, a marketing objective should be SMART (page 32).

For example, a marketing objective might be 'to increase sales by 10% by 2002'.

> **Key terms**
>
> A **marketing objective** is a marketing target. This will be derived from the overall corporate objective.

Marketing objectives often focus on sales. In most cases, firms want to increase their overall sales, but they may also set objectives for particular products or regions. For example, a firm might be very eager to promote some of its products to a greater extent in the North or it may want to boost sales of its latest brand in particular. A firm might want to smooth out sales over the year (if its existing sales are very seasonal). It may even want to reduce sales, if it knows it cannot meet the orders and that to accept them might lead to long waiting lists and dissatisfied customers.

Marketing strategy and tactics

As we have seen, a strategy is the means of achieving an objective. A marketing strategy is, therefore, a way of achieving a marketing objective. This means it is the long-term plan the firm has to ensure it meets its marketing target. A marketing strategy involves analysing markets, choosing which markets to operate in and which products to offer. The strategy is implemented through marketing tactics. These tactics involve detailed decisions about factors such as the price and the way the product is distributed.

For example:

- A firm's marketing objective might be to increase sales by 30% over the next five years.
- Its marketing strategy might be to launch some of its products abroad.
- The marketing tactics used might include launching the products at a low price in France and Germany first and gradually extending this to other countries.

> **Key terms**
>
> A **marketing strategy** is the long-term plan detailing how the marketing objective will be fulfilled.
>
> **Marketing tactics** are the short-term actions taken to achieve the marketing strategy.

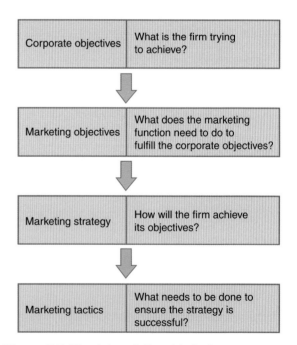

Figure 3.8 *The interrelationship between objectives, strategy and tactics*

Types of marketing strategy

There are many types of marketing strategies. These include niche marketing and mass marketing.

Niche marketing

This occurs when a firm focuses on a specific segment of the market with which the major competitors are not concerned. For example, a radio station may concentrate on playing a type of music which is not featured much on other radio stations. Classic FM focuses primarily on classical music, and probably appeals to older listeners; Saga radio specifically targets an older audience. A fashion company may focus on a particular item of clothing which most other firms do not, such as cufflinks or socks.

There are a number of advantages of operating in a niche market:

- A firm may be able to survive because it is offering a product or service that the larger firms are not bothered about supplying. If a small firm tried to compete in the mass market, the existing competitors might react aggressively.
- The firm may be able to operate on a small scale.

Many niche markets are relatively small and specialised. Small organisations are, therefore, able to meet the demand in this market, whereas they might lack the resources to meet demand in a mass market.

However, firms producing and selling in niche markets also face disadvantages:

- If the business earns high profits, other firms might enter the market, making it more competitive. In some cases, the niche producer will struggle to survive if larger, more powerful firms enter the market and sell at lower prices.
- The market as a whole may be quite small which may limit the overall returns a firm can achieve.
- The market may consist of a small number of customers. This may mean that the firm is vulnerable to the loss of one or two customers. In the mass market this is less of a problem: if one customer is lost, there are normally plenty more!

People in business

Charles Dunstone, the founder of The Carphone Warehouse, is widely acknowledged as the man who brought mobile phones to the mass market.

He was one of the first to spot a niche in the market in the late 1980s. In 1986 he was selling computers for NEC and reluctantly took a job at its mobile-phone division. He was selling 'transportable' phones to dealers and recognised the opportunities. NEC was targeting large corporate clients; Charles Dunstone saw the potential to sell to the self-employed: plumbers, builders and roofers, for example. At that time, phones were sold direct to corporate buyers and not through shops: the Carphone Warehouse changed all that.

Dunstone set up the business at the age of 24, renting a single room. Within four months he had his first retail site and two months later was advertising on the radio. The business really took off when Vodafone and Cellnet started offering different combinations of rental and call charges. Customers had to decide which tariff was best and the Carphone

Warehouse was one of the few retailers offering independent advice. Dunstone commented, 'This differentiated our business. The bottom line is we had empathy with our customers, who were confused by the choice in the market place and what package they should go for.'

In the first year the Carphone Warehouse made sales of £1m employing 30 staff. With demand booming he could sell stock before he had even paid for it. The business grew rapidly. He made the first profits (£1m on sales of £37m) four years after starting. By 1998 he was making £14m on sales of £160m with a staff of over 760. He now has over 50 stores in France, over 30 in Sweden and Switzerland.

'The important thing is to remain focused, have a passion and an understanding of what people want', says Dunstone.

Source: Excerpts from Sunday Times, 31 October 1999
For more information on The Carphone Warehouse, visit www.carphonewarehouse.com and look under corporate information.

Business in focus

Robin Webb set up his 'Vegetarian Shoes' shop in Brighton in 1990. Robin had taught himself to make shoes after leaving Art College and at first was only able to offer one style of hand-made shoe. Now he sells shoes, boots, sandals and belts. They are all made from a synthetic material rather than leather (which obviously is cow's skin and so would not be acceptable to vegetarians). Demand has become so great that his products are produced by factories and shipped all over the world.

1 Discuss whether other retailers are likely to copy Robin Webb's approach.

Mass marketing

This takes place when a firm aims a product or service at most of the market. ITV is a mass-market TV channel because it tries to cater for a majority of tastes. The Vauxhall Astra is aimed at the 'average' car user and, therefore, sells in a mass market.

To operate in a mass market, a firm must be able to produce goods on a large scale. This may require a heavy investment in equipment and in the recruitment of staff. The danger of mass marketing is that, if demand does fall, the firm may be left with unused resources. Machines may sit idle and there may not be enough work for employees. Before investing in the large-scale resources essential for a mass marketing strategy, a business must be sure that demand will be sustained.

The advantage of mass marketing is that the firm can produce large numbers of relatively standardised products. This means the production process is relatively repetitive and the cost per unit should be low. However, even though the firm will be producing many thousands of the same item it still needs to differentiate itself from the competition. Ariel, Daz, Surf and Radion all compete in the same market but try to make themselves different from each other – through the product itself or the price. This is product differentiation.

Products

	Existing	New
Markets Existing	Market penetration	New product development
New	Market development	Diversification

Figure 3.9 *Ansoff's matrix*

Key terms

Product differentation occurs when a product is distinguished from its competitors. For example, this could be achieved via a brand name or the design of the product. Emmerdale, Eastenders and Coronation Street are all soap operas, but they differ significantly in terms of where they are set, their storylines and their general approach to issues.

POINTS TO PONDER

Firms often seek to develop a USP – a Unique Selling Point (or Proposition). This is some feature of the product that differentiates it from the competition. Tyrrells Hand Fried Potato Chips, for example, are the only UK chip maker to grow their own potatoes.

Ansoff's matrix

Other marketing strategies can be highlighted by Ansoff's matrix. Igor Ansoff was a management writer who outlined four types of marketing strategy.

● Market penetration – using this strategy, a firm tries to gain more of its existing market. For example, if Coca-Cola tried to sell more of its products in the UK, this would be market penetration. To do this it may cut the price or launch a new advertising campaign.

People in business

Figure 3.10 *Akio Morita, co-founder of Sony*

Akio Morita was the co-founder of Sony and was a major influence on its amazing success from the 1950s onwards. He started the company with his partner, Masuru Ibuka, in 1946. Over the next 40 years their tiny electrical engineering firm grew into the huge Sony group. They transformed peoples' image of Japanese products from cheap and unreliable products to goods of the highest quality and value.

The first real success of Morita and Ibuka's company came with the transistor radio. Sony's work on transistors won one of its engineers the Nobel Prize in 1973 and allowed the company to dominate the electronics industry with cheap, well-made transistor radios.

Sony's success was followed in the 1970s with a major failure when it lost the video-cassette war. Sony's version of the video cassette (the Betamax) was soundly beaten by JVC's VHS technology which we still use today. Morita's greatest triumph came in 1979 with the launch of the Sony Walkman: much of its development was due to him alone. This was a classic example of new product development.

For more information on Sony, visit www.sony.net.

- Market development – this entails a firm selling its existing products in a new market. This may either be a new segment of the market or a new market geographically. For example, Johnson and Johnson's talcum powder, originally marketed for babies, has been sold to adults as well. Companies such as Unilever have been trying to sell much more of their products (such as Persil) in China in recent years as this is a very fast-growing market.
- New product development – firms pursuing this strategy develop new products to sell to existing customers. This may either be a modification of an existing product or a completely new one. For example, DVDs are replacing videos.

- Diversification – this strategy occurs when a firm offers a new product in a new market. This does not mean this product or market didn't exist before, but simply that this firm had not been involved before. For example, CAT is a producer of industrial equipment but has used its brand to move into the clothes market. Diversification is quite a high-risk strategy because it means the managers of a business are becoming involved in an area in which they do not have any experience.

Business in focus

Walker's Sensations

Walkers Sensations are 'Posh Crisps' from Walkers. They are an everyday treat, specially prepared crunchier crisps which are available in a range of indulgent flavours. They are designed for people who want to treat themselves

Flavours include Four Cheese & Red Onion, Sea Salt & Cracked Black Pepper, Oven Roasted Chicken & Thyme, Thai Sweet Chilli, Roast Lamb & Mint, Tangy Tomato & Red Pepper Salsa and Sea Salt & Malt Vinegar. The three flavours available in 40g bags are: Four Cheese & Red Onion, Sea Salt & Cracked Black Pepper and Oven Roasted Chicken & Thyme.

It is estimated that 11 million people will eat a Walkers product EVERY DAY.

Source: www.walkers.co.uk

Pilkington's self-cleaning glass

Pilkington Activ is the world's first self-cleaning glass. The glass has an active coating on the outside designed to absorb the ultraviolet light given off by the sun. The absorption process causes a reaction on the glass which breaks down and loosens dirt. Then, when it rains, the water pours off the glass and takes the dirt with it!

Source: with kind permission from www.pilkington.com

1 Examine three factors that you think determine the success of a new product.

What determines a marketing strategy?

1 As we have seen, a firm's marketing strategy must be derived from its marketing objectives.
2 The strategy must also be linked to the opportunities available within the market. If new technology brings new ways of selling a product (for example, via the Internet) the firm's strategy will change.
3 A firm's plan must also be related to its own strengths and resources. If, for example, a

business has a strong distribution network, it may seek to sell other products through its outlets. If, however, a firm has a strong brand name it may seek to use this asset in new markets.
4 A firm's strategy will also be influenced by what competitors are doing. If there are several large and powerful firms competing in one segment, a firm may want to avoid this and compete elsewhere.

Figure 3.11 *Influences on marketing strategy*

APPLICATION IN ACTION

The nature of the strategy will vary from industry to industry. Cars, washing powder and chocolate tend to be advertised heavily and on television. Local services tend to use the Yellow Pages or the local radio. Large-scale computer systems rely much more on personal selling. Musicians thrive on public relations.

 QUICK CHECK QUESTIONS

1 An example of a marketing objective could be:
a) to reduce production costs by 5%
b) to recruit five new staff
c) to increase sales by 10%
d) to cut the number of defects by 30 items per 10 000.
2 The plan to achieve the marketing objectives is called the marketing ....
3 A .... is a small segment of a market.

4 When a firm tries to distinguish its product from the competition this is called product
....

5 Mass marketing is likely to
focus on a small segment of the market
involve large-scale production.

6 What is on the axes of the Ansoff matrix?

7 Market development involves:
a) new products in new markets
b) new products in existing markets
c) existing products in existing markets
d) existing products in new markets.

8 Diversification involves:
a) new products in new markets
b) new products in existing markets
c) existing products in existing markets
d) existing products in new markets.

9 Name two factors that might influence a firm's marketing strategy.

10 What is meant by marketing tactics?

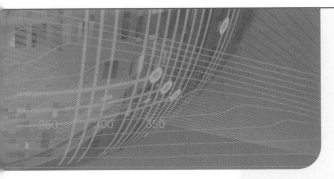

Progress questions

1 a) *What is meant by a 'marketing objective'?*
(2 marks)

   b) *What are the features of a good objective?*
(2 marks)

2 *What is meant by a 'marketing strategy'?*
(2 marks)

3 *Explain two factors which might influence a record company's marketing strategy.* *(6 marks)*

4 *What is meant by 'marketing tactics'?* *(2 marks)*

5 *Explain two possible benefits to a clothes manufacturer of niche marketing.* *(6 marks)*

6 *Explain two possible disadvantages to a pet food manufacturer of niche marketing.* *(6 marks)*

7 *What is meant by mass marketing?* *(2 marks)*

8 *Outline the possible benefits to a car manufacturer of mass marketing.* *(9 marks)*

9 *Explain what is meant by 'new product development'.* *(3 marks)*

10 *Explain what is meant by 'diversification'.* *(3 marks)*

Analytical and evaluative questions

11 *Examine the factors that might influence the marketing strategy of a new entrant into the shampoo market.* *(8 marks)*

12 *Discuss the factors a producer of luxury vegetable soups may take into account before*
moving from a niche strategy into a mass market. *(15 marks)*

13 *Banto's plc is a national chain of chemists. Its managers are considering moving into new markets and selling DVDs and music alongside its existing products. Discuss the factors the managers may take into account before making this decision.* *(15 marks)*

TLC plc is a manufacturer of trainers. The company has recently experienced a fall in market share. To find out why, the company has decided to undertake a combination of primary and secondary market research. The Managing Director of the company, Samantha Scully, believes the underlying problem is that the company's marketing strategy is no longer suitable for its marketing objectives. She believes that, following the findings of its research, the company needs to look again at its existing strategy.

Up until now, the company has tended to focus on specific niches in the market. Samantha wonders whether the firm should attempt a mass-market strategy in the future.

1 a) *Explain the difference between a marketing objective and a marketing strategy for a company such as TLC plc.* (3 marks)

   b) *Explain two factors which might determine TLC's marketing strategy.* (5 marks)

2 *Examine the factors which TLC might take into account before deciding whether to enter the mass market.* (7 marks)

3 *To what extent is primary research likely to be better than secondary research for TLC?* (10 marks)

>> The product life cycle and portfolio analysis

Looking at products

When deciding on its marketing strategy, a firm will have to examine the existing position of its products and services. Only by assessing how its products are doing, will it be able to decide what to do next.

This process of assessing the position of the firm makes use of techniques such as the product life cycle model and portfolio analysis.

The product life cycle

The product life cycle traces the sales of a product over its life. The typical path for a product can be divided into five stages.

1 Research and development

During this stage, the basic idea is developed and tested. This can be expensive for a firm and no revenue is being generated. The length of the research and development process will vary from product to product. In the case of new pharmaceuticals, it may take several years to develop

and test products before they can be launched. Developing a new design for a greeting card is likely to take months rather than years. Some products, such as newspapers, are modified on a daily basis. Some products never get beyond the development phase.

2 Introduction

This is the stage at which the product or service is put on sale. Many product ideas will never actually

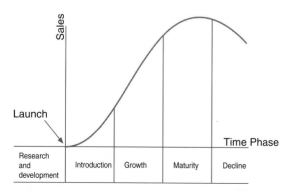

Figure 3.12 *The product life cycle*

reach this stage. They are abandoned after prototypes. At this stage, income from sales is unlikely to cover the initial launch costs. In the launch phase, distribution and promotion costs will be high. Sometimes products will be launched in one area of market first and then 'rolled out' to other markets. Digital TV and radio are still at the introduction stage in the UK.

3 Growth

If the product becomes known and accepted by customers, sales should grow. At this stage, it should be slightly easier to get distributors to stock the products, as they will be more confident of sales. The firm should begin to make profits at this stage, as revenues begin to outweigh costs. Sales of wine and anti-wrinkle creams, and sales of products by electronic commerce are in their growth stage at the

moment in the UK. Some products will never reach the growth stage.

4 Maturity and saturation

At this point in a product's life, sales tend to slow down. The product is likely to have been in the market for some time and competitors may well have launched similar products. Products such as washing machines and televisions are currently in their maturity stage. The maturity stage can last for years in some cases.

5 Decline

Eventually, the sales of any product will begin to fall. The firm may find it more difficult to get the product distributed and may be forced to cut the price to maintain sales. Think of the cassettes or books you sometimes see in the bargain area of

---

POINTS TO PONDER

Organisations are constantly reviewing their mix of products to ensure they have new ones coming on line when the sales of older ones are declining. In the table below you can see how sales of Sony Playstation 3 are expected to take over from Playstation 1, Gamecube 2 to take over from Gamecube and Xbox2 to take over from Xbox. The market as a whole is expected to start growing more slowly in 2007.

	2002	2003	2004	2005	2006	2007
Sony Playstation 3	0	0	0	2275	4095	5400
Sony Playstation 2	5642	4236	2982	1609	1103	476
Sony Playstation/PS One	350	216	83	0	0	0
Nintendo Gamecube2	0	0	0	900	1723	2250
Nintendo Gamecube	861	712	648	300	175	81
Microsoft Xbox2	0	0	0	1400	2720	3600
Microsoft Xbox	1576	1455	1420	764	477	176
Total	8429	6619	5132	7248	10292	11983
Annual growth	17%	−21.50%	−22.50%	41.20%	42%	16.40%

Table 3.2 *Game console revenue forecast 2002–2007 ($m)*

Sources: In-Stat/MDR

INTERPRETING DATA

	This year	Last year	Two years ago	Three years ago
Sales of product A	£250 000	£240 000	£200 000	£100 000

1 What stage of the product life cycle is product A at? Explain your reasoning.

Business in focus

Production of Doc Martens ended in 2003. The Northamptonshire shoe maker R Griggs, that make Doc Martens, announced it would close its five UK factories following a slump in the sales of its boots. Originally designed for industrial workers, the boots with their yellow stitching and air-cushioned soles were adopted by skinheads in the 1960s. In the late 1970s they were revived by punk bands such as The Clash. Doc Marten sales reached their peak in 1998, selling 10 million pairs. By 2003, sales were only 5 million and the company had had to make 1000 redundancies in the previous three years.

1 Why do you think sales of Doc Martens have gone into decline?

shops; the price has been reduced to try and increase sales. Products such as beer and board games are in their decline stages in the UK at the moment.

Extending the life cycle

A firm may try to prevent sales going into decline by using **extension strategies**. These might include the following:

- Increasing the use of the product – for example, in the 1980s the Milk Marketing Board stressed the benefits of drinking an extra pint of milk each day. Shampoo products always advise you to rinse and wash again, thereby doubling the usage rate.

- **Encouraging the use of the product on more occasions** – for example, Head & Shoulders was seen by consumers as a product to use when you had dandruff. The company tried to change this perception to get people to use it all year round to *prevent* dandruff.

- **Reducing the price** – as products approach the maturity stage, firms often cut the price to maintain sales.

- **Adapting the product** – look around a supermarket and you will see endless examples of 'new, improved' products or products with added X or extra Y (or less Z!). These are all ways of trying to keep the consumer interested in the product.

- **Introducing promotional offers** – another technique often used by firms to keep sales high is to have competitions to boost their sales.

- **Changing the image of the product** – this has been done with a number of drinks, such as vodka, which have had their image changed to appeal to a younger audience. New versions have been launched, such as vodka and mixers, and the branding and packaging has been changed.

INTERPRETING DATA

Shulters is a furniture manufacturer and retailer. When a new managing director was appointed she wanted more sales of the company's latest sofa range, called 'Extravaganza'. Shown below is the latest data on the Extravaganza range.

	This month	Last month	Two months ago	Three months ago
Monthly sales	£200 000	£120 000	£100 000	£120 000
Percentage of sales for which the customer is given an extended credit period	48%	30%	20%	20%
Marketing costs	£40 000	£35 000	£30 000	£10 000

1 Comment on the significance of the above data for Shulters.

Sales growth $=$
$$\frac{\text{change in sales}}{\text{original value of sales}} \times 100 = \%$$

For example, sales were £50 000 but have grown to £60 000

Sales growth $= \dfrac{(\text{£}60\,000 - \text{£}50\,000)}{\text{£}50\,000} \times 100$

$\qquad = \dfrac{\text{£}10\,000}{\text{£}50\,000} \times 100$

$\qquad = 20\%$

1 ABC Ltd has enjoyed sales of £600,000 this year. Last year's sales figure was £550 000. What is the growth in sales?

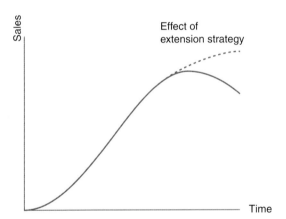

Figure 3.13 *An extension strategy aims to extend the product life cycle*

An **extension strategy** is an attempt to prolong the sales of a product and prevent it declining.

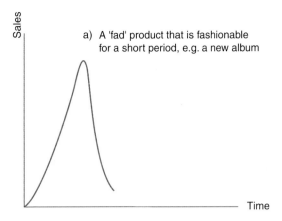

a) A 'fad' product that is fashionable for a short period, e.g. a new album

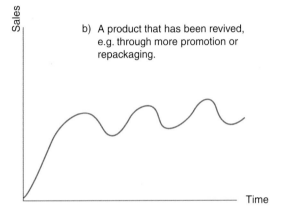

b) A product that has been revived, e.g. through more promotion or repackaging.

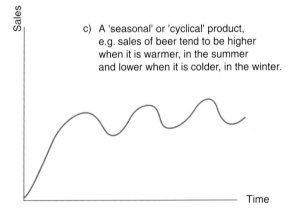

c) A 'seasonal' or 'cyclical' product, e.g. sales of beer tend to be higher when it is warmer, in the summer and lower when it is colder, in the winter.

Figure 3.14 *Different examples of the product life cycle*

Product launch and capacity utilisation

The capacity of a firm refers to the maximum amount it can produce at a moment in time. This will depend on the numbers and skills of its employees and its capital equipment and technology. Capacity utilisation refers to the amount that a firm is producing, compared with the amount it could produce. For example, a 50% capacity utilisation means that a firm is making half

Business in focus

Camelot plc is the operator of the National Lottery and is wholly owned by five shareholders: Cadbury Schweppes plc, Royal Mail Enterprises, De La Rue Holdings, Fujitsu Services and Thales Electronics. Since tickets first went on sale on 14 November 1994, the company has fought hard to try and maintain sales.

Extension strategies have included:

1995	the launch of Lottery Instants
1996	the launch of Lucky Dip
1997	the introduction of midweek draws
1999	the launch of Thunderball
31 December 1999	the special Millenium Draw
2000	Lottery Extra launched
2001	special Christmas Eve draw
2002	rebranding: The National Lottery is called Lotto
2002	launch of Lotto Hotpicks
2002	launch of midweek Thunderball

1 What factors do you think determine demand for Lotto?

as much as it could be making; 25% utilisation means it is producing a quarter of what it could produce.

Key terms

Capacity is the maximum amount a firm can produce at any given time, given its resources. **Capacity utilisation** measures existing output relative to potential output.

When a firm first considers launching a product, it must predict the level of sales because this will determine the capacity it will need. In the early stages of the life cycle, sales are likely to be less than

in the maturity phase, so the capacity utilisation will be low. This can be expensive because, although it has the resources to produce, say, 100 000 units, it may only be producing 20 000. This means the cost per unit will be high – the cost of the equipment and staff have to be covered by relatively few sales. As the sales grow over time, these costs can be spread over more units, thereby reducing the cost per item.

If sales continue to grow and exceed the firm's expectations, it must make a decision regarding its future level of capacity – should it increase its capacity or not? If it does it must be confident that sales will continue to grow to make sure this new higher level of capacity is utilised.

Product life cycle and cashflow

Cashflow at the start of a product's life cycle is likely to be negative. This is because cash has to be spent researching and developing the product before any sales have occurred. Even when the product is launched, the firm is likely to be spending more promoting it than is coming in as income.

As sales enter the growth phase, the cashflow should become positive. By this stage, there should be less need for extensive promotion because customers should be aware of the product and income will be higher. In the maturity phase, there may be a need to spend money re-promoting the product. As a result, cashflow may begin to fall, but should remain positive. With falling sales in the decline phase, cashflow will continue to drop.

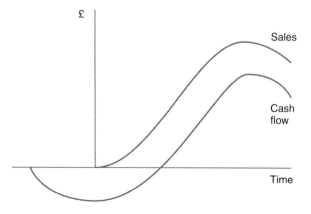

Figure 3.15 *Cashflow and product life cycle*

Business in focus

The soft drink Sunny Delight was the marketing success of the 1990s. It was launched in 1998 with a £10 million promotional campaign and quickly became the third-best selling drink behind Pepsi and Coke, with sales of over £160 million a year. The product was extremely popular with children who pushed their parents into buying it. Parents were willing to buy it because it had the image of being healthy orange juice, even though in reality a 200ml bottle had only 5% fruit juice and 14g of sugar – the equivalent of three and a half teaspoons – in it. An essential part of its marketing was to store it in chiller cabinets (even though it did not need to be stored there) to give the impression of being healthy orange juice. Then the media and the food regulatory authorities began to turn on the product, questioning how healthy it was; one news story even featured a girl whose skin turned orange after drinking 1.5 litres of Sunny Delight a day. Rather than fight back, the Sunny Delight team stayed quiet hoping the problems would go away – they didn't. Sales slumped by 40%.

In 2003 the product underwent a multimillion pound revamp, aimed at repositioning Sunny Delight as a health drink; however, this failed to impress the Food Commission, which said the marketing campaign was 'aimed at hoodwinking parents', and eventually its manufacturer, Procter & Gamble, put the brand up for sale.

1 Do you think that all products have to go into the decline stage eventually?

The value of the product life cycle model

The product life cycle model is valuable also because it highlights the fact that marketing policies have to be adjusted at different stages in the development of a product. For example, during the growth phase a firm may be able to launch different versions and have high prices. During the maturity or saturation phases, there is likely to be more competition and a firm may have to stress its price competitiveness.

Figure 3.16 *Barbie is looking good for her age – she has had a long product life cycle!*

However, it is important to remember the product life cycle is just a model and its shape will vary considerably between products. In the case of a new CD single, for example, the life span may be just a matter of weeks; Marmite was launched in the early twentieth century and is still in its maturity phase. Toys often, but not always, have short life cycles. Barbie dolls have sold in their millions for many years!

Problems with the model

There is a danger that the product life cycle model can be self-fulfilling. Managers who have studied the life cycle may actually make it happen to their own products! For example, *because* they expect the sales of a new product to enter the growth phase, managers may invest heavily in its promotion. The fact they have invested so heavily may actually bring about the very success they expected. Similarly, when sales growth starts to slow, managers may decide that decline is inevitable and cut back on marketing expenditure – this may then lead to the decline they predicted. This problem is known as determinism – if you think it will happen, you may make it happen!

The life cycle model must, therefore, be treated with some caution. It should not be regarded as always true or the same for every product. It is also important to distinguish between the life cycle of a particular brand and the product as a whole. Sales of individual brands of chocolate, for example, may have declined even though overall sales of the product are relatively stable.

Product portfolio analysis

Most firms have more than one product – some have thousands. At the time of writing, for example, Unilever owns a huge number of brands, including Bertolli, Birdseye, Findus, Hellman's, Knorr, Lipton, Slim-Fast, Comfort, Domestos, Dove, Lux, Pond's and Sunsilk, to name some. The range of products and services a firm has is known as its product portfolio. As part of its planning process, a firm should examine the position of these products in their markets. This is known as portfolio analysis. One of the most famous models of portfolio analysis was developed by the Boston Consulting Group and is known as the Boston matrix. This analyses the position of a firm's products in terms of their market share and the growth of the markets they operate in.

Key terms

A product portfolio is the collection of products and services that a firm produces.

The Boston matrix involves an examination of the existing position of a firm's products in terms of their relative market share and the growth of the markets they operate in.

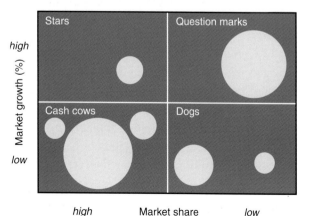

Figure 3.17 *The Boston matrix*

INTERPRETING DATA

Feranzi plc produces computer sports games. Below is a diagram showing its product portfolio.

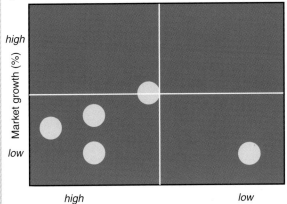

1 Comment on the significance of the above data for Feranzi

Business in focus

Although we tend to associate Coca-Cola with one main product, it does in fact have more than 300 drinks in its portfolio around the world.

Just a few of them are: Aqua, Alive, Bacardi Mixers, Beat, BlackFire, Cristal, Cappy, Cherry Coke, Dasani Water, Dorna, Eva, Fanta, H2OK, Hit, Hawai, Ice Mountain, Ice Dew, Jet Tonic, KMX, Lift, Lilt, Milo, Minute Maid, Nordic Mist, Oasis, OK, Powerade, Pulp, Quatro, Ramblin' Root Beer, Real Gold Rio, Samurai.

1 How many of these brands do you recognise?

2 In what ways could using the Boston Matrix help Coca-Cola?

3 Why do you think Coca-Cola has so many brands?

Relative market share

Each circle in the Boston matrix represents one particular product or service. The size of the circle illustrates the turnover of the product. The firm's products can be classified according to their market share and the growth of the market in which they operate.

- Cash cows – these are products which have a high market share and are sold in a slow-growing market. In some cases, this product-type will be the market leader in a mature market. Although the market may not be growing very fast, this may be because it has already grown quickly in the past leaving little room for further growth. For example, the market for washing machines is quite big but is not actually growing very fast. By comparison, the market for digital television is small but has potential for very fast growth. A cash cow already has a large market share and so much of the promotional work will have been done. The product is likely to have a good distribution system and people will already be aware that the product exists. The firm is used to producing it in relatively large volumes and, as a result, the cost per unit should be fairly low. So, this type of product is likely to bring in high levels of cash for the firm. This can be used to finance other areas.

- Question marks (or problem children) – these are products possessing a small market share of a fast-growing market. These products may go on to be very successful, but equally they may fail. They are quite vulnerable and their future is uncertain (hence the name). They need protecting by the firm and they require extensive marketing. Most new products are question marks because their future is so uncertain (although there are exceptions when a product takes off quickly).

- Stars – these products enjoy a large share of a market that is growing rapidly. They are highly successful products for the business; however they are usually expensive to market. Money must be spent to ensure they retain their position in a growing market.

- Dogs – these products have a low market share and are selling in a slow-growing market. A firm may want to get rid of these products unless they

Business in focus

The Wrigley Company is the world's largest manufacturer of chewing gum. In the US, Wrigley sells nearly half of all the gum sold. In 18 European markets Wrigley is the absolute market leader, with market shares of 80% or higher. Wrigley continues to innovate and develop new gums.

Relatively recent products have included Airwaves and Thin Ice. In 2000, Wrigley established the Wrigley Healthcare Division to develop and market products that deliver ingredients that provide health benefits. The Division's first product, Surpass, is designed to ease heartburn.

Wrigley's segments its products in the following ways:

- **Taste**: Juicy Fruit, Wrigley's Spearmint, Doublemint, Extra
- **Breath-freshening**: Winterfresh, Big Red, Eclipse, Eclipse Flash
- **Oral care** (e.g. teeth whitening): Orbit White, Orbit, Freedent
- **Wellness** (e.g. decongestant): Surpass, Airwaves, Alpine

'Quality, innovation and integrity'. That is the Wrigley way.

Source: www.wrigley.com

1 What factors do you think will determine how much Wrigley spends on developing new products each year?

think they can improve their sales. However, dogs can sometimes be revived. Lucozade used to be seen as a drink to help sick people get better, until it was very successfully repositioned as a sports and energy drink.

The value of the Boston matrix

The Boston matrix provides a snapshot of the position of all of a firm's products at a particular moment in time. The firm can see if it has a balanced portfolio – an appropriate mix of products. If it has too many 'dogs', the firm will have

insufficient new products to keep it going in the future. As a result, it may want to invest in new products quite quickly.

If it has lots of cash cows, it is generating relatively high levels of cash but, again, needs to think about the future; cash cows tend to be dominant products in markets that have already grown and a firm may want to be involved in newer markets as well.

If a firm has too many question marks it may be quite vulnerable – question marks need protective marketing and this may drain a firm's resources.

With an appropriate mix of products, the cash cows can be used to finance the development of question marks and turn them into stars; this way the firm uses money from established markets to enter new marks and so protects its future. Portfolio analysis, therefore, provides a good basis for marketing planning.

EXAMINER'S ADVICE

Remember that tools such as the product life cycle and Boston matrix do not guarantee that managers will make the right decision.

APPLICATION IN ACTION

- The product life cycle is often short in some industries, such as films and music, although for a few the sales can continue for years.
- Sales in some markets, such as fireworks, Easter eggs and greeting cards are likely to be very seasonal.
- At the moment, products such as anti-wrinkle cream, male cosmetics and cosmetic surgery are in the growth phase.

QUICK CHECK QUESTIONS

1 What are the different axes of the product life cycle model?

2 Outline the different stages of the product life cycle.

3 Efforts to prevent sales falling are called
……………. …………………..

4 In the early stages of the product life cycle, is cashflow likely to be positive or negative? Why?

5 Sales of a product have been:

2 years ago   £180 000
1 year ago   £190 000
now   £195 000

What stage of the life cycle is this product in? Explain why.

6 Capacity utilisation is likely to increase as a product moves through the stages of the life cycle. True of false?

7 The stages of the product life cycle may occur because firms think they are going to occur and because of the actions they then take. This is called:
a) fatality
b) determinism
c) inevitability
d) demonstrationism.

8 The Boston matrix is an example of product …………….. analysis.

9 What are on the axes of the Boston matrix?

10 A product with a low market share of a fast growing market is called a ….. product.

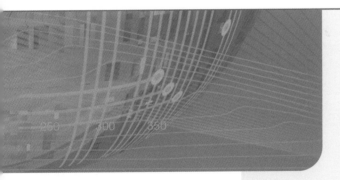

Progress questions

1 What are the different stages of the product life cycle? *(2 marks)*

2 Explain how the marketing of an energy drink may change at different stages of the product life cycle. *(8 marks)*

3 Explain how the cashflow of a film company may change at different stages of the product life cycle. *(6 marks)*

4 Explain how the level of capacity utilisation may vary at different stages of the product life cycle. *(6 marks)*

5 Outline two possible extension strategies for a particular brand of coffee. *(6 marks)*

6 Explain the possible value of the product life cycle model to a washing powder manufacturer. *(8 marks)*

7 What is meant by 'portfolio analysis'? *(3 marks)*

8 Explain what is meant by a 'cash cow' product in the Boston matrix model. *(6 marks)*

9 What is meant by a 'question mark' product in the Boston matrix model? *(6 marks)*

10 Explain two possible benefits of portfolio analysis to a firm such as Unilever. *(8 marks)*

Analytical and evaluative questions

11 *Jimbo, Joho and Rooster are the three founding members of Bling, a new boy band. Rather than sign with one of the big record labels, Bling have decided to set up their own company and launched their first record (Breaking Out) themselves. Examine the likely impact of the launch on their company's cashflow in the coming months.* (8 marks)

12 *Underlow plc is a leading producer of washing powders and liquids. Sales of one of its products, Umo, have been declining. Discuss the actions Underlow might take in such circumstances.* (15 marks)

13 *Mia Furrow has just set up a business selling a new kind of pram for babies. It is made of bright colourful plastic and looks very different from a traditional pram. Mia had the idea when she was pushing her own baby around in a rather boring blue pram. Before approaching the major stores, such as Mothercare, Mia went to evening classes to learn about business studies. As part of her course she learnt about the product life cycle. To what extent is the product life cycle model likely to help her in her marketing planning?* (15 marks)

Case study

25 marks

Sarah has just looked at the latest sales figures and is horrified. Sarah is the manager of the band 'Slightly Hazy'. The band has had three number one hits in the last two years but according to the figures in front of Sarah their latest single is only number 57 in the charts. Sarah cannot understand it – the band seemed to be doing so well. 'It's all about the product life cycle' said her younger brother, who studied Business Studies at school and liked to think he knew the answer to everything. 'It's obvious – they are in the decline phase. I'd drop them if I were you and get yourself another band. The growth phase of the product life cycle's very short these days and you've got to keep looking for new bands.'

'The problem with that is I'd be falling into the trap of determinism – the main reason the sales of products fall is because marketing managers believe they will act in a way which brings it about – which you would know if you studied properly,' said

Sarah. 'Anyway you've got to take an overview. It's not just how one product is doing. That's why we use product portfolio analaysis.' Her brother yawned and walked out.

1 *What is meant by 'product portfolio analysis'?* (2 marks)

2 *If 'Slightly Hazy' is in the decline phase of the life cycle, explain two marketing actions Sarah might take to maintain sales.* (5 marks)

3 *Analyse the factors which determine how long the growth phase of the product life cycle might last for a band such as 'Slightly Hazy'.* (8 marks)

4 *'The main reason the sales of products or services fall is because marketing managers believe they will act in a way which brings it about.' Discuss this view in the context of groups such as 'Slightly Hazy'.* (10 marks)

>> Marketing mix

What is the marketing mix?

The marketing mix includes all the elements associated with a product which affect whether the customer decides to buy or not. A broad range of factors may affect customers' purchasing decisions.

Consider why customers might choose one supermarket rather than another. The list below contains a number of factors affecting this decision.

- How far away is it?
- How easy is it to park?
- What is the range of products like?
- Are the prices competitive?
- What facilities are there (for example, a coffee shop)?
- Are the staff friendly and helpful?
- What services are provided (such as carrying shopping to customers' cars)?
- Does the supermarket offer a loyalty card?

There are clearly many factors which influence a consumer's decision to buy something and these are all part of the marketing mix.

The marketing mix is often simplified and is commonly described as the 4 Ps. This approach identifies four elements in the mix (all beginning with the letter P!):

> **Key terms**
>
> The **marketing mix** is the combination of all those factors combining to influence the customer's buying decision.

1 **Price** – how much are customers charged for the product and what are the terms of payment?
2 **Product** – this term includes the features of the product, such as design, quality, reliability, features and functions.
3 **Place** – this is the way the product is distributed. Is the product sold direct to the customer or through retail outlets?
4 **Promotion** – is the way in which the firm communicates information about the product to the customer. For example, it may use advertising or a salesforce. Promotion also includes the image customers have of the product.

An important thing to remember about the marketing mix is the way in which all the different

Figure 3.18a and b *What differences would you expect to find in the products and services offered by these two supermarkets?*

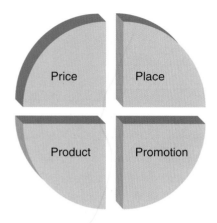

Figure 3.19 *The marketing mix*

items must work together for the customer to be satisfied. Part of the appeal of a well-known brand may be that it is quite expensive and that you cannot get it in every shop. If it is too cheap or too easily available, the brand may become less attractive. By comparison the success of Coca-Cola and Pepsi is due, not only to the product itself, but to the way the brand is promoted and the fact that the products are very easily available. So, the price, the way a product is promoted, the way it is distributed and all the other elements of the mix must all complement each other for the consumer to be satisfied.

The price

The price of a product or service plays an important part in our decision about whether or not to buy it. If the price is too high, we simply cannot afford the product even if we want to! However, the relative importance of price is likely to vary according to the product and the particular circumstances. As an example, if two garages opposite each other are charging different prices for petrol, we are likely to choose the cheaper one. When buying a wedding ring, however, we do not always go for the cheapest! In some cases it may be difficult to compare prices directly – just look at how complicated the price structure is for mobile phones. When considering the price, it is important to place it in the context of the other elements of the mix and the buyer's circumstances.

The price of a product will depend on the following range of factors:

The cost of producing a unit
Although in the short run a firm may sell an item at a loss to get it established in a market, in the long run a product usually has to generate a profit. This means the price has to be greater than the cost per unit. Some organisations (such as museums and hospitals) are non-profit making and so do not necessarily have to cover their costs. However, most firms in the private sector have to make a long-term profit to survive.

Competitors
The price a firm sets must take account of competitors' prices. If competitors are offering a similar product or service and it is easy to switch from one to the other, firms are likely to set similar prices. This is why, when two clothes shops on the high street are selling similar brands, the prices are similar. Wherever possible, a firm will stress the particular benefits of what it is offering so that it can justify a higher price. If the customer believes a product provides better value for money, he or she may still buy it even if it is more expensive. Stella Artois, for example, ran a very successful 'reassuringly expensive' campaign stressing that you pay more for high quality lager.

The firm's objectives
The price charged by a firm will be determined by its objectives. If a firm has a particular profit target, this will influence the price that is set per unit. If it wants to achieve £10 000 profit and expects to sell 20 000 units, it must make £0.50 profit per unit.

The level of demand
The price a firm can charge naturally depends on what people are able and willing to pay. If demand is high, the firm may be able to charge a higher price. However, it is not always easy to estimate demand in advance; for this reason many firms base their pricing on their costs.

The stage in the product life cycle
The price of a product is likely to be changed at different stages in the product life cycle. For example, when the product is in the maturity stage the price may need to be reduced to avoid losing sales to competitors.

The rest of the marketing mix

The price a firm charges depends on the other elements of the marketing mix. For example, if the product is heavily branded the firm may be able to charge a higher price.

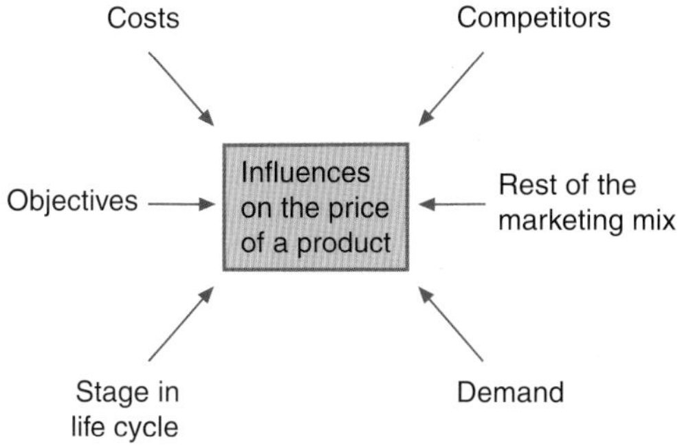

Figure 3.20 *Influences on pricing decisions*

When setting the price, the firm is likely to consider all these factors. The final price will be the result of all these influences.

Pricing strategies for new products

When a product is first launched into a market a firm will have to decide what price to charge.

Options include:

● Penetration pricing – this strategy uses a low price to enter the market and gain market share. This makes sense if there are cost advantages to producing on a large scale. It can also be beneficial if the market is price sensitive, so that a lower price generates significantly higher sales. In the late 1980s only the *Radio Times* and *TV*

Business in focus

The overall pricing strategy of Bryant Homes, the house builder, is to charge premium prices for its premium products (a higher price for a higher quality product). Its prices reflect the quality of the homes it builds. The purchase of a house is likely to be the largest expenditure in people's lives; they are likely to pay more if they think they are getting better value for money.

The following factors may affect the price of any particular house:

● The cost of buying the land; acquiring land is increasingly difficult due to problems with planning permission and this often forces up land prices.
● Costs associated with construction, including sewers, planning permission, and cleaning up the land.
● The quality of the property, including the design of the house, the labour costs and the construction costs.
● The state of the local property market, for example, the local level of demand for houses.

When choosing an area of land on which to build a group of houses Bryant Homes will consider issues such as:

● How much does an acre of land cost?
● How many houses can be built on each acre?
● What is the average cost of building each house?
● What are the legal and selling costs?
● What will consumers think is a fair price?
● What is the ideal competitive price to sell the houses quickly?

To achieve its target of a price premium of 5 to 10% (i.e. a price which is 5 to 10% higher than the average), Bryant's production and sales team must provide houses which:

● are in the most desirable locations
● have individual character rather than all being the same
● have fewer houses per acre than rivals
● have more features than rivals.

For more information on Bryant Homes, visit www.bryant.co.uk.

1 What does this example tell us about the links between the marketing and production functions of a firm?
2 Think of a clothing company which charges a price premium. How can it justify this price? Why do people pay it?

Times magazines were able to publish information on the week's television programmes. When the legislation was changed to allow other competitors, a number of firms entered the market with low prices to try and gain market share quickly.

- Price skimming – this strategy uses a high price to enter the market. Even though the price is high, some people may still be eager to try a new product. Once sales from this group of people have been exhausted, the price can be dropped to attract a new segment. When this segment is exhausted, the price can be cut again. A price skimming strategy is appropriate if the firm can protect its idea or invention so that competitors cannot enter with a cheaper version. It may be protected using a trademark (which protects the firm's logo) or a patent (which protects a new invention). Price skimming makes sense if the market is not particularly price sensitive, so that a price cut would not generate a particularly large increase in sales. This strategy is often used with new technology; the latest computer or computer accessory enters the market with a high price which then falls quite rapidly a year or so later.
- Competitive pricing – some firms set their price at the same level as their competitors. This makes sense if the market is highly competitive and consumers can easily compare the offerings of different firms. The John Lewis Partnership claims it is 'never knowingly undersold'. Esso operates a 'Pricewatch' to monitor competitors' prices. Competitive pricing is common when consumers can easily make a direct comparison between different products. Many retailers offer to refund the difference if you can find a similar

product cheaper in another local store. The rise in Internet usage has made it easier for customers to compare prices between firms. This puts more pressure on firms to be competitive.

Pricing strategies for existing products

For firms already competing in markets, pricing strategies may include:

- Price leadership – this tends to occur when a firm dominates a market and other competitors follow its lead. When leading petrol companies (such as BPAmoco) drop the price of their petrol, many smaller competitors follow suit.
- Price taking – price takers are firms that accept the price which dominates in the market. A small independent electrical retailer, for example, may have to accept the price set by the major sellers, such as Dixons. Independent bookshops may have to follow the prices of major bookstores, such as Waterstones.
- Predator pricing – this occurs when a firm sets out to destroy (or at least weaken) the competition through low prices. This usually occurs if the firm has more financial resources than the competition and so can sustain lower profits for longer.

Pricing methods

Pricing methods are the ways in which firms decide on the price they charge for a product.

Common methods include:

- Cost plus pricing – this method of pricing considers the total cost per unit and then adds on a percentage to arrive at the final price. For example, if the cost of producing a single unit of output is £20 and the firm has a 10% profit margin, the selling price will be £20 + 10% = £20 + £2 = £22. This method is simple to operate but does not consider the situation in the market. It ignores competitors' prices and what consumers might be willing to pay. Nevertheless, it is a simple method of pricing and is common in sectors such as retailing, where firms buy products in at a certain price and add on a percentage before selling it on.

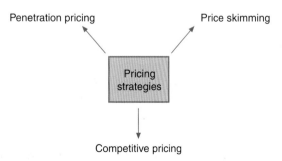

Figure 3.21 *Pricing strategies when a product is launched*

- Contribution pricing – the contribution of a product is the difference between the selling price and the variable cost per unit (such as the cost of materials). If the firm can cover the variable costs any remainder can be used to put towards its fixed costs (such as rent). This pricing method is often used when firms consider accepting a special order. Imagine a business receives a large order from a new customer; however, the price offered is below the normal selling price. Assuming the firm has sufficient capacity, it may accept the deal as long as the price covers the extra (or variable) costs involved in making the product. This special order decision can ignore costs such as the rent of the factory, the managers' salaries and interest payments on loans, because these are paid regardless of whether the order is accepted.
- Price discrimination – this occurs when different prices are charged for the same good or service. For example, the price charged for a train ticket can vary considerably according to when you book or what time you travel. Firms will charge different prices if demand conditions vary and provided they can separate out the different markets (they have to prevent people buying at the lower price and reselling at the higher one).

MATHS MOMENT
$1 + 1 = 2$

Imagine a firm sets its price by adding on a certain percentage to the cost of each unit. To calculate the amount it adds on use this equation:

$$\frac{x}{100} \times \text{cost per unit} =$$

For example, if a firm adds on 20% to its costs of £50:

$$\text{Amount added on} = \frac{20}{100} \times £50 = £10$$

So the final price = £50 + £10 = £60

1 If a firm produces its products at a cost of £30 each and decides to add on a 20% profit margin what will be its final selling price of a single product?

Pricing tactics
Pricing tactics are short-term policies aimed at achieving a particular objective. These include:

- Loss leaders – a loss leader is a product sold at a loss to generate business for other (profitable) products sold by the firm. For example, supermarkets often sell a few well-known products at a loss and publicise the prices of these few products heavily. This increases the number of people using their shop and boosts the sales of other products.
- Psychological pricing – this occurs when products are sold at prices intended to create a particular impression of the product. For example, selling a product at £49.99 instead of £50 makes customers think of it as 'less than £50'. Firms also use tactics which involve marking down prices, for example '*was* £60, *now* £49.99', to encourage people to buy. Alternatively, the firm may set a high price to convey quality – people often assume that a higher priced item must be better than a lower priced one.

Price and the rest of the marketing mix
The price that a firm chooses must fit with the other elements of the marketing mix and the firm's marketing strategy. Firms such as Asda, for example, have consistently pursued a strategy of low prices (Asda's slogan is 'permanently low prices forever'). This strategy has, therefore, determined its pricing policy.

The importance of price in the buying decision depends, only in part, on the nature of the product or service. For example, when you are buying a new house, the price is undoubtedly an important factor but you also pay a great deal of attention to the design, the number of rooms, the area, the local schools, and so on. You may well be willing to pay more if the other factors are positive. On the other hand, when buying light bulbs, there may be no obvious difference between the various brands and so the price may become more important in your buying decision.

The price is more likely to be important when you can compare goods easily. This is often the case with goods which are called shopping goods, such as fridges, microwaves and televisions.

Firms often try to build brand loyalty so that consumers are willing to pay more and pay less attention to prices; this is why famous brands in the clothing market can charge so much for their products.

Place for distribution

The distribution of a good or service refers to the way in which it gets from the producer to the consumer. In some cases, the product goes directly, for example, Dell computers supplies its customers direct, without intermediaries. Tesco sells through its supermarkets and direct via the Internet. In other cases, producers use intermediaries: most electrical good producers, such as Sony and Phillips, have intermediaries between the producer and the final seller.

It is common for manufacturers to use intermediaries to help them get their products to the market. These intermediaries include:

- Retailers – retailers such as Sainsbury and W H Smith are the final stage in the distribution chain. Most goods are sold through retailers.
- Wholesalers – wholesalers buy products in bulk from producers and sell these on to retailers, who then sell direct to the final consumer. Retailers use wholesalers because they offer a range of products and it is easier than dealing direct with individual manufacturers.

Distribution channels

The term distribution channel describes how the ownership of a good or service passes from the producer to the consumer. There are different types of retail channel:

- In a zero level channel, the good or service passes directly from producer to consumer without any intermediaries. For example, dentists, accountants and plumbers have zero level channels.
- A one level channel has one intermediary. For example, a retailer buys the product from the manufacturer and sells it to the consumer.
- A two level channel has two intermediaries. For example, a wholesaler buys the product from the manufacturer and sells it on to retailers, who sell to the final customers.

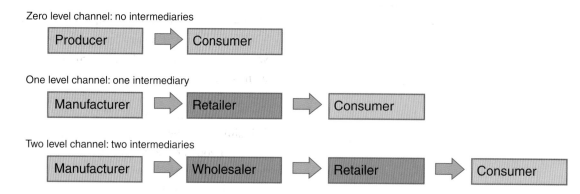

Figure 3.22 *Distribution channels*

Business in focus

Lands' End is 'a direct merchant of traditionally styled clothing for the family, soft luggage, and products for the home'. It offers products through catalogues, on the Internet and in a limited number of its own stores. It distributes nearly 300 million catalogues a year. Titles include: Lands' End Men; Lands' End Women; Lands' End Women, The Plus Size Collection; Lands' End Kids; Lands' End for School; Lands' End Home. Its website includes **My Virtual Model™**, where customers create a 3-D model of themselves by providing critical measurements; they can then use this to 'try on' items and outfits, to see how they will look on their body.

Lands' End's success is based on its willingness to 'go the extra mile'. For example:

- Lands' End offers one of the simplest guarantees in the industry – GUARANTEED. PERIOD.® – which allows customers to return items at any time, for any reason, for refund or replacement.
- Its phone lines for ordering and customer service are open 24 hours a day, 364 days a year.
- The company gets 40 000–50 000 calls on a typical day. During the Christmas season, it takes more than 1100 phone lines to handle over 100 000 calls a day. In one year, Lands' End answers the phone more than 15 million times.
- The company receives over 230 000 e-mails a year. Each e-mail receives a personal response.
- If a customer needs additional buttons, or luggage parts or repairs, they're all available free of charge.
- The company's Lost Mitten Club will replace any child's mitten lost in the same season as purchase at half the price of a pair, with free shipping.
- In-stock orders leave the Lands' End Dodgeville distribution center – the size of 16 football fields – the next business day after they're ordered.

Source: Adapted from www.landsend.com (© Lands' End, Inc. 2004. Used with permission.)

1 Examine the advantages and disadvantages to Lands' End of selling mainly through catalogues.

The distribution strategy will vary considerably from product to product. In the case of milk, newspapers and chewing gum, for example, the aim is usually to generate as wide a distribution as possible. These types of goods are called convenience items because consumers are not willing to travel far to buy them – they need them to be convenient. With products such as personal computers, vacuum cleaners, microwaves, and so on consumers usually want to compare the features and prices of different brands. Manufacturers of these products need to get them distributed to certain stores where customers expect to go to find them. These products do not need to be distributed to as many outlets as convenience items, but the firm may have to fight hard to get intermediaries to stock them. More exclusive products, such as Rolex and Porsche, have even fewer outlets, but the nature of these outlets is very important. They must reinforce the nature of the brand and so a great deal of time is spent ensuring they are well maintained and suitably exclusive.

Products that are sold to other firms rather than the final consumer are called industrial goods (rather than consumer goods). These tend to be distributed directly. This might include machinery, office equipment and specialised computer software.

The effects of distribution decisions

The decision about how to distribute a product can have a significant impact on a business:

- Cost – it may be cheaper to sell a product direct to the customer. If the product goes through various intermediaries, all of whom take their own profit margin, the final price may be higher.
- Market coverage – to get a wide coverage of the market, it may be necessary to use intermediaries. It is simply not possible for a manufacturer of electrical goods to reach all the potential buyers by itself. Much better to sell to a wholesaler who then sells on to a retailer.
- Control – the more intermediaries a firm uses to get its products to the market, the less control it has over the way it is sold at the end. The intermediaries may decide to promote, display or price the product as they wish.

The effective distribution of a product is essential to its success. After all, consumers cannot buy a product or service if they cannot actually get hold of it! Companies such as Amazon.com and Direct Line have turned the distribution of their services into a major competitive weapon. By distributing directly to the customer, they have cut their own costs (enabling them to offer better value) and provide a more convenient service for customers. You can now order your weekly shopping, buy your books, check your bank account and book your holiday from home.

Distribution targets

When developing a distribution strategy, firms often set themselves distribution targets. These might be in terms of the sales it hopes to achieve in different areas or through different types of store. To achieve these targets, the firm may need to convince intermediaries to take their products or promote their services. This is often the job of the salesforce. They meet with intermediaries, to persuade them to buy the firm's products.

EXAMINER'S ADVICE

Do not underestimate the importance of distribution. If a business cannot get its products to the market, it will not be able to sell them! You should also note that it can be quite difficult to get firms to stock new products. Retailers tend to be very short of space on their shelves, and have to be convinced or persuaded that stocking a particular product would actually help them.

Key issues

Distribution channels are always developing. Firms are not just finding new products and services to offer us, they are also finding new ways of getting them to us! Internet and telephone banking, and insurance mean we no longer need physical outlets to use these services. The Internet, in particular, is transforming the way in which we buy goods and services and the way they are distributed to us. The Internet allows many firms (even very small firms) to deal directly with their customers on a global basis.

Promotion

The promotion of a product involves the communication of various messages to existing or potential customers. These messages may be aimed at *informing* customers (e.g. telling them about modifications to the product or promotional offers), or *persuading* them (e.g. putting across a product's benefits compared with the competitors) or reassuring buyers they did the right thing. A firm can promote its products in various ways, including:

Advertising

Advertising involves paying for communications. Adverts can be placed in a range of media, such as television, newspapers, radio and the Internet. Advertising is often used as a long-term strategy to build brand loyalty. Advertising that uses independent media, e.g. TV or newspapers, is known as above the line promotion. All other forms of promotional activity, e.g. free samples or special offers, are known as below the line promotion.

Sales promotions

These are attempts to boost sales using techniques such as promotional offers, competitions and price cuts. Offers can include 10% extra free and buy one get one for free. Sales promotions may be used as a means of boosting sales in the short term.

Personal selling

Personal selling is based on face-to-face contact with customers. This may be used by manufacturers to get distributors to take their products or in industrial markets and the service sector, where the producer often deals directly with the customer. Financial services, such as pensions, insurance and mortgages, are often sold in this way. Similarly, the sale of products, such as photocopiers, often takes place through a salesforce.

Public relations (PR)

Public relations activities involve contact with the media and the various groups that the firms deals with. It attempts to send out particular messages about the firm or its products. This might involve press releases to the media, handling customer complaints and organising events to promote particular messages.

Figure 3.23 *Different forms of promotion*

Direct mail

This type of promotion involves sending mailshots to customers. With increasingly sophisticated database information, these can be carefully targeted.

Each of these methods of promotion has its own advantages and disadvantages, as shown in Table 3.3. For example, personal selling is obviously quite labour intensive and, therefore, expensive but the firm gets immediate feedback from its customers.

The promotional mix

Businesses use a combination of these five methods – this is known as the promotional mix. The composition of the promotional mix depends on numerous factors:

- The stage in the life cycle – when a product or service is first launched, the promotional message is likely to be informative. Once a product and the market is more established, promotion may

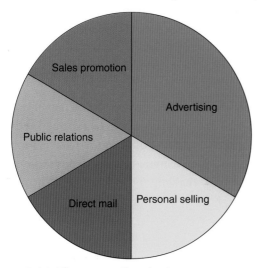

Figure 3.24 *The promotional mix*

focus more on how products differ from the competition. Thus, firms selling will promote the advantages of purchasing their *particular* product.

- The nature of the product – consumer durable products, such as televisions and washing machines, are likely to be advertised to the final customer. Firms usually use a sales team to deal with wholesalers and retailers but use advertising to get customers to demand the product in stores. By comparison, sales of heavy construction equipment are usually made direct to the customer and rely on the sales force.
- The marketing budget – inevitably, the budget acts as a constraint on all firms' promotional activities. Faced with a small budget, for example, a firm cannot even consider television advertising and may have to rely on local newspaper advertising instead.

To measure the effectiveness of a promotional campaign, it is important to consider the overall objectives. Was the intention to generate more sales or to increase awareness of the brand name in the short run, for example?

The product

The product itself is a crucial element of the marketing mix. Many marketing specialists argue that it is the most important element of the marketing mix.

A successful product will be designed to meet customer requirements. These requirements will have been identified, perhaps through market research. The design of the product will take account of the production process. A well-designed product can save on costs, can be made easily to a consistent quality and meets the needs of customers very precisely. Many firms try to rush the design and development stage because they are so eager to get the product out on to the market to earn money! However, it is often the case that more time spent developing the product results in a much greater chance of long-term success. Approximately four out of five new products fail, which shows how risky developing new products can be.

Method of promotion	Advantages	Disadvantages
advertising	• wide coverage • control of the message • can be used to build brand loyalty	• can be expensive, e.g. TV advertising
public relations	• can be relatively cheap	• control over the way the story is covered by the media
direct mail	• relatively cheap	• may not get read
sales promotions	• can entertain and interest the consumer	• often short-term effects • can encourage brand switching
personal selling	• two-way communication; can answer customer enquiries	• can be expensive • can only reach a limited number of customers

Table 3.3 *A comparison of promotional methods*

Business in focus

The Smart, car which began production in 1997, was the first car with an all-plastic chassis and plastic body panels. The company is jointly owned by Mercedes Benz and the makers of Swatch watches. The manufacturing approach for the Smart car is very different from traditional car manufacturing. Unlike most car companies, the components are all produced and assembled under one roof. An entire car can be produced in four hours and dismantled in two. As the chassis is bolted rather than welded onto the steel frame, parts such as bumpers can be switched for those of a different colour, for example. Owners can also clip in new seats, seat covers and door linings to reflect different tastes. At the same time, the significant weight reduction afforded by plastic body parts leads to lower fuel consumption for the motorist. The Smart is also revolutionary in terms of its size – at only 2.5 metres long and 1.51 metres wide, coupled with an excellent turning circle, parking anywhere is easy. Finally, the revolutionary design of the Smart car means that at end-of-life nearly 100 per cent of the car is recyclable – this may become extremely important with ever greater recycling directives being introduced by the EU.

1 How important is the design of a car to a customer?

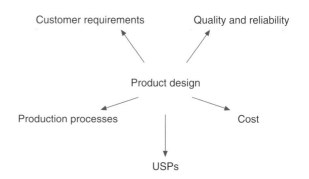

Figure 3.25 *Aspects of product design*

Key terms

*A product has a **Unique Selling Proposition** (or **Unique Selling Point**, **USP**) when there is some aspect of it that other products do not have. This could lie in the way it was designed, its features or the technology involved. If a product has a USP this helps to differentiate it from the competition.*

Firms may succeed in the market by launching products that meet new needs or existing needs more precisely, by offering a more reliable product or by producing it more cheaply than the competition, enabling the firm to lower the price.

An integrated mix

The key thing to remember when discussing the marketing mix is that it must be part of an

Business in focus

The Internet is changing many aspects of business – it makes it easier for customers to find what they want and compare prices and services, and it also provides a new way for firms to promote and sell their products. Although many 'dot.com' businesses have failed, Amazon has become one of the most famous brands in the world, even though it is still quite a young company.

In 1994 Jeff Bezos was working on Wall Street and noticed that the use of the web was growing by 2300% a year. Seeing the potential of the Internet, Bezos looked for the right product to sell and decided on books. Its first headquarters were in Bezos' garage, its first customers were his friends, and books were the first and best products to sell on the Internet.

Amazon.com opened for business in July 1995. Originally, the company installed a system that beeped every time a customer placed an order. The constant beeping drove employees mad, and the beeper was soon disabled. Orders, however, continued. In fact, it had its first 100-order day by October 1995. Its first 100-order hour came less than a year later; 100-order minutes are now common. In 1998 Amazon launched new businesses (including its Music and Video stores) in the US and opened sites in the UK and Germany. In 1999 it started offering Electronics, Toys & Games and Tools & Hardware. In July 2000 it served its 20 millionth customer and its US Books, Music and Video businesses had reached profitability for the first time.

Amazon.com seeks to be 'the world's most customer-centric company, a place where people can find and discover anything they might want to buy online'.

1 Analyse the possible advantages to Amazon of operating only as an online business.

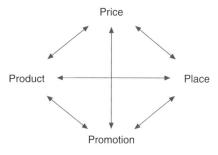

Figure 3.26 *Integration is the key to the marketing mix*

integrated approach. This means that all the different elements of the mix must work together and complement each other. There is little point trying to develop a high-priced, exclusive brand to target high-income earners if it is then distributed through bargain outlets. In a well-managed mix, the elements fit well together and enhance the overall value provided to the customer.

It is also important to see the 4 Ps model as a rather *basic* model of what influences a decision to buy, or not buy, a product. We are also influenced by the people who serve us, the way in which we buy the product, the ease with which the features of one product can be compared with others. The mix should be thought of as anything connected with a product or service which influences the buyers' decision.

Some business writers now talk of the 7 Ps, rather than the 4 Ps. In addition to the original 4 Ps, these include:

● people – a well-trained, polite staff can influence people to buy from one shop rather than another
● physical environment – factors such as the

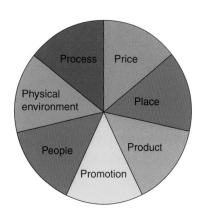

Figure 3.27 *7 Ps of the marketing mix*

What might make someone buy this product?

Is it:

- the brand name? Perhaps this is a brand they trust or have heard is good at producing this kind of product (perhaps friends have it).
- the design? Perhaps the size of it or the look of it appeal.
- the features? Perhaps the spin speed, the number and type of programmes, the energy usage appeal.
- the price? This may be competitive and be regarded as good value for money.
- the sale offer? Customer may want to buy now before the price goes up.
- the free delivery and installation? This may entice the customer to buy this product or from this shop rather than somewhere else because it makes the purchase more convenient.
- the payment terms, which enable the customer to spread the cost?
- the distribution? If the model was not in a convenient store, if the customer could not see it, he or she would be unlikely to buy it.
- the sales staff? Perhaps they advised the customer this was good product.
- a review of the product in a magazine.

The answer is that it may well be a combination of all these factors. The marketing mix is all the different factors that interrelate to influence the customer's decision to buy.

layout, decor and parking can be an important influence on which restaurant, pub or store a person chooses

- process – the ease of ordering and paying can influence a purchase. Many supermarkets are introducing self-scanning to reduce queues and attract customers.

APPLICATION IN ACTION

- The relative importance of elements of the marketing mix may vary from industry to industry. With convenience items, customers look for the nearest place to buy – they assume they know the product already and that prices will be roughly similar, so look for the nearest shop selling milk, newspapers or chewing gum. With shopping goods, customers will look for the lowest price and compare between sellers.
- Remember that producers often sell to intermediaries rather than the end customer. Producers of soups and frozen foods, for example, sell to shops and these are their immediate customers, so think what will make the shops want to buy it.
- Remember that the customer and consumer may be different – just think of petfood!

QUICK CHECK QUESTIONS

1   Give four factors that might influence the price of a product.

2   If a low price is set when a product is launched, this is known as …………… pricing.

3   If a high price is set when a product enters a market, this is called ………..……………..

4   Price discrimination occurs when:
a)   prices are changed over time
b)   prices depend on costs
c)   different prices are charged for different products
d)   different prices are charged for the same products.

5   Which of the following is not part of below-the-line promotion:
a)   television advertising
b)   competitions
c)   discounts
d)   special offers.

6   A retailer adds 30% to the cost of goods to set the selling price. If the retailer buys in a product at £40, what price will it sell for?

7   A product sold at a loss to get more people to come into the store is called a …………
…………………..

8   If a product is sold direct from the manufacturer to the customer, this means it has a …… ……….. distribution channel.

9   Public relations is:
a)   a form of distribution
b)   part of the promotional mix
c)   a pricing strategy
d)   a form of market research.

10   Most new products succeed. True or false?

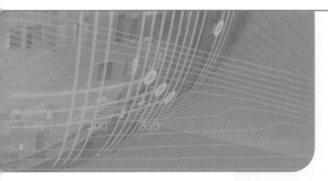

Progress questions

1   What is meant by the 'marketing mix'?   *(2 marks)*

2   What is meant by 'predator pricing'?   *(2 marks)*

3   Explain two factors which might influence the price of employing an accountant.   *(6 marks)*

4   What is meant by 'price skimming'?   *(2 marks)*

5   What is meant by 'promotion'?   *(2 marks)*

6   Distinguish between advertising and sales promotion.   *(5 marks)*

7   What is meant by a 'distribution channel'?   *(2 marks)*

8   Explain two ways in which the choice of distribution channel may benefit a computer manufacturer.   *(6 marks)*

9   Outline two factors a firm might consider when designing a television.   *(6 marks)*

10   Explain how the pricing of a brand of coffee may have to change as it moves out of a niche market into a mass market.   *(6 marks)*

Analytical and evaluative questions

11 *Examine the ways in which a new mobile phone from Nokia might be promoted.* *(8 marks)*

12 *Discuss whether distribution is the most important element of the marketing mix for a firm such as Wrigleys.* *(15 marks)*

13 *To what extent does the price determine the success of a new type of training shoe?* *(15 marks)*

Case study   **25 marks**

After months of development, the new computer game 'Cyberpunk' by Arcadia was ready to be launched. Focusing on a central character, Nasser Maddox, the game involved a series of gang fight scenarios set in the twenty-second century. Although fairly confident the game was distinctive and had the potential to do well, the marketing managers of Arcadia were unsure how to price the product. Some of them talked about cost plus pricing, others mentioned price skimming and penetration pricing. The company also had to consider the promotion of the product – would above the line or below the line be more effective? In addition, the competition's products seemed to be absolutely everywhere – walk into almost any games or computer shop and you would see 'Bulman Watt, King of the Dragon Slayers' for example. Arcadia's managers were very aware of the

need to ensure that 'Cyberpunk' was well distributed. 'Distribution can make or break a product such as this,' said Claudia, the Marketing Director of the company.

1 *Explain two factors Arcadia might have taken into account when designing 'Cyberpunk'.* *(3 marks)*

2 *Explain two methods of below the line promotion which might be used to increase sales of 'Cyperpunk'.* *(5 marks)*

3 *Analyse two factors which might influence the price set by Arcadia for the 'Cyberpunk' game.* *(7 marks).*

4 *To what extent is distribution the most important element of the marketing mix for a product such as 'Cyberpunk'?* *(10 marks)*

>> Elasticity of demand

What affects demand?

Of course, all firms are interested in what affects demand for their products and services. What is it that makes a firm's sales go up or down? Will sales alter if it changes the price or if incomes change? What is the strength of the relationship between, for example, price and sales? If the price is cut by 10%, will sales go up by 5% or 50%? Similarly, if average consumer income levels rise by 20%, what

impact will this have on demand for a firm's products?

The relationship between changes in demand and changes in price and income, is known as the elasticity of demand. There are two types of elasticity of demand: price elasticity and income elasticity.

The **price elasticity of demand** measures the sensitivity of demand to a change in price.

The income elasticity of demand measures how sensitive demand is to a change in income.

Why does elasticity matter?

By calculating elasticity, a firm can identify how changes in price and income may affect demand and, therefore, sales. This is important for planning. If, for example, a firm is planning a price cut, it will want to estimate the impact on demand and sales. This allows it to ensure it has sufficient stocks or capacity to meet demand. It may also have implications for workforce planning. The business may need to hire extra people or get staff to work overtime to meet orders. It will also want to calculate whether the price cut is worthwhile. Will it lead to higher profits?

MATHS MOMENT $1 \div 1 = 2$

The value of the price elasticity of demand is calculated using the equation:

$$\frac{\text{percentage change in quantity demanded}}{\text{percentage change in price}}$$

If sales rise by 10% following a 2% price cut:

the price elasticity of demand
$$= +\frac{10}{-2} = -5.$$

The answer is negative because price and sales have moved in different directions. All answers for **price** elasticity of demand are likely to be negative.

Similarly, if the economy is growing or shrinking, consumers' incomes will be changing. Businesses will want to estimate the possible effects on sales. Accurate forecasts ensure that the firm can meet the likely demand.

Price elasticity

Price elastic demand

Demand is price elastic if the value of the price elasticity of demand is greater than 1, i.e. every 1% change in price brings about a more than 1% change in quantity demanded.

For example, if demand rises by 20% when the price is cut by 10%, the price elasticity of demand will equal $\frac{+20}{-10} = -2$.

Remember that although the answer is -2, the part of this we are most interested in is the value of 2. This shows that for every 1% change in price, the quantity demanded changes by 2%, i.e. by twice as much. The negative sign simply shows that the price and quantity demanded more in different directions. If price goes down, quantity demanded rises, and if price rises, quantity demanded falls.

Price inelastic demand

Demand is price inelastic if the value of the price elasticity is less than 1, i.e. a 1% change in price leads to a less than 1% change in quantity demanded.

For example, a price cut of 10%, leading to an increase in demand of only 5%, will have a price elasticity of demand of $\frac{+5}{-10} = -0.5$. The negative sign shows that as price goes down, quantity demanded rises (i.e. they move in opposite directions). The 0.5 (which is less than 1) shows that every 1% change in price leads to a 0.5% change in quantity demanded.

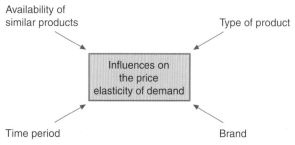

Figure 3.28 *Factors affecting the price elasticity of demand*

What determines the value of the price elasticity?

The price elasticity of demand will be affected by a number of factors.

The availability of similar products

If a consumer can switch easily from one product to another the demand is likely to be quite sensitive to price changes; hence demand will be price elastic. When buying a light bulb, for example, most customers do not care what brand they buy – faced with two types, they are likely to buy the cheaper one. Many firms attempt to differentiate their products so that consumers do not switch to competitors' offerings. Coca Cola, for example, has worked hard to establish its products as distinct from other cola drinks. Coca Cola hopes that relatively few consumers will switch brands even if its price is higher. Successful branding should, therefore, reduce the price elasticity of demand. The growth of the Internet, on the other hand, should make goods more price elastic because it is easier for buyers to compare prices and find alternatives. The Euro is also expected to increase price elasticity because, for consumers in member countries, it is easy to compare prices because they will all be in the same currency.

Time

Over time consumers may find more alternatives and be able to switch their purchases. In the short term customers are often loyal to their existing provider (for example, their credit card company, their bank or their insurance company). If, over time, they feel they are getting a bad deal, this will act as an incentive to switch.

The type of good

As mentioned previously, when buying convenience products, such as a pint of milk, purchasers tend to go to the nearest shop. Consumers do not spend much money on each item and are not too concerned about price. In comparison, shopping goods are likely to be much more sensitive to price.

Brand versus product

Demand for petrol as a whole is likely to be very price inelastic – most consumers would find it difficult or inconvenient to do without their cars. Conversely, demand for one company's petrol is likely to be fairly price elastic as it is easy to switch to another garage.

Price elasticity, revenue and profits

If a good is price elastic, a firm can increase its revenue by lowering the price. Although it earns less for each item, its overall income goes up because it is selling so much more. Whether this leads to an increase in profit depends on what happens to the costs when the firm produces and sells more. If, for example, a firm has to increase capacity it may incur expenses and so, although it is earning more, profits may fall. On the other hand, if revenue increases more than costs, profits will rise.

If demand for a good is price inelastic, revenue will fall when the price is cut. This is because the increase in sales is not big enough to compensate for the fact that each item is selling for less. In this situation, the firm could earn more by putting the price up. Although it would lose some customers, the fact that it is charging more per unit means its overall income will increase.

INTERPRETING DATA

The Wideworld Waxworks museum recently increased its charges.

	This month	Last month
Price	£15	£10
Revenue	£300 000	£250 000

1 Comment on the above data with reference to the price elasticity of demand.

Key terms

*The **revenue** or **turnover** of a firm is the value of its sales.*

*The **profit** of a firm equals its revenue minus its costs. Revenue may increase but, if costs increase by more, profit falls.*

Income elasticity

As we have seen, the income elasticity of demand measures the sensitivity of demand to a change in income. The income elasticity of demand is calculated using the equation:

$$\frac{\text{percentage change in quantity demand}}{\text{percentage change in income}}$$

If demand is income elastic, this means that every 1% change in income will lead to a change in quantity demanded of more than 1%. If demand is income inelastic, every 1% change in income will lead to a less than 1% change in quantity demanded.

The sensitivity of demand to income changes depends on the type of product. Goods and services such as holidays abroad, health clubs and sports cars, are mostly income elastic. With an increase in income the increase in demand is likely to be relatively large. Goods and services such as matches, lemonade and newspapers, are income inelastic. An increase in income is unlikely to lead to a bigger percentage increase in sales of these goods.

Inferior goods

Most goods have a positive income elasticity of demand. As income increases so consumers purchase more of the good. However, some goods and services have negative income elasticity. As income increases, people buy less not more! These sorts of products are called inferior goods. When people get more money, they switch to better-known brands or more luxurious products.

The use of income elasticity

If firms know the income elasticity of demand for their products, they target appropriate areas, change their products and generally plan ahead. For example:

- If demand is income elastic (sensitive to income), and the income of the target market is set to grow, the firm may need to increase capacity and recruit staff to meet the demand.
- If demand is income elastic, the firm may target fast growth regions or countries to boost sales.
- If the economy is set to go into a recession, and decline, the firm may change its product mix and focus more on basic or inferior goods.

Calculating the elasticity of demand

Percentages

To calculate elasticity you need to be able to work out percentages.

> **EXAMINER'S ADVICE**
>
> *Although the concept of elasticity can be applied to many different variables, it is important to distinguish between the different types, such as price elasticity and income elasticity. One shows how sales vary in relation to price changes; the other shows how they vary in relation to income changes. They are, therefore, measuring very different things. Take the demand for luxury sports cars, for example; this demand is not likely to be sensitive to price changes (given it is so expensive anyway) but probably will be sensitive to income changes (because many of us would like one if we had enough money!).*

To calculate a percentage you can use the following equation:

$$\frac{\text{the change in value}}{\text{the original value}} \times 100 = \%$$

For example, if price changes from 20 to 22 pence, this is a change of 2 out of an original value of 20. (Remember to use the original value not the new one!) So, the percentage change in price is:

$$\frac{+2}{20} \times 100 = +10\%$$

If, as a result of this price increase, sales fall from 50 units to 40 units, this is a change of 10 out of 50. Thus:

percentage change in demand =

$$\frac{-10}{50} \times 100 = -20\%$$

Price elasticity

As we have seen, to calculate the price elasticity of demand we use the equation:

$$\frac{\text{percentage change in quantity demanded}}{\text{percentage change in price}}$$

Remember to put demand on the top line (one of the most common mistakes is to get the equation the wrong way around).

In this case, the price elasticity of demand

$$= \frac{-20\%}{+10\%} = -2$$

Remember that the negative sign shows that price and quantity demanded move in different directions. The value of 2 shows that for every 1% change in price, quantity demanded changes by 2%.

Another example

Income increases from £20 000 to £25 000. Demand and sales increase from 40 000 to 48 000 units.

Percentage change in demand

$$= \frac{+8000}{40\,000} \times 100 = +20\%$$

Percentage change in income

$$= \frac{+£5000}{£20\,000} \times 100 = +25\%$$

Income elasticity of demand

$$= \frac{\text{percentage change in demand}}{\text{percentage change in income}}$$

$$= \frac{+20}{+25}$$

$$= +0.8$$

Note:

- The change in demand is on the top line again.
- The answer shows the good is income inelastic because it has a value of less than one. For every 1% change in income, the quantity demanded changes by 0.8%.
- The answer is positive because sales have gone up with an increase in income, i.e. both have moved in the same direction.

Problems with elasticity

It is important to remember that the values for elasticity are usually estimates and, therefore, need to be treated with some caution. The firm may look at what has happened in the past or what happened in a test market and base the estimate on this. However, conditions may have changed since the estimate was made, or the test market may not have been representative of the whole market, in which case the wrong decision may be made.

It is also important to remember that markets keep changing and these changes can all affect demand. New products, changes in consumer tastes, developments in distribution and competitors' marketing campaigns will all affect the demand for a product. This can make it difficult to know exactly what caused a change in sales. Was it the price change? Was it government policies, or consumer confidence? While it may appear that a price cut of 1% increased sales by 2%, suggesting a price elasticity of −2, in reality the sales may have gone up for completely different reasons.

APPLICATION IN ACTION

- Income elastic products may include: health clubs, private healthcare, swimming pools, sports cars, game park holidays, holiday homes.
- Price inelastic products may include: cigarettes, car parking fees, train fares in rush hour, food and coffee at motorway service stations, milk.

INTERPRETING DATA

The owners of Monarch Cruise Holidays has produced the following data:

	This year	Five years ago
Price elasticity of demand	−0.6	−0.8
Income elasticity of demand	+2.5	+2.0

1 Comment on the significance of the data above for Monarch Cruise Holidays and explain how it might affect the firm's marketing.

QUICK CHECK QUESTIONS

1 State three factors that may affect the demand for a product.

2 If the value of the price elasticity of demand is 0.8, this means demand is price inelastic. True or false?

3 Demand is likely to be more price elastic if there are few substitutes:
a) a product has a unique selling proposition
b) it is easy to compare prices between different firms' products.

4 If demand increases when income rises, this means that the product is income elastic. True or false?

5 If the price elasticity of demand is 2.4:
a) a 1% change in income changes demand by 2.4%
b) a 1% change in price changes demand by 2.4%
c) a 1% change in demand changes price by 2.4%
d) a 1% change in price changes income by 2.4%.

6 If price falls when demand is price inelastic, revenue will increase. True or false? Explain

7 If price falls when demand is price elastic, revenue will increase. True or false? Explain.

8 If the income elasticity is 4 and income grows by 2%, what will happen to demand?

9 Luxury products are likely to be income elastic. True or false? Explain.

10 Sales are 200 units. Price elasticity is −2. The price is cut by 10%. Sales will now be:
a) 160
b) 240
c) 20
d) 40.

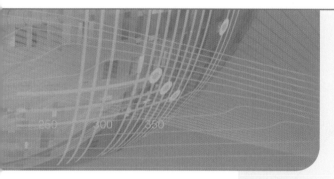

Progress questions

1 What is 'price elasticity of demand'? *(3 marks)*

2 What is meant by 'price inelastic'? *(2 marks)*

3 Explain two factors which might determine the size of the price elasticity of demand. *(6 marks)*

4 The price of a product is cut from £5 to £4. Sales increase by 50%. Calculate the price elasticity of demand. *(3 marks)*

5 The price elasticity of demand is −1.5. What would be the effect of a price cut on the firm's revenue? What about its profits? Explain your answers. *(4 marks)*

6 What is 'income elasticity of demand'? *(3 marks)*

7 What is meant by 'income elastic?' *(2 marks)*

8 Income in a country rises by 5%. The sales of a product increase from 20 000 units a week to 22 000 units. What is the income elasticity of demand for this product? *(3 marks)*

9 What is meant by an 'inferior' good? *(2 marks)*

10 Explain why an understanding of elasticity might be useful for a firm. *(6 marks)*

Analytical and evaluative questions

11 *Slater plc produces a range of washing-up liquids and soaps. Analyse the factors that might influence the price elasticity of demand for its products.* (8 marks)

12 *To what extent is the concept of elasticity useful to a major retailer such as Tesco?* (15 marks)

13 *The demand for overseas holidays is income elastic. To what extent will changes in income determine the success of holiday companies?* (15 marks)

Case study   **30 marks**

Amanda Whitworth is one of the UK's up-and-coming young designers. Her clothes have already been on display at fashion shows all over the world, from New York to Paris to Tokyo. At the top end of the range, her clothes sell for thousands of pounds. However, she has recently signed a deal with a major high street retailer to design a range of clothes, called Whitworth, which will sell for much less than this.

The marketing manager of the stores has estimated that for the Whitworth range:

● if the average price of an item is £200, sales would be 200 000 items.
● if the average price of an item is £250, sales would be 180 000 items.

The marketing manager also believes the income elasticity of demand will have a value of +1.8.

By comparison, the marketing manager estimates that for the store's own label range of clothing (sold under the name of 'Bland') the price elasticity of demand is −1.3 and the income elasticity is +1.1.

1 a) *Calculate the apparent price elasticity of demand for the new clothing range called Whitworth.* (3 marks)

b) *Comment on your findings.* (3 marks)

c) *Calculate the change in revenue which would occur if the price was increased from £200 to £250.* (2 marks)

d) *The marketing manager estimates the price elasticity of demand for the store's own label clothing is −1.3. Explain one way in which this price elasticity of demand might have been estimated.* (3 marks)

e) *Explain one reason why the price elasticity of demand for the Whitworth range may differ from the Bland range.* (3 marks)

2 a) *What is meant by the 'income elasticity of demand'?* (2 marks)

b) *Assume that the firm's sales of the Whitworth range are 200 000 items. Then incomes increase by 10%. What would the new level of sales be?* (4 marks)

3 *Discuss the ways in which the concept of the elasticity of demand may be useful in the marketing planning of a retailer.* (10 marks)

End of chapter questions

When Hissam and AB set up HAB Toys Ltd in 1992, they focused on a particular niche market. They both left their jobs working for the council and put all their savings into the firm. The company produced old-fashioned wooden toys, such as spinning tops and yo-yos. These tended to appeal to parents who remembered them from their childhood and seemed to buy them as much for themselves as for their children! The idea for the business came from AB's mother who was a collector of original antique toys and had noticed how much interest they attracted from her friends. She had felt there was a gap in the market. When AB and Hissam told her they were looking for a way of leaving their jobs and setting up in business, it seemed an ideal opportunity. AB's mother could provide the ideas for the products and Hissam, who was an excellent craftsman, could make them. To begin with they could work from home.

The company did fairly well in its early years attracting quite a bit of publicity and signing agreements with retailers such as Past Times and various gift catalogue companies. The two founders were closely involved with the day-to-day business and people dealing with the company liked its personal touch. 'It's so rare these days for the managers of a company to recognise you. Businesses have just got too big,' said one of their distributors, 'But Hissam and AB take real interest in their company and their customers.'

Although the company's profits were reasonable, AB felt it should be growing much faster. She pointed to the success of other toys in the past, such as Teletubbies and Beanie Babies and felt that HAB should be competing in mass markets like these. Hissam was not so sure and felt that they needed to think about it a bit more. 'The first thing we need to establish,' he said, 'is our marketing objective. Then we need to think about our strategy. Changing to fight in the mass market is one option but there are other alternatives.'

1 *What is meant by a 'marketing objective'?*
(3 marks)

2 *Examine two possible reasons why Hissam and AB may have decided to target a niche market when they first set up.* *(7 marks)*

3 *AB is eager for the company to compete in a mass market. Would you advise the company to do this or not? Justify your answer.* *(10 marks)*

4 *Discuss the factors which might cause a firm, such as HAB Ltd, to alter its marketing strategy.*
(10 marks)

Fianti plc is a UK producer of a range of carbonated (fizzy) soft drinks. Its most famous products are 'Appley-Dappley' and 'Orang-E-Tang'. Although the total sales of these two products remain high (for example, Orang-E-Tang sales of £29m in 2004 mean it has 1.2% of the non-cola, carbonated drinks market) their growth rate has been slowing up in recent years. Orang-E-Tang seems particularly vulnerable with the recent entry of two significant competitors – Jucy and Oringee – which are well-established brands in the USA and have now been brought into the UK. The market also seems to be moving away from the very sweet taste, which is a prominent feature of both Orang-E-Tang and Appley-Dappley. Anita Feathershaw, Orang-E-Tang's brand manager is presently working on possible extension strategies for the product.

Until now Fianti has avoided competing in the cola market because of the fierce levels of competition in this segment. However, having seen the success of supermarket brands and being worried by the performance of 'Appley- Dappley' and 'Orang-E-Tang,' it has decided to risk entering with its own product. After several months of test marketing, it is now ready to launch its 'Coola Cola' nationally. To be able to match expected levels of demand, the firm has invested in a new production line; inevitably, in the introduction stage of the life cycle capacity utilisation will be low.

The management is eager to encourage more planning on a company-wide basis. According to Nina Strachan, the Managing Director, 'we have tended to operate on a product-by-product basis; each brand manager has made their own plans

without necessarily considering other elements of the business.' Nina Strachan has also announced ambitious long-term plans for the firm which will involve a significant increase in the number of product lines and brands it has on the market, as well as entry into several new markets.

1 *What is meant by 'capacity utilisation'?* (2 marks)

2 *Calculate the value of the non-cola carbonated drinks market in 2004.* (2 marks)

3 *Explain two ways in which Fianti might try to extend the life of Orang-E-Tang.* (4 marks)

4 *Examine how Frianti's cashflow might be affected at different stages of Coola Cola's life cycle.* (7 marks)

5 *Discuss the ways in which portfolio analysis might benefit the marketing planning of a firm such as Fianti.* (10 marks)

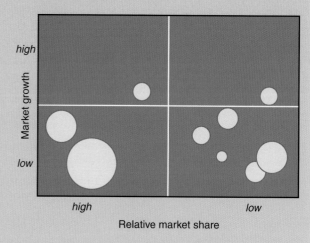

Figure 3.29 *Boston matrix for Fianti plc 2004*

Sandhia left school after her A levels and worked in a local music shop called Listen In. She enjoyed her job and, in many ways, it was what she wanted. She loved music and liked dealing with customers. However, she did not really get on with Mike Hatchet, her boss, and thought she could run the shop better herself. Eventually, after a couple of years working there, she decided to set up a shop for herself in the area – she was convinced she could make it successful.

However, when she visited the bank she found the people there were not so sure and wanted far more information than she had available. Eva Moen, the Bank Manager, advised Sandhia to find out more about her potential market before making the decision to set up on her own. 'You need to undertake a proper quantitative analysis of the market. Do you know about market segmentation, for example? Which segments will you be targeting? What market share are you aiming to achieve in your first year?'

Sandhia knew that the business could work and felt she just had to find the figures to prove it! Eva had advised her to use primary research so she decided to take a sample of 20 people who she knew from Listen In. She interviewed them whenever they were in the shop and Mike was not around –

she did not want him to know what she was planning. Inevitably, it meant the survey was quite rushed but the findings were overwhelming: 96% of those asked said they would visit her shop, for example, and 50% said they bought CDs regularly. With her research complete, Sandhia rushed back to show Eva she had been right all along. Eva did not seem quite so excited as Sandhia and asked her whether the results were at a 95% or 98% confidence level. Sandhia hesitated for a minute and wondered which one would sound better . . .

1 *What is meant by:*

   a) *a '95% confidence level'* (2 marks)

   b) *market share.* (2 marks)

2 *Explain two possible advantages to entrepreneurs such as Sandhia of using primary research as opposed to secondary research.* (6 marks)

3 *Analyse the ways in which market segmentation might benefit Sandhia.* (8 marks)

4 *The bank manager was very keen for Sandhia to undertake research. To what extent can market research guarantee the success of would-be entrepreneurs?* (12 marks)

Figure 3.30 *Relationships between Marketing and other topics in the AS specification*

Accounting and finance

4

Introduction

- Why is financial data important and who is it for?

- What are the different forms of data and how are they used?

>> Profits, costs and revenues

The relationship between profit, cost and revenue

One of the most important relationships for a business is:

$$\text{profit} = \text{total revenue} - \text{total costs}$$

Profit is a very important objective for many businesses. This formula allows businesses to calculate whether they might make a profit and, if so, how much it might be.

> **Key terms**
>
> *Revenues* are the earnings or income generated by a firm as a result of its trading activities.

Business costs

What is a cost? It is simply the expenditure a firm makes as part of its trading. Some of the expenses or costs firms face include payments for raw materials, fuel and components, as well as for labour (in the form of wages and salaries).

Firms face many costs or expenses. Some occur before the business starts trading (for example, the legal costs of setting up a business) whilst others

have to be paid throughout the life of a business (wages and rent fall into this category). The costs faced by a business can be classified in a number of ways, though the most common is to divide them into fixed and variable costs.

> **Key terms**
>
> *Fixed costs* are costs that do not alter when the business alters its level of output. Examples include rent and rates.
> *Variable costs* alter directly with the business's level of output, for example, fuel costs.
> *Total costs* are fixed and variable costs added together.

Fixed costs

Fixed costs do not change when a business alters its level of output. As an example, a business's rent will not vary if there is an increase or decrease in the level of production. Other examples of fixed costs include management salaries and interest payments made by the business.

It is not uncommon for businesses to incur fixed costs over which they have little or no control. For example, in 2003 the EU introduced a law to ensure that filling stations install and operate equipment to disperse petrol vapours, which are potentially harmful to health. Many independently owned filling stations argued that the equipment would cost thousands of pounds to install. Loans will be needed, adding to fixed costs in the form of interest payments.

The graph below relates to XYZ Computers plc – a manufacturer of computers. You can see that whether the factory produces 10 000 or 70 000 computers each year, the fixed costs faced by the business will remain the same – £5m.

The reason that fixed costs do not alter is that XYZ Computers simply uses its *existing* facilities fully at times when it is receiving more orders. As a further example, in the run up to Christmas a

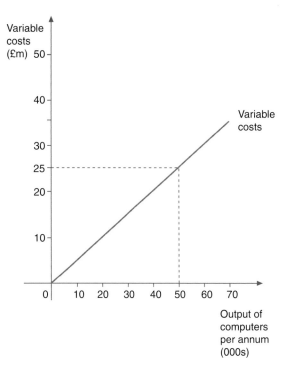

Figure 4.2 *Variable costs for XYZ Computers plc*

chocolate manufacturer might increase its output, thereby using its existing production facilities more fully. The firm's rent, rates and other fixed costs will be unchanged.

Variable costs

In contrast to fixed costs, variable costs alter directly with the level of a firm's output. This means that, a firm which is increasing its output is likely to have to pay higher variable costs, whereas one reducing output could expect variable costs to fall. Expenditure on fuel, raw materials and components are all examples of variable costs.

The XYZ Computer company faces variable costs of £500 for each computer it manufactures (see Figure 4.2); this is necessary to pay for the electronics, case and monitor. Thus, to produce 20 000 computers, the company faces variable costs of £10m (20 000 × £500); to manufacture 50 000 results in variable costs of £25m (50 000 × £500).

Variable costs are usually shown as a straight line (Figure 4.2). This suggests that expenditure on items such as fuel, labour, raw materials and components rises directly along with output. Variable costs are drawn this way for simplicity. In the real world, the line may gradually flatten out as

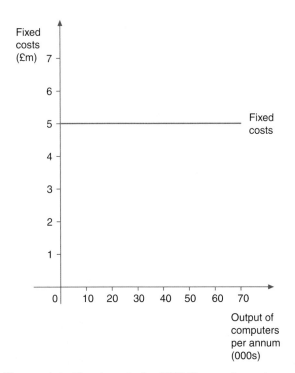

Figure 4.1 *Fixed costs for XYZ Computers plc. Looking at this graph, can you think of any two benefits XYZ Computers might gain from producing 60 000 computers rather than 30 000 computers annually?*

businesses frequently negotiate lower prices when placing large orders. Thus, XYZ Computers may be able to purchase components more cheaply, so the variable costs associated with an output of 50 000 computers might be £22.5m. This means that the variable cost of one computer is actually £450, not £500.

EXAMINER'S ADVICE

It is common in Business Studies examinations to be asked to define terms such as fixed costs and variable costs. In answering this type of question it is important to give a general definition of the term and to support it with examples. It is not sufficient to answer such questions just using examples.

Fixed costs and prices

As we have seen, the cost of making any product is made up of two parts:

1 fixed costs
2 variable costs.

A firm can help to keep costs of production for each individual unit to a minimum by producing on the largest possible scale. Consider the following two scenarios for the Loddon Bicycle Company. This Company has fixed costs of £100 000 and each bicycle has variable costs of £50 for materials and labour.

Scenario A

The company produces 1000 bicycles during the year. Total production costs are £100 000 + (£50 × 1000) = £150 000

Average cost of producing one bicycle = £150

Scenario B

The company produces 5000 bicycles during the year. Total production costs are £100 000 + (£50 × 5000) = £350 000

Average cost of producing one bicycle = £70

Manufacturing in the circumstances of Scenario B would allow the company to set lower prices for its bicycles or to enjoy higher profits – or both.

Semi-variable costs

Some firms face costs which should be classified as semi-variable: they have fixed and variable elements.

Telephone costs are an example of a semi-variable cost. Most businesses pay a fixed, quarterly charge for line and equipment rental. In addition, they face charges for each call made. The line and equipment rentals are fixed as they do not change as the firm increases or lowers its production levels. However, call charges are variable – they are likely to increase along with output as more calls are made to suppliers and customers, for example. Thus, taken together these elements mean telephone charges are semi-variable.

Total costs

The calculation of total costs assumes that all the costs faced by a business are either fixed or variable. This means total costs can be calculated simply using the following formula:

$$\text{total costs} = \text{fixed costs} + \text{variable costs}$$

Total costs of production are an important piece of information for a business. Managers of a business can use this information when taking decisions on levels of output and prices to be charged. For example, firms that have very high levels of fixed costs, perhaps due to expensive equipment, will seek to produce large quantities of output. This reduces the effect of fixed costs on selling price by spreading them over a large quantity of sales.

Table 4.1 below shows the cost information for XYZ Computers plc set out in the form of a table, rather than graphs as in Figures 4.1 and 4.2.

MATHS MOMENT

1+1=2

At an output of 10 000 computers per year, XYZ Computers have total costs of £10 million. This means that, on average, it costs the business £1000 to manufacture each computer (£10 million divided by 10 000). What is the average cost of producing each computer when output is 50 000 per annum? Why does the average cost of production change when the level of production alters?

Level of production (thousand computers)	Fixed costs (£ million)	Variable costs (£ million)	Total costs (£ million)
0	5	0	5
10	5	5	10
20	5	10	15
30	5	15	20
40	5	20	25
50	5	25	30
60	5	30	35
70	5	35	40

Table 4.1 *Fixed, variable and total costs of production for XYZ Computers*

Other categories of costs

An alternative way of classifying the costs encountered by a business is to divide them into direct and indirect costs. Direct costs can be attributed to the production of a particular product and vary directly with the level of output. Examples include the costs of raw materials and fuel.

Indirect costs cannot be allocated to the production of a particular product and relate to the business as a whole. Indirect costs include the costs of marketing and administration. Indirect costs are generally recognised as being difficult to control.

A manufacturer of motor cars may incur direct and indirect costs as set out below.

Direct Costs
- Direct materials, e.g. sheet steel and engine parts.
- Direct labour, e.g. wages paid to employees on the production line.

Indirect Costs
- Indirect labour costs, e.g. management salaries and wages paid to security staff.
- Other indirect costs, e.g. administration and distribution.

Direct costs + indirect costs = total costs of production

Indirect costs are also called overheads and are always fixed costs. Direct costs tend to vary with the level of production and are normally (but not always) variable costs.

Opportunity costs

There is another way of looking at costs, rather than giving a monetary value to the resources used by a business. Economists use a concept called opportunity cost, which values a product in terms of *what has been given up to obtain it.* Thus, an accountant might value a factory extension at £250 000, based on the resources necessary to build it. An economist might say that the opportunity cost of the extension was a training programme for employees. This is because the management team of the business decided on an extension to the factory, rather than a training programme for employees.

Why do businesses calculate costs of production?

There are a number of reasons why it is important for a business to know the level of costs they are incurring as a result of their trading activities.

- Most businesses draw up financial forecasts or budgets which set out their production plans and the costs they expect to pay. It is an important part of management to ensure that costs are being kept within agreed limits.
- Businesses benefit from knowledge of their costs of production to allow them to set a price that ensures that they make a profit. This is known as 'cost-plus' pricing and is considered in more detail in Chapter 3.
- Sometimes businesses are not able to control the price at which they sell their products – they might be a small firm in a very competitive

market. In these circumstances it is important to know costs of production to decide whether it is possible to sell products at a profit.

Business revenues

A business's revenue is its income or earnings over a period of time. You may also encounter the term sales revenue, which has the same meaning. Businesses calculate the revenue from the sale of a single product and from their entire product range. In either case the calculation is the same:

revenue = quantity sold × average selling price

In most circumstances, a firm can exercise some control over the quantity it sells and hence over its revenue.

- If a business reduces its selling price, it can normally expect to sell more. Whether this increases its revenue depends on the number of additional sales it makes as a result of reducing its price. If competitors also reduce their prices, then few extra sales will result and revenue will be relatively unchanged.
- Similarly, a rise in price can be expected to reduce sales. The size of the fall in sales will depend on many factors, including the loyalty of customers and the quality of the products. The amount by which sales fall will determine whether the firm receives more or less revenue following its price rise. Some businesses sell products which are unique or regarded as highly desirable, perhaps because they are fashionable. Thus, some clothes producers, such as Gucci (*www.gucci.com*), can charge high prices and still enjoy relatively high sales. Price and sales revenue are related to the concept of the price elasticity of demand (see page 105).

EXAMINER'S ADVICE

Business studies is an integrated subject. It is important to explore the links that exist between the various modules of the subject when responding to questions. There are obvious links between the topic of business revenues and price elasticity of demand. It may be worth revising such linked topics together to allow you to explore the relationships in your examination.

Profits

A business makes a profit when, over a period of time, its revenue exceeds its total costs of production. The formula necessary to calculate profit is set out below.

profit = total revenue − total costs

A company's profits depend upon two main factors: profit margins and the amount (or volume) of sales.

- A profit margin is the amount or percentage of the final selling price that is profit. Thus, if a business sells a particular T-shirt for £10 and the average cost of producing that product is £8, the profit margin is £2 or 20% (£2/£10 × 100%).
- The quantity a firm sells will also affect the amount of profits it earns. In our example above, if the firm in question sells 5000 T-shirts in a month it will earn £10 000 in profits. If sales rise to 7500, profits will also rise to £15 000.

MATHS MOMENT

1+1=2

Last year the same T-shirt company sold 20 000 T-shirts at an average price of £11. This year it increased its price to £12. As a result sales fell by 5%. Calculate the effect on this company's revenue of this increase in prices.

Key issues

One of the most important decisions taken by businesses is how to use their profits. The uses of profits can be divided into two categories.

- **Distributed profits** – these profits are paid to shareholders or other owners, normally in the form of **dividends**.
- **Undistributed profits** – this portion of a business's profits are kept for investment in the business. Such profits may be used to purchase new machinery or properties.

The key issue in distributing profits is the balance between the short term and the long term. Distributing a high proportion of profits may keep shareholders happy in the short term, but might not be in the interests of those looking for a long-

Business in focus

In 2003, Marks & Spencer announced that its sales had grown strongly during the previous November and December. Compared with the same period in the previous year, sales rose by up to 9% for some lines, including clothing. The company was still disappointed as the rise was below expectations and this affected its profits. The company was forced to sell surplus stock in the January sales. However, a spokesperson from Marks & Spencer said that despite sales being below expectations over the Christmas period, it expects profit margins to rise by about 1% compared with the previous year.

1 If Marks & Spencer's profit margins on clothes increased by 1% and sales by 9%, what would be the overall percentage effect on the company's profit?
2 Why would selling surplus stock in the January sales have affected Marks & Spencer's profit margins?

term investment. Such shareholders want to see the company grow over a number of years and to benefit from rising share prices which increase the value of their investments.

The importance of profit

For many businesses, especially those that are privately owned, profits are very important and are often used as a measure of success. People and institutions (such as insurance companies and pension funds) that buy shares in a company hope to receive a share of the business's profits in the form of a dividend on their shareholding. In many cases high profits mean large dividends and satisfied shareholders.

Earning a profit is not always important. A number of businesses are not established with the aim of making profits. Charities, some building societies (for example, the Nationwide) and organisations such as schools, colleges and trade unions do not seek to make profits. Charities seek

to raise the maximum amount of income possible, whilst other non-profit making organisations aim to provide a high-class product, whilst earning enough to cover costs.

EXAMINER'S ADVICE

Examinations in AS Level Business Studies always ask a number of questions requiring you to make some judgement (or evaluation). These questions are designed to make you think a little more deeply about the subject. So, an obvious question to ask might be whether high profits are always an indication of a successful business. When answering this question, you are expected to cover circumstances in which high profits might represent success and situations in which other measures might indicate success.

QUICK CHECK QUESTIONS

1 Complete the following formula: Profit = ? − total costs
2 Which one of the following is the best definition of variable costs?
a) costs that do not change when output changes
b) costs that do change when revenue alters
c) costs that have no relationship with output
d) costs that change directly with output.
3 Is the following statement true or false? 'When drawn on a graph, variable costs always start at the origin (where the two axes intersect).'
4 Which **two** of the following may be considered to be semi-variable costs?
a) rent for the factory
b) the costs of running a delivery vehicle

c) telephone charges

d) salaries of the management team.

5 The opportunity cost of a product is best defined as

a) the fixed cost of buying that product

b) what has been given up to obtain the product

c) the total cost of buying the product

d) the cost of a competitor's product.

6 Complete the following formula: Sales revenue = ... × average selling price.

7 Is the following statement true or false? 'An increase in price will always increase a business's sales revenue.'

8 For which one of the following businesses is profit unlikely to be an important concept?

a) Marks & Spencer

b) Barclay's Bank

c) Oxfam

d) Norwich City Football Club.

9 Complete the following sentence: Distributed profits are paid to shareholders, normally in the form of ....

10 Is the following a definition of direct or indirect costs? '............ costs can be attributed to the product of a particular product and vary directly with the level of output.'

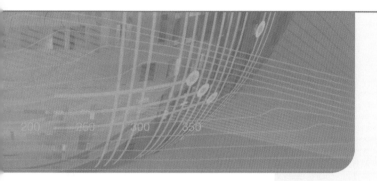

Progress questions

1 Identify three costs that might have to be paid when a business is first established. *(3 marks)*

2 For each of the costs listed here state whether they are fixed or variable: wages paid to shop-floor labour, business rates, a three-year lease on a photocopier, supplies of gas, the salary of maintenance staff and the business's annual payment to a local charity. *(6 marks)*

3 What is meant by the term 'semi-variable cost'? *(3 marks)*

4 A business's variable costs are normally drawn as a straight line on a graph. Explain why, in reality, this might not be the case. *(6 marks)*

5 A manager notes the following cost information relating to her business.

Level of production (000s)	Total costs (£m)
0	20
25	50
50	75

For this business:

a) What are its fixed costs? *(2 marks)*

b) What is its average cost of production at 25 000 and 50 000 units? *(4 marks)*

c) Why might the average cost of production fall for this company? *(4 marks)*

6 Explain why the costs associated with a business's delivery vehicle might be classified as semi-variable. *(5 marks)*

7 Explain why a firm's revenue is unlikely to rise by 10% if it increases all its prices by the same percentage. *(7 marks)*

8 Outline two factors that may determine the effect on a firm's revenue of an increase in their prices. *(6 marks)*

9 What is a 'profit margin'? State two factors that may determine the amount of profit a firm makes. *(4 marks)*

10 Explain two reasons why a business might not aim to earn the highest possible profits. *(6 marks)*

Analytical and evaluative questions

11 *Waller Electronics plc manufactures electrical equipment such as lights, switches and timers. The company has grown over recent years and has entered several overseas markets, including Japan and the US. Analyse **two** reasons why profit might be important to this company.*

(8 marks)

12 *Vodafone is one of the UK's largest businesses. It sells mobile phone services throughout the world. Discuss factors that might influence the profits Vodafone makes.*

(10 marks)

13 *McDonald's made a loss in 2003. Evaluate the ways in which the company might return to profitability.*

(10 marks)

>> Break-even analysis

What is break-even analysis?

The break-even output is that level of output at which a firm's sales generate just enough revenue to cover all the costs of production. At the break-even level of output a business makes neither a loss nor a profit. Firms may use break-even analysis for a number of reasons:

- To help people setting up a business to decide level of output and sales necessary to provide a profit.
- The results of break-even analysis can be used to support an application by a business for a loan from a bank or other financial institution.
- To assess the impact of changes in the level of production on the profitability of the business.
- To calculate the likely profitability of one of a range of products produced by a business.

MATHS MOMENT

1 + 1 = 2

Until last month, Mercer Furniture Ltd sold one style of wooden chair (the Pendle) for £80. This price was just sufficient to break even. However, the company has taken the decision to increase the price of Pendle chairs to £96. Use this information to calculate the following:

a) the percentage by which the company has increased the price of Pendle chairs
b) the profit Mercer Furniture would receive from selling 150 Pendle chairs at the new price.

Contribution

Contribution is an important part of break-even analysis. Contribution can be defined as the *difference between sales revenue and variable costs of production*. This is illustrated in Figure 4.3.

Contribution is calculated through the use of the following formula:

$$contribution = revenue - variable\ costs$$

Contribution can be used to pay the fixed costs

incurred by a firm. Once these have been met fully, contribution provides a business with its profits.

Contribution can be calculated in two different ways.

1 If a business produces more than one product, it may calculate the contribution made by each product to paying fixed costs and providing profits. Using contribution avoids the need to divide up fixed costs between the firm's various products. This assists firms in assessing the financial performance of each of their products.

2 Contribution can be calculated for the sale of a single product. It is calculated by using the formula:

contribution per unit =
selling price of one unit of output − variable cost of producing that unit

It is this second method of calculating contribution that is useful when calculating the break-even point.

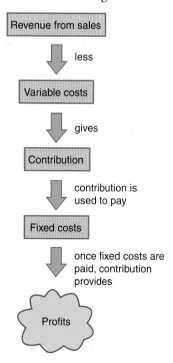

Figure 4.3 *Contribution; where it comes from and what it is used for*

Calculating the break-even point

A manager wishing to calculate the break-even point will require the following information:

● the selling price of the product
● the variable cost of producing a single unit of the product
● the fixed costs associated with the product – remember, fixed costs do not change as the level of production alters.

This information is used within the formula set out below:

$$\text{break-even output} = \frac{\text{fixed costs}}{\text{selling price per unit} - \text{variable cost per unit}}$$

This formula can be rewritten given that contribution is the result of taking away variable cost from the selling price of a product.

$$\text{break-even output} = \frac{\text{fixed costs}}{\text{contribution per unit}}$$

Calculating break-even: a case study

Maria Elphick owns and manages the famous Elphick's restaurant in Soho, West London. Elphick's has a worldwide reputation for serving high quality meals in the beautiful setting of a Georgian house. At weekends, the restaurant is always turning people away; at other times it is unusual for there to be any empty tables.

Maria is aware that she could open another restaurant nearby to increase the number of customers she could serve each month. Maria appreciates that she would have to take out a loan to buy a lease on another property. She has already looked at a building about a mile away which would seat up to 30 diners. She produced the figures set out in Table 4.2.

Business in focus

After a lengthy period during which it has not made a profit, India's film industry (nicknamed Bollywood), is expected to generate a profit by 2004. Management consultants KPMG have forecast an improved financial position for the industry because it has concentrated on making fewer, but more popular, films recently. Bollywood anticipates increased sales revenue from overseas sales of films and videos as well as increased cinema advertising.

1 How can the Bollywood industry produce fewer films, and at the same time make more revenue and break even?

Type of cost or revenue	Amount
Average selling price per meal at Elphick's	£60
Variable costs per meal – ingredients, fuel, wages	£35
Additional fixed costs associated with opening a new restaurant – carpets, furnishing, crockery and lease on property	£10 000

Table 4.2 *Maria Elphick's analysis for a new restaurant*

Using this information, Maria was able to calculate how many additional meals she will need to sell in her new restaurant if the project were to break even.

$$\text{break-even output} = \frac{\text{fixed costs}}{\text{contribution per unit}}$$

Maria knows her fixed costs will rise by £10 000 each month and this figure is entered into the top of the formula. To fill in the bottom Maria has to take away the variable cost of producing a meal from the price the customer pays for a meal. The contribution earned from each meal in Maria's new restaurant is £25 (£60 − £35). Thus:

$$\text{Monthly break-even output} = \frac{£10\,000}{£25}$$
$$= 400 \text{ meals}$$

So, Maria knows that, if her plan for a second restaurant is to break-even, she will need to attract at least 400 new customers each month. If she attracts more than 400 customers, the project will make a profit. Maria normally opens Elphick's on 25 evenings each month and would, therefore, break even if she had an average of 16 customers each night in the new restaurant.

Whilst this calculation gives Maria a quick guide to the number of customers her new restaurant will need to break even, it tells her little more about the level of profit or loss the new Elphick's might make. A break-even chart is one way to work out the level of profits the business will generate if her estimate is proved to be correct.

Break-even charts

We can use a break-even chart to illustrate Maria's plans to open a second branch of Elphick's.

> **EXAMINER'S ADVICE**
>
> *Time constraints mean that it is unlikely that you will be asked to draw a complete break-even chart in an examination. You should practise adding lines to incomplete charts and reading profit or loss at specified levels of output.*

Drawing a break-even chart

The first stage in constructing a break-even chart is to mark scales on the two axes. Maria knows that her new restaurant (Elphick's Too) can seat a maximum of 30 customers per night and that she normally opens for 25 evenings each month. Thus her maximum number of customers each month is 750 (30 customers × 25 nights). So her scale on the horizontal axis runs from zero to 750.

The vertical scale on a break-even chart records costs and revenues. Normally revenues are the highest figure. Thus Maria has to calculate the highest possible revenue she could earn from Elphick's Too. At most she could attract 750 customers paying an average of £60 each. So the highest revenue she could possibly receive is (£60 ×

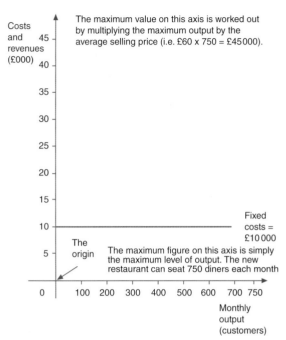

Figure 4.4 *Fixed costs on Maria's break-even chart*

750) = £45 000. If she marks her vertical scale from zero to £45 000, Maria will have an appropriate range of values.

Having marked her scales, the first line to be drawn onto the chart is fixed costs. This is relatively simple as fixed costs do not change whatever the

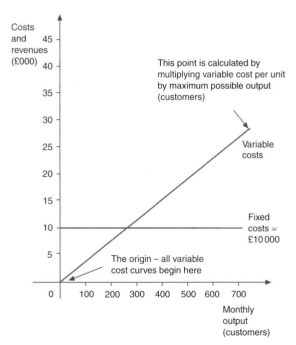

Figure 4.5 *Adding variable costs to Maria's break-even chart*

number of customers. Thus Maria marks a horizontal line on the chart to show the monthly fixed costs she will have to pay – £10 000. This is illustrated in Figure 4.4.

The next stage is to include variable costs. As variable costs are expenditure on items such as components and raw materials, these costs will rise along with output. If Maria has an increasing number of people dining in Elphick's Too she will need to buy more food and her wage bill will also rise.

Variable costs always start at zero. It is not necessary to plot variable costs at each level of production. Maria can simply calculate variable costs for the highest possible level of output. This would occur if Elphick's Too was full every night and the restaurant had 750 customers each month. Thus, the highest variable costs Elphick's Too could encounter are to provide 750 meals each having a variable cost of £35. The highest variable cost would therefore be £26 250 (£35 × 750). Maria marks this point onto her break-even chart as shown in Figure 4.5 and draws a straight line from this point to the origin.

The next task for Maria in drawing her break-even chart is to add together fixed and variable costs. The results can be entered onto the chart as total costs. Maria will calculate total costs at zero output and maximum output (750 customers per month). She can mark these two points onto her chart and join them with a straight line.

1 If Elphick's Too has no customers in a month, it will not incur any variable costs. At zero output, total costs are the same as fixed costs. In Maria's case, this will mean a total costs figure of £10 000 per month.
2 At the other extreme, Elphick's Too might be full with 750 customers each month. Maria will add together fixed costs (still £10 000, of course) and variable costs at full capacity (750 customers' meals each having variable costs of £35) equal to £26 250. Thus, total costs for the restaurant in these circumstances will be £36 250 (£10 000 = £26 250).

The line connecting these two points is equal to total costs. If it is drawn correctly, it should be parallel to the variable costs curve.

Business in focus

Smart is a brand of the Daimler-Chrysler company. The original Smart car was introduced in 1999 and is about half the size of a standard family car, measuring just 2.5 metres from bumper to bumper. The expensive status symbol car was designed for use in crowded cities, where being small offers many advantages.

Figure 4.6 *The Smart car range is being expanded despite not yet breaking even*

In 2003 the brand was extended with the launch of a more traditional supermini – the Smart Forfour. This car is much more conventional than the original Smart car and operates in a more price-competitive market. Apart from some shocking colours and a boldly designed dashboard, the Forfour is unlikely to stand out in a crowd. The company has plans to launch more new vehicles, including a tiny four-wheel-drive off-road vehicle in the United States in 2006. Plans to expand the range of vehicles in the Smart brand are surprising given that it has yet to break even.

Source: Adapted from The Electronic Telegraph (www.telegraph.co.uk), September 2003

1 Why might Daimler-Chrysler have decided to expand the range of Smart cars when the brand 'has yet to break even'?

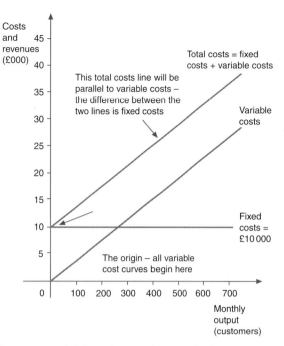

Figure 4.7 *Adding the total costs line to Maria's chart*

The last stage in constructing Maria's break-even chart is to add on a line showing the revenue Elphick's Too will earn. Maria has already calculated that an average customer spends £60 on a meal in her restaurant. Following the approach we used for costs, Maria works out her revenue if the restaurant has no customers and if it is full every evening during a month.

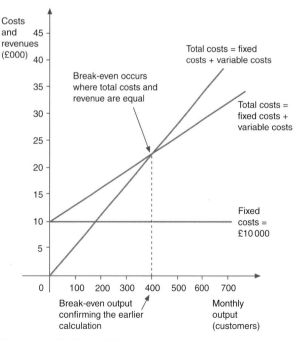

Figure 4.8 *The full break-even chart*

1 The first situation is easy. If Elphick's Too does not have any customers, it will not have any revenue. Thus the revenue line begins at the origin.

2 If the restaurant is full, Maria expects each of the 750 customers to pay £60 on average. If Elphick's Too attracts this level of custom, it will earn £45 000 (£60 × 750).

Figure 4.8 shows the break-even chart with the revenue line included. To make the chart easier to read, the variable costs line has been left out in this case.

The break-even chart tells Maria that she needs 400 customers each month if Elphick's Too is to break even. This confirms the calculation we carried out earlier. However, a break-even chart provides much more information. Maria can use it to read off the level of profit or loss her new restaurant will make according to the number of customers it attracts. Figure 4.9 summarises how to draw a break-even chart.

Reading break-even charts

Figure 4.10 shows the break-even chart for Elphick's Too. We have indicated on the chart the following scenarios.

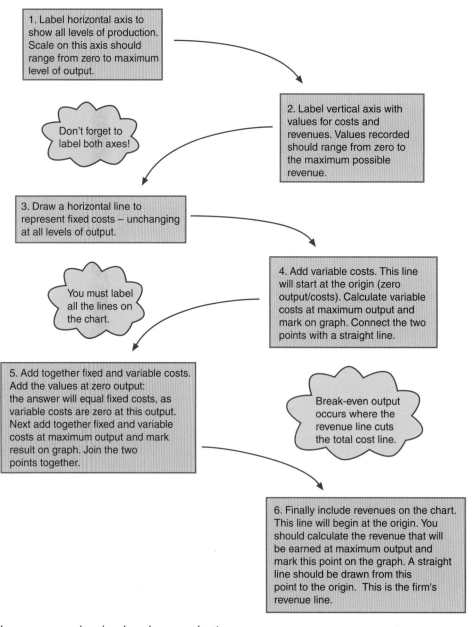

Figure 4.9 *In summary: drawing break-even charts*

- If Elphick's Too attracts 200 customers each month, the restaurant will make a loss as this figure is less than break-even output. The financial position of the business will be:

Revenue (200 customers paying £60 each) =	£12 000
Total costs [costs of £10 000 + (200 × £35)] =	£17 000
With 200 customers Elphick's Too will make a loss =	£5000

This loss is illustrated on the vertical axis.

- If Elphick's Too attracts 600 customers each month, the restaurant will make a profit as this figure is greater than break-even output. The financial position of the business will be:

Revenue (600 customers paying £60 each) =	£36 000
Total costs [costs of £10 000 + (600 × £35)] =	£31 000
With 200 customers Elphick's Too will make a profit =	£ 5000

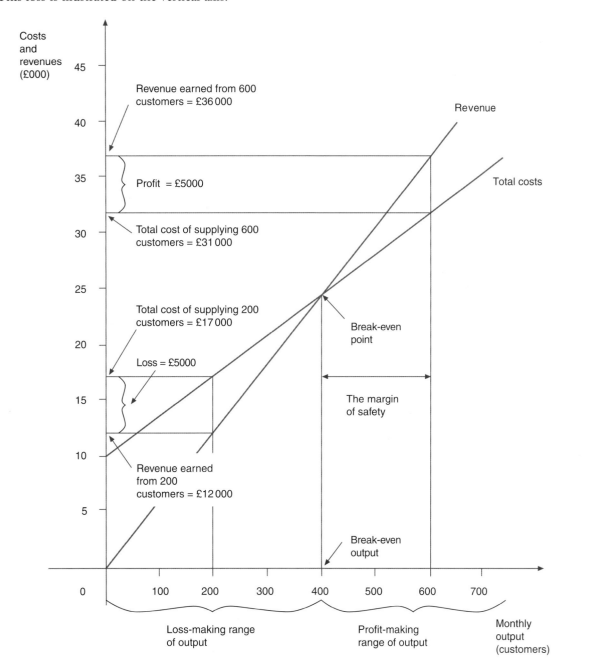

Figure 4.10 *Reading break-even charts*

The amount of profits at this level of output is shown on the vertical axis.

It is, of course, possible to read off the level of profit that Maria's new restaurant will make whatever the number of customers it attracts each month.

EXAMINER'S ADVICE

Reading data from break-even charts is an important skill. Because of the limited time available in examinations, examiners often ask students to read off levels of profit or loss for a business at selected levels of output. You may also be asked to mark the loss or profit on the chart as shown in Figure 4.10. Finally, a common question is to ask you to mark break-even output on the graph.

The margin of safety

A break-even chart can be used to show the **margin of safety**. The margin of safety is the amount by which a firm's current level of output exceeds the level of output necessary to break even.

If Maria's new restaurant is successful and attracts 600 customers each month, the margin of safety will be 200 customers. This means that, in these circumstances, Elphick's Too could lose 200 customers monthly before it began to make a loss.

INTERPRETING DATA

Using Figure 4.10, read off the level of profit or loss that Elphick's Too might make if it attracted 300 customers each month. Carry out calculations to confirm your answer.

Key terms

The margin of safety *is the amount by which a firm's current level of output exceeds the level of output necessary to break even.*

The advantages and disadvantages of break-even analysis

Most financial techniques have advantages and disadvantages, and break-even analysis is no

exception. The advantages offered by break-even analysis include the following:

- It is a simple technique allowing most managers to use it without the need for expensive training. Because of this it is particularly suitable for small businesses.
- It is a technique that can be completed quickly, providing immediate results.
- Its use can be of value in supporting a business's application to a bank for a loan.
- By using break-even charts a business can forecast the effect of varying numbers of customers on its costs, revenues and profits.

Break-even analysis has a number of shortcomings:

- It assumes that all products are sold. Thus Maria might *assume* that she will attract 600 customers each month. She will order the necessary food and hire sufficient staff. However, if only 500 turn up, she will not make the profit indicated for 600 customers on the break-even chart.
- It is a simplification of the real world. Businesses do not sell all their products at a single price and calculating an average is unlikely to provide accurate data. The technique is also difficult to use when a business sells a number of different products.
- Costs do not rise steadily as the technique suggests. As we have seen, variable costs can rise less quickly than output because of the benefits of buying in bulk.
- A break-even analysis will only be as accurate as the data on which it is based. If costs or selling prices are incorrect, then the forecasts will be wrong.

Analysis and marketing

To be most effective, break-even analysis should be supported by market research.

EXAMINER'S ADVICE

Knowing the advantages and disadvantages of financial techniques such as break-even analysis can help you to write analytical answers. Thus, if you are asked the benefits of break-even analysis to a particular firm, you should be able to apply the information above to the circumstances of the question.

QUICK CHECK
QUESTIONS

1   Which one of the following statements relating to break-even output is true?
a) It is the level of output at which sales revenue equals total costs.
b) It is the level of output at which variable costs equal sales revenue.
c) It is the level of output at which variable costs and total costs are equal.
d) It is the level of output at which profits are greatest.

2   Complete the following formula: Contribution = sales revenue − ....

3   Which of the following statements relating to contribution is not true?
a) Contribution can be used to pay fixed costs.
b) Contribution can be calculated for a single unit of output.
c) Contribution always equals profits.
d) Once fixed costs are paid, contribution provides a business with profits.

4   Complete the following formula:
    Break-even output = fixed costs divided by .... per unit.

5   Which one of the following statements about break-even charts is true?
a) Fixed costs lines always slope upwards from left to right.
b) The total cost and variable cost lines are always parallel.
c) Variable costs are always lower than fixed costs.
d) The total cost and fixed costs lines are always parallel.

6   Is the following statement true or false? 'At levels of output below break even, the total revenue line will be below the total costs line, while at output greater than break even, the total revenue line will always be above the total cost line.'

7   Fill in the missing three words to complete the following definition. 'The .... / ... / .... is the amount by which a business's current level of output exceeds the level of output necessary to break even.'

8   Is the following statement true or false? 'The level of profit or loss on a break-even chart can be shown by the vertical distance between sales revenue and variable costs.'

9   Which of the following statements about the technique of break even is **not** true?
a) It is a simple technique requiring little training.
b) It can be used by businesses to support an application to a bank for a loan.
c) Break even is a simplification of the real world.
d) Break even takes into account the level of demand from consumers.

10 Is the following statement true or false? 'On a break-even chart, costs do not rise steadily with output.'

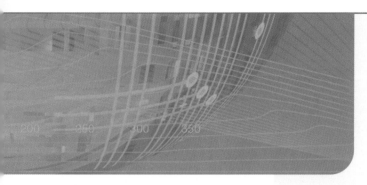

Progress questions

1 State two reasons why a business might carry out a break-even analysis. *(2 marks)*

2 Carefully distinguish between contribution and profits. *(5 marks)*

3 Outdoor Ltd manufactures jackets. It has annual fixed costs of £100 000, sells its jackets at £50 each and estimates the variable cost of producing a single jacket to be £30. Calculate the level of contribution made from the sale of a single jacket. *(4 marks)*

4 Using the above example, calculate the annual break-even output for Outdoor Ltd. *(4 marks)*

5 If Outdoor Ltd manufactured 7500 jackets during the year, what would be its margin of safety? Why might this information be important to the managers of the business? *(10 marks)*

6 Norris Newspapers produce a local newspaper. They face fixed costs amounting to £20 000 a month, sell their newspapers at £0.50 each and the variable cost of printing a single newspaper is £0.25. At full capacity, they can print 150 000 newspapers each month. Construct a break-even chart and illustrate Norris Newspaper's break-even point. *(10 marks)*

7 Using the chart you have drawn in answer to question 6, indicate Norris Newspaper's level of profit or loss if:
   a) They print and sell 50 000 newspapers per month. *(3 marks)*
   b) They print and sell 100 000 newspapers per month. *(3 marks)*

8 Outline two reasons why a small business such as Norris Newspapers might make use of break-even analysis. *(4 marks)*

9 A firm's break-even analysis has been shown to be inaccurate. Explain three factors that might have caused this outcome. *(6 marks)*

10 Explain the benefits that a small business might gain from the use of break-even analysis. *(7 marks)*

Analytical and evaluative questions

11 Winger Ltd manufactures a range of wooden doors and window frames for the UK construction industry. Examine two actions the company might take to increase its total contribution to fixed costs. *(8 marks)*

12 A newly established kebab shop is operating below its break-even output and is making a loss. Discuss **two** actions the manager of the shop might take to ensure it makes a profit. *(10 marks)*

13 Trish and Paul own a hotel in the Lake District. The business is very seasonal, with 50% of revenue earned in June, July and August. To what extent is break-even analysis a useful decision-making took for Trish and Paul? *(10 marks)*

Cash flow forecasting and >> management

What is cash flow?

A potentially profitable business can fail because of poor management of cash flow. Equally, an unprofitable business can enjoy a period in which it has plenty of cash – before the bills arrive!

Cash flow and profits are two very different concepts:

- A business makes a profit if, over a given period of time, its revenue is greater than its expenditure. A business can survive without making a profit for a short period of time, but it is essential that it earns profits in the long run.
- Cash flow relates to the timing of payments and receipts. Cash flow is important in the short term as a business must pay people and organisations to whom it owes money.

Unless a business manages the timing of its payments and receipts carefully, it may find itself in a position where it is operating profitably but is running out of cash regularly. This could be because it is forced to wait for several months before receiving payment from customers. In the meantime, it has to settle its own debts.

MATHS MOMENT   1+1=2

Dave Chell manages a small business making garden furniture. His business has made a steady profit over a number of years. In January, Dave received a large and unexpected order from a local garden centre. He agreed to supply the furniture in March and April; payment was due in May and June. Figures 4.11a and 4.11b show Dave's cash flow over the period and the cash problems that growth (or accepting a large order) can create for a business.

1 Calculate the profits for Dave's business over these six months by comparing cash inflows and outflows over the period.

Businesses are especially vulnerable to cash flow difficulties in their first years of trading or when starting a major new project. It is for this reason that many financial institutions demand evidence that businesses have planned the management of their cash during periods of particular risk.

Key terms

Cash flow is the movement of cash into and out of a business over a period of time.

EXAMINER'S ADVICE

The distinction between proft and cash flow is vital. It is useful when answering financial questions to consider the short-term effects of an action on cash flow and the long-term effects on profits. Thus, a business offering a discount for prompt payment may improve its cash flow, but (in the longer term) could damage its profitability.

Key terms

Cash flow forecasts state the inflows and outflows of cash that the managers of a business expect over some future period.

Why do businesses forecast cash flows?

Businesses undertake cash flow forecasting for a variety of reasons:

1 To make sure that they do not suffer from periods when they are short of cash and are unable to pay their debts – by forecasting cash flows, a business can identify times at which they may not have enough cash available. This allows them to make the necessary arrangements to overcome this problem.

2 To support applications for loans – businesses

often require loans when they are first established and when growing. Banks and other financial institutions are far more likely to lend money to a business that has evidence of financial planning.

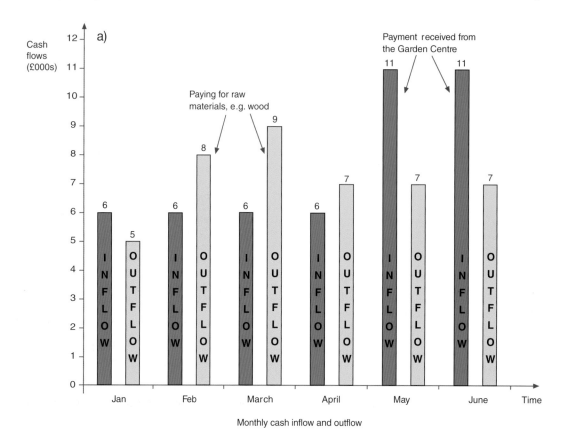

Monthly cash inflow and outflow

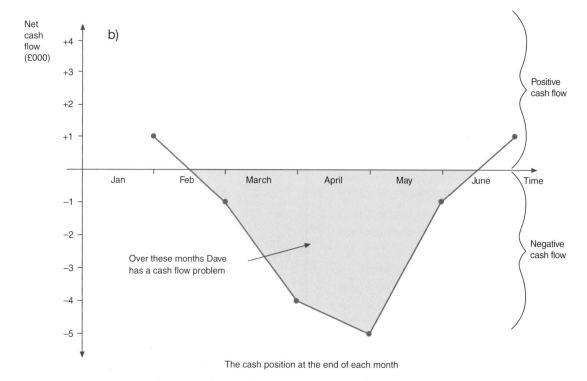

The cash position at the end of each month

Figure 4.11a and b *Cash flow graphs for Dave's garden furniture*

Constructing cash flow forecasts

A simplified cash flow forecast is illustrated in Figure 4.13. Although cash flow forecasts differ from one another, they usually have three sections and are normally calculated monthly. An essential part of cash flow forecasting is that inflows and outflows of cash should be included in the plan at the time they take place.

1 **Cash in** – the first section forecasts the cash **inflows** into the business, usually on a monthly basis. This section includes receipts from **cash sales** and **credit sales**. Credit sales occur when the customer is given time to pay: normally 60 or 90 days.
2 **Cash out** – the cash out (or expenditure) section will state the expected expenditure on the goods and services. Thus, a typical section might include forecasts of expenditure on rent, rates, insurance, wages and salaries, fuel, and so on. At the end of this section the total expected outflow of cash over the time period in question would be stated. The net monthly cash flow is calculated by subtracting the total outflow of cash from the total inflow.
3 **Net monthly cash flow** – the final section of the forecast has the opening balance and the closing balance. The opening balance is the business's cash position at the start of each month. This will, of course, be the same figure as at the end of the previous month. The net monthly cash flow is added to the opening balance figure. The resulting figure is the closing cash balance for the

month. It is also the opening balance for the following month.

Constructing cash flows – a case study

Tony Tuck owns a bookshop. Tony forecasts his cash flow to help him to identify times when he might experience problems. Knowing when he is likely to be short of cash gives him the chance to arrange an overdraft or short-term loan.

> **Key terms**
>
> An **overdraft** is a flexible loan on which a business can draw when necessary up to some agreed limit.

Tony has made the following forecasts about his business for the four months June to September.

- Tony expects his business to have an opening cash balance of £500 at the start of June.
- Tony anticipates his cash sales to be £8000 for each of the four months. However, in June he received an additional order to supply books to a local College. The order was worth £10 000. He expects payment in September.
- Each month Tony orders books to the value of £4500 from his suppliers. In June this figure was £11 000 because of the order received from the College.
- He has to pay his own wages and those of a part-time assistant. These amount to £1500 each month.

		January	February	March	April	May	June
1 Cash in	Cash sales						
	Credit sales						
	Total Inflow						
2 Cash out	Raw materials						
	Wages						
	Other costs						
	Total outflow						
3 Net monthly cash flow	Net monthly cash flow						
	Opening balance						
	Closing balance						

Figure 4.12 *A typical format for a cash flow forecast*

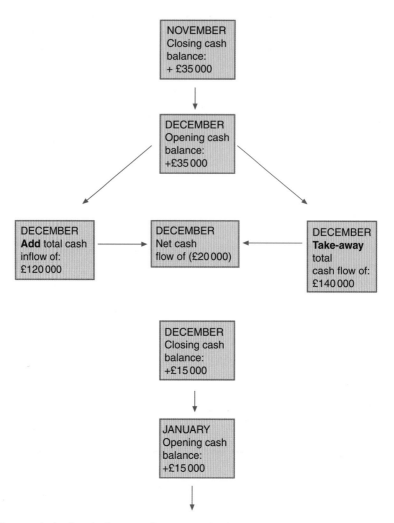

Figure 4.13 *Opening and closing balances. Suppose, in this example, the cash outflow forecast for December is £160 000. What would be the closing balance for December in these circumstances?*

● Other costs, including his rent, rates, heating and lighting amount to £1500 each month.

Tony's cash flow forecast is shown in Figure 4.14. Tony's cash flow forecast illustrates many of the key principles. An important figure for each month is shown in the row entitled 'Net monthly cash flow'. This simply records the balance between the inflow and outflow for the month: June is a good example of how this operates. In June, Tony expected to receive £8000 from book sales. At the same time he planned to spend £14 000 on books, wages, rent, etc. Thus, in June he expected his net cash flow (cash inflows less cash outflows) to be minus £6000 (£8000 − £14 000). In cashflow forecasts, negative figures are usually shown in brackets. Hence, the figure entered for net monthly cash flow in June is (£6000).

This case study also highlights one of the key advantages of cash flow forecasting. Tony's business will be short of cash during July and August. The

	June	July	August	September
Cash in				
Cash sales	8000	8000	8000	8000
Credit sales				10000
Total inflow	8000	8000	8000	18000
Cash out				
Raw materials – books	11000	4500	4500	4500
Wages	1500	1500	1500	1500
Other costs, e.g. rent	1500	1500	1500	1500
Total outflow	14000	7500	7500	7500
Net monthly cash flow	(6000)	500	500	10500
Opening balance	500	(5500)	(5000)	(4500)
Closing balance	(5500)	(5000)	(4500)	6000

Figure 4.14 *Cashflow forecast for Tony's bookshop. (NB: figures in brackets are negative)*

closing balances for these months indicate that he will require approximately £5000 to enable him to pay his rent, wages, and so on. Knowing this in advance means that Tony can take steps to avoid a cash crisis, possibly by agreeing an overdraft with his bank.

People in business

Figure 4.15 *Richard Branson*

Richard Branson is a businessman who has masterminded the development of a highly popular and diverse group of companies, avoiding the cash flow difficulties commonly experienced by rapidly growing companies.

Born in 1950, Branson founded Virgin in 1970 as a mail order record company, later building a recording studio. The first artist signed to the Virgin label was Mike Oldfield of *Tubular Bells* fame. This record was Branson's first success, selling over 5 million copies. Following this, Virgin signed a series of superstars including Phil Collins and the Rolling Stones. Branson sold the Virgin Music Group to EMI in 1992.

In the meantime, Branson has developed a range of other activities under the Virgin name. In 1984, he founded Virgin Atlantic Airways. This company has engaged in fierce (and controversial) competition with British Airways on the transatlantic routes. Other ventures have included Virgin cola, Virgin vodka and Virgin Direct selling financial services.

In recent years, Richard Branson has attracted much publicity for his Virgin empire through his attempts to fly a hot air balloon around the globe, his plan to buy Concorde and keep it in service, and his attempts to take control of the UK's National Lottery. Less well known are his charitable activities, notably his involvement in 'Parents Against Tobacco', a pressure group aiming to restrict tobacco advertising.

Causes of cash flow problems

A major cause of cash flow problems is a lack of planning. Many businesses, once established, do not forecast in this way and frequently face unforeseen problems.

A number of other factors can contribute to cash flow difficulties.

- Overtrading – this occurs when a business expands quickly without organising funds to finance the expansion. Rapid growth normally involves paying for labour and raw materials several months before receiving payment for the final product. If this occurs over a prolonged period, a business can face severe cash flow problems.
- Allowing too much credit – most businesses offer trade credit – allowing customers between 30 and 90 days to pay. This helps to win and keep customers. However, if a firm's trade credit policy is too generous, it may lead to cash flow difficulties.
- Poor credit control – a firm's credit control department ensures that customers keep to agreed borrowing limits and pay on time. If this aspect of a business's operation becomes inefficient, cash inflows into the firm may be delayed. In some cases, customers may not pay at all (this is known as bad debts). In these circumstances it is highly likely that a firm will encounter problems with its cash flow.

Figure 4.16 *In 2003 Lloyds TSB reported an 18% drop in profits, partly caused by bad debts on its operations in Argentina*

Monitoring cash flow

It would be foolish for businesses to imagine that their cash flow forecasts will always prove to be accurate. A number of factors can lead to incorrect cash flow forecasts:

- Inaccurate assumptions – people may make mistakes regarding the future levels of sales for the business or the prices they will receive for their products. A firm's forecasts of the cash it will earn can, of course, be too low or too high. If a competitor suddenly increases prices, for example, this may lead to higher cash sales than expected.
- Unexpected costs – prices of raw materials may increase without warning. The cost of labour may rise due, for example, to the minimum wage. Similarly, machinery breakdowns can impose unanticipated pressures on a business's cash flow.
- Inexperience – this is often the cause of poor quality cash flow forecasting. Many people set up firms with relatively little experience of managing a business. Forecasting sales and costs accurately in this situation is very difficult.

Researching cash flow

Researching the market carefully can reduce the risk of inaccurate cash flow forecasting. Research can establish the prices customers are prepared to pay and the probable level of demand for a firm's products.

Figure 4.17 shows Tony's cash flow forecast for June and the actual figures. It can be seen that Tony's cash position is slightly worse than he expected. This may mean that he needs to increase his overdraft or to try to negotiate a larger discount on the books he buys from his suppliers.

Most modern businesses use spreadsheets to construct and monitor their cash flow forecasts. This technology makes analysing cash flows simpler and quicker.

EXAMINER'S ADVICE

There are important links between cash flow and the following unit – Sources of finance. This is especially relevant when considering ways in which cash flow can be improved. It would be helpful to read these two units together.

	June	
	Forecast	Actual
Cash in		
Cash sales	8000	7950
Credit sales		
Total inflow	8000	7950
Cash out		
Raw materials – books	11000	11650
Wages	1500	1498
Other costs	1500	1532
Total outflow	14000	14680
Net monthly cash flow	(6000)	(6730)
Opening balance	500	500
Closing balance	(5500)	(6230)

Figure 4.17 *Monitoring Tony's cash flow forecast*

Methods of improving cash flow

Identifying potential cash flow problems is only part of the solution. Businesses have to decide how they are going to improve their cash position. A number of techniques can be used to improve cash flow.

Improved control of working capital

Working capital is the finance available to the business for its day-to-day trading activities. Working capital is available to a business when customers pay for the products they have received. Working capital is used to pay wages, and for fuel and raw materials. There are a number of techniques a business may use to improve its working capital.

Negotiate improved terms for trade credit

Most firms receive some trade credit from their suppliers. This means they are given 30 or 60 days to pay for supplies. If a business can persuade suppliers who have previously been reluctant to offer trade credit to do so, it will improve its cash position. Remember, cash flow management is a matter of timing – delaying payments always helps. Another important move might be to extend existing trade credit agreements from, say, 30 to 60 days, or 60 to 80 days.

Offer less trade credit

Similarly, a business can help its cash flow position by offering its customers less favourable terms for trade credit. This may require all customers to pay for products within 30 days, whereas in the past trade credit was for 60 days.

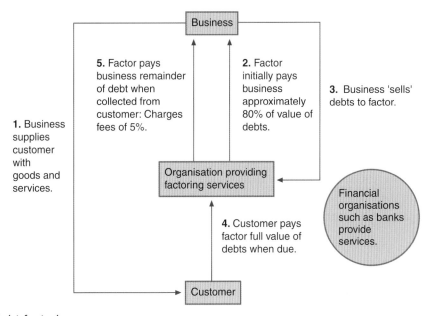

Figure 4.18 *Debt factoring*

Debt factoring

A firm can receive cash earlier by 'selling' its debts to a debt factor. Under such an arrangement the debt factor will pay up to 95% of the value of the debts immediately. This can assist a firm's cash flow position, but reduces its profits. We look at debt factoring in more detail later (see page 142).

INTERPRETING DATA

Look again at the cash flow forecast (Figure 4.14).

- Identify **two** reasons why Tony might have experienced cash flow problems.
- Suggest **two** solutions that would be suitable for his business.

Arrange short-term borrowing

The majority of businesses have an agreed overdraft with their bankers. An overdraft allows a business to borrow flexibly according to its needs up to an agreed limit. Overdrafts can be expensive, but are reasonably economical and flexible when a business only borrows a set amount for a short period.

Sale and leaseback

This method of improving cash flow has been widely used by businesses over recent years. It entails a business selling a major asset – for example, a building – and then leasing it from the new owner. This provides a significant inflow of cash into the business, improving the cash position, but commits the firm to regular payments to lease the asset.

Effective planning and monitoring of cash flow reduces the risk of a cash crisis. However, it does not remove the risk completely. Even experienced and highly-trained managers can make errors. In particular, changes in the external environment, especially sudden change, can result in inaccurate cash flow forecasts.

APPLICATION IN ACTION

High quality answers to questions about solving cash flow problems take into account the circumstances of the firm in the scenario. Selecting the most appropriate solution(s) is a good example of the skill of application and you should think carefully when answering this type of question. For example, a business with plenty of assets (such as property and vehicles) may be able to use sale and leaseback as a means of raising finance. Retailers and hotel chains could use this technique. In contrast, a large, well-established business may be able to negotiate improved trade credit terms with suppliers.

QUICK CHECK QUESTIONS

1   Which one of the following statements is true?
a) Cash flow is the movement of cash into and out of a business over time.
b) Cash flow compares costs and revenues over a period of time.
c) Cash flow problems cannot cause the failure of a business.
d) Cash flow problems are always beyond the control of a business's managers.

2   Is the following statement true or false? 'Businesses are particularly vulnerable to cash flow difficulties in the first few years of trading or when starting a major new project.'

3   For which two of the following reasons might businesses construct cash flow forecasts?
a) To increase the profit made per unit of production.
b) As a means of investigating the previous year's trading profit.
c) To support applications for loans.
d) To avoid suffering from periods when they may be short of cash and unable to pay suppliers.

4   Complete the following sentence by filling in the missing word. 'An .... is a flexible loan on which a business can draw, whenever necessary, up to some agreed limit.'

5   If Balmer Ltd has an opening cash balance in May of £24 750 and a net cash flow for May equal

to (£14 250), which one of the following will be its opening balance for June?
a) £39 000
b) £24 750
c) £38 500
d) £10 500.

6   Is the following a description of cash sales or credit sales? 'These occur when a business allows customers time to pay, normally 30, 60 or 90 days.'

7   Complete the following formula: Opening balance − net monthly cash flow =
.................\.................

8   Is the following statement true or false?

'Negative figures in cash flow forecasts are normally shown in brackets.'

9   Of what is the following a definition? 'This can occur when a business expands quickly without organising funds to finance the expansion.'

10 Which one of the following might **not** help a business to improve its working capital position?
a) Offering customers shorter periods of trade credit.
b) Using the services of a debt factor.
c) Persuading suppliers to provide extended periods of trade credit.
d) Stockpiling raw materials in preparation for future production.

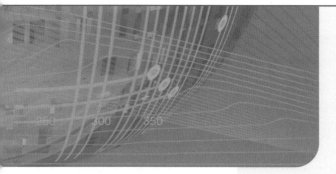

Progress questions

1   Explain the difference between 'cash flow' and 'profit'.   *(5 marks)*

2   Outline two circumstances in which a profitable business might encounter cash flow problems.
                                                           (6 marks)

3   Stuart Merrills is planning to set up his own business as a painter and decorator. Explain two reasons why a cash flow forecast might be particularly useful to him.   *(6 marks)*

4   A small business has the following information relating to a month's cashflow: opening balance – £4500, cash sales – £7500, credit sales – £20 000, closing balance – (£1500). What is the value of the firm's cash outflow for this month?   *(5 marks)*

5   Explain the meaning of the term 'working capital'.   *(3 marks)*

	January	February
Cash in		
Cash sales	65500	70000
Credit sales		24500
Total inflow	97500	
Cash out		
Raw materials	25000	27000
Wages	35000	39000
Other costs	29000	29000
Total outflow		95000
Net monthly cash flow		
Opening Balance	(1000)	
Closing Balance		

6   Complete the missing figures in the above forecast.   *(7 marks)*

7   Outline two factors that may lead to a business experiencing cash flow problems.   *(6 marks)*

8   Explain how a newly-established business might improve its cash flow position.   *(7 marks)*

9   Explain two ways in which change in a business's external environment may affect the accuracy of a firm's cash flow.   *(6 marks)*

10 Give two actions a business might take to improve the accuracy of its cash flow forecasts.
                                                           (2 marks)

Analytical and evaluative questions

11 Harvey's Ltd manufactures high-quality soups for the restaurant industry. The company sells fresh products in a highly competitive market. Examine problems Harvey's Ltd might face when trying to improve its cash flow through better control of working capital. *(8 marks)*

12 Applegate Juices Ltd opens next month. The company will supply retailers with freshly pressed fruit juice. Discuss the benefits of cash flow forecasting to the managers of Applegate Juices Ltd. *(10 marks)*

13 British Airways operates aircraft on routes throughout the world. In recent years, the company has faced tough competition from low-cost airlines such as easyJet. To what extent do you think British Airways' cash flow is under control? *(10 marks)*

Case study

25 marks

Paul Flash has just opened a small manufacturing business. He is in the process of drawing up his cash flow forecast and has assembled the figures below.

- Sales are expected to be £200 000 a month; 50% will be paid in cash; 50% is sold on credit and will be paid two months later.
- Materials are expected to be £90 000 in January, £80 000 in February and £85 000 in March.
- Labour costs are £70 000 a month.
- Rent is £25 000 a month but is paid quarterly (i.e. three months at a time) in January, April, July and October.

	January	February	March
Cash sales	100 000	100 000	100 000
Credit sales			
Total cash in			
Materials	90 000		85 000
Labour costs	70 000	70 000	70 000
Rent			
Total cash out			
Opening balance	50 000		
Net monthly cash flow			
Closing balance			

1 What is meant by credit sales? *(2 marks)*

2 Using the information above, complete the cash flow forecast shown above. Show all your workings. *(5 marks)*

3 Analyse two ways in which Paul might improve the cash position of his business. *(8 marks)*

4 Discuss whether cash is more important than profit for a firm. *(10 marks)*

>> Sources of finance

Managing money

From where can a business raise funds? There are a number of sources available, but the one chosen will depend upon several factors:

- the amount of money required by the business
- the risk associated with lending money to the business
- the time period over which the loan is required.

Short-term finance

A business may need short-term finance to pay its bills and to keep its suppliers happy. Managing cash flow can be difficult if a firm's customers are late in making payment for goods and services they have purchased or if sales are unexpectedly low. In either case, the firm is likely to be short of funds to purchase raw materials and pay wages and salaries. Sudden increases in the costs of raw materials can also create a need for short-term finance. Short-term finance of this kind is usually repayable within a one-year period.

There are many possible sources of short-term finance for businesses.

Trade credit

It is common for suppliers to offer their customers 30 days or so in which to pay for goods and services they have received. In effect it is a short-term loan by the supplier and it is called trade credit. If there is enough trade credit, a business may not need to seek other forms of short-term finance.

The typical credit period offered to customers is 30 days. In practice, however, businesses take usually nearer 75 days to make their payments. This can cause cash flow problems for their suppliers, who may be unable to meet their own commitments. Because of this, the government has launched a campaign encouraging businesses to pay their bills promptly.

Trade credit is attractive to businesses because it is free, although some suppliers may offer a discount for paying quickly.

Business in focus

Glasgow Zoo has been forced to close down after nearly 60 years as a major attraction and its animals have all been re-housed. Calderpark Zoo has faced a cash flow crisis partly because it has not received any financial support from the Government since 2000. Despite selling land to house builders, the Zoo's revenue declined. Simultaneously costs increased as requirements for animal welfare became more stringent. Eventually, unable to pay its debts (estimated at £3.5 million), the Zoo closed its gates for the last time in 2003.

1 Might Calderpark Zoo have been more able to solve its cash problems by cutting its cash outflow, rather than increasing its inflow?

POINTS TO PONDER

Electricity generators in the Ukraine have developed a novel way of persuading businesses to pay overdue accounts. Companies have used billboards to 'name and shame' slow-paying customers and blame them for power cuts.

Overdrafts

An overdraft is a facility offered by banks allowing businesses to borrow up to an agreed limit for a negotiated period of time. Overdrafts are a very flexible form of finance as the amounts borrowed can vary, as long as they are within an agreed figure. They are also simple to arrange – established business customers can often arrange, or increase their limit, without completing any forms.

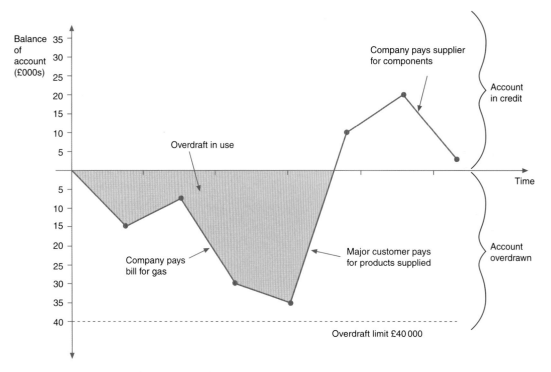

Figure 4.19 *The operation of an overdraft*

Business in focus

A report has revealed that British firms deliberately delay payment of their bills. Of the companies contacted by accountants Grant Thorton and the Business Strategies Group 54% admitted to withholding payment. This was revealed as the highest rate in Europe, well ahead of the average figure of 39%.

On average British firms take 49 days to pay their bills, which is better than the European figure of 61 days, but still causes frustration amongst suppliers. The policy of delaying payment hits small businesses particularly hard as they have very limited cash reserves and rely on customers paying promptly. Government ministers have spoken out regularly against intentional late payment.

1 Explain two reasons why a large firm might intentionally delay payment to a small supplier.

However, overdrafts can be quite expensive with interest being charged at between 4% and 6% over the bank's normal lending rate. This may not be a problem unless a business seeks to borrow on an overdraft over a long period of time.

Debt factoring

Factoring is a service offered by banks and other financial institutions. If businesses have sent out bills (also termed invoices) which have not yet been paid they can 'sell' these bills to gain cash immediately. Factoring debts in this way provides up to 80% of the value of an invoice as an immediate cash advance. The financial institution then organises the payment of the invoice and makes a further payment to the business concerned. It is usual for the financial institution to retain about 5% of the value of the invoice to cover their costs.

Many small firms believe that to lose up to 5% of their earnings means that factoring is uneconomic – it can eliminate much of their profit margin. However, factoring does offer a number of benefits:

- The immediate cash provided by the factor means that the firm is likely to have lower overdraft requirements and will pay less interest.

- Factoring means businesses receive the cash from their sales more quickly.

EXAMINER'S ADVICE

These short-term sources of finance are appropriate to solve cash flow difficulties for businesses. The links between cash flow and sources of finance are important and can be drawn on when answering examination questions.

Medium-term finance

Medium-term finance is appropriate when funds are required for between approximately one and seven years. It is commonly used to replace some short-term finance, for example an overdraft that has been difficult to pay off.

Leasing

This method of finance can be used to buy a range of assets that businesses need. With this method, a business simply leases (or rents) a fixed asset (e.g. vehicles) rather than buying it. Throughout the period of the lease, the finance company still owns the asset that has been purchased.

Key terms

Assets are anything owned by a business from which it can benefit. Assets might include land, vehicles, stocks and brand names.

Businesses may lease assets, for example vehicles or photocopiers, rather than purchasing them outright, because this allows the business to avoid spending a large amount of money at one time. Leasing also offers firms the chance to update their equipment at relatively little extra charge. Also, the nature of some lease agreements means that the firm is able to purchase the asset for a relatively low price at the end of the lease period.

Leasing has disadvantages. Because the finance company providing the asset has to make a profit, leasing an asset may prove to be more expensive than purchasing.

Bank loans

It is common for businesses to purchase assets by raising loans from banks or building societies. The financial institution lends the business a sum of money and the business makes repayments over an agreed period of time. Bank loans are relatively straightforward to arrange. If the bank lending the capital considers the loan to be in any way risky, then it is likely to charge a higher rate of interest. Small businesses, in particular, suffer from this effect. Normally, banks charge about 2% over their usual lending rate for loans such as these.

Banks often require security for their loans. This is known as collateral, and this will usually be in the form of property. If the business fails to repay its loan, the bank would sell the property to recover the money that it was owed.

Key terms

Collateral is the security offered to back up a request for a loan. Usually this is in the form of property, which is unlikely to lose value.

Fixed and variable interest rates

The interest rates charged on bank loans may be fixed or variable. Some businesses prefer fixed rates because they know exactly what their repayments will be. Others choose variable rates in case interest rates fall after the loan is agreed and they end up paying higher charges than is necessary.

When taking out loans, firms have to be careful that they do not borrow too much and make themselves vulnerable to rises in interest rates.

Long-term finance

Sometimes businesses need to purchase major fixed assets such as land and buildings. To do this they will require long-term finance. There are a number of ways in which businesses can raise long-term finance.

Reinvesting profits

Arguably, this remains the major source of long-term finance, particularly for smaller businesses. By using profits for reinvesting, a business avoids paying interest on a loan. But using profits for reinvestment may not be popular with shareholders who receive a lower dividend as a result. This method of finance is only available to firms making a profit. Even then, the profits may not be sufficient to purchase expensive capital assets.

Mortgages

Mortgages are long-term loans for the purchase of land and buildings. The land or building is used as security for the loan – it acts as collateral. These loans can be for long periods of time, often in excess of 20 years. Mortgages can have fixed or variable rates of interest and are particularly suitable for a business wishing to raise a large sum of money.

Some businesses may choose to remortgage their premises to raise capital. A remortgage either increases the existing mortgage or establishes a mortgage where one did not exist before.

Key issues

Deciding what proportion of profits to retain within the company for future investment and what proportion to distribute to shareholders as dividends is always a tricky decision for a board of directors.

There is no single answer to this question. In a rapidly growing company shareholders may be prepared to accept relatively low dividends to allow the company to have sufficient funds to promote growth. They can reasonably expect to receive the benefits of a rising share price as the company expands. However, this approach may not be suitable for a large and established business where shareholders may expect income in the form of dividends.

Microsoft, the American software supplier, is an example of a company moving from a reinvestment strategy to a dividends strategy. In late 2003 the company took the decision to double its dividends to shareholders. The company was in a strong financial position with cash reserves of approximately $50 billion (£31.25 billion). Shareholders had argued that some of this cash should be paid out to them in the form of dividends. Microsoft is unusual amongst technology firms in the United States as

most of them have never paid dividends to shareholders, preferring to re-invest profits (if they have made any).

Share or equity capital

Firms raise capital by selling, quite literally, a share in their business to investors. The investors can gain in two possible ways from their purchase of shares:

- If the business is successful, the price of the shares might rise allowing them to be sold at a profit.
- It is likely that the company will pay the shareholders a proportion of their profits, known as a dividend.

There are two main types of shares:

1 **Ordinary shares** – these give a variable dividend from year to year according to how well the company has done. They do, however, allow the shareholder a vote at the company's Annual General Meeting.
2 **Preference shares** – as their name suggests, these shares have priority over ordinary shares when it comes to paying dividends. If profits are small it is the holders of ordinary shares who are likely to lose out. Preference shareholders usually receive a fixed dividend.

> **Key terms**
>
> *Ordinary shares give shareholders ownership of part of a company. They may also have a share of any profits distributed and the right to vote at Annual General Meetings.*

A share is simply a certificate giving the holder ownership of part (or a share) of a company. Shareholders purchase shares. By selling large numbers of them, companies raise significant sums of capital. However, shareholders usually have the right to a say in the running of the company and, by selling too many shares, the owners can lose control of the company. Issuing shares is often administratively very expensive, which means it is only appropriate for raising very large sums of capital.

There are a number of benefits of raising capital through the selling of shares. A major one is that a business selling shares does not commit itself to a fixed annual payment to shareholders. Companies will be expected to pay an annual return to shareholders. However, the value of this dividend is not fixed and, in an unprofitable year, it may be possible for the company to avoid paying any dividends.

Government grants

Government grants to businesses can take a number of forms. Some grants are only available in selected areas of the UK. These areas are shown in Figure 4.20.

The benefits offered by the EU or the UK government, or by agencies on its behalf, can be summarised as follows:

- Selective Regional Assistance – under this system the government offers grants to firms who move to an assisted area and create jobs.
- Enterprise Grants – these are for firms with less than 250 employees who create jobs in development areas. The aid can help with investment up to a maximum of £75 000.
- European Structural Funds – this funding from the EU is available to improve the infrastructure and the skills of the workforce in certain parts of the UK. The UK's allocation for 2000–2006 is £10 billion.
- Enterprise Zones – designed to revitalise inner cities, these are areas of a few hundred acres offering financial incentives to firms who locate within them. Benefits include tax incentives and subsidised premises.

The government has also offered substantial and undisclosed financial packages to a number of multinational companies in order to persuade them to locate in the UK. These grants and loans can be a significant source of finance for a company expanding within the UK.

Figure 4.20 *Businesses locating in the areas shaded on the map are likely to receive some financial assistance from the government. The exact amount will depend upon the circumstances*

Source: Department of Trade and Industry (www.dti.gov.uk)

Debentures are often mentioned along with shares. They are in fact a special type of loan. They are long-term loans on which businesses have to pay a fixed rate of interest. Raising money through debentures allows the existing shareholders to retain control of a company, but make it vulnerable to changes in interest rates – when market rates are falling, the business is committed to fixed payments. Public limited companies rely heavily on selling shares to raise the capital they need. They enjoy the privilege of selling shares on the Stock Exchange, making it possible to raise large sums of money.

Type of business organisation	Possible sources of finance	Key issues for consideration
Sole trader	Owner's savings, banks, suppliers, government grants and loans	• security for those lending funds • loss of control by owner • evidence that business has potential to develop • financial history of business/owner
Partnership	Partners' savings, banks, suppliers, government grants and loans, hire purchase and leasing companies	• problems of introducing new partner • lack of collateral • potential expense of raising large sums of money • should they form a limited company?
Private limited company (Ltd)	Dependent upon the size of the private limited company, suppliers, banks, factoring, leasing and hire purchase companies, govenment grants and loans, venture capital institutions, private share issues	• disagreement amongst existing shareholders • difficulty of finding suitable shareholders • loss of control by existing shareholders • lack of collateral and security for those lending funds • element of risk in the loan
Public limited company (plc)	Suppliers, banks, factoring, leasing and hire purchase companies, government grants and loans, venture capital institutions, public share issues via the Stock Exchange	• state of economy and stock market • ability to move to area receiving government aid • recent financial performance • reputation of company and senior managers
Non-profit making organisation	Charitable donations, Lottery money, government and EU grants	• public profile • relationship with government

Table 4.3 *Analysis of business type and suitability of different forms of finance*

Key issues

The UK is Europe's most attractive location for international business. However, the amount of overseas investment has declined since 2001, as eastern European countries have become a more popular target. The entry to the EU of countries such as Poland and Hungary has accelerated this trend.

Invest UK is the only investment agency covering the whole of the UK. It helps the world's companies to set up or expand business from a British base quickly and smoothly. In some cases financial support is available to businesses choosing to locate in the UK.

Why Britain offers competitive advantages for the world's leading companies:

• economic stability avoiding severe recessions and inflationary booms
• fast access to markets
• skilled and adaptable workforce
• Europe's financial centre
• English-speaking workforce
• low rates of business taxation.

Source: Adapted from Invest UK, www.investuk.com

The existence of Invest UK shows how important investment by foreign firms is to the UK government. It also suggests how important financial support from the government is to firms taking decisions to relocate or to expand.

APPLICATION IN ACTION

It is vital to propose appropriate sources of finance for the circumstances of the business and to explain your decision in order to earn high marks for application. For example, you might suggest that a growing but successful company could use retained profits as a source, while this may not be an option for a newly established business. Similarly, a family-owned private limited company may be reluctant to raise large sums of money through share issues as they may lose control of the business as a consequence.

You should also relate the source of finance to the purpose for which the capital is to be used. Thus, you might argue that a business that requires funds to replace vehicles may consider leasing, especially if it does not have ready access to large amounts of capital.

QUICK CHECK QUESTIONS

1 Is the following statement true or false? 'Businesses only need to raise funds when first established or when expanding.'

2 For which one of the following situations would trade credit be a suitable source of finance?
a) to purchase a new factory
b) to buy a new fleet of 20 lorries
c) to redesign and re-equip a company's IT system
d) to purchase raw materials and components.

3 Which one of the following is a major disadvantage of using debt factoring?
a) It can result in a loss of up to 5% of earnings.
b) Customers may be dissatisfied as a result.
c) It can take time to arrange with debt factoring agencies.
d) It can result in a higher overdraft.

4 Fill in the missing word to complete the following sentence. 'Banks often require security for their loans – this is known as ....'

5 Which of the following assets would **not** normally be acquired through leasing?
a) company cars
b) land
c) photocopiers
d) IT systems.

6 Which of the following groups of stakeholders are **most** likely to be dissatisfied if a company decides to re-invest large proportions of its profits?
a) employees
b) managers
c) shareholders
d) the government.

7 Fill in the missing word from this statement. 'A .... is a special type of loan. It is a long-term loan on which businesses have to pay a fixed rate of interest.'

8 Is the following statement true or false? 'Ordinary shares give a variable dividend to shareholders and do not give shareholders a vote at the company's Annual General Meeting (AGM).'

9 Which **two** of the following statements about Enterprise Zones are true?
a) They are located in small inner-city areas in the UK.
b) They are areas with high levels of employment.
c) These areas contain many prosperous businesses.
d) The government offers firms in these areas financial benefits.

10 Complete the following sentence by filling in the missing word. 'A .... is a certificate giving the holder ownership of part of a company.'

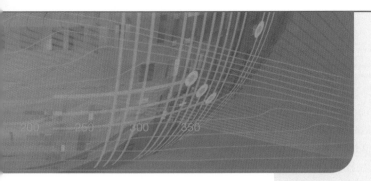

Progress questions

1 Bearing in mind the advice above, identify the best sources of finance in each of the situations below.
   a) A business wishes to finance a new fleet of cars for its salesforce.
   b) A company wants to build a major new factory costing £350m.
   c) A firm wishes to purchase more raw materials in order that it might increase its output.
   d) A small business needs to pay suppliers now but its customers are not expected to pay for a further two months.
   e) A large public limited company wishes to finance the development of a new range of products.
   f) A company wishes to install a new IT system but is conscious that the technology is changing rapidly.
   g) A firm has little cash to spare and pays all its bills promptly.
   h) A business that wishes to invest a substantial sum, but anticipates steady profits over the next few years.
                                    (1 mark for each)

2 State one advantage and one disadvantage to a business of using an overdraft as a source of finance.   *(2 marks)*

3 Explain why a small business might be reluctant to use factoring as a method of raising finance.   *(6 marks)*

4 Distinguish between 'leasing' and 'factoring'.   *(5 marks)*

5 Outline why leasing might be an appropriate form of finance for a company requiring new computers.   *(6 marks)*

6 Outline one advantage and one disadvantage that may result from a company deciding to reinvest its profits.   *(6 marks)*

7 Outline two ways in which the government may assist a firm to raise finance.   *(6 marks)*

8 Explain why a public limited company might choose to raise funds by issuing more shares.   *(6 marks)*

9 Outline the role played by business angels in providing finance to businesses.   *(5 marks)*

10 Explain the possible sources of finance available to a sole trader planning to open a corner shop.   *(7 marks)*

Analytical and evaluative questions

11 Sarah Parker plans to open a new restaurant in Ipswich. She has £30 000 of her own money and her aunt is willing to invest £10 000. She needs £75 000 to open the restaurant. Analyse two possible sources of finance Sarah might use.   *(8 marks)*

12 Discuss whether it is better for a large, established company, such as Marks & Spencer, to rely on internal sources of finance rather than external finance.   *(10 marks)*

13 Darby and Sons Ltd is a small family business. Discuss the case for and against the company raising a large sum of money through a share issue.   *(10 marks)*

Wigg Ltd was in a terrible financial state. The last Financial Director had suffered from poor health and had taken a lot of time off work. Rather than get anyone else in to take over, the Managing Director, Bob Wigg (grandson of the founder), had decided to muddle through. The result was chaos!

The company faced two major problems. First, its short-term financial position was poor: it simply did not have enough money to pay its bills. The second problem was its long-term financial position. The company desperately needed to update its facilities and production equipment, but this would need major investment. Although the company, which produced office furniture, had been in existence for over 50 years its recent profits had been poor and the family was struggling to keep it going. Some members were said to be keen to sell out. However, the older generation wanted to keep it going as it was. Even so, there were rumours of take-overs.

In a heated management meeting last week, it was decided that a replacement for the Finance Director must be found as a matter of urgency.

Meanwhile, the directors had to decide how to raise the finance they needed so urgently. What should they do: Get an overdraft? A loan? Sell debentures? The company certainly needed external rather than internal finance, but what was the best way of raising it? Some of Wigg's managers felt that in the long term the company would need to sell shares to raise the money it needed. Bob Wigg was not sure this would work. Someone also mentioned the idea of venture capital but no one really knew much about it.

1 *What is meant by a 'debenture'?*   *2 marks)*

2 *Outline two ways in which the firm might be able to raise finance internally.*   *(6 marks)*

3 *Analyse two factors Wigg Ltd might take into account before raising finance by selling shares.*   *(8 marks)*

4 *Discuss the factors a bank might take into account when deciding whether or not to give Wigg Ltd a long-term loan.*   *(9 marks)*

>> Budgets

Introduction
What are budgets?

Budgets are financial plans for a future period. Firms plan their earnings and revenues using budgets. Budgets are usually drawn up on a monthly basis, over the period of a year.

Budgets help the business achieve its objectives. If, for example, a business has growth as a major objective the budgets will reflect this with higher revenues (and costs, of course) being planned.

Sales revenue budgets set out the firm's planned revenue from selling its products. These are often calculated on a monthly basis over the period of a year. Important information here includes the expected level of sales and the likely selling price of the product. Businesses also need to plan their expenditure on labour, raw materials, fuel and other items which are essential for production. Plans relating to a business's costs are termed production or expenditure budgets.

The process of creating budgets

Before firms can start to write their budgets for the coming year, they need to carry out some research. This may involve:

- analysing the market to predict likely trends in sales and prices to help plan sales revenue
- researching costs for labour, fuel and raw materials by contacting suppliers, and considering government estimates for wage rises and inflation.

Once a business has collected the necessary data, it is normal to draw up expected revenues from selling products – the sales budget. This is the first budget because, once a firm knows its expected sales, it can plan production levels. This enables the business to forecast the costs associated with producing enough to match planned sales. Once production budgets and sales budgets are completed, expected profits can be estimated.

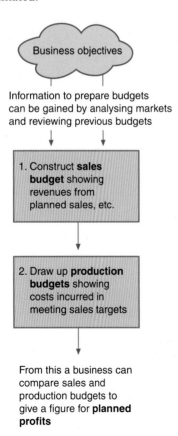

Figure 4.21 *Drawing up budgets*

EXAMINER'S ADVICE

A number of links exist between finance and other areas of the specification, notably marketing. One such link is between revenue budgets and various aspects of marketing. Whether a firm gains more revenue from reducing its prices will, for example, depend upon the price elasticity of demand for the products in question. Equally, market research may play an important part in developing a firm's sales revenue budgets. It is important to explore links such as these when writing answers to examination questions.

Why do businesses draw up budgets?

There are a number of reasons for planning future costs and revenues using budgets:

- Budgets assist businesses to control their finances by planning their expenditure over a future period, usually a year. It is not unusual for businesses to have budgets of many millions – or even billions of pounds. It is impossible for a single person (a budget-holder) to effectively manage these budgets to ensure costs are controlled and planned revenues earned. A system of delegated budgets allows a large number of people within the organisation to take a share of responsibility for finances.
- Budgets are an effective way of ensuring that a business does not spend more than it should. As long as every employee ensures that they do not spend in excess of their budget, costs should not get out of control.

Key terms

A budget-holder is responsible for the use and management of a particular budget.
Delegated budgets exist when firms give control over budgets to relatively junior employees.

Setting and monitoring budgets
Difficulties in setting budgets

If budgets are set incorrectly it can be harmful to the organisation.

- If sales budgets are set too high and are unachievable, they can demotivate sales employees and damage the sales performance of the business.
- Production budgets which are set impossibly low might be ignored. This may mean that the organisation fails to control its expenditure resulting in lower profits or even a loss.
- Equally, budgets that are very simple to achieve will not motivate employees or improve their performance.

Firms may find it difficult to estimate their sales when setting the sales budget. Changes in tastes and fashions can occur rapidly, especially in music and clothing industries. Equally, the pace of change in high technology industries, such as personal computers, makes the process of planning sales very tricky.

Planning expenditure on labour and raw materials can be difficult, especially if prices are changing rapidly, perhaps due to inflation.

Zero budgeting

An alternative approach used by a number of firms is zero budgeting. Using this system, each budget is set at zero at the start of the budget setting process. Managers responsible for the areas covered by the budget have to bid for a budget and to justify the money they request.

Key terms

Zero budgets *exist when budgets are automatically set at zero and budget-holders have to argue their case to receive any funds.*

EXAMINER'S ADVICE

This section of text highlights an important aspect of AS Business Studies. You will be expected to have some understanding of the advantages and disadvantages of techniques such as budgeting. This type of understanding helps you to write analytically.

MATHS MOMENT

1+1=2

Freemantle Furniture produces high quality wooden furniture. They sell a wide range of products, but have recently introduced two new lines, oak coffee tables and rocking chairs.

The company's Sales Director has forecast sales for these two products over the next six months as shown below.

	March	April	May	June	July	August
Coffee tables	£9375	£10 500	£11 250	£12 000	£11 100	£11 475
Rocking chairs	£4050	£4500	£4410	£4590	£4410	£3420
Total	£13 425	£15 000	£15 660	£16 590	£15 510	£14 895

Table 4.4 *Budget for Freemantle Furniture*

1 Coffee tables are sold for £75 each. How many did the firm sell in April and July? Would reducing the price of coffee tables automatically cut the firm's sales revenue?
2 Rocking chairs are sold for £90 each. What would the firm's planned revenue have been in June if they had sold all their chairs for £100 each?
3 Assume the costs (fixed and variable) of producing each chair are £75. How many chairs would they need to sell in a month to earn a profit of £400 on this product?

Monitoring Budgets

Setting budgets is only the first stage in the process. Once a business has planned its revenue and expenditure, it is essential to *monitor* the accuracy of these financial plans. If the business's plans go wrong due, for example, to lower sales revenue or higher production costs, then remedial action will be necessary.

The process for monitoring budget is known as variance analysis. A variance occurs when an *actual figure* for sales or expenditure *differs* from the *budgeted figure*. Actual sales and cost figures can be higher or lower than planned. The two categories of variance are shown in Table 4.6.

Key terms

Variance analysis is the process of investigating any differences between forecast data and actual figures.

EXAMINER'S ADVICE

Questions asking you to analyse variances are common in AS Business Studies examinations. It is important for you to identify those areas in which major differences between planned and actual expenditure or revenue have occurred. This will help to give a focus to your answer. It is also very likely that you will be asked to suggest possible causes (or cures) for the variances. Avoid simply describing the data you are given. Few, if any marks, will be awarded for this.

Carrying out regular variance analysis can give a business advance notice that their financial plans are inaccurate. Variance analysis can be carried out each month and will show before the end of the financial year that the firm's finances are not as planned. Some possible responses to adverse variances are shown in Figure 4.22.

Revenue/cost	Budget figure (£)	Actual figure (£)	Variance
Sales revenue	840 000	790 000	£50 000 – adverse
Fuel costs	75 000	70 000	£5000 – favourable
Raw material costs	245 000	265 000	£20 000 – adverse
Labour costs	115 000	112 000	£3000 – favourable

Table 4.5 *Calculating variances*

Favourable variances	Adverse variances
A favourable variance exists when the difference between the actual and budgeted figures will result in the business enjoying higher profits than shown in the budget.	An adverse variance occurs when the difference between the figures in the budget and the actual figures will lead to the firm's profits being lower than planned.
Examples of favourable variances include: ● actual wages less than budgeted wages ● budgeted sales revenue lower than actual sales revenue ● expenditure on fuel is less than the budgeted figure	Examples of adverse variances include: ● sales revenue below the budgeted figure ● actual raw material costs exceeding the figure planned in the budget ● overheads turn out to be higher than in the budget
Possible causes of favourable variances: ● wage rises lower than expected ● economic boom leads to higher than expected sales ● rising value of pound makes imported raw materials cheaper	Possible causes of adverse variances: ● competitors introduce new products winning extra sales ● government increases business rates by unexpected amount ● fuel prices increase as price of oil rises

Table 4.6 *Favourable and adverse variances*

Firms may also need to respond to favourable variances. Production costs which are lower than planned may be regarded as beneficial. But sales revenue which is greater than anticipated might be caused by the firm selling more products than planned. In these circumstances, the business might not have sufficient supplies to meet customer requirements. This could result in the loss of long-established customers and should be avoided.

INTERPRETING DATA

Look at the budgetary data presented in Table 4.5 and answer the following questions.

a) Why might the manager responsible for this budget be surprised that sales revenue has an adverse variance whilst labour costs recorded a favourable variance?

b) Why might this have occurred?

c) Explain why raw material costs might be higher than expected.

Key issues

Recently, firms have given control of budgets to individuals and teams at all levels within the business. This has been accompanied by a reduction in the number of managers and an attempt to give workers more control over their working lives. Allowing them to take some decisions relating to finance through delegated budgets is an important part of this. The intentions behind these changes are:

- to reduce the number of managers, cutting wage costs
- to motivate employees by giving them more diverse and responsible jobs
- to help encourage employees at all levels to play a part in decision-making and problem-solving.

Many companies, such as Vauxhall (see *www.vauxhall.co.uk/companyinformation/factpage*), have made use of delegated budgets. Their use has also been extended to organisations in the public sector, for example schools and colleges.

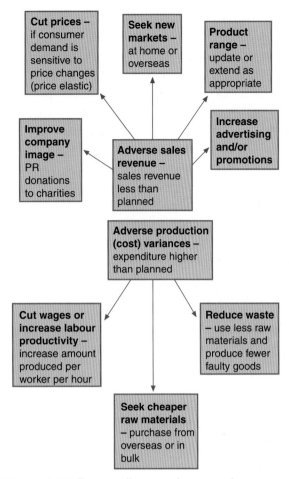

Figure 4.22 *Responding to adverse variances*

Advantages and disadvantages of budgets

The advantages of Budgets

Control of finances

Production or expenditure budgets allow managers to ensure that a business does not overspend. Senior managers receive their own budgets and can allocate these between the various parts of the department or area for which they are responsible.

Figure 4.24 illustrates this process. As long as each individual budget holder makes sure that she or he does not spend more than the agreed figure, the businesses overall expenditure should remain under control.

Budgets allow senior managers to direct extra funds into important areas of the business. Thus, if a business is concerned that its product range is not selling well, it may increase its budgets in the areas of market research, and research and development.

Motivation and appraisal
Budgets can be used to motivate employees. Employees can gain satisfaction from being given responsibility for a budget. They may also gain satisfaction from keeping within a budget. As a result their level of motivation and their performance may improve, benefiting the firm as a whole. We will consider motivation in more detail later (see page 180).

Sales revenue budgets can also be used as targets for employees, possibly as part of the appraisal process. Employees may be motivated to improve their performance by the existence of targets in the forms of sales revenue budgets.

The disadvantages of budgets
Training requirements
If a business intends that a significant proportion of its employees should manage budgets (known as delegating budgets), then training will be required. The cost of the training could be substantial, depending on the skills of the workforce. Furthermore, there could be teething problems as employees adjust to the new roles and responsibilities.

Allocation of funds
Allocating budgets fairly and in the best interests of the business is difficult. Some managers may be skilled at negotiating large budgets for the areas for which they are responsible. This might be at the expense of more worthy areas. Thus, for example, a manager responsible for the sales force in existing markets may receive a large budget allocation, whilst insufficient funds are given to developing new markets.

Short-term versus long-term planning
Budgets normally relate to the current financial year only. Thus, managers might take a decision to keep within the current budget which is not actually in the longer-term interest of the business. For example, a decision to reduce the size of a workforce for budgetary reasons might result in competitors gaining more of the market over the next few years.

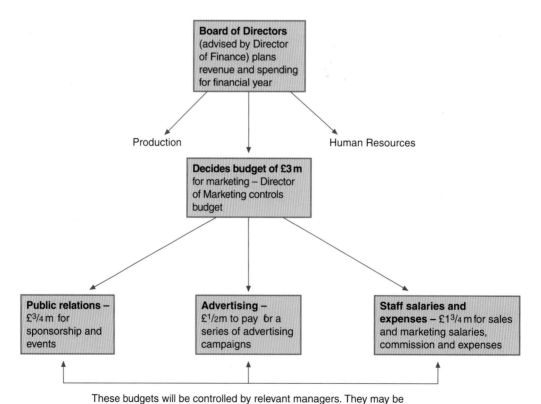

These budgets will be controlled by relevant managers. They may be further divided into, for example, a budget for expenses for the sales force.

Figure 4.23 *An example of using budgets within a company*

QUICK CHECK QUESTIONS

1   Drawing up budgets involves a series of activities. Place the four statements below in the correct order.
a)   Draw up production budgets.
b)   Construct sales budgets.
c)   Establish the business's objectives.
d)   Analyse markets and previous budgets to gather information.

2   Complete the following sentence by filling in the missing words. 'A .... budget exists when firms give control over budgets to relatively .... employees.'

3   Which of the following statements is **not** a reason why firms draw up budgets?
a)   To ensure that a business does not spend more than it should.
b)   As a means of sharing responsibility for financial management amongst a large number of employees.
c)   To ease the pressure on senior managers in an organisation.
d)   To give senior managers tighter control over expenditure.

4   Which of the following factors might cause a sales budget to be lower than forecast?
a)   a rise in variable costs
b)   a competitor introducing a new product unexpectedly
c)   a fall in overheads
d)   a competitor closing down.

5   Is the following statement true or false? 'Under a system of zero budgeting, all managers are guaranteed an increase in their budgets.'

6   Of what is the following a definition: 'The process of investigating any differences between forecast data and actual figures.'

7   Complete the following sentence by filling in the missing word. 'An .... variance exists when the difference between the actual and budget figures will lead to the firm's profits being lower then expected.'

8   Which one of the following is an adverse variance?
a)   sales revenue higher than forecast
b)   expenditure on wages lower than forecast
c)   raw material costs higher than stated in the budget
d)   fuel costs lower than forecast in the budget.

9   Is the following statement true or false? 'Managers do not need to take any action if variances are favourable.'

10   Which of the following is **not** a disadvantage of using delegated budgets?
a)   Relatively junior employees may take financial decisions.
b)   There are additional training requirements for employees.
c)   They encourage managers to focus on short-term planning and to pay less attention to long-term issues.
d)   Teething problems may occur when delegated budgets are first introduced.

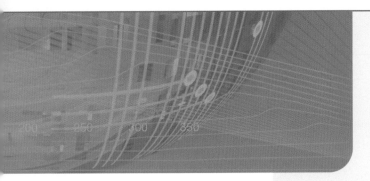

Progress questions

1 Explain two reasons why a business might use budgets as part of its management. *(6 marks)*

2 Outline the stages a business might pass through when drawing up a budget. *(5 marks)*

3 Explain two problems a business might encounter when setting budgets. *(6 marks)*

4 Outline why a business in the fashion clothing industry might face problems when setting its sales revenue budget. *(6 marks)*

5 Explain why a firm might decide to use zero budgeting. *(3 marks)*

6 Distinguish, with the aid of examples, between 'favourable variances' and 'adverse variances'. *(7 marks)*

7 The following variance data has been produced for Robinsworth Ltd.

Item	Budget (£)	Actual (£)
Sales revenue	950 000	1 100 000
Labour	275 000	382 500
Rent and rates	190 000	225 000
Raw materials	240 000	302 000

Identify and explain the possible causes of two of the variances within the data above. *(6 marks)*

8 Outline two possible courses of action open to a business facing an adverse sales revenue variance. *(6 marks)*

9 Explain two arguments in favour of using budgets as part of a business's financial control. *(6 marks)*

10 A medium-sized manufacturer is considering delegating budgets for the first time. Explain some of the problems that the business might face in these circumstances. *(7 marks)*

Analytical and evaluative questions

11 Sharrocks plc is a clothes retailer with 120 branches across the UK. The company has a reputation for selling highly fashionable products. Examine the benefits the company might gain from delegating budgets. *(8 marks)*

12 Protect is one of the UK's leading child welfare charities. It plans to divide the UK into 12 regions and to delegate budgets to each region. To what extent might this be an effective long-term strategy? *(10 marks)*

13 The Chief Executive of a large manufacturing business has stated that 'traditional budgets are outdated; we should use zero budgets'. Discuss the case for and against his view. *(10 marks)*

Case study

25 marks

When Kiri Bulman set up her first nightclub in 1993 (The Warehouse in Camden Town) she had little idea quite how successful it would be. Numbers attending the club just grew and grew. The right DJs, the right decor and the right music soon made it the place to be. The club's popularity was such that she was soon turning people away. Strangely, this seemed to make people more eager to get in! Over the next five years Kiri built a business on 'The Warehouse' name. She released CDs of the club's music, started a magazine and launched a range of clothing using this brand name.

Although the profits seemed to keep increasing, Kiri felt uneasy that there were no real controls on what was being spent in different areas. She did not set targets for the business or have any real ideas about its future direction. Her managers were basically left to do whatever they felt was right at that time. Neither Kiri nor they felt entirely comfortable with this approach.

As a result, she decided to introduce a budgeting system throughout the business. This was done in full consultation with staff to explain the benefits of the system. Most seemed to agree it was a good idea, although some were rather suspicious of the process. As part of her attempts to bring more financial control into the business, Kiri established four main profit centres: the club, music, magazines and clothing. At the end of the first year she undertook a variance analysis of the clothing business:

£m	Budgeted	Actual
Revenue	50	60
Production costs	30	35
Marketing costs	5	6
Other costs	3	3.5

Having analysed the results for the business as a whole, it was necessary to set next year's targets. Kiri was particularly interested in the marketing budget for the club. She was eager to keep The Warehouse fresh and seen as the place to be. The place was certainly busy but she was afraid the customers might all disappear one day. She was also aware of the large number of new clubs opening up around the country.

1 *What is meant by an 'adverse variance'?*

(2 marks)

2 a) *Calculate the overall variance for the clothing.*

(2 marks)

b) *Explain one reason for the possible difference in the budgeted and the actual figure for the production costs.* *(5 marks)*

3 *Analyse the factors that might determine the size of the marketing budget for The Warehouse.*

(7 marks)

4 *Discuss the case for and against Kiri Bulman introducing a budgeting process into her organisation.* *(9 marks)*

>> Cost centres and profit centres

What is the difference between a cost and a profit centre?

In many ways cost centres and profit centres are similar. But there is a distinct difference.

> **Key terms**
>
> *A cost centre* is a distinct part (perhaps a division or department) of a business for which costs can be calculated.
>
> *A profit centre* is similar to a cost centre, being a part of a business for which costs and revenues (and thus profits) can be determined.

For a cost centre it is only possible to calculate the associated costs. Thus, the accounts department or the department providing IT services to a business could be cost centres. For these areas it is straightforward to calculate costs such as wages and salaries. However, it is impossible to calculate the *revenues* earned by areas of the business such as the accounts department, as they do not charge separately for their services.

Profit centres can calculate costs *and* revenues. So, it is possible to determine the *profit* generated by this aspect of the business's operation.

Creating cost and profit centres

1 Some large businesses might operate a number of factories, offices or branches. In these circumstances, profit centres can be developed on a geographical basis. High street banks, for example, expect branches (or groups of branches) to achieve agreed levels of profits.

2 In manufacturing industries, it is possible to operate smaller cost or profit centres relating to a particular product or even a single production line.

3 A relatively simple approach is to use departments or divisions as cost or profit centres. Hospitals use wards and individual departments such as X-ray to develop cost and profit centres, for example.

4 Profit and cost centres can also relate to individual products or brands.

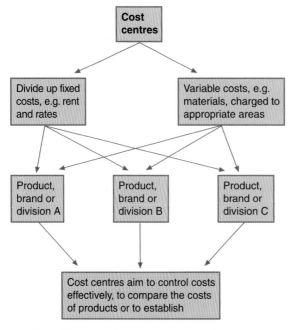
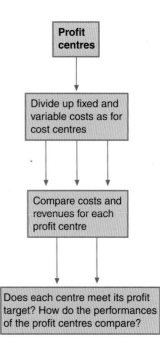

Figure 4.24 *The difference between cost and profit centres*

Business in focus

Gregory Walton owns and manages a chain of restaurants in North and West London. The restaurants are American theme restaurants selling ribs, burgers, fried chicken and similar foods. Greg has announced plans to open his fifth diner in Tottenham within a few weeks.

Greg runs his restaurants as separate profit centres so he is able to calculate the costs and revenues for each diner. The figures for the last financial year are shown below.

Location of diner	Revenues (£)	Costs (£)	Profit (£)
Edmonton	125 750	98 550	27 200
Harrow	180 000	141 950	38 050
Ruislip	129 500	118 000	11 500
Stanmore	155 900	131 675	24 225

Table 4.7 *Profit centres for Greg's Diners chain*

Greg's business is managed from a head office where he is supported by a staff of three. Between them they carry out all the accounting, marketing and personnel duties needed by the firm. Greg's head office is simply run as a cost centre because it does not earn any revenue directly. It supports the diners and assists them (and the business as a whole) in earning a profit.

1 Greg's staff like their restaurants to operate as profit centres. Can you explain two reasons why they might feel this way?
2 Look at the data given for profits and costs in Greg's Diners above. Clearly, the Harrow diner earns the highest profit. But which earns the highest profit as a percentage of revenue?
3 Why might this be a useful piece of information for Greg?

Why operate cost and revenue centres?

There are three broad categories of reason why businesses decide to operate cost and profit centres:

1 financial reasons
2 organisational reasons
3 motivational reasons.

Financial reasons

Businesses gain more detailed information from running a number of separate cost and profit centres, rather than merging all the figures into a single set of financial statements. Having separate cost centres allows managers to compare the costs incurred by various parts of the business. This enables managers to identify the less cost-efficient parts of the business. Senior managers can then attempt to reduce costs in this area, perhaps through more training of staff, creating a more profitable business overall. Cost centres can also play a part in setting prices – once the cost is known, it is possible to set a price to make sure that the brand, product or division earns a profit.

EXAMINER'S ADVICE

There are a number of important links between this part of the business studies specification and the people and organisations chapter (see page 169). Adopting cost or profit centres may result in a different organisational structure, as well as changing responsibilities for employees and possibly bringing about a reduction in the number of middle managers. It is useful to understand and explore such interrelationships within the subject.

Organisational reasons

The financial data provided by cost and profit centres gives managers more in-depth information about the operation of their business. Using this information, managers might be able to organise the business more effectively and make higher profits.

Many businesses are made up of a number of separate elements. If a company wishes to expand, having information on the relative financial performance of each of the divisions of the business

People in business

Michael Dell founded Dell Computers in 1984 with $1000 while still a student at the University of Texas. At the end of 2003, the Corporation employed over 41 000 people globally, earned a revenue in excess of £23 billion and sells in 80 countries. In 2002, Dell Computers became the leading seller of computers in the world.

Michael showed entrepreneurial skills from an early age. At 9 he had a cheque book; at 12 he was managing a profitable mail-order business and by age 13 was speculating in gold, silver and shares. Michael Dell studied biology at university, but spotted a business opportunity retailing computers. Initially, he sold computers through small adverts in the newspapers, but soon established the Dell Computer Corporation.

Michael's fundamental idea was to cut out the middleman in selling computers. By 1985, Dell Computers was manufacturing and selling its own products directly to the consumer. Selling computers via the Internet was a natural development for Michael Dell's business. The company is the leading online seller of computers – in 2002 its global web pages received 4 billion hits.

Dell's success and vision have earned him many awards. In 2001 he was named chief executive of the year, and in 2003 the *Financial Times* published a poll which showed him to be the fourth most respected business leader in the world.

will be helpful. It might be argued that they should focus on their profitable activities.

Companies can also use information from cost or profit centres in other ways. Some part of employees' pay may be linked to the success of the division, department or branch in keeping costs down, or in achieving profit targets.

Motivational reasons

Many psychologists recognise that giving people greater responsibility is an effective way to motivate them. This responsibility can take the form of achieving cost or profit targets within cost or profit centres. Businesses have increasingly recognised this and have sought to allow employees a greater role in managing budgets. When managing a profit or cost centre, employees have more varied and interesting jobs, as well as the satisfaction of achieving cost or profit targets.

Advantages and disadvantages of cost and profit centres
The advantages of cost and profit centres

- Cost and profit centres allow firms to assess the performance of individual parts of their business. Managers can identify those elements that are successful and those parts that are relatively unsuccessful. As a consequence, it is easier for managers to take appropriate actions and to concentrate their efforts on those parts of the organisation that are less efficient.

POINTS TO PONDER

In 2003 Ebookers, an online travel group, announced that its financial position had improved although it was still making a loss. The company, which sells holidays on the Internet, has transferred its administration to India. Its Indian operation is a cost centre and the move has helped to improve the company's financial position.

- Profit and cost centres allow businesses to take appropriate decisions at a local level. Thus, a large business may be able to set prices at a local level and to charge locally what the market will bear. This should lead to higher profits. Businesses may also enjoy more success in controlling costs if people at a local level are responsible for them.
- Many firms have decided to give greater responsibility to more junior employees as part of a policy designed to motivate all employees. By reducing the number of managers and giving junior employees more diverse and interesting jobs, it is hoped to improve their performance and the business's profitability. People cannot take more control over their working lives, as these initiatives intend, without having more financial responsibility.

The disadvantages of cost and profit centres

- Delegating authority down the organisation, including delegating budgets, is currently popular within many businesses. However, this places greater demands on junior managers and other employees who might be unprepared for the new responsibilities. Unless careful planning (including training) precedes delegating budgets and creating cost and profit centres, employees may struggle to cope with the additional demands placed upon them.

Figure 4.25 *Starbucks has over 5000 outlets across the globe, and each one operates as a profit centre*

- Creating a number of profit or cost centres within a business can develop rivalry between the areas. This type of competition can be a positive factor, although it can be destructive if taken too far.
- In some circumstances it is very difficult to divide up costs to create a cost or profit centre. Thus, a manufacturing firm might find it difficult to divide up costs such as rent and rates between the three products that it produces.

APPLICATION IN ACTION

A useful point is that cost and profit centres do not automatically suit all businesses. The following types of business may not be suited to managing their finances in this way:

- single-product businesses
- businesses with strong, autocratic leaders
- firms employing mainly unskilled workers.

Business in focus

Mouncey Engineering produces components for gas and oil companies operating rigs in the North Sea. Their factory manufactures three components – the automatic valve, the pressure sensor and the sea-bed monitor.

The managers of the business operate profit centres for each of the three products, but find it difficult to decide how to divide up the factory's rent and rates between the three products. The cost of rent and rates each year is £300 000 and this cost has to be split between the three products. It is easy to identify costs such as wages, raw materials and fuel for each of the three products, but rent and rates remain a problem. The Managing Director, Patricia Mouncey, has suggested three possible approaches:

1 Simply split the costs into three – that is allocate costs of £100 000 to each of the three products (and profit centres).
2 Divide up the cost of rent and rates according to the number of employees working on each of the products.
3 Divide up the cost of rent and rates according to the value of sales of each of the products.

She gave an example of the amount each profit centre will be charged for rent and rates if they were divided up according to the number of employees. The number of employees is as follows:

● the automatic valve – 15 employees
● the pressure sensor – 30 employees
● the sea-bed monitor – 15 employees.

The total number of employees is 60. Thus the automatic valve profit centre should carry (15/60 × £300 000) £75 000 of the cost of rent and rates. The pressure sensor profit centre would be charged (30/60 × £300 000) £150 000. Finally, the amount charged to the sea-bed monitor profit centre would be (15/60 × £300 000) £75 000.

Patricia Mouncey commented that this revealed a weakness in their use of profit centres: the profit earned by each of the three centres will vary according to the way in which the business's rent and rates are divided up between the three areas.

1 Assume that Mouncey Engineering decide to divide up the costs of rent and rates between the three profit centres according to the value of sales revenue earned by each of the products. Their sales revenue for the last year were:

● the automatic valve – £400 000
● the pressure sensor – £800 000
● the sea-bed monitor – £600 000.

Using this approach, how much should each profit centre pay towards the business's rent and rates?

QUICK CHECK QUESTIONS

1 Complete the following sentence by filling in the missing two words. 'A .... centre is a part of a business for which costs and revenues (and hence ....) can be determined.'
2 Is the following statement true or false? 'A hospital can only operate cost centres.'
3 Which one of the following aspects of a business's operation might be a profit centre rather than a cost centre?

a) its accounts department
b) a newly launched brand
c) the security and maintenance teams
d) the administration section of the business.
4 Which of the following might not be a profit centre?
a) a well-established product
b) a restaurant
c) a the company's delivery vehicles
d) a production line in a factory.

5   Is the following sentence false or true? 'Cost and profit centres allow managers to identify less financially efficient aspects of the business and to take good decisions.'

6   Which of the following is **not** a reason for operating cost and profit centres?
a)   to improve the motivation of employees
b)   to reduce the workload of more junior employees
c)   to give a basis on which an appraisal system may be operated
d)   to compare the performance of various elements of the business.

7   Is the following statement true or false? 'Operating cost and profit centres is often accompanied by the delegation of authority down the organisation.'

8   Complete the following sentence by inserting the missing word. 'If junior employees are to manage cost and profit centres efficiently, the company may need to increase its expenditure on ……………'

9   Is the following statement true or false? 'Creating cost and profit centres may develop an unhealthy sense of rivalry between teams, areas or sections within the business.'

10   Complete the following sentence by inserting the missing word. 'Cost centres can play a part in setting …………, as once the cost is known it is possible to set a ………… to ensure that a business makes a …………'

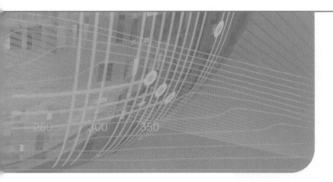

Progress questions

1   *Explain the distinction between a 'cost centre' and a 'profit centre'.* (5 marks)

2   *Outline the circumstances in which a business might decide to operate cost centres rather than profit centres.* (5 marks)

3   *Outline three ways in which a business might divide up its activities to create profit centres.* (6 marks)

4   *Explain two financial benefits that managers might expect as a result of creating cost centres within a business.* (6 marks)

5   *What benefits might the junior employees of a business receive as a result of the organisation adopting cost and profit centres?* (5 marks)

6   *Explain why a business might be able to improve its pricing policies (and profits) as a result of introducing cost and profit centres.* (7 marks)

7   *Outline the benefits that senior managers might gain from the widespread use of cost and profit centres within their business.* (7 marks)

8   *State two additional costs that a business might incur as a consequence of using cost and profit centres.* (2 marks)

9   *Explain two difficulties that a firm might encounter when attempting to divide up costs between several cost centres.* (6 marks)

10   *Outline two business situations in which cost and profit centres may be inappropriate.* (6 marks)

Analytical and evaluative questions

11 Naylor Ltd manufactures double-glazed doors and windows and operates in a highly competitive market. Analyse the benefits to the company of introducing cost centres. (8 marks)

12 Starbucks is a fast-growing coffee chain operating over 5000 outlets across the globe. Every one is operated as a profit centre. Discuss the case for and against this policy. (10 marks)

13 Cartwrights is a long-established family business. A recently appointed Chief Executive has decided to introduce cost centres into the organisation. Discuss reasons why employees might resist his move. (10 marks)

End of chapter questions

Case study

25 marks

Paul and Sarah Brooke run a garage in Leicester. The garage has a good reputation amongst local people for supplying quality second-hand cars at reasonable prices. Over the past six years, the garage has built up a steady custom in South Leicester. On reviewing the garage's accounts for the past year, Sarah calculated the key costs and revenues for the garage.

Cost or revenue	£
Fixed costs per annum	75 000
Average selling price per car	5000
Average costs of purchasing a car	3500

Sarah included all variable costs when calculating the average cost of buying a car from an individual or another garage. She pointed out to Paul that, because their fixed costs were high, it was worthwhile trying to sell as many cars as possible. She proposed that they should consider selling their cars at a lower average price – £4500 rather than the current £5000 per car. Sarah estimated that, if they had offered their cars at this lower price they might have sold an additional 40 cars over the past year. Paul was less sure about Sarah's proposal. 'People are interested in other things when buying a used car, apart from price. Anyway, I am not sure that making the largest profits possible means that your business is successful.'

1 What is meant by 'variable costs'? (2 marks)

2 Brooke Garage sold 112 cars during the last year.
   a) Calculate Sarah and Paul's profits using the data above.
   b) Calculate their profits, assuming that they reduced their average price by £500 as suggested by Sarah, and sold an additional 40 cars as a consequence. (6 marks)

3 Sarah and Paul are uncertain whether reducing the prices of their cars will increase the company's sales revenue. Examine the factors that may influence whether a price cut will increase Brooke Motors' sales revenue. 7 marks)

4 There are a number of ways to measure the success of a business. Discuss whether or not the level of profits is a good indicator of business success. (10 marks)

Case study

25 marks

It had seemed so promising just a few short months ago. Jon Plum had fulfilled his ambition to start up his own business building and supplying computers to local businesses and private customers. Jon had taken the plunge after he was made redundant. He had raised sufficient capital to purchase a lease on a shop with a large workshop at the back and to pay the start up costs of his business.

During the first few months, Jon had struggled to earn enough revenue to pay the business's bills. However, he was not disheartened – the bank manager had told him to expect this. Then he had some great news! A local college wanted him to supply 20 computers for a new teaching block they had just finished constructing. Jon thought that an order of this size was just what he needed to establish his business. He promised that he would have the computers installed by the middle of August.

A few months later Jon's business was in deep financial trouble. He had completed the order for the college and overseen the installation of the computers. The Principal of the college praised the quality of his work and promised more business in the future. However, he was still awaiting payment. In the meantime his business account had exceeded its overdraft limit by a large figure. Jon realised his business had been overtrading. And he had not paid the rent yet either . . .

1 What is meant by the term 'overtrading'. *(2 marks)*

2 Explain one benefit a small firm might gain from operating an overdraft. *(2 marks)*

3 Complete the table below by calculating:
   a) the closing balance for August
   b) the net monthly cash flow for September
   c) the net monthly cash flow for November. *(3 marks)*

4 Examine the sources of finance available to someone like Jon who is establishing a small business. *(8 marks)*

5 Discuss the actions that Jon might have taken to avoid the cash flow problems that he experienced. *(10 marks)*

	August	September	October	November
Cash sales	5500	7750	8000	8500
Credit sales		1000	500	950
Total inflow	5500	8750	8500	9450
Rent	2500	2500	2500	2500
Wages	1000	1000	1000	1000
Raw materials	10300	3500	4000	4250
Other costs	500	1500	1700	1750
Total outflow	14300	8500	9200	9500
Net monthly cash flow	(8800)	?	(700)	?
Opening Balance	500	(8300)	(8050)	(8750)
Closing Balance	?	(8050)	(8750)	(8800)

The Chalfont Gallery opened a year ago. Located in the prosperous village of Chalfont St Giles, the Gallery sells a range of works of art, such as oil paintings, water colours and sculptures. Jane Sawkins, the owner of the Gallery, is aware that her business has not made a profit during its first year of trading. Her accountant has advised her that she needs to carry out some financial planning to help improve her financial position. Acting on her accountant's advice, Jane has decided to set herself sales and profits targets for the coming financial year.

In its first year, the Gallery faced higher costs than Jane had expected. Her rent and rates were £110 000, insurance for the Gallery was £7500 and other overheads amounted to £32 500.

The Chalfont Gallery does not make a large number of sales, but normally earns a considerable profit on each sale. Jane has calculated that, on average, she pays £5000 for each work of art and sells it for £10 000.

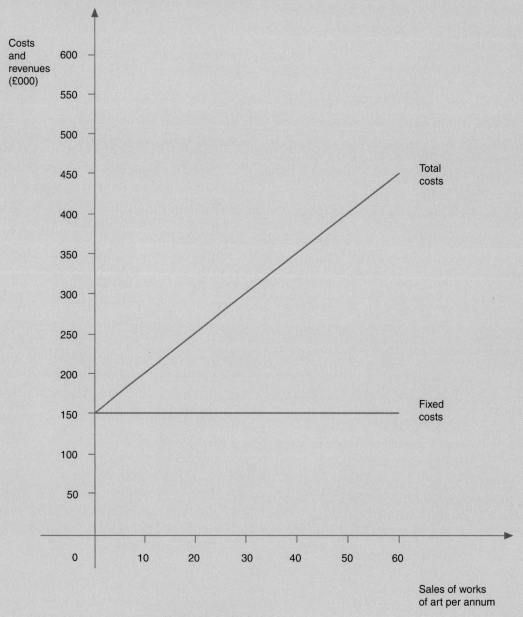

Figure 4.26 *Break-even chart for the Chalfont Gallery*

25 marks

1 *Explain the meaning of the term 'contribution'.*
(2 marks)

2 *Calculate the average contribution made to fixed costs from the sale of a single work of art.*
(5 marks)

3 a) *On the break-even chart (Figure 4.26) draw in the sales revenue line for The Chalfont Gallery and mark the level of break-even output.*
(4 marks)

b) *Jane has set herself a sales target of 50 works of art for the year. Illustrate and state the level of profits that The Chalfont Gallery would earn if it achieves this target.*
(5 marks)

4 *Jane's accountant advised her to use financial planning techniques such as cashflow forecasts and break-even analysis. Discuss the case for and against using such methods of financial planning.*
(9 marks)

Case study

80 marks

In spite of the take-over of many British car manufacturers, Britain retains a major, independent manufacturer of components for the motor industry. Perry-Carr Components was established in the 1930s by two engineers, Chris Perry and Stephen Carr, who realised that demand for the motor industry for components such as lights, exhausts and dashboards was likely to increase rapidly. The two engineers thought this was too good an opportunity to miss.

The company expanded rapidly in the 1950s, in spite of increasing competition from overseas. The 1970s saw Perry-Carr fight off a number of take-over bids, before becoming a public limited company in 1981. Since that time, and in spite of suffering a series of cash flow crises, Perry-Carr Components has steadily improved its position in the European motor components market.

The current Chief Executive, Ian Walker, was appointed two years ago with the task of developing a strategic plan for the company over the next five years. Previously, Walker had made his name doubling the sales of an electrical engineering group over a four-year period. He has won a reputation for being adventurous and tough, and is expected to introduce policies to continue Perry-Carr's growth.

The creation of the European Single Market offered the company a number of opportunities. The removal of many barriers to trading with the other members of the European Union made it easier for the company to sell their products to motor manufacturers throughout Europe. Perry-Carr Components eventually negotiated a large contract to supply components to the Volkswagen group. This has posed difficult questions for the company and has led Ian Walker to make the proposals set out below.

Ian Walker's Proposals – Selected Key Points

- The company should close its smallest UK factory and operate the others as separate profit centres.
- Perry-Carr needs further production capacity if it is to supply Volkswagen's increasing demand for components. A large-scale factory near to the Channel Tunnel would be an ideal base from which to meet the growing demand from Europe.
- The company should introduce a number of changes to the way the company is managed, including the delegation of budgets to managers of individual product lines within the company. The company also plans to extend the use of zero budgeting.
- The company would need to raise £100m to finance the closure of the small existing plant and the construction of a large factory near to the Channel Tunnel.
- The company expects to have to undertake considerable training to implement the proposals within this plan.

Some members of the Board of Directors are alarmed at Ian Walker's proposals. They fear that his plans for the company are too ambitious and that the company could face a number of financial problems during a period of rapid growth. Walker's opponents remember the company's previous cash flow difficulties and argue that a steady rate of expansion would be more manageable and less risky.

The table below shows selected budget figures for Perry-Carr's Reading factory 2002/2003.

Revenue/cost	Budget figure (£000)	Actual figure (£000)	Variance (£000)
Sales revenue	85 000	88 450	3 450
Overheads	14 615	14 837	(222)
Labour costs	21 225	24 115	(2 890)
Fuel costs	7 500	7 650	(150)
Raw material costs	24 500	27 000	(2 500)
Marketing costs	6 000	6 115	(115)
Other costs	2 100	2 035	65

1 Outline the possible reasons which might have led to the company suffering '... a series of cash flow crises ...'. *(8 marks)*

2 Discuss three ways in which Perry-Carr Components could raise the £100m they need to expand their business. *(18 marks)*

3 Consider the preparations that Perry-Carr Components would need to take before using profit centres in each of their factories. *(15 marks)*

4 a) Using the table above identify and explain possible causes of three significant variances. *(9 marks)*

b) Examine how the use of zero budgeting might help to improve Perry-Carr's financial management. *(12 marks)*

5 Discuss the financial problems that a large manufacturing business might encounter '... during a period of rapid growth'. *(18 marks)*

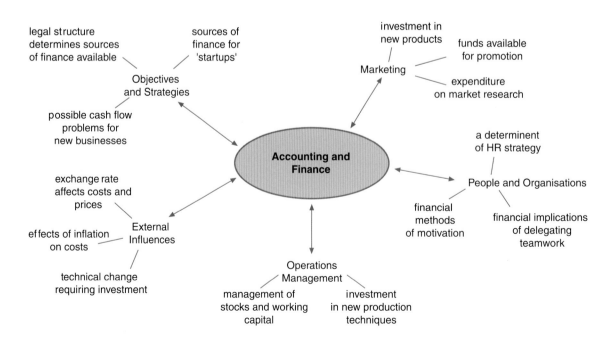

Figure 4.27 *Relationship between Accounting and Finance and other topics in the AS specification*

Introduction

- What are the different types of organisational structure and when are they used?
- How can businesses make effective use of human resources and how can they motivate their staff?
- What makes a good leader?
- How do different managers manage their staff? Is there a best style for a particular situation?

>> Organisational structures

What is an organisational structure?

An organisational structure is the way in which a business is arranged to carry out its activities. The organisational structure, which may be shown in an organisation chart, sets out:

- the routes by which communication passes through the business
- who has authority (and power) and responsibility within the organisation
- the roles and titles of individuals within the organisation
- the people to whom individual employees are accountable and those for whom they are responsible.

Figure 5.1 illustrates a simplified organisational chart for a large business.

Businesses change the structure of their organisation rapidly and regularly; some entrepreneurs believe that they should be continually reorganising their firms to meet the demands of a dynamic marketplace.

Key terms

Authority and responsibility – it is possible for a manager to delegate authority to a subordinate. However, responsibility must remain with the manager.

Organisation charts are diagrams representing the job titles and formal patterns of authority and responsibility within an organisation.

Shop-floor employees operate at the lowest level within an organisation and are normally directly involved in the production and supply of goods and services.

POINTS TO PONDER

In 2003 Tomkins, the engineering group, announced the completion of a three-year programme to restructure its organisation. The changes involved shutting 19 factories and the loss of 3400 jobs.

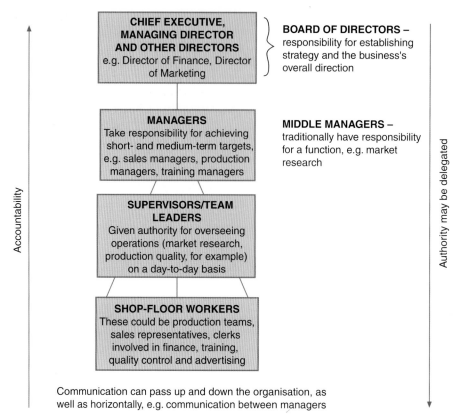

Figure 5.1 *A simplified organisational chart*

A principal reason for the regular change in organisational structures is the pace of external change. All businesses have to ensure that they are able to compete with rival firms. Keeping costs to a minimum is an important part of competing successfully and is a common factor causing businesses to change their organisational structures.

Key issues in organisational structures

Factors determining the structure adopted by an organisation include the number of levels or layers of hierarchy used and the extent of the span of control.

> **Key terms**
>
> **Levels of hierarchy** *refer to the number of layers of authority within an organisation. That is, how many levels exist between the Chief Executive and a shop-floor employee.*
> **A span of control** *is the number of subordinates directly responsible to a manager.*

Levels of hierarchy

Organisations with a large number of layers (or levels) of hierarchy are referred to as 'tall'. That is, there are a substantial number of people between the person at the top of the organisation and those at the bottom. Figure 5.2a and b illustrate both tall and flat types of structure.

Traditionally, UK businesses have tended to be tall. Such businesses have long chains of command from those at the top of the organisation to those at the bottom. Businesses with many layers of hierarchy frequently experience communication problems as messages moving up and down the organisation pass through many people.

> **Key terms**
>
> *The **chain of command** is the line of communication and authority existing within a business. Thus, a shop-floor worker reports to a supervisor who is responsible to a departmental manager, and so on...*

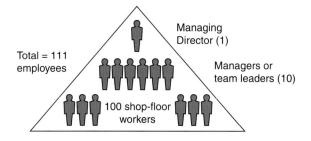

(a) A 'flat' organisational structure has few levels of hierarchy (three) and a wide span of control. Many UK businesses have implemented this form of organisational structure.

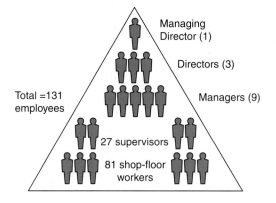

(b) A traditional 'tall' organisational structure has five layers of hierarchy and a narrow span of control (3). In spite of the firm employing more people, it has less shop-floor employees from the 'flat' stucture above.

Figure 5.2 a and b *'Flat' and 'Tall' organisational structures. Surveys of employees have shown that the majority prefers to work within a 'flat' organisation. Why might this type of structure be particularly popular with junior employees?*

Perhaps attracted by the prospect of faster and more effective communication, and influenced by Japanese and American companies, UK businesses have moved towards flatter organisational structures. This process of flattening structures (commonly termed delayering) has led to businesses operating with significantly wider spans of control. We consider delayering in more detail later in this unit.

Spans of control

Figure 5.3 illustrates a broad and a narrow span of control. An organisation with a wide span of control will have few layers of hierarchy – the 'flat' organisation in Figure 5.2a. Conversely, 'tall' organisations have many layers of hierarchy, but narrow spans of control.

A narrow span of control allows supervisors and managers to keep close control over the activities of the employees for whom they are responsible. As the span of control widens, the subordinate is likely to be able to operate with a greater degree of independence. This is because it is impossible for an individual to monitor closely the work of a large number of subordinates. A traditional view is that the span of control should not exceed six, if close supervision is to be maintained. However, where subordinates are carrying out similar duties, a span of control of 10 or even 12 is not unusual. It is normal for a span of control to be less at the top of organisation. This is because senior employees have more complex and diverse duties and are, therefore, more difficult to supervise.

Delayering

Delayering occurs when businesses remove one or more layers of hierarchy from the organisation. A number of businesses have implemented large-scale delayering programmes over recent years. Many businesses have removed middle managers from their organisational structures.

POINTS TO PONDER

Not everyone is impressed by delayering. In 2003, Cadbury Schweppes confirmed its intention to delayer its organisation to improve efficiency. Shareholders were wary of the policy and the company's shares fell by 6% in value.

The increasing level of competition in international markets, and particularly from businesses in the Far East, has forced UK firms to reduce their costs. Delayering the organisational structure is one way in which costs have been lowered.

Delayering has been encouraged further by the acceptance of management theories emphasising the benefits that may result from having fewer layers of hierarchy. Modern business writers have identified significant competitive benefits to be gained from giving relatively junior employees greater authority and control over their working lives. This combination of the need to reduce costs and the move to enhance the role of shop-floor employees has led to cuts in middle managers' jobs. Delayering creates 'flatter' organisations which some describe as 'leaner and more responsive'.

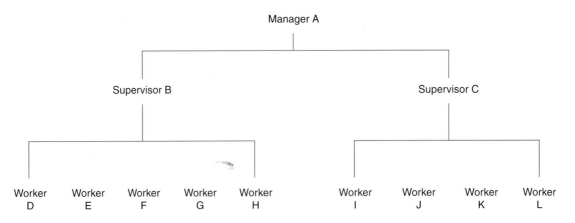

Figure 5.3 *Spans of control*
Manager A has a span of control of two. This is because the two supervisors B and C are the only employees directly responsible to her. Supervisor B has the widest span of control – five workers are responsible to him.

Centralisation and decentralisation

Centralisation and decentralisation are opposites. A centralised organisation is one where the majority of decisions are taken by senior managers at the top (or centre) of the business. Centralisation can provide rapid decision-making, as few people are likely to be consulted. It should also ensure that the business pursues the objectives set by senior managers.

Decentralisation gives greater authority to employees lower down the organisational structure. In the 1980s and early 1990s many businesses decentralised for a number of reasons.

Advantages	Disadvantages
● Delayering reduces costs by removing a number of expensive middle managers.	● Delayering can lessen organisational performance as valuable knowledge and experience may be lost.
● Delayering can improve responsiveness by bringing senior managers and customers closer together.	● Morale and motivation may suffer because employees feel insecure.
● Delayering can motivate employees lower down in the organisation by giving them greater authority and control over their working lives.	● Some businesses may merely use the excuse of delayering for making a large number of employees redundant.
● Communication may improve as a consequence of delayering since there are less levels of hierarchy for a message to pass through.	● Because delayering means employees have to take on new roles within the organisation, extensive (and expensive) retraining may be required.
● It can produce good ideas from a new perspective as shop-floor employes take some decisions.	● Delayering can lead to intolerable workloads and high levels of stress amongst employees.

Table 5.1 *The advantages and disadvantages of delayering*

- Decentralisation provides subordinates with the opportunity to fulfil needs such as achievement and recognition by working on **delegated tasks**. This should improve motivation and reduce the business's costs by, for example, reducing the rate of labour turnover.
- Decentralisation is doubly beneficial to management. It reduces the workload on senior managers allowing them to focus on strategic (rather than operational) issues. At the same time it offers junior managers an opportunity to develop their skills in preparation for a more senior position.

The government has encouraged organisations in the public sector to decentralise. For example, it has championed the cause of foundation hospitals, which would be run by local communities rather than the National Health Service.

> ### Key terms
>
> **Delegation** *is the passing of authority (but not responsibility) down the organisation structure. Thus, a junior manager might be given the authority to conduct a market research campaign, but responsibility for the overall success of the campaign remains with the senior employee.*

Organisational structures

Businesses can adopt a number of structures according to the size of the organisation, the environment in which it operates and the personal preferences of the owners and senior managers.

Formal or traditional hierarchies

This structure gives all employees a clearly defined role, as well as establishing their relationships with other employees in the business. It is common for this type of organisational structure to be based on departments and, because of the dependence upon agreed procedures, it can be bureaucratic.

This type of structure normally has a number of other associated features:

- It is a relatively 'tall' hierarchy with narrow spans of control.

- The organisation will be centralised with the most important decisions taken by senior managers.
- Hierarchy is important and senior managers expect to be treated with respect.
- Tradition is important and change is often implemented slowly.

Communication in formal organisations is principally downwards and uses established routes moving down from senior to junior employees.

Traditional hierarchies allow specialists to operate within their area of expertise, such as marketing. They can generate new and very innovative ideas, but other areas of the business may be unaware of such developments. Employees understand lines of command and communication, and the position of their department or unit within the organisation. All employees appreciate the possibilities for promotion existing within the business.

The disadvantages of this structure can become more apparent as the organisation grows in size. Departments may bid for resources in an attempt to increase their prestige within the business, rather than because this will benefit the organisation. Furthermore, as the business becomes larger, decision-making can become slower as communication has to pass through many layers. Coordinating the business's attempts to achieve its objectives become difficult. Senior managers can become remote and may take decisions inappropriate to local situations or to the needs of particular groups of customers.

Traditional organisational structures can be found in the following types of businesses.

- Long-established businesses, such as merchant banks in the City of London.
- Family businesses operating on a relatively small scale.

Matrix structures

This type of organisational structure is task-orientated and is intended to overcome many of the problems associated with the traditional or hierarchical structure. It is a combination of a vertical chain of command operated through department or units and horizontal organisation of

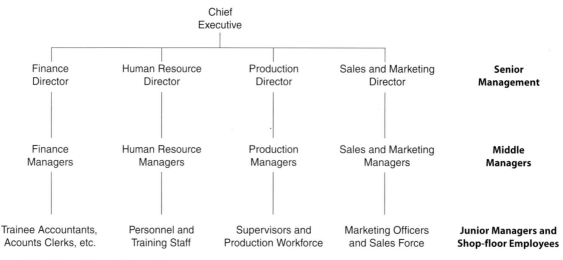

Figure 5.4 *A traditional hierarchy*

project or product teams. A typical matrix structure is illustrated in Figure 5.5.

Businesses using matrix structures develop teams of individuals with the specialist skills necessary to complete a given project. Each individual within the project team brings a particular skill and carries appropriate responsibilities. The aim is to allow all individuals to use their talents effectively, irrespective of their position within the organisation. So, a project manager looking to develop a new product may be able to call on IT and design skills from relatively junior employees elsewhere in the organisation.

Matrix structures focus on the task in hand. Launching a new product, opening new retail outlets, closing down factories or entering overseas

Advantages	Disadvantages
• Authority and responsibility are clearly established.	• The organisation can be slow to respond to customer needs.
• Specialist managers can be used effectively.	
• The promotion path is clearly signposted.	• Communication, and especially horizontal communication, can be poor.
• Employees frequently very loyal to their department within the business.	• Inter-departmental rivalry may occur at expense of performance of business as a whole.

Table 5.2 *The advantages and disadvantages of traditional hierarchies*

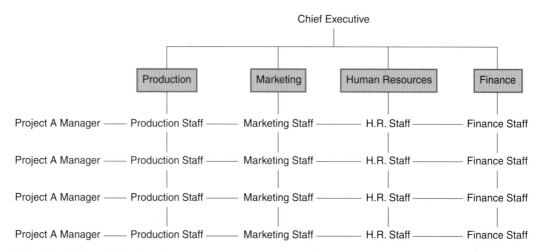

Figure 5.5 *A typical matrix structure*

Advantages	Disadvantages
● Focuses on tasks necessary for business success.	● Employees can have divided responsibilities.
● Encourages organisations to be flexible and responsive to customers' needs.	● Conflict can occur between project and departmental managers, reducing the performance of the organisation.
● Motivates and develops employees by providing varied and challenging tasks.	● Heavy expenditure on support staff may be required.

Table 5.3 *The advantages and disadvantages of matrix structures*

markets are examples of projects. Project groups often have strong senses of identity, despite being drawn from various areas in the business. This is because they are pursuing a clearly defined objective which provides team members with a sense of purpose and responsibility.

Matrix structures are often used by businesses such as advertising agencies who manage a number of customer projects simultaneously.

Entrepreneurial structures

These are frequently found in businesses operating in competitive markets and particularly in those where rapid decisions are essential. News organisations, for example Sky News, often operate with an entrepreneurial structure. A few key workers at the core of the organisation – frequently the owners in the case of small businesses – make all the major decisions. The business is heavily dependent upon the knowledge and skills of these key workers. Power radiates from the centre under this structure as illustrated in Figure 5.6.

Entrepreneurial structures are suited to markets where rapid decisions are essential and where organisations are small enough to be controlled effectively by a few trusted employees. It is a structure frequently used by charismatic and dynamic leaders: Alan Sugar used this approach to manage his electronics company Amstrad during the

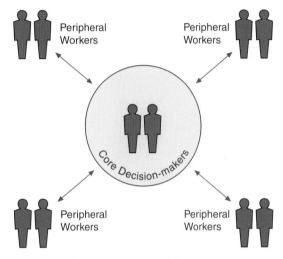

Figure 5.6 *The entrepreneurial structure*

early years of the business. Because all-important decisions are taken at the centre, little use is made of hierarchies and the organisation is relatively 'flat'.

However, there are distinct drawbacks to the entrepreneurial structure. Its effectiveness depends upon two factors:

1 The quality of management and decision-making by the 'core' employees. If decisions are delayed or if the workers lose touch with the market, the business is unlikely to perform effectively.
2 As the business grows, the 'core' employees experience increasing difficulty in managing the business. The work may overwhelm them and the quality (and speed) of decisions may suffer. At this point the business may adopt another structure.

Informal structures

This type of structure exists where the organisation does not have an obvious structure. This is common in the case of professional practices (lawyers, for example) where members operate as a team. The

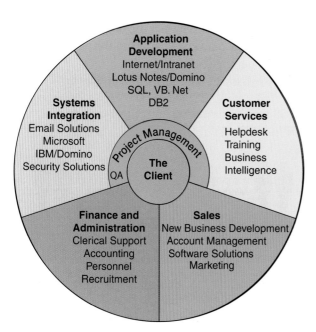

Figure 5.7 *The informal organisational structure at Nexus Technology Ltd*

Source: www.nexus-technology.com

professionals normally receive administrative support from others within the organisation.

This form of organisational structure allows highly trained and motivated employees to organise their working lives and to take decisions with a high degree of independence. However, it is less appropriate for many businesses as it lacks co-ordination and control by senior managers.

Factors determining organisational structures

When deciding upon an organisational structure a business will be subject to both internal and external influences.

Internal factors

The following internal factors all influence the organisational structure to some extent.

The size of the business

As the scale of the business increases, an

entrepreneurial structure, for example, becomes unsuitable. As the business grows further, the chain of command is likely to be lengthened, encouraging the removal of some layers of hierarchy and broader spans of control.

The nature of the product

If the firm supplies a diverse range of products it may organise itself traditionally – perhaps in the form of divisions reporting to the board of directors. The Rank Organisation operates in this way with key areas of the business, such as film services and leisure activities such as the Hard Rock Cafes, having some degree of independence.

The skills of the workforce

The higher the level of skill the typical employee has, the more likely it is that businesses will organise along matrix or informal lines. A small group of professionals may simply carry out their professional duties with administrative support from the organisation. Less skilled employees may respond better to a more formal structure with more authority retained further up the hierarchy.

The culture of the organisation

This is a major influence on the structure the firm adopts. If a business has a highly innovative culture whereby it wishes to be a market leader selling advanced products, it may adopt a matrix structure to minimise bureaucracy and to allow teams to carry out the necessary research and development, and market research. On the other hand, an organisation which places importance on tradition (and wants to appear conventional) may be best suited to a formal, hierarchical structure. This structure places emphasis on positions rather than people and this factor encourages the continuance of existing policies and practices. Some high-class hotels may fall into this category.

The strategic objectives of the business

An innovative and highly competitive organisation may opt for a matrix structure in order to complete tasks effectively. On the other hand, a business focusing on quality of design and production (as opposed to growth) may suit an entrepreneurial

Business in focus

Information resources and research services for corporate and private clients.
Good morning! How are you?

Professional Researcher supplies online support to lecturers, journalists and writers researching a variety of subjects and especially those relating to business and politics. The business was started as a collaboration of Lancaster University students, who started out by pooling knowledge to help each other find information online.

The Professional Researcher website was first launched on 22 August 1999. The site was developed pretty much as a 'hobby' with limited resources and very limited manpower available.

For the first couple of years the business struggled because of its 'virtual organisation' status. Professional Researcher has no central office and no 'business address'. Every member of the team works from home and communicates via email, instant messaging and via the telephone. Some of the team work from home offices, some from computers in the bedroom and in one case from a computer in the kitchen.

Professional Researcher does not have an organisation chart. It has minimal structure. The latter structure may be appropriate for businesses in a craft industry.

'organisation' in terms of hierarchy and job titles. Those titles that we do have were often created solely to provide those outside of the firm with a framework within which to work. For example, when one of the team speaks with a client about a proposed research project he acts as a Research Manager. When he speaks with the Bank Manager or a supplier he uses the title CEO or Managing Director. These titles reflect to 'outsiders' the fact that he is authorised to make certain decisions on behalf of the organisation, but they are all meaningless within the organisation.

Professional Researcher has eight employees who are organised around the functions that are carried out. In essence there is an accounts department and a marketing department, etc., but none of the team is labelled accounts staff or marketing staff – these roles are carried out by the team as required.

Source: Adapted from Professional Researcher,
www.pro-researcher.co.uk

1 What factors have influenced Professional Researcher's structure (or lack of it)?
2 What are the advantages and disadvantages of operating an unstructured organisation?

External factors

The environment in which the business is operating is important. Fierce competitive pressures may encourage delayering in an effort to reduce costs, whilst rapid change may require a matrix structure to ensure that the organisation can remain competitive. The matrix structure would also eliminate the possibility of inflexible hierarchies getting in the way of rapid decision-making.

Business in focus

Lloyds TSB is to become the latest British financial services group to move jobs to India, expanding its workforce in the country to 1500 staff by the end of next year. The high street bank said a pilot programme it began in Bangalore in May to process new bank account and credit card applications had been highly successful, convincing management that a larger operation could provide a swift and effective service to its customers.

As a result, Lloyds TSB will expand the Bangalore site, where it currently has 250 staff, and build a new operation in Hyderabad, India's fifth largest city. Lloyds TSB said the Indian jobs being created could include back-office processing and work currently carried out by British call centres. About 20 000 of Lloyds TSB's 79 000 staff work in these operations in Britain.

Source: Adapted from www.telegraph.co.uk, 25 September 2003

1 Many businesses are moving part of their operations overseas. Discuss the implications of this trend for the types of organisational structures that are used.

QUICK CHECK QUESTIONS

1 Which of the following will be shown on an organisational chart?
a) the roles and titles of people within the organisation
b) the names and addresses of customers
c) details of suppliers
d) the business's stakeholders.

2 Complete the following sentence by filling in the missing words. 'It is possible for a manager to .... authority to a subordinate. However, ... must remain with the manager.'

3 Of what is the following a definition: The number of layers within an organisation?

4 Of what is the following a definition: The number of subordinates directly responsible to a manager?

5 Which of the following is **not** associated with a 'tall' hierarchical structure?
a) many levels of hierarchy within the organisation
b) wide spans of control
c) a long chain of command
d) a large number of people between the person at the top and those at the bottom of the organisation.

6 Complete the following sentence by filling in the missing terms. 'A ...... organisational structure contains few levels of hierarchy but a ...... span of control.'

7 Which group of employees are most likely to lose their jobs as a result of a policy of delayering?
a) directors
b) senior managers
c) middle managers
d) supervisors.

8 Complete the following sentence by filling in the missing terms. 'A .... organisation is one where the .... of decisions are taken by senior managers at the ...... of the organisation.'

9 Which type of organisational structure gives employees a clearly defined role, as well as establishing their relationships with other employees in the organisation?
a) formal or traditional structure
b) matrix structure
c) entrepreneurial structure
d) informal structure.

10 Which type of organisational structure might be most suitable for a business trading in a competitive market where rapid decisions are needed?
a) formal or traditional structure
b) matrix structure
c) entrepreneurial structure
d) informal structure.

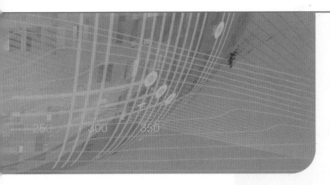

Progress questions

1 State two factors that can be discovered about a business from examining its organisational chart. *(2 marks)*

2 Explain the benefits a business might gain from operating wider spans of control. *(7 marks)*

3 Outline two reasons why a business might choose to delayer its organisational structure. *(6 marks)*

4 Explain why the drawbacks of delayering might be experienced in the short term whereas the benefits would only be felt in the long term. *(7 marks)*

5 Outline one advantage to junior employees and one advantage to senior managers that may result from an organisation decentralising. *(4 marks)*

6 Outline three common features found in organisations with traditional hierarchies. *(6 marks)*

7 Explain the circumstances in which a business might benefit from the use of a matrix structure. *(6 marks)*

8 Explain why an entrepreneurial structure becomes more difficult to operate effectively as the organisation grows. *(6 marks)*

9 Explain why an informal structure is appropriate to organisations employing professional and highly-skilled employees. *(6 marks)*

10 Do you consider internal or external factors to be more important in determining the structure adopted by an organisation? Explain your answer. *(7 marks)*

Analytical and evaluative questions

11 GX Consulting Ltd provides specialist financial advice to companies trading internationally. Examine the benefits the company might receive from operating an informal structure. *(8 marks)*

12 Jaguar, one of the UK's leading manufacturers of luxury cars, enjoyed record sales in 2002 and 2003. The company has delayered in recent years. To what extent might delayering have contributed to the company's recent success? *(15 marks)*

13 A major UK supermarket uses wide spans of control throughout the organisation. Discuss the case for and against this approach. *(15 marks)*

>> Theories of motivation

Why is motivation important?

Motivation can be the will to work due to enjoyment of the work itself. This implies that motivation comes from within an individual employee. An alternative view of motivation is that it is the will or desire to achieve a given target or goal. The first of these definitions assumes that motivation lies within employees, the other that it is the result of some external stimuli.

Whatever its nature, motivation is an important factor for all businesses. Organisations whose workforces possess high levels of motivation might show a number of characteristics including :

- a low level of absenteeism by employees at all levels within the business
- relatively few employees deciding to leave the organisation giving a low level of labour turnover
- good industrial relations

- high levels of productivity from the labour force.

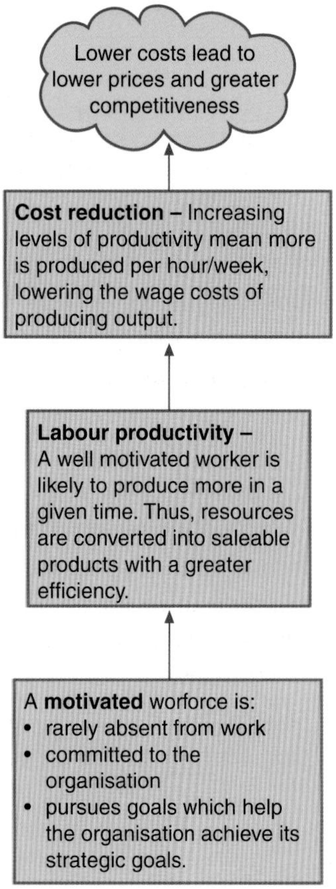

Key terms

Motivation describes the factors within individuals that arouse, maintain and channel behaviour towards a goal. More simply, it is the will to work.
Productivity measures the relationship between the resources put into an activity and the resulting output.

It is factors which lead to improved productivity that are perhaps most important. A business that enjoys the benefit of a highly motivated workforce is also likely to have a productive workforce. Low production costs offer firms two opportunities:

1 to sell their products more cheaply
2 to maintain price levels and enjoy greater profits.

Figure 5.8 *How motivation can aid productivity*

MATHS MOMENT $1+1=2$

Month	Worker hours	Output	Labour productivity per hour
January	12 000	360 000	30
February	12 500	375 000	30
March	12 500	400 000	?
April	12 000	390 000	?
May	13 000	422 500	?

Table 5.4 *Productivity measures for Shire Products Ltd*

1 Complete the table above by calculating labour productivity for March, April and May.
2 If Shire Products Ltd achieved a rate of labour productivity per hour of 34 in June, how many worker hours would be needed to produce an output of 448 800 units during the month?

A high level of motivation within a workforce offers a business other benefits too:

- Motivated employees are normally contented, making it easier for businesses to attract other employees – the firm will have a reputation as a 'good' employer.
- Modern businesses protect their public image and spend vast sums of money to enhance it. The motivation (and thus the performance) of the workforce can be an important element of creating a positive corporate image.
- Over recent years, firms have become increasingly aware of the need to compete in terms of quality and customer service. If businesses are to compete in these ways, motivated employees are essential.

POINTS TO PONDER

Employers and employees do not agree about what motivates people at work. A survey revealed that nearly 90% of employers believe that money is the main motivator whilst employees only rank pay fourth (behind interest, security and achievement).

Source: Adapted from Bulletpoint, 1996

How can businesses motivate employees?

Many different views exist on motivation, and they differ because it is not clear why people work. Is it to gain money, to enjoy social interaction with other humans or to fulfil personal needs such as achievement and recognition? If managers can identify why people work they can determine how best to motivate them at work. The varying reasons why people work underpins the theories put forward by the various **schools of thought** on motivation.

Key terms

Division of labour is the breaking down of production into a series of small tasks carried out repetitively by relatively unskilled employees.

The School of Scientific Management

Motivating workers became an important issue as the size of businesses increased in the late nineteenth century. Managers developed the **division of labour** to its fullest extent in an attempt to increase efficiency and improve competitiveness. The introduction of mass production methods along with the use of division of labour increased

School of thought	Key writers	Essential ideas
Scientific School	Frederick Winslow TAYLOR (1856–1917)	Motivation is an external factor achieved through money. Employees should be closely supervised and paid piece-rate. **Time and motion** studies determine efficient means of production and workers are trained and told how to operate.
Human Relations School	Elton MAYO (1880–1949)	This brought sociological theory into management and accepted that employees could be motivated by meeting their social needs. More attention was given to the social dimension of work (e.g. communication, working as groups and consultation between managers and employees).
The Neo-Human Relations School of Management	Abraham MASLOW (1908–1970) and Frederick HERZBERG (1923–2000)	This school highlighted the importance of fulfilling psychological needs to improve employee performance. Motivation, according to Maslow and Herzberg, depended upon designing jobs to fulfil psychological needs.

Table 5.5 *Schools of thought on motivation*

People in business

Taylor was born in Philadelphia in March 1856, the son of a lawyer. Taylor was a brilliant scholar and, after attending Harvard University, trained as an engineer. He spent many years working for Midvale Steel Company in Philadelphia, eventually becoming chief engineer.

Whilst at Midvale, he introduced work-study. Under this technique he observed employees at work and suggested ways of eliminating wasted time and effort by workers. This became the basic principle of his scientific approach to management.

Taylor was a talented inventor, but he decided to become a consultant to spread his ideas on scientific management. His most notable work was at the Bethlehem Steel Company, where his ideas achieved enormous increases in productivity.

Taylor retired at the age of 45. He spent much of his remaining life as a writer and lecturer. His most notable book was The *Principles of Scientific Management*, published in 1911. Taylor died in 1915, having had a profound impact upon the management of business.

Figure 5.9 *F. W. Taylor*

the numbers of people working in factories. At the same time, their tasks became monotonous.

Against this background, managers began to investigate ways of increasing employee motivation to improve competitiveness and employee satisfaction. Frederick Winslow Taylor was the most notable of these early writers on motivation and became known as 'the father of scientific management'.

Taylor began to advise and lecture on management practices and became a consultant to car manufacturer Henry Ford. Taylor's theories were based on a simple interpretation of human behaviour, that people were motivated solely by money – his term was 'rational man'. He combined this principle with a simple interpretation of the role of the manager: to operate the business with maximum efficiency.

The key elements of Taylorism

1 The starting point of Taylor's approach was work-study. He measured and analysed the tasks necessary to complete the production process. He used a stopwatch to measure how long various activities took and sought the most efficient methods of completing tasks. He encouraged the use of the division of labour, breaking down production into small tasks.

2 From this he identified the most efficient employees and the approaches they adopted. Using these as a basis, he then detailed 'normal' times in which duties should be completed and assessed individual performance against these norms.

3 Employees were provided with the equipment necessary to carry out their tasks. This principle extended to giving stokers (men shovelling coal) a shovel of a size appropriate to their physique to maximise their efficiency. They were also given elementary training and clear instructions on their duties.

4 Because, according to Taylor, employees were only motivated by money, the final stage of the system was to design and implement a piece-rate pay system. Under a piece-rate system employees are paid according to the amount they produce. Taylor, however, developed differential piece-rate systems to encourage efficiency amongst employees.

Taylor also believed in close supervision of the workforce to ensure that they continued to make the maximum effort possible, motivated by pay.

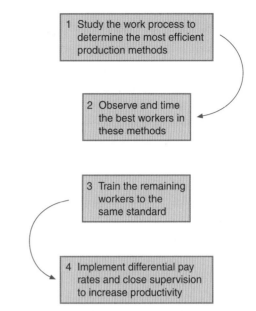

Figure 5.10 *The essential features of Taylorism*

Taylor's views were unpopular with shop-floor employees. His systems forced them to work hard and, by raising productivity levels, placed the jobs of the less efficient workers under threat. Taylor's approach raised efficiency and productivity. Therefore, businesses did not need as many employees. Taylor's ideas resulted in strikes and other forms of industrial action by dissatisfied workers.

Taylor's legacy
It is easy to dismiss Taylor and his ideas. His entire philosophy was based on the belief that employees were motivated only by money. He ignored any social dimension of employment and made employees work very hard for what was a meagre wage. His ideas resulted in workers endlessly completing monotonous tasks. There was considerable hostility towards his ideas and opposition from politicians and the business community.

However, Taylor made a significant and enduring contribution to the management of business organisations. He established management as a scientific subject worthy of research and study. His approach was adopted by many premier figures in the business community in the early decades of the century, including Henry Ford. His techniques encouraged the use of mass production and the conveyor belt system. Furthermore, his work provided a starting point for a later and more people-centred approach to management.

MATHS MOMENT

$1 + 1 = 2$

Under a piece-rate system, employees are paid according to the quantity they produce. Taylor supported several bands of payment, such as that set out below.

Output range (units per day)	Payment per unit of production
0–50	£0.50
51–80	£1.00
80+	£1.50

Table 5.6 *Taylor's pay system*

Under this system, an efficient and productive employee could earn a reasonable wage by producing say, 60 units of output daily. In these circumstances, he or she would earn £35 (50 × £0.50 + 10 × £1.00). On the other hand, a less productive employee might struggle to earn an acceptable wage.

1 Calculate the earnings of an employee *per five-day week* if he produced (a) 46 units and (b) 87 units.

The Human Relations School of Thought

A fundamental weakness of the Scientific School was that its work ignored the social needs of employees. This, and the obvious unpopularity of the ideas of Taylor, led to the development of the Human Relations School. This school of thought concentrated on the sociological aspects of work. Its foremost member was an Australian-born psychologist, Elton Mayo (1880–1949). Initially, Mayo was one of Taylor's disciples, believing in the importance of scientific management to business efficiency.

The Hawthorne effect

Mayo's views altered as a result of research he conducted at the Western Electric Company in Chicago. The research was to examine the effects of changes in lighting on the productivity of workers at the company's Hawthorne plant. Previous experiments on lighting and productivity had produced unexpected results. Researchers had anticipated that improving lighting would increase productivity because giving workers better working conditions would allow them to work harder and earn more money. They were astonished when productivity increased in the group enjoying improved lighting and amongst a group whose lighting had not changed.

It became apparent that the employees were responding to the level of attention they were receiving as part of the investigations and because they were working together as a group.

This became known as the 'Hawthorne effect'. As a result of this and similar experiments, Mayo stressed the importance of 'social man' within the workplace. From these experiments Mayo concluded that motivation was dependent upon:

- the type of job being carried out and the type of supervision given to the employee
- group relationships, group morale and the sense of worth possessed by individuals.

The implications of the 'Hawthorne effect'

Following the publication of Mayo's findings, managers gradually became more aware of the importance of meeting the social needs of individuals at work. Social environments at work and informal working groups were recognised as having positive influences upon productivity.

The acceptance of Mayo's views led to a number of developments in businesses during the 1940s and 1950s, many of which remain today:

- Personnel departments were established to ensure that employees' social needs were met at work wherever possible.
- Employees were provided with a range of sporting and social facilities to foster the development of informal groups amongst employees.
- Works outings and trips became a familiar part of an employee's year – Marks & Spencer organises short-break weekends for its employees.
- Managers gave more attention to teams and **teamworking**.

Mayo's recognition of the importance of teamworking is perhaps his most enduring testimony. Many firms have organised their workforce into teams, for example, John Lewis and Toshiba (for more information about John Lewis, visit *www.john-lewis-partnership.co.uk*). We shall consider teamworking in more detail later in this chapter.

By 2003 over two million employees worked at home using modern technology. The Department of Trade and Industry has published guidelines on motivating teleworkers, and especially on overcoming the effects of isolation.

Many students just think of Mayo in terms of communicating with bosses, and also social and sporting facilities. This is only part of his work. He advocated the benefits to employers and employees of working in teams – this aspect of his work is an important issue within many businesses today.

Mayo's work took management in general and motivation in particular forward. He moved the focus onto the needs of employees, rather than just the needs of the organisation.

Business in focus

A survey, conducted in 2003, has shown that money is not the most influential factor when people are choosing a job. Over 30% of the 4000 respondents preferred flexible working hours to an increase in salary of £1000 a year.

Making sure that they were able to devote sufficient time to their families as well as to work was a crucial matter for employees at all levels within businesses.

Many businesses are offering employees more flexible working weeks and the government is supporting this development. A Department of Trade and Industry spokesperson commented that employees would be more productive if they were motivated by being able to balance working and domestic lives successfully. Since April 2003 parents with children aged under six have had the legal right to request flexible working hours. Employers are only able to refuse this request for 'good business reasons'.

1 Does this survey indicate that the techniques needed to motivate employees change over time?

The Neo-Human Relations School of Thought

This could also be called the new Human Relations School. Abraham Maslow and Frederick Herzberg are recognised as key members of this particular school. They began to put forward their views in the 1950s. Whilst the Human Relations School, associated with Elton Mayo, highlighted the sociological aspects of work, the Neo-Human Relations School considered the psychological aspects of employment. This school argued that motivation lies *within* each individual employee: managers merely need the key to unlock the motivational force.

By focussing on the psychological needs of employees, Maslow and Herzberg encouraged managers to treat their employees as individuals with different needs and aspirations. Their work emphasised that, because people are different, the techniques required to motivate individuals will also differ.

Maslow's hierarchy of needs

In 1954, Maslow published his 'hierarchy of needs' setting out the various needs that, he argued, every one attempted to meet through working. Maslow presented his hierarchy of needs as a triangle with basic needs shown at the bottom and his so-called higher needs towards the top. Maslow's hierarchy of needs is illustrated in Figure 5.11.

Maslow's argument was a relatively simple one. Employees, he argued, have a series of needs they seek to fulfil at work. These are in a hierarchy – once a lower level need is satisfied, individuals strive to satisfy needs further up the hierarchy. Abraham Maslow established five levels of human needs that can be satisfied through employment.

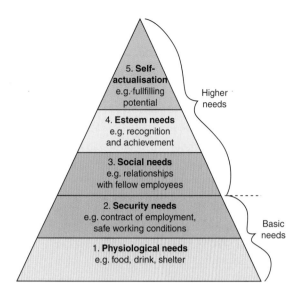

Figure 5.11 *Maslow's hierarchy of needs*

The key point of Maslow's argument was that a business could motivate its employees by offering them the chance to fulfil a higher level of need once a lower one was satisfied. Thus once an employee's basic needs had been met, perhaps through a fair pay system, he or she could be motivated further by the offer of secure and continuing employment. Similarly, a worker whose social needs were met through employment could next be motivated by the opportunity to satisfy self-esteem needs. This could be achieved by taking responsibility for a major project, offering the chance of achievement and recognition.

Maslow's theory was attractive to managers from the outset. It offered a more individualistic approach to motivating employees, recognising that not all people are the same. Managers had long realised that what motivated one person, would not motivate for another. Maslow's theory offered an explanation and an alternative approach for managers.

Frederick Herzberg's two-factor theory

Herzberg's two-factor theory was the result of a study designed to test the view that people face two major sets of influences at work. Herzberg's resulting theory was based on the results to questions asked of 200 accountants and engineers in the USA.

The first part of Herzberg's motivation theory is related to the environment of the job. He identified a range of factors that shaped the environment in which people work and he called these influences hygiene or maintenance factors. These factors are all around the job, but are not a part of the job itself. Herzberg's research identified a number of hygiene factors, including the following:

- company policies and administration
- supervision of employees

Maslow's level of need	Examples	Means of satisfying needs
1 Physiological needs	Food, water, shelter, clothing	Through pay and a warm and dry working environment
2 Security needs	A safe and secure working environment for employees	Implementing a proper health and safety policy, providing employees with contracts of employment
3 Social needs	Contact and friendships with other employees	Social and sporting facilities, opportunities to work in groups
4 Esteem needs	Achievement, recognition and self-respect	Delegating authority to junior employees, offering promotion opportunities
5 Self-actualisation	To fulfil one's potential completely	Providing opportunities to take new responsibilities and to develop new skills

Table 5.7 *An explanation of Maslow's hierarchy of needs*

- working conditions
- salary
- relationship with fellow workers (at the same level).

Herzberg's crucial finding was that hygiene factors do not lead to motivation, but without them employees may become dissatisfied. Thus, according to Herzberg, an employee cannot be motivated by pay, but might be dissatisfied by inadequate financial rewards. Hygiene factors were so named because Herzberg believed attention to them would prevent hygiene problems. It is important to note that Herzberg's research classified pay as a hygiene factor and, therefore, as unable to motivate.

The second finding of Herzberg's research established those factors with the ability to motivate – the motivators. These factors relate to the job itself and can be used to positively motivate employees. He identified the following factors as motivators:

- personal achievement of goals and targets
- recognition for achievement
- interest in the work itself
- responsibility for greater and more complex duties
- personal growth and advancement.

Herzberg believed that these approaches (hygiene and motivation) must be used simultaneously. Employees should be managed so they have a minimum of dissatisfaction. They should get achievement, recognition for achievement, take interest in their work and be given responsibility to allow them to grow and develop within their work.

Assessing the work of the Neo-Human Relations School

The research and writing of Maslow and Herzberg has had a major impact on the way in which businesses have managed their employees. Although there are differences in their approaches, many similarities also exist. As illustrated in Figure 5.15, Herzberg's motivators broadly correspond with Maslow's higher needs.

Both have the major advantage in that they were not simply theoretical writings – practical implications for management were within the

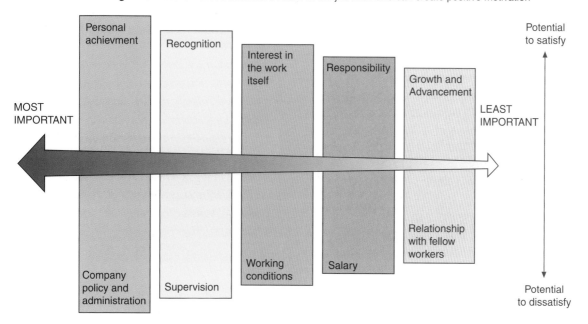

Herzberg's motivators – these **satisfiers** relate to the job itself and can create positive motivation

Herzberg's hygiene factors – these relate to the job environment and have the potential to dissatisfy

Figure 5.12 *Herzberg's hygiene and motivational factors*

Business in focus

Union leaders in the United States have voiced criticisms of the giant global retailer Wal-Mart. Jill Cashen of America's United Food and Commercial Workers Union (UFCW) commented: 'The Wal-Mart future is bleak. In our country, it is a future with not much money, few health benefits and little job security. We would encourage workers in the UK to avoid Wal-Mart.'

Figure 5.13 *In 2000 Wal-Mart purchased ASDA, one of Britain's leading supermarkets*

The company insists it will accept its prospective British employees' union arrangements, pointing out it has earned plaudits in the UK for good employee relations since acquiring ASDA. Nonetheless, Wal-Mart's workforce in America is completely non-union; unions staged anti-Wal-Mart rallies in 40 American cities in 2002. The only union success at a Wal-Mart branch was short lived. In 2000, staff in the butcher's department at a store in Jacksonville, Texas, voted to join a union. Shortly afterwards, in what Wal-Mart insists was an unrelated move, it closed the department.

Wal-Mart acknowledges that it keeps a close eye on wage costs, but argues that it motivates employees with flexible hours, consultation and fast promotion. The company is also popular for making large donations to charities.

1 To what extent do the actions of Wal-Mart support the views of Maslow and Herzberg regarding theories of motivation?

	Maslow	Herzberg
Motivation Factors (higher needs)	• Self-acualisation needs • Esteem needs • (Higher needs)	• Achievement • Recognition • Responsibility • Interest in work • Personal growth
Maintenance Factors (lower needs)	• Social needs • Security needs • Physiological needs • (Mainly lower needs)	• Company policy and administration • Supervision • Working conditions • Relationship with fellow workers

Figure 5.14 *Herzberg and Maslow compared*

theories. Both authors encouraged managers to utilise their employees' abilities by giving them challenging tasks.

Weaknesses do exist within these theories, of course. Herzberg's assertion that pay cannot be used to motivate might be true of many employees in wealthy, developed economies. However, this may not be the case with workers in poorer, developing countries. Equally, Maslow's theory is based upon a hierarchy and the assumption that individuals move from one level to the next. Maslow's work has been criticised on the grounds that people do not move through these needs in the same order. It also assumes that, once a need is fulfilled, it loses its power to motivate. This may not be the case, especially with the higher needs.

EXAMINER'S ADVICE

Motivation is a popular topic in examination questions and a popular subject with students. However, many answers receive low marks because students do not apply their knowledge to the scenario in the question. Many questions on motivation ask you to consider whether the events in the scenario can be explained in terms of relevant theory. The skill is, therefore, to analyse whether the theory 'fits' the scenario.

QUICK CHECK QUESTIONS

1   Read the following two statements and then decide which of the four options set out below is correct.

Statement A: the will to work due to the enjoyment of work itself.

Statement B: the will or desire to achieve a given target or goal.

a)   Only statement A is a correct definition of motivation.

b)   Only statement B is a correct definition of motivation.

c)   Both statements are correct definitions of motivation.

d)   Neither statement is a correct definition of motivation.

2   Is the following statement false or true? 'A highly motivated workforce can help a business to improve its corporate image.'

3   Which writers on motivation were responsible for the following two concepts?

● rational man

● social man

a)   Taylor and Maslow

b)   Taylor and Mayo

c)   Mayo and Herzberg

d)   Maslow and Herzberg.

4   Which two writers on motivation argued that motivation lies within each individual employee and that managers merely need to use appropriate techniques to stimulate this motivational force?

a)   Taylor and Maslow

b)   Taylor and Mayo

c)   Mayo and Herzberg

d)   Maslow and Herzberg.

5   Place these essential elements of Taylorism in the correct order:

a)   Implement differential pay rates and close supervision.

b)   Study the work processes to determine the most efficient production methods.

c)   Train all the workers to master the most efficient methods.

d)   Observe and time the most efficient workers.

6   Mayo would have supported the use of the following techniques to motivate employees with one exception. Which one is the exception?

a)   works outings and trips

b)   the provision of sports facilities

c)   the use of teams within businesses

d)   the use of piece-rate pay systems.

7   The Hawthorne experiment was investigating:

a)   working in teams

b)   levels of lighting and productivity

c)   the role of supervisors

d)   the effects of all-female workforces.

8   Place the following four needs from Maslow's hierarchy in the correct order (from lowest to highest).

a)   esteem needs

b)   security needs

c)   physiological needs

d)   social needs.

9   Which of the following, according to Herzberg, is not a hygiene factor?

a)   salary

b)   working conditions

c)   company policies and administration

d)   recognition for achievement.

10   Is the following statement true or false? 'Maslow's higher needs roughly correspond with Herzberg's motivators.'

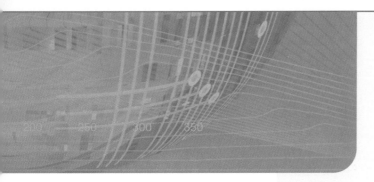

Progress questions

1 Outline the two views of motivation that exist.
(4 marks)

2 Explain two benefits that a business might gain as a consequence of having a highly motivated workforce.
(6 marks)

3 Fully explain **two** different reasons why people work.
(6 marks)

4 Outline the role that work-study played in F. W. Taylor's theory of Scientific Management.
(7 marks)

5 Outline the 'Hawthorne Effect'.
(5 marks)

6 Explain the fundamental difference in views between the Human Relations School and the Neo-Human Relations School.
(6 marks)

7 Outline why Maslow's higher needs might be more relevant than his lower needs to businesses in the UK today.
(7 marks)

8 State one major weakness in Maslow's theory of the hierarchy of needs.
(2 marks)

9 Explain why Herzberg believed that pay would not positively motivate an employee.
(5 marks)

10 Explain the difference between Herzberg's motivators and his hygiene factors.
(4 marks)

Analytical and evaluative questions

11 Analyse the possible implications of Herzberg's two-factor theory for the management team at one of the UK's largest house building companies.
(8 marks)

12 'All low-paid workers are motivated solely by money.' Discuss this statement.
(15 marks)

13 Shell employs thousands of people in jobs ranging from administrative to engineering to management. To what extent is it possible to motivate such a diverse workforce?
(15 marks)

Case study !

35 marks

The company William O'Connor worked for, Fischel Media, had recently undergone a major restructuring to increase efficiency, with the result that William's span of control had increased from 6 to 12. As part of the changes, all senior managers had to attend a management training course on motivation. William had spent three days learning about theorists such as Mayo, Herzberg and McGregor. The only one he had ever heard of was Taylor and his scientific management approach.

William's Chief Executive suddenly started talking about the value of people as resources. At the same time William was ordered to establish a committee in which employees could meet to discuss ways of improving their area of the business. Attendance would be out of company time with a small financial reward for attending.

The Chief Executive publicly announced that these groups were a major step forward in terms of employee involvement. However, William had overheard him saying: 'Most people don't come to work to actually work: they come to get away with what they can and to get some money. The role of management is to control them. We may get a few

people turning up to these committees, and you never know some ideas could come from it. I don't hold with all this nonsense written by people such as Maslow. Did he ever manage a business?'

William was not convinced the Chief Executive really understood what people wanted from work and realised that the course had made him think about what actually motivated him and what *he* could do to motivate his staff. The mood in the firm had not been good recently; the restructuring had caused a great deal of bad feeling and insecurity. What could he do to change things?

1 What is meant by the 'span of control'? (2 marks)

2 Explain the possible benefits of scientific management to Fischel Media. (8 marks)

3 Examine the possible reasons why a chief executive might ignore the theory put forward by Abraham Maslow. (10 marks)

4 With reference to motivational theorists, discuss how William might be able to increase the motivation of his staff. (15 marks)

>> Motivation in practice

Why put theory into practice?

Competition from European and Asian businesses poses an ever-greater challenge to British producers. UK businesses have come under increasing pressure to supply high-class products at low prices.

A highly motivated workforce can help to give a business a competitive edge over its rivals. This need to enhance competitiveness has been the driving force behind many of the practical attempts to improve employee motivation.

Monetary forms of motivation

Managers and organisations use a variety of pay systems in an attempt to improve the performance of their workforce. Despite publicity given to the views of Herzberg, suggesting that monetary methods of motivation are of limited value, pay remains a major incentive.

Piecework

Under this pay system, employees are paid according to the quantity they produce. Thus, an employee on a production line might receive an

Advantages	Disadvantages
• Little supervision is required as employees complete tasks as quickly as possible • Helps to keep wage costs under control – if workers' output falls so will their wages. • Piecework employees are frequently not entitled to holiday and sick pay, reducing employment costs.	• The system can lead to low quality products as employees strive to maximise their output. • A high proportion of output may be scrapped if it fails to meet quality standards. • Employees may ignore health and safety regulations in their attempts to increase their output.

Table 5.8 *Advantages and disadvantages of piecework*

agreed amount for each unit of production they complete. Piecework is common in a number of industries in the UK including textiles, electronics and agriculture.

POINTS TO PONDER

Even the industry associated with the Internet uses a piecework system. People operating websites often receive some of their payment through commission. Many websites carry adverts for other linked sites and receive a payment for each customer who clicks on the advert to enter the linked site.

Piecework offers businesses a number of advantages and disadvantages.

Since the implementation of the minimum wage, employers have faced additional problems in using piecework. Employers using piecework have to ensure that their employees earn at least the minimum wage rate per hour.

Salaries and wages

Most employees in the UK receive their payment in the form of salaries or wages. Salaries are expressed in annual terms (e.g. a production manager might be paid a salary of £30 000 per year) and are normally paid monthly. Salaried employees are not normally required to work a set number of hours per week though their contract of employment may state a minimum number of hours.

On the other hand, wages are usually paid weekly and employees are required to be at work for a specified number of hours. Employees are normally paid a higher rate (known as overtime) for any additional hours worked.

 ## Key Issues

The UK government introduced the minimum wage on 1 April 1999. This legislation covered full- and part-time employees as well as temporary workers and those on piecework. Since then the wage has increased steadily and at rates above inflation and the average increase in wages. This has benefited low-paid employees, but has imposed an additional cost burden on businesses.

When the minimum wage was initially introduced, businesses argued that it would result in around 80 000 job losses. These fears have

Writer	Opinions on the motivational powers of pay
Frederick Taylor	Taylor saw pay as the primary motivating factor for all workers. He referred to workers as 'economic animals' and supported the use of piece-rate.
Abraham Maslow	He saw pay as a reward permitting employees to meet the lower needs on their hierarchy.
Frederick Herzberg	Pay is a hygiene factor and a possible cause of dissatisfaction. In a few circumstances pay might be a motivator if, for example, it is used as a recognition for merit.

Table 5.9 *Opinions on pay*

Date	Hourly rate for employees aged over 21	Hourly rate for employees aged 18–21
April 1999	£3.60	£3.00
October 2000	£3.70	£3.20
October 2001	£4.10	£3.50
October 2002	£4.20	£3.60
October 2003	£4.50	£3.80
October 2004*	£4.85	£4.10

Table 5.10 *The UK minimum wage*
* Agreed, subject to confirmation

Source: Low Pay Commission

proved to be unfounded and the government has raised the minimum wage rates every year since its introduction, as shown in Table 5.10.

Key terms

Fringe benefits are rewards received by employees in addition to their wages or salary. Common examples include company cars and private health care.

Performance-related pay exists where some part of an employee's pay is linked to the achievement of targets at work. These targets might include sales figures or achieving certain grades in his or her annual appraisal.

MATHS MOMENT   1 + 1 = 2

Chedgrave Furnishings manufactures pine furniture. Employees are paid £5.50 per hour for a basic week of 40 hours and overtime at 'time-and-a-half' for any hours worked in excess of this. Thus, if an employee works 46 hours in a week his wages are as follows:

40 hours at £5.50 per hour	£220.00
6 hours at £ 8.25 per hour	£ 49.50
Total weekly wage	£269.50

1 How much would any employee earn if he or she worked 50 hours in a particular week?
2 In these circumstances, calculate his average hourly rate.

Fringe benefits

These are sometimes referred to as 'perks'. Fringe benefits are those extras an employee receives as part of their reward package. Examples include the following.

- a company car (or a mileage allowance for an employee's own car)
- luncheon vouchers
- private health insurance
- employers' contributions to pension schemes
- discounts for company products.

Firms tend to use fringe benefits to encourage employee loyalty and to reduce the proportion of employees leaving the firm. A danger of the widespread use of fringe benefits is that costs can increase quickly, reducing profitability.

Performance-related pay (PRP)

Performance-related pay (or PRP) has become more widely used over recent years and has developed along with employee appraisal systems. PRP is only paid to those employees who meet or exceed some agreed targets. Under PRP employees are paid for their contribution to the organisation, rather than their status within it.

Key terms

Piecework (also called piece-rate) is a system whereby employees are paid according to the quantity of a product they produce.

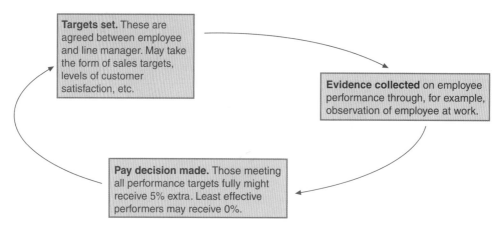

Figure 5.15 *The operation of a typical performance-related pay system*

Performance-related pay can demotivate too! In 2003, 450 employees of Caledonian McBride (a ferry company that provides shipping services to the Scottish Islands) threatened strike action because their pay rise contained an element of performance-related pay.

A number of large-scale manufacturers, such as Cadbury's and Nissan, and public-sector industries, for example, schools and colleges have introduced PRP schemes. PRP remains popular, and many employees support linking some element of pay to performance. However, there have been criticisms of huge bonuses paid to senior managers and directors of moderately successful companies. For example, in 2003 Marks & Spencer's directors could earn bonuses of between 40% and 100% of their normal pay.

Criticisms of PRP

A number of criticisms of performance-related pay have been put forward:

- Many employees perceive PRP as fundamentally unfair. This is particularly true of those working in the services sector where employee performance is difficult to measure. Employees fear that they might be discriminated against because they do not get on with the manager conducting their appraisal interview. This can result in their performance worsening, not improving.

- A majority of businesses operating PRP systems do not put sufficient funds into the scheme. Typically, the operation of a PRP scheme adds 3–4% to a business's wage bill. This only allows employees to enjoy relatively small performance awards, which may be inadequate to change employee performance.

Key terms

Employee appraisal schemes assess and evaluate the performance of workers over a period of time with the intention of improving their performance.

Developments in PRP

Increasing numbers of firms are implementing a system known as variable pay. Companies such as Levi-Strauss in America and Unilever in Britain recognise that company performance often depends upon the achievements of the few.

Staff at the Philip Electronics Group in Holland are convinced of the benefits of variable pay. In 2002 they took the company to court to challenge its policy of restricting variable pay to managers. The employees won!

Variable pay is really a development of PRP. It is similar in that it rewards employee performance, but there are differences. PRP operates according to a formula used throughout the company. Variable pay is far more flexible and the potential rewards for star employees are greater. However, management consultant Peter Newhouse & Co believe that variable pay has a limited impact on motivation, and that a recent survey shows poorly designed variable pay systems can demotivate. (For more details, visit *www.peternewhouse.com/services/services-motivational*.)

Key terms

Variable pay is a flexible form of performance-related pay which offers employees a highly individual pay system related to their performance at work.

POINTS TO PONDER

PRP is generally applied to individuals. But the increasing attention being paid to developing good teamwork is encouraging some organisations to concentrate more on team pay, usually through some form of group bonus scheme.

Business in focus

IBM bases its PRP system on a four-category rating system for employees. Employees are placed into one of these categories according to their achievement in a number of objectives. The four categories are:

- **1.5 rating** – for employees who exceeded all their objectives
- **1.0 rating** – those who achieve all their objectives
- **0.5 rating** – for employees who met some of their objectives
- **0 rating** – for those who achieved few, if any, objectives.

Performance-related pay is directly linked to the rating each employee achieves. Employees awarded a zero rating would not receive any PRP award. During successful periods, many employees can enjoy an increase in income as PRP is an addition to salary.

A criticism of the IBM system was that, since the PRP system was introduced, there had been no increase in basic pay.

Some managers remain unconvinced of the value of PRP, no matter how sophisticated the scheme. The widespread use of PRP may, in part, be an attempt by managers to keep pay rates *down* for the majority of employees. PRP, or variable pay, treats employees as individuals limiting the ability of trade unions to bargain collectively.

Key terms

Collective bargaining takes place when a trade union or other representative body negotiates pay and conditions on behalf of a group of workers.

Profit sharing

Profit sharing is a system whereby employees receive some of the business's profits. This is a type of performance-related pay, but one that may not discriminate between the performances of individual members of staff. Such payments, which may vary according to salary or wage, are distinct from and additional to regular earnings.

Profits are paid out to employees immediately in the form of cash or company shares. Profit sharing in the form of ownership of shares in the firm has, in a few cases, also involved participation by employees in the firm's management.

EXAMINER'S ADVICE

PRP remains a highly topical issue. Whilst there are a number of arguments in favour of it, a central weakness remains. This can be explained in terms of the theory we covered in the previous unit. Writers such as Maslow and Herzberg argued that money has limited power to motivate employees. PRP, no matter how it is implemented, has more in common with Frederick Taylor's views of motivating employees.

POINTS TO PONDER

Employee shareholders in Corus, the Anglo-Dutch steelmaker, reacted furiously to an announcement in 2003 that it is to shed a further 2200 jobs. The firm will have made 12 000 redundancies since it was formed by a merger in 1999.

Profit-sharing schemes may improve employees' loyalty to the company. These schemes can help to break down the 'them and us' attitude. Under profit-sharing schemes, a greater level of profit is regarded as being of benefit to all employees, and not just senior managers and shareholders. Employees may be more willing to accept changes designed to improve the business's profitability.

The danger with profit-sharing schemes is that they can be too small and fail to provide employees with a worthwhile payment. On the other hand, if schemes are too generous, the company may have insufficient funds for capital investment.

Share ownership

This can be a development of profit-sharing schemes. Some businesses pay their employees' share of the profits in the form of company shares. Share ownership schemes vary enormously in their operation. We shall consider two of the main schemes operated by UK companies.

Some businesses, such as Asda, offer employees the opportunity to purchase shares after saving for a period of time. After say, five years, employees can purchase shares at the price they were at the start of the savings scheme. This is a popular type of scheme, though tax changes introduced in the Chancellor's 1999 budget will make it more difficult to operate in the future. Other businesses offer employees free shares as an incentive.

Share options are a form of share ownership normally aimed at senior managers. About 14% of UK companies operate share option schemes, according to a recent survey.

Under share options, managers have the opportunity to buy company shares at some agreed date in the future, but at the current share price. Thus, the current share price might be £2.50 and the manager is given the option to purchase 1000 shares in three years' time at this price. In three years the market price of shares may have risen to £3.50. This offers the manager the chance to purchase the 1000 shares for £2500 (£2.50 × 1000) and to sell them immediately for £3500, giving a profit of £1000. If the share price falls over the three-year period the manager will choose not to buy the shares.

Business in focus

During 2003, Tesco's stakeholders received good news about profits. Shareholders would have been delighted by the company's announcement that profits had risen by 13% to £1.3 billion. However, 75 000 of the supermarket's employees also received good news. They are to receive a £34 million payout from the company's profit sharing scheme.

The shares had been held in trust for three years, thanks to the retailer's on-going growth and performance. When the shares were first allocated to staff three years ago they were worth 184p each. But when they are released, the share price value will have grown by 31%.

Tesco staff had to decide whether to keep their shares or cash them in. Tesco Chief Executive, Terry Leahy, commented: 'Once again Tesco staff can share in our exceptional performance. The profit share scheme is a great way for us to recognise and reward the enormous contribution of our staff, and is a big thank you for everyone's hard work.'

The supermarket chain is also giving staff more free shares under its new *Shares in Success* scheme, under which eligible staff receive free shares worth up to 3.6% of their salary. Employees can sell these shares in 2008.

Source: Adapted from Guardian Unlimited (www.guardian.co.uk) 21 June 2003 and www.tesco.com

1 To what extent does Tesco believe that money motivates?

(See http://www.tesco. com/ everylittlehelps/csourpeopledetail.htm for more information.)

POINTS TO PONDER

A change in accounting rules proposed in 2003 will make share options appear as a liability to the company. This is likely to depress the company's share price. As a result, share options will be less common in the future if the new rules are agreed.

Advantages	Disadvantages
● Employees may work harder as they have a stake in the company's performance and share price. ● Employees are less likely to leave the company saving on recruitment and retraining costs. ● Employees paying into share ownership schemes provide the company with capital for investment.	● Some schemes (especially share option schemes) are only available to senior employees, causing resentment. ● Some firms receive bad publicity from operating generous share option schemes solely for senior employees.

Table 5.11 *Advantages and disadvantages of share ownership schemes*

Non-monetary forms of motivation
What makes a good job?
Non-monetary methods of motivation tend to focus upon the design of employees' jobs. Employees can be motivated by asking them to do a job that is challenging and interesting. A good job should have at least a number of the features listed below.

● Employees carry out duties that result in a definite end product.
● Clear and challenging goals give employees something to aim at. Goals should be demanding, but not unattainable.
● Employees should be able to identify easily their contributions to the organisation.
● Jobs should be designed so jobholders are involved in planning their own schedules of work, choosing their work methods, and coping with problems as they arise.

The main methods of non-monetary motivation attempt to incorporate some of these features into the working lives of employees.

> **Key terms**
>
> *Job design* is the process of grouping together individual tasks to form complete jobs.

Job enrichment
Job enrichment occurs when employees' jobs are redesigned to provide them with more challenging and complex tasks. This process, also called vertical loading, is designed to use all employees' abilities.

The intention is to enrich the employee's experience of work.

Frederick Herzberg was a strong supporter of job enrichment. He believed that enrichment provided employees with motivators that increase the satisfaction they might get from working.

Job enrichment normally involves a number of elements:

● redesigning jobs so as to increase, not just the range of tasks, but the complexity of them
● giving employees greater responsibility for managing themselves
● offering employees the authority to identify and solve problems relating to their work
● providing employees with the training and skills essential to allow them to carry out their enriched jobs effectively.

Job enrichment involves a high degree of skill on the part of the managers overseeing it. They must ensure that they do not ask employees to carry out duties of which they are not capable.

> **Key terms**
>
> *Job enrichment* occurs when employees' jobs are redesigned to provide them with more challenging and complex tasks.

> **POINTS TO PONDER**
>
> In 2003, Marks & Spencer agreed to over 600 two-week work experience placements. These placements were offered to homeless people in 13 UK cities in an attempt to enhance their job-related skills.

Business in focus

A small but growing number of companies are offering their staff limitless holiday entitlement. Surprisingly, employees can take as many days off as they want. Their bosses are saying, 'Think you might have a hangover tomorrow? Stay in bed. Dying to spend five weeks in Australia this summer? Go for it.'

The concept, known as 'trust breaks' or 'zero-allocation policy', originated in the US with firms such as law firm Baker & McKenzie. Nick Candler, human resources and finance director of drinks company Allied Domecq, explains the idea. 'We are an extremely high-performing company, not least because we take that attitude. It's all about us saying to our staff, "We will give you the freedom to choose how you achieve your goals, but the bottom line is that you must achieve them. If you don't you can't remain in the organisation." That is the contract, one of trust.'

Supporters of the 'trust breaks' approach argue that employees should be judged by their achievements and not by the number of hours they work.

Source: Adapted from Guardian Unlimited/Kate Hilpern, www.jobs.guardian.co.uk 10 March 2003

1 What preparations might a company need to make before introducing a system of 'trust breaks'?

Job enlargement

Job enlargement does not increase the complexity of tasks carried out by an employee. Instead it increases the number of similar duties. It is also termed 'horizontal loading'.

Key terms

Job enlargement entails giving employees more duties of a similar level of complexity.

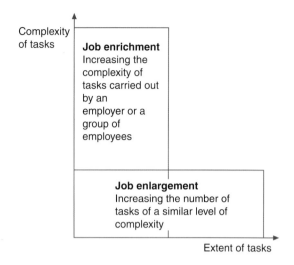

Figure 5.16 *Job enrichment and job enlargement*

A number of firms operating a policy of job enlargement simply require employees to carry out a number of similar tasks. Thus, a receptionist might be asked to carry out a number of duties in addition to dealing with telephone and personal enquiries from customers. The receptionist may also be asked to maintain records of petty cash and update customer records for example.

Job enlargement offers benefits to the employee in that carrying out a range of duties, rather than a single one repeatedly, may stimulate their interest. The business gains an advantage from having an employee able to carry out a wider range of duties, possibly reducing their labour costs.

Job rotation is a particular type of job enlargement. Under this system employees switch regularly from one duty to another. Thus, a supermarket may require employees to spend a week on the checkout, a week stacking shelves and a week dealing with customer enquiries. Rotation may reduce the level of monotony, but does not increase the challenge of the job.

Employee empowerment

Empowerment involves redesigning employees' jobs to allow them greater control over their working lives. Empowerment gives employees the opportunity to decide how to carry out their duties and how to organise their work.

POINTS TO PONDER

BAE systems, the UK defence and aerospace equipment manufacturer, brought in a complete management team in 2003 to help on a project that was behind schedule. The US team was hired to use its skills to ensure that the development of the Astute submarine is not delayed further.

Empowerment can make work more interesting as it offers opportunities to meet a number of individual needs. Empowered workers can propose and implement new methods of working as they bring a new perspective to decision-making. They may spend a part of their working lives considering the problems they face and proposing solutions.

Vauxhall Motors operates empowered teams at its Luton plant. In 1998, one team improved productivity by designing a swing chair to improve access to cars on the production line. Using this chair made it easier for employees to move in and out of the cars when adding components and improved productivity.

Empowerment would receive the approval of Maslow and Herzberg. It provides motivators, as well as offering employees the opportunity to fulfil higher needs.

POINTS TO PONDER

Research conducted into the activities of 100 UK companies revealed that, in those companies which implemented extensive policies of empowerment, sales revenue increased by 30% and profit per employee rose by more than £5000 as a consequence of this decision.

Employees require training if they are to be empowered. They are unlikely to have the skills necessary to schedule tasks, solve problems, recruit new employees and introduce new working practices. It takes time to implement empowerment and teething problems are common.

Teamworking

Teamworking exists when an organisation breaks down its production processes into large units instead of relying upon the use of the division of labour. Teams are then given responsibility for completing the large units of work. Team members carry out a variety of duties including planning, problem-solving and target-setting.

A number of different team types operate within businesses:

● Production teams – many production lines have been organised into distinct elements called cells. Each of these cells is staffed by teams whose members are multi-skilled. They monitor product quality and ensure that production targets are met.
● Quality circle teams – these are small teams designed to propose solutions to existing problems and to suggest improvements in production methods. The teams contain members drawn from all levels within the organisation.
● Management teams – increasingly, managers see themselves as complementary teams establishing the organisation's objectives and overseeing their achievement.

There has been a major trend in businesses towards teamworking over recent years. Teamworking is a major part of the so-called Japanese approach to production and its benefits have been extolled by major companies such as Honda and John Lewis (visit *www.john-lewis-partnership.co.uk* for further details of the business).

Teamworking offers employees the opportunity to meet their social needs, as identified by Maslow; Herzberg identified relationships with fellow workers as a hygiene factor. However, much of the motivational force arising from teamworking comes with the change in job design that usually accompanies it. Teamworking requires jobs to be redesigned, offering employees the chance to fulfil some of the higher needs identified by Maslow such as esteem needs. Similarly, teamworking offers some of the motivators, for example achievement.

Which motivators are best?

The type of non-monetary forms of motivation used by businesses depends upon a number of factors.

The style of leadership

Some managers are content to give employees greater freedom in organising their working lives in an attempt to motivate them. Others prefer to retain control and rely on monetary techniques of motivation.

The culture of the business

If a business has a dynamic, flexible and competitive culture, then employees are likely to be motivated by the jobs that they do, rather than external factors such as pay. Alternatively, a more traditional and hierarchical culture might encourage employees to operate with less freedom. Techniques such as job enlargement may be used.

 QUICK CHECK QUESTIONS

1 'Under this pay system, employees are paid according to the quantity they produce.' Of what is this a definition?

2 Which of the following best describes the term 'overtime'?
a) The amount paid for each unit of production.
b) The hourly wage rate paid to supervisors who oversee other workers.
c) The hourly wage rate paid for any hours worked over the normal amount.
d) Any hourly wage rate in excess of the minimum wage.

3 Which of the following is **not** a fringe benefit?
a) overtime payments paid to employees
b) private health insurance
c) discounts on company products
d) a company car.

4 Complete the following sentence by filling in the blanks. 'Performance-related pay (PRP) rewards employees for their

.... to an organisation rather than their .... within it.'

5 '................. / ...... is a development of PRP. It rewards performance, but it is more flexible and offers far greater rewards for "star" performers.' Which of the following terms could be inserted in the space?
a) piecework pay
b) hourly pay
c) bonus pay
d) variable pay.

6 Which of the following is **not** a possible benefit of profit sharing?
a) Such a scheme may increase the company's ability to reinvest profits.
b) Profit sharing schemes may improve employees' loyalty to the company.
c) Under profit sharing, employees may be more willing to accept changes designed to improve the company's performance.
d) A profit sharing scheme can help to break down 'them and us' attitudes.

7 Which of the following should **not** be a feature of a well-designed job?
a) Employees carry out a variety of duties.
b) Employees earn an hourly pay rate in excess of the minimum wage.
c) Employees are given clear and challenging goals.
d) Employees are able to identify their contribution to the organisation.

8 Complete the following sentences by filling in the missing words. '...... / ....
occurs when employees' jobs are redesigned to provide them with more ....
and .... tasks.'

9 Which of the following is an alternative name for job enlargement?
a) vertical loading
b) employee empowerment
c) job redesign
d) horizontal loading.

10 Of what is the following a definition? 'This involves redesigning employees' jobs to allow them a greater degree of control over their working lives.'

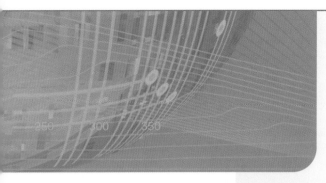

Progress questions

1 *Explain the difference between 'wages' and 'salaries'.* *(3 marks)*

2 *Outline the arguments in favour of piecework as a method of motivating employees.* *(5 marks)*

3 *Explain two problems a business might encounter when operating a performance-related pay system.* *(6 marks)*

4 *Outline why a number of businesses have replaced performance-related pay with variable pay.* *(5 marks)*

5 *Outline the factors that managers should consider before introducing a share option scheme.* *(6 marks)*

6 *Explain three features of a good job.* *(6 marks)*

7 *Outline why job enrichment is more likely to improve employee motivation and performance than job enlargement.* *(7 marks)*

8 *Outline the preparations managers might need to take before empowering the workforce.* *(6 marks)*

9 *Examine the reasons why Maslow and Herzberg would approve of the implementation of teamworking within businesses.* *(7 marks)*

10 *Maslow and Herzberg both argued that money has limited use as a motivator. Explain two reasons why, in spite of this, many firms continue to use pay systems in an attempt to motivate their workforces.* *(6 marks)*

Analytical and evaluative questions

11 *Gibble & Co Ltd produces high-quality fountain pens. Analyse the possible disadvantages of the company introducing a piecework system onto its production line.* *(8 marks)*

12 *Erskine Moore plc is a London-based firm of management consultants. It offers advice and support to a wide range of UK businesses.*

Discuss the factors the firm might take into account when designing its own payment system. *(15 marks)*

13 *Philly plc manufactures bottles using a piece-rate pay system, and encourages its employees to specialise in particular tasks on the production line. A new Chief Executive has commented 'redesigning our employees' jobs is the only way to motivate our workforce in the long term'. To what extent do you agree with this statement?* *(15 marks)*

Case study !   35 marks

Mink Pongsapas took over the Rhino Printing Company in 1995 and within four years had completely transformed the business. 'The key to a firm's success is its people. Once I took over I knew that what had to be done was to motivate the staff.'

Mink inherited a traditionally run and highly inefficient business. Delegation was limited, spans of control were small and production process involved a high degree of specialisation and division of labour.

Just four years later the company is regarded as the industry leader. The changes Mink introduced included a job enrichment programme and significant investment to improve communications. She also ended the payment of employees on piecework in favour of a salary scheme, 'Piecework is not a sensible option for an organisation interested in innovation, quality and employee commitment,' she said.

Mink's achievement was all the more impressive given the rapid change that had occurred in the industry, the threats of takeover by competitors and a demotivated workforce. Many managers would have avoided such drastic changes at this time but she felt strongly that '. . . a firm's ability to compete ultimately depends on the motivation of its employees.'

1 What is meant by 'piecework'?   (2 marks)

2 What is meant by 'job enrichment'?   (2 marks)

3 Explain why Mink might have switched the payment system from piecework to a salary scheme.   (8 marks)

4 Analyse the ways in which a manufacturing company might enrich the jobs of its shop-floor employees.   (8 marks)

5 'A firm's ability to compete ultimately depends on the motivation of its employees.' To what extent do you agree with this view?   (15 marks)

Planning and developing the
>> workforce

What is Human Resource Management?

Human Resource Management (HRM) is the process of making the most efficient use of an organisation's personnel. HRM covers a broad range of business activities:

- assessing future labour needs
- recruitment and selection
- training
- appraisal
- motivation and reward of employees.

Until recently, most businesses have relied on the concept of personnel management. Latterly, the influence of Japanese management techniques has encouraged the adoption of at least some elements of HRM. The most enthusiastic supporters of HRM are foreign-owned companies operating in the EU. However, many firms do not engage in human resource planning and management.

Key terms

Human resource management is the process of making the most efficient use of an organisation's personnel.
Personnel management describes a range of discrete tasks necessary to administer the human dimension of business activities.

HRM views activities relating to the workforce as integrated and vital in helping the organisation to achieve its objectives. People are viewed as an important resource to be developed through training. Thus, policies relating to recruitment and training, for example, should be formulated as part of a coordinated human resource strategy.

Conversely, personnel management considers the elements that comprise managing people (recruitment, selection, and so forth) as separate elements. It does not take into account how these parts combine to assist in the achievement of organisational objectives. At its simplest, personnel management within businesses carries out a series of unrelated tasks.

Planning the workforce

Before a business recruits or trains employees, it must establish future labour needs. This is not simply a matter of recruiting sufficient employees. Those recruited must have the right skills and experience to help the organisation achieve its corporate objectives.

Managers will draw up a human resource plan to detail the number and type of workers the business needs to recruit.

The plan will also specify how the business will implement its human resource policies. An important element of the plan is a skills audit to identify the abilities and qualities of the existing workforce. This may highlight skills and experience of which managers were unaware.

Businesses require specific information when developing human resource plans:

- They need to research to provide sales forecasts for the next year or two. This will help identify the quantity and type of labour required.
- Data will be needed to show the number of employees likely to be leaving the labour force in general (and the firm in particular). Information will be required on potential entrants to the labour force.
- If wages are expected to rise, then businesses may reduce their demand for labour and seek to make greater use of technology.
- The plan will reflect any anticipated changes in the output of the workforce due to changes in productivity or the length of the working week.
- Technological developments will impact on planning the workforce. Developments in this field may reduce the need for unskilled employees whilst creating employment for those with technical skills. Human resource plans are also called workforce plans.

Business in focus

Sony, one of the world's largest manufacturers of electronic consumer products, has announced that it will be reducing its workforce by between 15 000 and 20 000 people by autumn 2006.

The Japanese manufacturer has announced a major reorganisation of its operations including large-scale redundancies and the closure of several factories, though it has yet to confirm all the details. 'Job cuts and plant closures definitely will be included, but details, like the time frame for the plant closures, have not been finalised,' one company source told Reuters.

The reorganisation follows the announcement of a quarterly loss of almost £650 million in April 2003. The company's financial position was weakened due to declining demand, increasing stock levels and difficulty in controlling costs.

1 What other factors might have influenced Sony's human resource management?
2 Discuss whether this article suggests that human resource planning usually responds to events rather than anticipating them.

Key terms

Redployment occurs when an employee is moved from one job to another within the same organisation.
An employee is made **redundant** when the job no longer exists and, therefore, work is not available for the person who held that post.

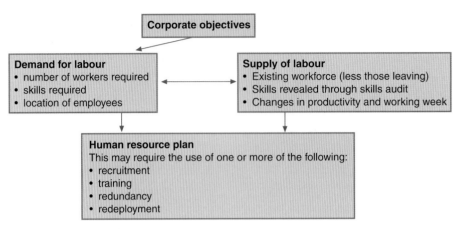

Figure 5.17 *Human resource planning*

Developing the workforce

One strategy to improve the performance of employees requires businesses to recruit employees with the appropriate skills from outside the organisation. An alternative is to train existing staff to develop their skills and knowledge. This option can be expensive and takes time.

Recruiting and selecting employees

Firms can alter the composition of their workforce through recruitment. The process of recruitment is summarised in Figure 5.18 below.

The human resource department normally plays a key role in the recruitment and selection process. However, the increasing influence of Japanese business practices on British organisations has meant that some firms no longer have a separate human resource department. In these circumstances, managers or teams responsible for the relevant area of the business may oversee the process of recruitment.

Recruitment

The start of recruitment is to draw up job descriptions and person specifications.

Job descriptions relate to the *position* rather than the *person*. Typically, job descriptions might contain the following information:

- the title of the post
- employment conditions
- some idea of tasks and duties.

Person or job specifications set out the qualifications and qualities required in an employee. They refer to the *person* rather than the *post* and include:

- educational and professional qualifications required
- character and personality needed
- skills and experience wanted.

These documents form an important part of recruitment and selection. Candidate's applications should be compared against the person specification

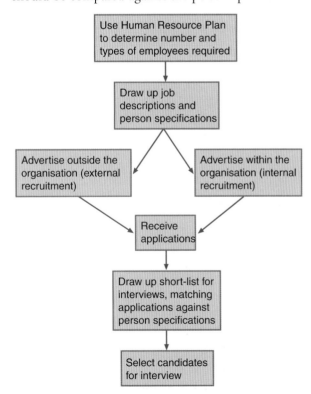

Figure 5.18 *The recruitment process*

and those applicants having the 'best fit' should be invited to interview. At interview, the job description might form the basis for the interviewer's questions.

Key terms

Recruitment and selection is the process of filling an organisation's job vacancies by appointing new staff.
Job descriptions list the duties and responsibilities associated with a particular job.
Person specifications outline the skills, knowledge and experience necessary to fill a given position successfully. These are also termed job specifications.

EXAMINER'S ADVICE

It is easy to get bogged down in the detail of recruitment and selection procedures. There will normally be relatively few marks available for describing different approaches. It is more important to focus on how recruitment and selection will help a business to fulfil its workforce plan and achieve the corporate objectives.

Internal and external recruitment

Key terms

Internal recruitment takes place when a business looks to fill a vacancy from within the existing workforce.
External recruitment occurs when a business invites applications for vacant posts from any suitably qualified candidates.
Training is the process whereby an individual acquires job related skills and knowledge.

Firms may recruit internally through promotion or redeployment from within existing employees. This offers a number of benefits:

- candidates will have experience of the business and its culture and will be familiar with the firm's procedures
- internal candidates may not require induction training

- internal recruitment provides employees with opportunities for promotion
- it avoids the need for expensive external advertising
- selection may be easier as more is known about the candidates.

However, internal candidates are drawn from a limited pool of employees and the skills and experience of this group of people may be insufficient to meet the business's needs. This is more likely in the case of senior appointments.

Managers may be keen to have a wider choice of candidates and may seek to recruit externally. This can result in applications from higher quality candidates, especially if recruitment is through national media or nationally-based recruitment agencies. External recruits may bring fresh ideas and enthusiasm into the business. This can be a vital factor in an organisation with a low level of labour turnover.

Key terms

Labour turnover is the proportion of a business's workforce leaving the organisation over a given period.

External recruitment is likely to be very expensive. It also carries a greater risk as candidates are not known to the business.

POINTS TO PONDER

Alan Milburn, the government minister responsible for health, announced in 2003 that he is to appoint headhunters to recruit hundreds of young managers for the NHS. The headhunters will raid the private sector for suitable candidates in an attempt to make the NHS more entrepreneurial.

Firms can recruit externally by using a range of methods.

- Firms 'headhunt' employees who are currently working for other organisations in order to offer them employment. Those employees who are headhunted are usually either senior managers or people with specialist skills, perhaps in short

Business in focus

Scientific Sales Representative

StemCell Technologies Inc is the world leader in the development and manufacture of haematopoietic and other specialized tissue culture reagents and we provide unique and powerful cell separation technology to researchers in the life sciences. We are a dynamic, rapidly growing biotechnology company, expanding its sales force and we have an opening for a field sales representative in the Northern United Kingdom.

The Role:
* Leadership role and the candidate must seek new opportunities to expand StemCell's customer base to increase revenue.
* Utilize your understanding of the basic research marketplace to communicate key market information back to the Scientific Staff and Management.
* Provide exceptional customer service and technical support.
* Develop strong customer relationships.
* Travel is a requirement.
* Report directly to the UK Sales Manager.
* Liaise with head office in Canada and our European office in France.

The Candidate:
* 1+ year's sales experience in life science research sector.
* BSc, MSc, or PhD. in Immunology, Haematology, Cell Biology or an allied science.
* A strong work ethic and exceptional interpersonal and organizational skills are required.
* We are looking for candidates with strong scientific and technical backgrounds.
* Must be able to work independently, with little supervision.
* Fluency in French would be a bonus.

You will be rewarded by a generous compensation and benefit package, including a non-capped commission plan. The company is in a rapid growth phase and offers many opportunities for advancement to its valued employees.

If you are interested in exploring a challenging and rewarding career opportunity, please forward your resume by 7 November, 2003 to:

Human Resources, StemCell Technologies,
PO Box 35727, London, E14 9YE
humanresources@stemcellgb.com
Fax: +44-(0) 20-7515-5408
www.stemcell.com

Source: The Guardian, 23 October 2003

Figure 5.19 *A job advert for a sales representative, placed by StemCell Technologies*

1 How might a sales representative help a company such as StemCell to carry out market research?
2 Why would it by easy to draw up a job description and person specification for this post?

Business in focus

According to a study published in 2003 by the Royal College of Nursing (RCN), there are 42 000 foreign nurses in the UK – more than double the number in 2000. Some NHS hospitals in southeast England rely on overseas staff for up to 50% of their nursing needs. In private hospitals, that proportion can be as much as 65%. One unidentified London NHS trust reports that it employs nurses and midwives from 68 other countries.

The RCN study, *Here to Stay?*, finds that some NHS employers are reliant on foreign nurses, considering them no longer a mere short-term solution to nursing shortages but as 'core' to their medium-term workforce planning strategies. Some hospitals expect up to 35% of their nursing needs to be met by 'imports' over the next five years. A London NHS manager was quoted as calling overseas recruits 'the saviours of the organisation'. Without them, in other words, the health service would grind to a halt.

And it is not just nursing. Within the NHS, doctors, radiographers, physiotherapists and occupational therapists are all actively sought from overseas to overcome domestic shortages. This internationalisation of the public services workforce is apparent also in social work, where a quarter of all new social workers in 2001–2002 were from other countries. And the trend is evident in teaching and, on a smaller scale, in areas such as town planning and environmental health.

Source: Adapted from Guardian Unlimited, 19 February 2003

1 What problems might a business such as an NHS hospital face when recruiting employees from many different countries?

intending to recruit. Job centres may also advise on training available to workers.

- **Employment agencies** provide employers with details of suitable applicants for posts they may have vacant. Agencies usually charge considerable fees for bringing together employers and potential candidates.

- The government operates a number of training schemes to improve the skills and knowledge of the workforce. Participating in schemes such as New Deal offers firms a chance to consider the skills and aptitude of possible employees whilst they are on a training scheme. This is a relatively low-risk strategy and a cheap means of recruitment.

POINTS TO PONDER

The New Deal programme for the young unemployed is costing the taxpayer more than £11,000 for each job created, according to a recent study.

Source: Adapted from The Electronic Telegraph 26 November 1999

Recruitment can be an expensive exercise, but is less costly than appointing the wrong employee and perhaps having to repeat the process.

Selection

A number of selection techniques exist. Because of the high costs resulting from recruiting the wrong people, firms are investing more resources and time in the recruitment and selection process.

Interviews remain the most common form of selection technique. Interviews can involve one or two interviewers, or even a panel. They are relatively cheap and allow the two-way exchange of information, but are unreliable as a method of selection. Some people perform well at interview, but that does not necessarily mean they will perform well at work.

Psychometric tests reveal the personality of a candidate. Questions are used to assess candidates' honesty, commitment or ability to fulfil a particular role.

As managers become more aware of the high costs of poor selection decisions, they have made increasing use of **assessment centres**.

supply. Specialist executive recruitment agencies exist which can target precisely the right type of candidates, but normally charge high fees.

- **Job centres** are run by the Department for Education and Employment (DfEE) to bring together those seeking work and businesses

In such centres, a number of candidates are subjected to a variety of selection techniques over a period of between two and four days. These might include some or all of the following:

- **simulations** of circumstances that might occur within the job
- a variety of interviews
- **role-plays** involving a number of the candidates and assessment centre staff
- psychometric tests.

Evidence suggests that assessment centres are efficient at selecting employees for managerial positions. They are substantially more expensive than operating interviews, but their better performance compared with more traditional selection techniques might make them more cost effective in the long run.

Training

Training is a process whereby an individual acquires skills and knowledge. This can help him or her to develop, as well as assisting the organisation in achieving its objectives.

Almost all employees receive training at some point during their working lives. For example, they may receive training when commencing a new job. This is known as **induction training** and is intended to introduce an employee to the business.

Induction training may provide employees with information on the following:

- important policies such as health and safety, and disciplinary procedures
- the layout of the factory or office
- their new colleagues
- the basic duties of the job.

Induction training enables a new recruit to become more productive quickly. It can prevent costly errors resulting from employee ignorance and make a new employee feel welcome, thereby reducing labour turnover.

Types of training

Off-the-job training

This involves training outside the workplace, either at a college, university, or some other training agency.

Off-the-job training can take the form of external courses in the form of lectures and seminars, self-study or open learning.

On-the-job training

This form of training does not require the employee to leave the workplace. He or she learns from experienced employees through observation and work shadowing. The trainee may work through instruction manuals or receive guidance from senior employees.

In spite of being expensive, and sometimes disruptive, training does offer organisations a number of benefits (see Table 5.12).

Government support for training

The government encourages training in various ways. It funds a range of training schemes such as modern apprenticeships and the New Deal. It also promotes the cause of training through its 'Investors in People' scheme.

Firms that meet the requirement for training of employees (in particular for training employees to assist in meeting corporate objectives) are entitled to use a logo identifying them as meeting this particular standard. This may assist the business in its dealings with customers and other businesses.

It is important to appreciate the benefits and drawbacks of techniques such as training. Questions with high mark allocations will often require students to assess the strengths and weaknesses of particular techniques in given circumstances.

It will, therefore, be necessary to apply information such as that set out above when responding to this type of question.

APPLICATION IN ACTION

Training needs and the amount spent on training can vary considerably according to the type of business. Companies offering few opportunities for delegation, empowerment or enrichment are likely to invest less in training.

Costs	Benefits
• Training uses up valuable resources that could be utilised elsewhere in the organisation. • Training means that employees are unavailable to the organisation for a period of time. • Employees, once trained, often leave for better jobs. • Some managers avoid training their staff as it can lessen the degree of control they have over their subordinates.	• Training can improve employee performance and hence the competitive position of the business. • Training should improve employee motivation and productivity. • Training is a core component of HRM and assists organisations in achieving strategic objectives. • A reputation for training will assist organisations in attracting and retaining high quality employees.

Table 5.12 *The costs and benefits of training*

The failure of the labour market

The labour market relates to the supply of labour services by individuals and the purchase of those services by thousands of businesses, large and small.

An important aspect of the labour market is training. In an efficient labour market, each firm would pay to train its own employees to provide them with the necessary skills and knowledge. However, at times in the UK training has resulted in the market not working effectively.

Particularly during economic upswings, businesses have 'poached' employees with the necessary skills from rival organisations. This saves both the time and expense of training.

However, the danger is that poaching, if too common, may dissuade employers from training their staff for fear of losing such a valuable asset. In such circumstances the labour market would not operate effectively. This could be described as market failure.

QUICK CHECK QUESTIONS

1   Which of the following activities is **not** a part of HRM?
a) training
b) recruitment and selection
c) appraisal
d) factoring.

2   Complete the following sentences by filling in the missing words. 'A .... / .... is an important part of a human resource plan. It identifies the abilities and qualities of the .... workforce.'

3   Which of the following is **not** likely to be used as part of a human resources plan?
a) recession
b) redeployment
c) redundancy
d) recruitment.

4   The following list contains four activities undertaken by businesses during the recruitment process. Place them in the correct sequence:

a) Draw up short list.
b) Draw up job description and person specification.
c) Place job adverts in the media.
d) Use assessment centre to select candidates.

5   Which business term does the following sentence define? 'These outline the skills, knowledge and experience necessary to fill a given position successfully.'

6   Which of the following is an advantage of internal recruitment?
a) The business has access to a larger pool of candidates.
b) It helps businesses to bring in new ideas.
c) There is less likely to be a need for induction training.
d) It is particularly suitable for a firm that is expanding quickly.

7   Complete the following sentences by filling in the missing words. 'On-the-job-training does not require the employee to .... the workplace. He or she learns from .... employees through observation and .... shadowing.'

8   Which of the following is **not** a means by which the government encourages training?
a) psychometric testing
b) New Deal
c) Modern Apprenticeships
d) Investors in People.

9   Of what business term is the following a definition? 'The process whereby an individual acquires job-related skills and knowledge.'

10 Which of the following is a type of off-the-job-training?
a) observing other employees
b) lectures at a local college
c) work shadowing
d) receiving guidance from senior employees.

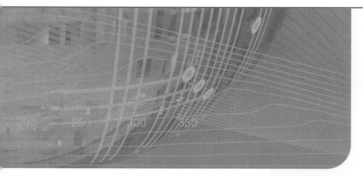

Progress questions

1   Distinguish between 'human resource management' and 'personnel management'.
(4 marks)

2   Outline two pieces of information a business might require before drawing up a human resource plan.
(6 marks)

3   Explain the difference between a 'job description' and a 'person specification'.
(5 marks)

4   Explain two benefits to a firm that may arise from internal recruitment.
(6 marks)

5   Outline three reasons why a business might choose to recruit new staff externally.
(9 marks)

6   Explain two techniques of selection that an organisation might opt to use when employing new staff.
(6 marks)

7   What is meant by the term 'induction training'?
(3 marks)

8   Explain three benefits a business might receive as a result of a substantial increase in its expenditure upon training.
(9 marks)

9   Outline possible implications for a firm of a decision to impose significant cuts in the training budget.
(7 marks)

10 How might headhunting contribute to the failure of the labour market?
(7 marks)

Analytical and evaluative questions

11 *Sandlers is a large retail chain in the UK. The firm is expanding rapidly. Examine the ways in which the firm may recruit staff to work in its stores.* (8 marks)

12 *Matalan plc is a discount store offering consumers competitively priced clothes and*

household goods. Discuss the factors that might affect the company's decision regarding the size of its training budget. (15 marks)

13 *HSBC is one of the UK's largest banks, trading in an increasingly competitive market. To what extent might the bank's recruitment and selection process determine the overall performance of the business?* (15 marks)

Leadership and management >> styles

What is the difference between leadership and management?

A significant feature in modern businesses is that the distinction between management and leadership is becoming blurred.

Key terms

Management is the process of setting objectives and making the most efficient use of financial, human and physical resources to achieve these objectives. Key tasks include planning, control and coordination.

Leadership is influencing others to achieve certain aims or objectives. Effective leadership skills can help a manager to carry out their duties.

Some companies have moved towards bringing these roles together and presenting managers as leaders. Major businesses such as Levi Strauss have adopted the principle of managers as leaders and place great emphasis on developing leadership skills amongst their employees. Good leadership skills can help a manager to be successful.

What do leaders do?

Leaders or managers have a broad range of duties. Their tasks may include:

- Deciding objectives for the organisation – leaders have to establish a sense of direction for the organisation.
- Providing expertise and setting standards for the organisation – the leader will have to show enthusiasm in difficult times and take a major role in solving problems.
- Canvassing opinion – leaders have to draw on all the expertise within the organisation when taking decisions.
- Deciding structure – the leader will play a key role in determining the structure of the organisation and in shaping the culture of the business.

What makes a good leader?

Some people believe great leaders are born. This is known as trait theory. Supporters of this theory have attempted to identify the features of personality that one would expect to find in a good leader. The following list contains some qualities a good leader should have:

- being informed and knowledgeable about matters relating to the business
- having the ability to think creatively and innovatively and to solve problems
- possessing self-motivation and the desire to achieve great things
- showing the ability to act quickly and decisively when necessary
- possessing an air of authority
- demonstrating excellent communication skills (including listening!).

POINTS TO PONDER

In 2002 the Council for Excellence in Management and Leadership criticised the quality of British business leadership. They argued that poor leadership had led to unmotiviated workplaces and poor training and development.

Source: Adapted from Guardian Unlimited/Nic Paton, www.guardian.co.uk, 22 February 2003

Styles of leadership

Another view of leadership is that people can be taught to be good leaders through training.

There are three basic categories of leadership style. These are:

1 autocratic or authoritarian leadership

2 paternalistic leadership
3 democratic leadership.

EXAMINER'S ADVICE

Textbooks often present a number of styles of leadership. However, in reality there is a range or spectrum of styles. The types we have looked at represent points on that spectrum. Thus, a range of democratic leadership styles exists. Leaders can be mildly democratic or strongly democratic, for example. Good answers recognise that any leadership 'label' in fact covers a variety of styles.

Authoritarian or autocratic leadership

Authoritarian or autocratic leaders would have considerable sympathy with the views expressed by F. W. Taylor (see page 182). Leaders using this style normally show a number of the following features:

- They like to retain control over the organisation and do not allow other employees much freedom of action.
- They tend to pass down instructions to junior employees and offer few opportunities to subordinates to discuss ideas and issues.
- Autocratic leaders set objectives, allocate tasks and expect obedience from subordinates.

	Leadership Style		
Features	Authoritarian	Paternalistic	Democratic
Description	Senior managers take the decisions with little involvement of junior employees	Dictatorial, but decisions are taken in the best interests of the employes	Running a business on the basis of majority decisions
Key features	• Sets objectives • Allocates tasks • Leader retains control throughout	• Explains decisions • Ensures employees' social and leisure needs are met	• Encourages employees to take part in decision-making • Uses delegation
Communication used	One-way communication – downwards from leader to subordinate	Generally from leader downwards, though some feedback takes place	Extensive, two-way communication between senior and junior employees
Circumstances in which style may be appropriate	Useful when quick decisions are required or when large numbers of unskilled employees are involved	Can appear democratic, but is really autocratic leadership with a human face	Useful when complex decisions are made requiring a range of specialist skills

Table 5.13 *Types of leadership style*

- Employees in an autocratically-led organisation often become very dependent upon their leader as they do not have the necessary information to act on their own initiative.

Organisations managed in an authoritarian style may face a number of difficulties. Mistakes by subordinates can result in criticism and, sometimes, disciplinary action. Hence, people avoid making decisions and these are passed up to be made at a higher level. Senior managers tend to be overworked, and staff turnover is often high.

> ## POINTS TO PONDER
>
> BHP Billiton, the world's largest mining company, announced the shock departure of Chief Executive Brian Gilbertson only six months after he was appointed. Reports suggest that Mr Gilbertson, who has a reputation as an autocratic leader, clashed with other directors on the Australian mining company's board.
>
> *Source: Adapted from www.telegraph.co.uk,*
> *7 January 2003*

Autocratic styles of management *do* have a part to play and might be appropriate in the following circumstances:

- when a rapid decision is needed
- when it is important that everyone in the organisation gives out the same message – maybe as part of crisis management
- when managers are responsible for a large number of (possibly unskilled) subordinates.

The term autocratic leadership covers a range of styles from the extremely autocratic approach used in the armed forces to a more benevolent autocratic style known as paternalistic leadership.

Paternalistic leadership

Paternalistic leadership is autocratic in approach but leaders take decisions in what they consider to be the best interests of the workforce. In these circumstances leaders will explain decisions and may engage in a limited amount of delegation. However, paternalistic leaders are unlikely to delegate extensively or to empower their workforces.

The paternal company treats its workforce as family, and places great emphasis on meeting the social and leisure needs of its staff. This approach was common in Victorian times with famous examples such as Rowntree and Cadbury. Both companies exhibited a strong social conscience.

Paternalistic leaders do gain the loyalty of their subordinates and paternalistic businesses frequently have a low rate of labour turnover.

On the other hand, a very low rate of labour turnover is not always an advantage. It may mean that new ideas and energy do not enter the business, damaging its performance and competitiveness. Paternalistic leaders do not encourage their employees to use their creative and imaginative skills, nor do they encourage the use of initiative.

Democratic or participative leadership

Democratic leadership (or participative leadership) occurs when a business's decisions are based on the majority view. Decisions may be agreed through a voting system, but are more likely to be the result of informal discussions. Democratic leadership encourages some or all of the following:

- The leader delegates and encourages the development of leadership skills in subordinates.
- Leaders and subordinates discuss issues and employee participation is actively encouraged.
- The leader acts upon advice, and explains the reasons for decisions.

The successful operation of this style requires excellent communication skills on the part of the leader and the ability to generate effective two-way communications. A considerable amount of management time may be spent on communicating.

Democratically-led groups usually offer constructive ideas and suggestions and can gain great satisfaction from their employment. Such groups have high levels of self-motivation and may require relatively little supervision.

There has been a move towards democratic leadership in many businesses over recent years (though there are still many autocratically-led businesses around). This trend might have taken place because leadership has become more complex.

Businesses are larger and more complicated organisations, the environment in which they operate is dynamic and changes rapidly. In these circumstances individual leaders are more likely to need the support that democratic leadership can provide.

Style versatility

Many managers believe that there is not a single perfect style of leadership. It may be that the best managers are those who adopt a style suitable to the circumstances. Thus, the most talented managers might be the most versatile; able to call on one or more styles.

Douglas McGregor's Theory X and Y

Douglas McGregor was an American psychologist who researched into management in large companies. McGregor published *The Human Side of Enterprise* in 1964. This book has become famous for examining how leaders' attitudes may influence their behaviour. In particular the book is noted for its comparison of two types of leader that McGregor called Theory X and Theory Y leaders.

McGregor's research revealed that many leaders assumed their workers were motivated solely by money. McGregor referred to this type of manager as Theory X. He also discovered a less common type of manager: the Theory Y leader. Such leaders believed employees wanted more than financial gain from working. Thus, a poor performance by a group of workers may be the result of a work environment lacking stimulation and challenge. The

People in business

William (Bill) Gates is Chairman and Chief Executive officer of the Microsoft Corporation. In the 2002–2003 financial year, the company enjoyed revenues in excess of £20 billion. The company has over 50 000 staff.

Bill Gates was born in 1955 and grew up in Seattle. Gates showed his first interest in computers as a 13-year-old schoolboy. Even at this age he was able to program computers. In 1973 Gates entered Harvard University. However, in 1975 he dropped out of university to concentrate on developing Microsoft, a company he had formed in partnership with Paul Allen. Microsoft was established with a mission statement to put a personal computer on every desk and in every home.

Gates has operated a democratic management style at Microsoft. He has actively involved employees in key management and strategic decisions, and has played an important role in the technical development of new products. Much of his time is devoted to meeting with customers and staying in contact with Microsoft employees around the world by email.

Figure 5.20 *Bill Gates*

behaviour of employees, argued McGregor, is often the result of the way they are treated.

In the early 1950s, Douglas McGregor used the results of his research to design a factory for Proctor and Gamble in the United States. The factory used self-managing teams and Theory Y principles and soon became Proctor and Gamble's best-performing factory.

McGregor did not believe in the views expressed by Theory X leaders. In his mind his Theory X managers assumed that workers were 'mediocre' and lacked talent and commitment. He argued that many businesses were making a mistake in using control and authority to achieve the best performance from their workers. McGregor presented this theory only to disprove it as part of his support for Theory Y managers.

McGregor's work set out the leadership style likely to introduce the methods of motivation proposed by Maslow and Herzberg (see page 185). Figure 5.21 summarises the links between the theories of the three writers.

Although McGregor wholeheartedly supported the Theory Y view of leadership, this does not mean that the Theory X approach has no place. A Theory X view of leadership would be appropriate under the same circumstances as an autocratic style (see page 212). A Theory X manager is likely to adopt an autocratic style, whilst a Theory Y leader would be expected to use a more democratic approach.

Management by objectives

In 1954 Peter Drucker published *The Practice of Management,* including his theory of Management by Objectives (MBO). This emphasised the central role of objectives in business management (see Chapter 2).

According to Drucker's theory of management by objectives, managers should:

- identify and agree targets for achievement with subordinates
- negotiate the support that will be required to achieve these targets
- evaluate over time the extent to which these objectives are met.

POINTS TO PONDER

'A manager's job should be based on the task to be performed in order to achieve the company's objectives ... the manager should be directed and controlled by these objectives ... rather than by his boss.'
Peter Drucker, The Practice of Management, 1954

The objectives set for each individual should be co-ordinated to ensure that the business achieves its corporate objectives. Each member of staff, therefore, makes a contribution towards the business objectives.

In Figure 5.22 a business has a mission statement giving the organisation's overall target of becoming the 'premier supplier of bottled beer in Europe'. The business's corporate objectives contribute to

Theory X leaders believe:	Theory Y leaders believe:
- The average employee dislikes work and will avoid it if possible. - People must be controlled and directed and punished, if necessary, to put in a real effort at work. - The typical worker wants to avoid responsibility and has little ambition. - Employees look for security above all else at work.	- Working is as natural as play or rest for the average employee. - The typical worker does not have an in-built dislike of work. - Other means exist to motivate workers rather than control and punishment. - In the right circumstances, workers seek responsibility. - Most employees have imagination and creativity that may be used to help organisations achieve their goals.

Table 5.14 *The views of Theory X and Theory Y leaders*

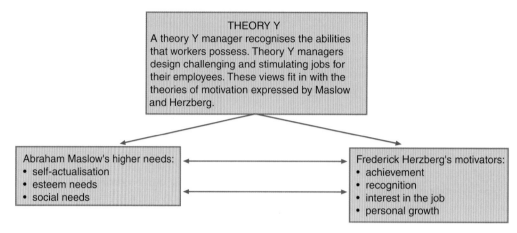

THEORY Y
A theory Y manager recognises the abilities that workers possess. Theory Y managers design challenging and stimulating jobs for their employees. These views fit in with the theories of motivation expressed by Maslow and Herzberg.

Abraham Maslow's higher needs:
• self-actualisation
• esteem needs
• social needs

Frederick Herzberg's motivators:
• achievement
• recognition
• interest in the job
• personal growth

Figure 5.21 *Theory Y and the ideas of Maslow and Herzberg*

Mission Statement
e.g. 'To become the premier supplier of bottled beer in Europe'

Corporate objectives, once achieved, allow the business to fulfil its **mission statement**
e.g. 'To increase sales in Europe by 5% in each of the next 5 years

Business functions pursue objectives to assist the business in achieving its **corporate objectives**
e.g. (marketing function) to achieve a 10% share of the bottled beer markets in Italy and Spain within 5 years

Attaining **departmental objectives** contributes to the business achieving its corporate objectives
e.g. (market research) to develop a plan to research customers' views on bottled beer in Italy and Spain

Individuals and teams negotiate **targets** which assist departments in achieving their goals
e.g. to design questionnaires as part of market research campaign

Objectives stated in greater detail

Figure 5.22 *Management by objectives*

this mission – one objective might be to increase sales in Europe by a certain percentage each year. The business comprises functions such as marketing, finance and production. These functions should contribute to the achievement of corporate objectives by doing their bit. Finally, the departments, teams and individuals should all make their coordinated contribution to the attainment of

the objectives of the functional area of the business in which they work.

An important element of the operation of MBO is the review of the extent to which targets have been met and the development of new goals, targets and objectives in the light of this experience.

The advantages and disadvantages of MBO

MBO offers a number of advantages to businesses:

● It can improve communication within the organisation as the target-setting and evaluation process takes place.
● Employees may be motivated by understanding what they are trying to achieve, and how it helps the business achieve its overall goals.
● MBO can highlight training needs for managers and subordinates, improving their performance and productivity.
● The attainment of goals can help all employees to fulfil some of the higher needs identified by Maslow.

Drucker recognised at the outset that MBO had a number of potential drawbacks:

● Some employees may see the setting of targets as threatening. A manager might set targets that the subordinate considers unachievable.
● All employees within the organisation must be committed to the technique if it is to succeed and benefit the business.
● Setting targets for highly specialised employees

can be difficult and tends to remove the focus from the mainstream corporate objectives.

- Modern businesses operate in a business environment that changes rapidly. Objectives can quickly become out of date.

Issues in leadership

The previous section reviewed some of the theory relating to leadership in modern businesses. However, a number of important factors influence the day-to-day approach used by managers.

Team-based leadership

Teamworking occurs when production is organised into substantial units of work. This is in contrast to the division of labour that requires employees to carry out simple tasks repeatedly. The team of people is likely to be working on a large task, for example, installing the engine into a car.

Teamworking is common within organisations and often accompanies delayering (see page 171). Major multinational organisations, such as Volvo and Toshiba, have organised their business on the basis of teams. Businesses may assemble teams to solve problems and propose new working methods (quality circles or kaizen groups) or to manage major projects such as developing a new product.

Part of the art of leading a successful team is ensuring the correct balance of people within the team. To succeed, a team must have individuals who can between them carry out a range of duties. Not only must they be multi-skilled, their skills and personalities must blend together and be

complementary. Successful teams need people with drive and motivation, as well as people with administrative skills to ensure that all tasks are completed.

Potential problems with teams

It is important for leaders to make sure that teams are all pursuing the organisation's objectives. Teams may aim for goals that are different from the corporate objectives. Alternatively, they may become too competitive and the desire to beat the rival team within the organisation may become the primary objective.

Teams can become complacent, confident in their own success and unaware of major changes taking place outside the team. This can result in failure to achieve targets. Successful team-based management may, therefore, require regular changes in the personnel of teams.

Key terms

Quality circles *are teams of employees drawn from all levels in the organisation and given the task of solving operational problems. The Japanese term for these groups is sometimes used:* **kaizen***.*

Single status

Team-based leadership may also require the implementation of single status into the workplace. Single status leads to the removal of all barriers distinguishing between different grades of staff within the organisation.

Under single status all employees within an organisation:

- use the same canteen and other facilities
- work similar hours, irrespective of their roles within the organisation
- are entitled to similar holiday arrangements
- wear the same clothing – often a company overall.

The only distinction remaining in single status organisations should be the level of pay received by the various grades of employee. The adoption of single status is intended to remove the 'them and us' mentality within businesses.

Delegation and consultation

Delegation and consultation are important elements of an individual's style of leadership. Delegation means managers give junior employees the authority to carry out particular tasks. For example, teams on a production line may be given authority to recruit new team members. Consultation allows a manager to retain more control. A consultative manager would seek employees' views on important issues. Their views would play a part in decision-making but with consultation managers keep authority. A consultative style is often a feature of paternalistic leadership. Democratic leaders tend to use delegation.

Key issues

The government is keen to improve the performance of British workers in an attempt to close the productivity gap between British workers and those from other industrialised countries. The government's own figures suggest that output per worker is 42% higher in the USA, 14% higher in France and 7% higher in Germany.

The government has invested heavily in improving the skills of the workforce and the latest announcement came in the Budget in the spring of 2003. The Chancellor of the Exchequer revealed that a scheme to compensate businesses for employee time lost due to training would be extended. He allocated an additional £40 million to support this initiative, bringing the total expenditure on it to £170 million.

This is a small part of the Government's strategy to improve workplace skills. In total, nearly £60 billion will be spent on education in the UK by 2006, with an increasing proportion being spent on vocational training and major initiatives such as the New Deal.

Source: Adapted from www.guardian.co.uk/Nic Paton, 22 February 2003 and http://bbc.co.uk, 9 April 2003

Forms of Consultation

Consultation can take place informally within an organisation when managers have discussions with employees. As an organisation grows, consultation is likely to become more formal. Paternalistic leaders often use works councils to gain employees' views on major issues.

The degree of delegation used may depend on the skill and experience of managers and subordinates, as well as on the philosophy of the company concerned. Experienced managers leading highly trained employees will be more inclined to use delegation, especially if the organisation's senior managers are democratic leaders.

Advantages	Disadvantages
• Delegation frees senior managers for other (possibly strategic) matters.	• Trusting subordinates can be risky and responsibility remains with the senior manager.
• Delegation may breed a sense of responsibility and help to motivate.	• Delegation can involve expensive training for subordinates.
• Controlling subordinates is expensive, for example, supervisors may be needed. Delegation relaxes control.	• Once trust is given, it is impossible to withdraw it without loss of face.
• Delegation allows individuals to develop skills and careers.	• Some managers may be reluctant to use delegation as they have to relinquish control.
• Without delegation there is no training for prospective managers.	

Table 5.15 *The advantages and disadvantages of delegation*

1 Complete the following sentences by inserting the missing words. '...................... is the process of setting objectives and making the most efficient use of financial, human and physical .... to achieve these objectives. .... is influencing others to achieve certain aims or ....'

2 A certain manager is dictatorial but takes decisions in the best interests of her employees. Which of the following best describes this style of leadership?
a) autocratic
b) democratic
c) paternalistic
d) authoritarian.

3 Which of the following types of leader is most likely to rely upon extensive two-way communication between senior and junior employees?
a) autocratic
b) democratic
c) paternalistic
d) authoritarian.

4 Which of the flowing writers would be most likely to be in sympathy with an autocratic style of leadership?
a) Herzberg
b) Maslow
c) Mayo
d) Taylor.

5 Which style of leadership may be most appropriate when rapid decisions are required?
a) autocratic
b) democratic
c) paternalistic
d) participative.

6 Read the statements below. In each case say whether they would be associated with Theory X or Theory Y leaders.
a) Workers are motivated solely by pay.
b) Work is as natural as rest or play for the average employee.
c) In the right circumstances, employees seek responsibility.
d) If workers are to make an effort at work they must be controlled and directed.

7 Which of the following is **not** an advantage of management by objectives (MBO)?
a) Employees may be motivated by understanding what they are trying to achieve.
b) Setting targets for highly specialised employees may lead to objectives that do not fit in with corporate objectives.
c) MBO may highlight considerable training needs for managers.
d) Setting targets may result in employees fulfilling some of Maslow's higher needs.

8 Of what is the following a definition: the process of removing all barriers that distinguish between different grades of staff within an organisation?

9 Complete the following sentences by inserting the missing words. 'Delegation occurs when senior managers give .... employees the .... to carry out particular tasks. .... takes place when managers ask for, and take into account, the .... of subordinates.'

10 Which style of leadership is most likely to make use of consultation?
a) autocratic
b) democratic
c) paternalistic
d) participative.

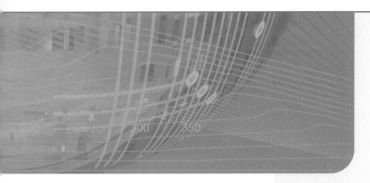

Progress questions

1 Explain the difference between 'leadership' and 'management'. *(5 marks)*

2 Outline two key duties of a leader. *(6 marks)*

3 Fully explain two circumstances in which autocratic or authoritarian leadership might be considered appropriate. *(6 marks)*

4 Explain the problems a paternalistically-led business might encounter as a result of a decision to increase the scale of its operations. *(7 marks)*

5 Outline three problems a business might encounter as a result of adopting a democratic style of leadership. *(9 marks)*

6 'Democratic leadership is the most efficient style.' Do you agree with this statement? Explain your answer. *(7 marks)*

7 Explain one advantage and one disadvantage to a business of using Management by Objectives. *(6 marks)*

8 Distinguish between 'delegation' and 'consultation'. *(4 marks)*

9 Outline two implications for a business's management style of a decision to implement teamworking throughout the organisation. *(6 marks)*

10 Explain the relationship between management styles and the extent to which delegation is employed. *(6 marks)*

Analytical and evaluative questions

11 Parsley & Sons Ltd is a medium-sized business manufacturing components for the electronics industry. The firm employs mainly unskilled labour and has several large customers who place large regular orders. Examine the case for and against the company's use of an autocratic style of leadership. *(8 marks)*

12 Microsoft is one of the world's largest businesses, employing in excess of 50 000

people in 60 countries. To what extent can Bill Gates' leadership guarantee the company's success? *(15 marks)*

13 Howard & Duncan Ltd operates several factories in locations throughout the UK. Each factory operates independently and manufactures different products. The company employs 10 000 people and has a newly appointed Chief Executive. Discuss whether this business would benefit from the introduction of management by objectives (MBO). *(15 marks)*

End of chapter questions

Healeys, a major producer of soaps, detergents and washing powders, operates throughout Europe. The company is renowned for its paternalistic management style. Until the last few years, the company had about 20% of the UK market but sales have fallen. In particular, sales have been lost to L & T manufacturing. Commentators have noted that Healeys is too product-oriented. They also highlight the rather cumbersome management structure with many layers of hierarchy and short spans of control which they believe has significantly hindered competitiveness.

At the recent Annual General Meeting Saskia Papagna, the Managing Director, announced radical change and restructuring. 'We will be delayering and reorganising within the group.' However, the problems at Healeys may be deep rooted and a change in structure may not be able to provide a quick fix solution. Commentators point to the lack of delegation at the firm which may have contributed to a demotivated workforce. Papagna recognises this problem within the firm and ordered all managers to make more use of their subordinates immediately. Some senior managers are wary of such change and doubt its likely effectiveness.

1 *What is meant by the term 'layers of hierarchy'?* (3 marks)

2 *Explain two likely implications of 'paternalistic management' for Healey's employees.* (6 marks)

3 *Analyse the possible implications for a firm of having a demotivated workforce.* (10 marks)

4 *To what extent is more delegation desirable in a firm such as Healeys?* (15 marks)

Research conducted in autumn 2003 showed that since 1993 the pay of the UK's senior managers has risen six times as quickly as that of typical employees. In 2002 the chief executives of Britain's largest 100 companies enjoyed pay increases of over 16%. Over the last ten years the chief executives of the UK's major companies have experienced pay increases of 288% whilst the average earnings of a UK employee have risen by a paltry 45%.

Incomes Data Services, the consultants who carried out the research, say the rapidly widening pay gap could cause tension over pay structures within firms. If companies reveal the salaries that bosses are receiving it is likely to boost pay claims by shop floor workers.

The pay of the UK's top managers has been a controversial issue for some time and in 2003 the Department of Trade and Industry set out a range of options for tackling excessive pay-offs in its paper *Rewards for Failure*.

Leaping to the defence of bosses' pay, the Confederation of British Industry (CBI), said that UK companies were legally obliged to reveal full details of top managers' pay in their annual reports. A spokesman said that the increase in executive pay reflected the market value of high quality managers. The 17% rise in chief executives' salaries and bonuses in 2002 compares with 11% in the previous year.

EXAMPLES OF REWARDS FOR TOP MANAGERS

GlaxoSmithKline chief Jean-Pierre Garnier received £22m as a pay-off

HSBC pays director William Aldinger £25m per annum

Reuters Tom Glocer receives a £612000 bonus for 2002 whilst the company records a loss

---

Some businesses have spoken out in support of the CBI's position. They argue that they can only attract world-class managers by paying salary packages comparable with those available elsewhere in the world. The market for managers is global. Top managers' pay packages often include health insurance, company cars and share options as well as the highly publicised high salaries

1 *What is meant by the term 'share options'?*
(2 marks)

2 *Explain **two** factors that may influence the salary levels paid to senior managers.* (6 marks)

3 *Analyse the advantages and disadvantages to high street bank HSBC of awarding director William Aldinger a £25 million pay deal.* (9 marks)

4 *Frederick Herzberg believed that pay could not be used to motivate people. Discuss whether the payment of large salaries to senior managers in the UK's largest companies indicates that his theory has little relevance today.* (15 marks)

Case study

32 marks

Cadbury Schweppes plc has become one of the world's largest drinks and confectionery companies, selling its products throughout the world. The company has pursued an objective of growth over recent years, and this was reflected in its purchase of the American sweets manufacturer Adams. In 2002 Cadbury's profits rose 6% to £935 million. Disappointingly, 2003 proved less profitable as the company has faced more intense competition in the vital American market. However, the manufacturer of Dairy Milk chocolate and Schweppes tonic water expected this, and said it would not meet its 10% growth target in 2003. The company expects sales in America to remain virtually unchanged over the next few months.

The company was also criticised for its policies of directors' pay. The National Association of Pension Funds described this aspect of Cadbury Schweppes operation as 'falling well short of current UK best practice'. The NAPF particularly highlighted easy performance targets for senior managers and generous offerings of company shares.

Cadbury Schweppes also confirmed plans to delayer its company structure and to reorganise its management. Its new, simpler organisation structure was introduced in February 2003, to clarify accountability and enable swifter decision-making. Cadbury Schweppes now operates five geographical regions rather than ten as in the past. Although this resulted in job losses, a more centralised structure aids control. Under the new structure ten key executives report directly to the company's Chief Executive.

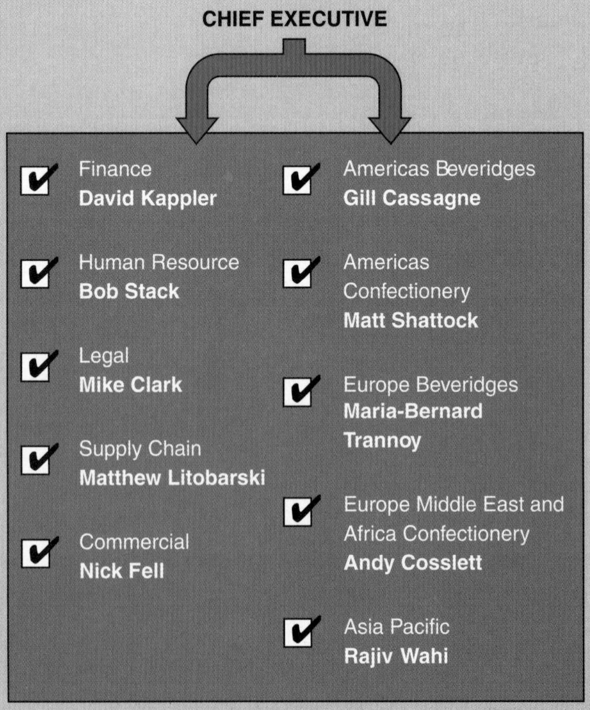

CHIEF EXECUTIVE

☑	Finance David Kappler	☑	Americas Beveridges Gill Cassagne
☑	Human Resource Bob Stack	☑	Americas Confectionery Matt Shattock
☑	Legal Mike Clark	☑	Europe Beveridges Maria-Bernard Trannoy
☑	Supply Chain Matthew Litobarski		
☑	Commercial Nick Fell	☑	Europe Middle East and Africa Confectionery Andy Cosslett
		☑	Asia Pacific Rajiv Wahi

Source: www.cadburyschweppes.com/EN/AboutUs/ Glance/OrganisationStructure

Figure 5.23 *Cadbury Schweppes organisation structure*

It is likely that the company will only receive the benefits of delayering in the long run. Chief executive John Sunderland said '2003 will be a year of transition'. The restructuring had cost the company £140 million.

Source: Adapted from (Cadbury Schweppes plc)
www.cadburyschweppes.com and www.telegraph.co.uk, 3 May 2003

1 *What is meant by the term 'delayering'? (2 marks)*

2 *Explain two benefits that Cadbury Schweppes might enjoy as a consequence of delayering its organisation.* *(6 marks)*

3 *Analyse the case for Cadbury Schweppes offering its senior managers generous salary packages.* *(9 marks)*

4 *To what extent is it likely that Cadbury Schweppes will only receive the benefits of its restructuring in the long term.*

(15 marks)

Case study

34 marks

A leader is someone who has the ability to inspire others and to make them willing workers. Fortunately, leaders are made as well as born, but all leaders have to understand the difference between leaders and bosses.

Leadership has three key aspects: managing yourself, leading the individual and leading the team. Training in these areas can produce men and women who are capable of encouraging others in the pursuit of organisational objectives.

- Managing yourself involves planning, setting objectives, managing change and problem-solving.
- Leading the individual involves motivation, recruitment and induction, consultation, delegation and reviewing performance.
- Leading the team involves meetings, training the team, team leadership and team building.

Leadership requires that a positive view is taken of employees and that good communication skills are used at all times. Effective leaders take a Theory Y view of their employees. The boss approach can lead to a lowering of morale; an essential element of being an effective leader is providing motivation for employees.

1 *Explain the difference between delegation and consultation.* *(5 marks)*

2 *Outline the skills that a leader in a small business needs to carry out the role effectively.* *(6 marks)*

3 *Analyse why effective leaders in the banking industry might '… take a Theory Y view of their employees'.* *(8 marks)*

4 *All a person needs to be an effective leader of a multinational business is good communication skills. To what extent do you agree with this statement?* *(15 marks)*

The boss's approach	The leader's approach
1 I'm at the top in a controlling and directing role	1 I'm at the bottom in a supporting and coaching role
2 I tell people what to do	2 I consult with my people and agree decisions
3 I get results from my people	3 I get results through my people
4 My people have confidence in me	4 My people have confidence and self-esteem
5 I improve organisational performance by supervising people	5 I improve the organisation's performance by developing people
6 I provide solutions to problems for individuals	6 I encourage individuals and teams to solve problems
7 I instruct people	7 I motivate people
8 I tell my people my views	8 I listen to my people's views

Amersham Insurance boss Usha Gupta has announced that the financial services group is reorganising following a period of sustained growth. The announcement was received well in the City and the company's share price rose by 14 pence to a new high of 282 pence. The company's expansion plans follow two years of trading during which the business has seen its sales of pensions, insurance policies and other financial products increase by over 32%.

The Buckinghamshire-based company is expected to recruit 900 employees over the next 18 months. Ms Gupta commented yesterday that the board has approved a new human resource plan designed to take the company forward over the next ten years. The objective of being '... a major player in the financial services market' is 'definitely achievable' according to Ms Gupta. 'We have set ourselves tough corporate objectives based on strengthening our position in the financial services market and our human resources plan is an integral component of this. We are a services business and rely heavily upon the quality and motivation of our staff. I am convinced that training is the key to improving Amersham Insurance's performance over the coming years.'

Year	Expenditure on training (£ million)
2002	1.50
2003	1.65
2004	2.05
2005	2.64
2006	3.15

Table 5.16 Expenditure on training by Amersham Insurance 2002–2006 (the figures in italics are forecasts)

The company's plans are based upon continuing the policy of empowering the workforce and the widespread use of teams in designing and selling financial services. Amersham Insurance's culture has changed significantly alongside the development of a new organisational structure. The company has sought to eliminate bureaucracy and to become more task-orientated in response to the increasing competitiveness of the financial services market.

Amersham International remains unique amongst financial services businesses for operating a flat organisational structure and using wide spans of control. This has led to criticisms from a number of former employees about being expected to cope with excessive workloads.

1 Outline the process by which Amersham Insurance might have developed its human resources plan. *(6 marks)*

2 a) Calculate the percentage increase in expenditure on training forecast to take place between 2002 and 2006. *(6 marks)*

b) Explain why Usha Gupta might believe that '... training is the key to improving Amersham Insurance's performance ...'. *(8 marks)*

3 Evaluate the case for and against an organisation using wide spans of control. *(15 marks)*

4 Amersham International intends to recruit 900 new employees into a business operating empowered teams. Examine the problems the company might encounter during this process. *(10 marks)*

5 Discuss the factors that might have influenced Usha Gupta and her fellow directors when redesigning the organisational structure of Amersham Insurance. *(15 marks)*

Figure 5.24 *Relationships between People and Organisations and other topics in the AS specification*

Operations management 6

Introduction

- What is operations management?
- How do businesses decide on the right production technique, scale of production and stock level?
- How do businesses ensure good productivity *and* good quality?

>> What is operations management?

The aim of operations management is to ensure the right quantity of goods are produced at the right time at the right cost and with the right quality. This involves managing all the business's resources to make sure:

- the right inputs are there when they are needed
- the most effective method of production is used to provide high quality products at minimum cost
- the firm can produce an appropriate range of goods and services
- the goods are produced on time for the customer.

Operations management therefore involves decisions about:

- how to produce products
- what people, equipment and machinery are required
- the level of materials and components the firm needs to have available at any given moment.

Productive efficiency

One of the ways in which the success of operations management can be assessed is known as **productive** efficiency. Productive efficiency measures the cost of producing an item in terms of resources used. The more productively efficient a firm is, the lower the cost per unit; the less efficient it is the higher the cost per unit.

Operations management will aim to increase the firm's productive efficiency whilst also meeting a given quality target. There is no point in cutting costs if the result is a poor and unreliable product that customers do not want. In some cases, the firm's strategy will be to produce items which are much more expensive than the competition because they have far more benefits to the customers. A luxury car such as Rolls Royce will inevitably cost more to produce than a mass market, high-volume car such as Nissan Micra.

The cost per unit will depend on many factors:

- The way in which the output is produced – for example, it is more expensive to make items by hand than it is using machinery.
- The cost of materials – cars with leather seats will be more expensive than ones with plastic seats.
- The number of items being produced – it is often cheaper per item to produce goods on a large

Business in focus

Operations management includes finding the right quality and amount of supplies at the right price. The Wrigley Company, for example, has to find huge amounts of mint each year to flavour its chewing gum. A vast area of farmland is required to grow all the mint the Wrigley Company needs. If added together, this farmland would equal 53 square miles, or 30 550 American football fields.

The mint is grown in areas of America such as Indiana, Michigan and Wisconsin. One acre of mint produces about 34.5 kg of oil. It is harvested from mid-June to late September. The mint is cut and and left to dry. Then it is placed in tubs and pressurized steam is shot through the tubs, vaporising the mint oil. Samples are then tested and the oil is either bought or rejected. Oils accepted for purchase are stored in a temperature-controlled warehouse. Numerous tests are performed to create the right blend of the different oils from the various regions. Then the 'master blend' is mixed with the other flavour ingredients required by the brand's formula and mixed with other chewing gum ingredients.

Source: Adapted from www.wrigley.com/products

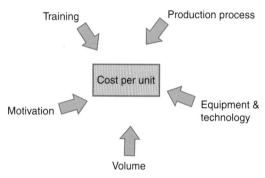

Figure 6.1 *Cost per unit*

POINTS TO PONDER

In an attempt to become much leaner, Sony announced in 2003 a strategy that included the reduction in the number of parts it uses for its consumer electronics products by nearly 90%. It set out to reduce the number of components used in its complex manufacturing processes from 840 000 to 100 000 within two years. Sony's aim is to free up product developers to spend more time on developing new products rather than new parts. This need to reduce costs is forced on the firm by the fierce competition in the market.

scale rather than make a small quantity because the initial design and cost of setting up the process can be spread over more units.

A major influence on the productive efficiency of a firm is its workforce. If employees are motivated, they are likely to produce more units than if they are demotivated. Motivated employees are likely to produce better quality products with less mistakes and rejects because they will take more interest in the work.

The amount and quality of the training employees receive and the investment in equipment is also important. There is little point in having motivated employees, if they do not actually have the skills or tools they need to do the job.

Operations management and competitiveness

The competitiveness of a firm depends on its ability to offer customers better value for money than its rivals. This means it must offer more benefits than the competition and/or produce goods at a lower price. For a firm to be successful, customers must think its products or services offer good value for money and are worth buying.

Business in focus

UK companies use an estimated £800m worth of nuts, bolts and fastener products each year. Approximately half are made in Britain and the rest are imported, mainly from South East Asia, where production costs are lower. Forty years ago Britain was almost self-sufficient in nuts and had dozens of factories. Now most UK plants concentrate on relatively expensive items such as lightweight rivets for the aerospace industry.

One of the few remaining businesses in this market in the UK is Philidas, which now operates in a niche market. 'We have to focus on quality and high technology products,' says the company's Managing Director. 'Above all we have to be good at solving customers' problems.' For example, the company has devised a wheel nut for Ford vans that contains an in-built washer, making assembly easier and the vehicles safer.

Philidas has also developed 'team-based' manufacturing methods in which individual workers do a variety of machining and forging steps and are each responsible for quality. Such ideas encourage worker involvement and cut the number of defective parts, enabling the firm to maintain its competitiveness.

Source: Financial Times, 3 November 1999
(For more information on Philidas, visit
www.infastusa.com/artman/publsh/philidas-intros.html)

1 Most nuts and bolts are now imported into the UK rather than being produced here. Why do you think this is?
2 How have firms such as Philidas survived?
3 In what ways do you think team-based manufacturing methods might help a firm to become more competitive?

Operations management can improve a firm's competitiveness in several ways:

- by reducing the cost per unit so the firm is able to lower its prices
- by providing better quality goods which meet the needs of customers more effectively than other firms
- by producing more reliable goods with less faults
- by producing goods faster than the competition so they can get them to the customer more quickly
- by developing new products quickly so that customers are offered new models or new varieties ahead of the competition.

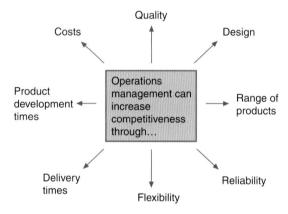

Figure 6.2 *Operations management can improve a firm's competitiveness*

Operations management and other functions of the business

Operations managers have to work closely with the other functions of the firm.

Marketing

The marketing function determines what needs to be produced and when by focusing on customer's needs. It also influences the amount the firm can afford to spend on producing the item, because it knows how much customers are prepared to pay for the goods or services. Marketing, therefore, influences the design of the product, the required output levels and the timing of production.

Human Resources

The human resource function is important because a business needs the right number of employees with the correct skills in order to meet its production targets. Planning to ensure the firm has the appropriate workforce is a vital support to operations management.

Production

Production has an impact on the firm's finances. A business may need to raise finance to buy stocks of raw materials, to build a new factory or move into new offices. Production costs are likely to have a significant effect on profits.

Integration

The operations manager must coordinate the production plans with the other functions. Without this coordination, the firm may find that:

- it is producing goods even though there is not enough demand for them
- it does not have the right number of employees or workers with the right skills to produce the goods it wishes
- it does not have the money it needs to buy in components
- it is producing items which are not profitable.

POINTS TO PONDER

The UK is increasingly moving towards a service economy. The fast-growing areas of the economy are music, entertainment, computers and finance, rather than manufacturing. Operations management is, therefore, focusing more on the management of people, ideas and knowledge, than on traditional manufacturing processes.

QUICK CHECK QUESTIONS

1   Operations (or production) is one function of a business. Name two others.

2   State three ways in which operations management can improve the competitiveness of a firm.

3   Which of the following in not part of operations management?
a)   output levels
b)   quality
c)   staff recruitment
d)   production methods.

4   Which is the best definition of productive efficiency?
a)   It measures the level of sales in relation to revenue.
b)   It measures the level of output in relation to the inputs used up.
c)   It measures profits.
d)   It measures output.

5   The resources of a business do not include:
a)   land
b)   labour
c)   entrepreneurship
d)   finished goods.

6   Which of the following is not an operations objective?
a)   reduce unit costs
b)   improve quality
c)   increase production flexibility
d)   increase sales.

7   Which of the following might increase the productive efficiency of a business?

APPLICATION IN ACTION

- When answering questions about operations management, think carefully about what really matters in the given industry.
- Some production processes produce huge volumes of goods (think of a Coca-Cola bottling plant) and keeping the production line going is essential. In other sectors, such as accountancy, each project is unique and this requires a great deal of direct contact with the customer to understand their specific requirements. In some industries, coping with seasonal demand is a major issue (e.g. sunglasses); in others rapid product development is the key (e.g. consumer electronics). In manufacturing, organising stocks may be important. In services, coping with queues may be the priority.
- Remember to think of the key operational issues in the market you are studying.

a) less output per worker
b) the same output achieved with more machines
c) maintaining output but reducing staff
d) less output per input.

8 Which of the following is the direct responsibility of operations management?
a) stock control
b) pricing
c) training
d) market research

9 The objective of operations management is always to produce as cheaply as possible. True of false? Explain.

10 Increasing efficiency means:
a) increasing the revenue per unit
b) reducing the cost per unit
c) increasing sales
d) decreasing the volume of outputs.

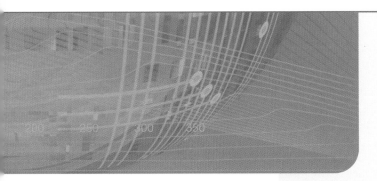

Progress questions

1 What is meant by 'operations management'?
(2 marks)

2 What are the possible objectives of operations management? (5 marks)

3 What is meant by 'productive efficiency'?
(2 marks)

4 Frank Bruno is desperate to increase the productive efficiency of his toaster factory. Explain two ways in which his firm might increase its productive efficiency. (6 marks)

5 Explain two ways in which decisions made by the operations manager of a toy manufacturer might affect the marketing function. (6 marks)

6 Explain two ways in which decisions made by the operations manager of a mobile phone manufacturer might affect the human resource function. (6 marks)

7 Examine how operations management of a furniture store can affect the competitiveness of a firm. (8 marks)

8 Jessica Cheung is the Human Resources Director of Allendale Country Casual Clothing. In recent months Jessica has found it difficult to recruit new staff. Explain how these problems may affect the firm's production. (6 marks)

9 Operations management is often concerned with the cost of producing. Explain two factors that might affect the cost of producing yoghurts. (6 marks)

10 Zanti Fanti produces animated cartoons for the television. The firm is eager to increase in size and produce far more cartoons in the coming years. Explain how an increase in the size of the firm might affect the other functions of the business. (8 marks)

Analytical and evaluative questions

11 *Andrew Longfellow has just been appointed as Operations Manager at the Fretin plc bottling plant in Scotland. The factory bottles soft drinks for one of the major manufacturers. Analyse the activities Andrew is likely to be responsible for in his job.* (8 marks)

12 *Discuss the ways in which increased productive efficiency might benefit a car manufacturer.* (15 marks)

13 *To what extent can effective operations management influence the success of a new retail store?* (15 marks)

>> Types of production

Production and operations

Many types of production exist in a modern economy. All, however, take inputs, transform these in some way and produce outputs, whilst varying tremendously in how they do this. Making computer games is very different from running a hotel; producing a film is different from operating a soft drinks bottling plant. These processes will differ in terms of the number and range of goods produced, how they produce them and the nature of their inputs and outputs.

Although there are many different types of production process they are often classified under three headings:

1 Job production.
2 Batch production.
3 Flow production.

Job production

Job production occurs when a firm produces specialised or one-off items for its customers. An artist and an architect, for example, both provide a service which is tailor made to the needs of their clients. Although the principles of painting or designing buildings are essentially the same for all customers, the precise service offered must be adapted for different needs. Similarly, recording a new album or fixing someone's car are all examples of job production.

Job production is usually an expensive way of making something as the firm must plan each project individually. The business also needs to have the skills and equipment available to meet a wide range of different needs. In many cases, job production relies on specialist skills and is labour intensive, involving a high level of labour in relation to the amount of equipment and machinery. The benefit of job production is that each item can be altered for the customer; this can be a useful marketing asset and may provide a Unique Selling Proposition.

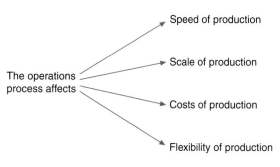

Figure 6.3 *Aspects of production which are controlled by operations management*

Business in focus

'It requires the ultimate in skill and 12 weeks' total dedication to quality and excellence, precision, painstaking care and meticulous attention to detail by the craftsmen at Newport Pagnell to build an Aston Martin and complete the 438 quality checks which are applied to every new car which leaves the world famous Buckinghamshire factory. The resultant product is as perfect as possible. Each car has:

- 12 coats of paint, each one carefully checked and rubbed down by hand
- hand-finished aluminium body panels
- ten cow hides used in each interior
- highest quality Wilton carpet inside
- a small brass plate on the engine carrying the name of the engine builder.

'When commissioning an Aston Martin, personal expression is only limited by the imagination. Customers are encouraged to take time in selecting colours and textures in the same way and with the same attention to detail as the craftsmen who build the car. As a result, very few cars are the same; each one an individual and unique statement of personal choice.' Truly job production!

Source: Aston Martin prospectus and website (for more information on Aston Martin, visit www.astonmartin.com)

1 Aston Martins are obviously produced using job production techniques. What implications does this have for the marketing of the car?

Batch production

In this type of production, groups of items move through the different stages of the production process at the same time. Imagine you have to photocopy 50 copies each of several different documents: you will have to set the machine up for the first item and run off 50 copies; then you will copy the next item. For some of the items you may need to change the set up of the machine – you may want a different type of copy (one-sided, two-sided, enlarged or reduced). This is a good example of batch production. Paint and wallpaper rolls are also produced in batches. When you go to buy these items you can usually find a batch number on the packaging.

POINTS TO PONDER

In expensive restaurants diners choose different dishes from the menu, specifying exactly how they want each one cooked. The chef will produce to order: this is job production. In a fast-food restaurant or fish and chip shop there is a limited choice of items and these are produced in batches.

Batch production involves a great deal of planning to decide how the firm's machines will be used and what batch will be produced when. It is also likely to involve high levels of stock, as the firm must wait for all of the items to finish at one stage before they are moved on to the next.

Another key issue in batch production is the time it takes to switch from producing one batch to producing another. For example, settings on machines may have to be changed.) This is known as **down time**. The longer the down time, the more expensive it is for firms to produce because the machinery is not being used during this time.

Flow production

In this production system, products move continuously from one stage of the process to another. This type of production is appropriate when a firm is looking to produce large volumes of very similar items (e.g. cans of cola, bottles of mineral water).

Flow production tends to be very capital intensive. This means that the amount of machinery involved is high compared with the number of employees involved. Flow production uses production line techniques.

Another consideration is that, once the process is set up, it is difficult to switch from one type of product to another. Flow production is only really suitable when there is a high demand for a very

Job	Batch	Flow
• one-off production	• production in batches or groups	• continuous production
• can produce tailor-made products	• involves high level of pre-planning to coordinate batches	• economies of scale involved in mass production
• suitable for niche marketing	• can produce a variety of products needing different marketing	• suitable for mass marketing
• needs wide range of machines and skills to meet requirements of each job	• needs fairly wide range of equipment and skills for different batches	• needs one set of machines to produce standardised product
• highly flexible process	• fairly flexible process	• inflexible process
• often labour intensive	• usually relatively capital intensive	• capital intensive

Table 6.1 *A comparison of job, batch and flow production*

Business in focus

Pirelli, a tyre manufacturer, has been trying to improve its profit margins through a strategy of targeting high value-added markets, while retaining a stake in the more mass market business. With new flexible manufacturing technology it is now commercially viable to produce tyres in batches of as low as 150–200 units. Pirelli believes it is in a particularly strong position, thanks to its new production system, the first to require no direct labour input! It can be contained in a space that is only one-fifth the floor area of a conventional factory.

The new technology is initially for high performance tyres, where it will cut the cost of the finished product by 25% compared with conventional processes. A plant capable of producing 1 million tyres a year with just 104 employees spread over five shifts to supervise the production process, occupies just 3500 square metres and has an investment cost of €41 million excluding the basic building, according to Pirelli.

(For more information on Pirelli, visit www.pirelli.com)

1 How might Pirelli's new technology help it compete against other producers?
2 Pirelli can produce 1 million tyres a year with 104 employees. What is the productivity of its workforce?

standardised product. It is not appropriate when demand is changing all the time or the overall level of demand is small.

In flow production, the aim is to keep the process moving at all times; any delay or stoppage is extremely expensive because the whole line must wait for any fault to be fixed.

Key terms

A *capital intensive* process has a high level of capital equipment, such as machinery, relative to the labour input, e.g. car manufacture.

A *labour intensive* process has a high level of labour input relative to the capital input. Teaching and hairdressing are examples of this.

Which is the best type of production process?

The best or most appropriate type of production process for a firm depends on a variety of factors such as:

• the type of product
• the expected level of demand
• the variety of goods expected by the customer.

If, for example, customers want products tailor made to their exact needs, the firm will need to adopt a job production process. Job production is flexible but expensive, so the firm needs to make sure that the customer is willing to pay for this specialised service.

If, on the other hand, there is a huge demand for a product, then it may be feasible to produce on a large scale and adopt a flow process. Hundreds of thousands of litres of Coca-Cola are produced and bottled every day, for example.

Production process and competitiveness

A firm's ability to compete will depend on whether it can provide better value for money than the competition. In the case of job production, a firm may achieve this by offering a more specialised product. In the case of flow production, it may be achieved by offering the product at a lower price than the competition. A firm must select the appropriate production techniques for the specific requirements of its market.

Business in focus

An early and one of the most famous examples of flow production is the Model T Ford. When Ford's engineers introduced the assembly line to Model T production in 1913 the amount of labour time spent making a single car dropped from 12 hours and 8 minutes to 2 hours and 35 minutes. Six months later Model Ts could roll off the assembly line at the rate of 1000 a day, with the average labour time dropping to just over an hour and a half.

However, the example of the Model T also highlights the potential problems of flow production. One of Henry Ford's famous sayings about the Model T was 'You can have any colour you want as long as it's black!'. Although the assembly line flow process provided high volumes and enabled a lower price to be charged, it produced a highly standardised product. In the 1920s the Ford company struggled under the attack from General Motors which offered a much wider range of choice to customers.

1 Does the experience of Ford suggest that flow production techniques are a good or bad thing?

The future of production

With developments in technology, firms are increasingly able to use flow production techniques but still offer some of the flexibility of batch and job production. Technological developments enable firms to make the same basic parts but assemble them in different ways to produce products that appear different, but are essentially very similar. Whirlpool, for example, produces a range of standardised elements for its fridge; these are combined in different ways (the door may open to the left or right, the fridge may be on top and the freezer below or vice versa). Thus the customer has a range of choices and can purchase products to meet their particular requirements.

 ## Key issues

Developments in technology have in recent years transformed operations management. Communication is easier between retailers, distributors, manufacturers and suppliers, speeding up the whole process of order to delivery. Manufacturing is easier and better quality products can be achieved with computer-aided machinery. Computer Aided Design and Computer Aided Manufacture are the result of new technology.

Technology also enables people within the organisation to share information and experiences much more easily. Rather than having to solve each problem from scratch every time, employees can quickly find out whether anyone else in the organisation has had similar problems before.

APPLICATION IN ACTION

When choosing the right type of production, managers must weigh up factors such as the need for flexibility compared with the need for high volumes. Flow production is most suitable for mass-marketed products that sell large quantities of similar products. If, however, a unique service has to be provided each time (e.g. tax advice, interior design, architect, hairdresser) then job production is the more suitable.

QUICK CHECK
QUESTIONS

1   Producing individual items to order is called
……….. production.

2   Flow production involves low volumes of
production. True or false?

3   A process that has high levels of staff relative
to machinery is called ……………..
……………..

4   Batch production:
a)   produces one-off items
b)   produces large volumes of identical products
c)   involves adjusting machinery to produce
different groups of items
d)   is a form of flow production.

5   The period when machinery is sitting idle as it
is prepared for a different production runs is called
……….. …………….

6   Flow production tends to be labour intensive.
True or false?

7   If firms are targeting a mass market, the most
appropriate form of production would be:
a)   individual
b)   batch
c)   flow
d)   unique.

8   Job production is more flexible than flow
production. True or false? Explain.

9   Stocks of work in progress are likely to be
high-batch production. True or false? Explain.

10   Which of the following types of production is
likely to be able to justify a premium price for its
output?
a)   job
b)   batch
c)   flow
d)   volume.

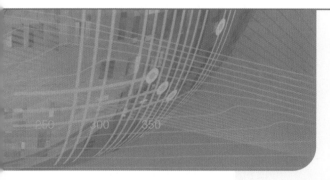

Progress questions

1   What is meant by 'job production'?   *(2 marks)*

2   Outline two advantages of job production over
other forms of production processes.   *(6 marks)*

3   What is meant by 'batch production'?   *(2 marks)*

4   Explain two advantages of batch production
over other forms of production processes.
(6 marks)

5   Distinguish between 'job production' and 'flow
production'.   *(4 marks)*

6   Outline the arguments for and against
introducing a flow production process into a
firm.   *(8 marks)*

7   'The most appropriate type of production
process depends on the size of the market and
how much variety customers want.' Explain this
view.   *(8 marks)*

8   Lucia Vialli is about to set up in business in the
clothing industry. Outline three factors which
might influence his decision about which form
of production process to use.   *(9 marks)*

9   Sam Butcher runs a design company
specialising in designing CD covers for bands.
Explain whether job, batch or flow production is
the most suitable form of production for his
business.   *(4 marks)*

10   'The choice of production process is a trade off
between costs and flexibility.' Explain this
statement.   *(7 marks)*

Analytical and evaluative questions

11 *Examine the possible problems for a food manufacturer of adopting a flow production process* (8 marks)

12 *Joanne Cobley makes hats using job production. Her hats are often worn by the stars at major events, such as first nights for a new film and the Oscars. Discuss the advantages and disadvantages for Joanne of using job production.* (15 marks)

13 *Warsany Ltd has developed a flat-screen, wall-mounted combined television and DVD player. Discuss whether batch or flow production is the most appropriate type of production for this new product.* (15 marks)

>> The scale of production

Output and capacity

When we talk about the scale of production, we are referring to a firm's output level; this will depend on its capacity. The capacity is the maximum output that an organisation can produce at any moment, given its resources.

The capacity of a firm will depend on:

* its level of machinery and equipment
* the existing level of technology
* the numbers and skills of its employees.

> **Key terms**
>
> The **capacity** of a firm is the maximum output that a firm can product given its existing resources.

Deciding on the correct level of capacity for an organisation is a critical decision for its managers. If the level of capacity is too low compared with demand, they will have to turn away orders, possibly losing customers. If the level is too high compared with demand, they will have idle equipment and machinery.

The desired level of capacity will depend on the expected levels of sales. The higher the level of demand, the greater the desired capacity. It will also depend on the costs involved. In some cases the scale of production a firm chooses will be limited by the availability of finance. The organisation may not be able to produce on the scale it wants because it does not have the money to buy all the equipment it needs. The capacity level may also be constrained by the labour market: firms may not be able to recruit sufficient numbers of staff.

A firm can increase its capacity by:

* investing in new equipment and technology
* training the workforce
* hiring more employees.

Figure 6.4 *The Morgan sports car*

Business in focus

The Morgan Motor Company has been making sports cars in the English spa town of Malvern for nearly 90 years. The family-owned business which employs just over 140 people recently expanded production and launched a modernisation programme aimed at reducing its waiting list to just two years. In the past, customers have had to wait for up to five or six years!

The company's current models – the 4/4, Plus-4 and Plus-8 have undergone successive under-the-skin engineering changes for several decades but have changed little in appearance since the late 1940s.

Output has traditionally been about 450 cars a year; the aim now is to increase production by 50% to more than 700 cars. However, this requires more staff and this will not happen quickly because of the high level of skills involved in the jobs.

(For more information on the Morgan Motor Company, visit www.morgan-motor.co.uk)

1 Why do you think the company has operated with a waiting list of five to six years for so long?

2 Why do you think the aim is only to reduce this to two years rather than a few weeks?

Key terms

The **unit cost** is the average cost of one unit. If total costs are £100 and output is 20 units the unit cost is £5.

Economies of scale occur when the cost per unit falls as output expands.

Diseconomies of scale occur when the cost per unit increases as output expands.

There are several types of economy of scale.

Technical economies of scale

As a firm expands, it may be able to adopt different production techniques to reduce the unit cost of production. For example, a business may be able to replace employees on the production line with technology as it increases its output. This will enable the firm to reduce the unit costs of production.

Specialisation

As firms get bigger, they are able to employ people to specialise in different areas of the organisation. Instead of having managers trying to do several jobs at once or having to pay specialist companies to do the work, they can employ their own staff to concentrate on particular areas of the business. For example, they might employ their own accountants or market researchers. By using specialists rather than buying in these services from outside firms, the business can make better decisions and save money. For example, a specialist purchasing manager may be able to find cheaper supplies.

Economies and diseconomies of scale

Economies of scale occur when the cost of producing a unit (the **unit cost**) falls as the firm's output increases.

Purchasing economies

As firms get bigger, they need to buy more resources. As a result, they should be able to

INTERPRETING DATA

Helter Ltd produces carpet tiles. It has produced the following estimates of the unit costs of production at different levels of output per week.

	20 000 units	40 000 units	60 000 units	80 000 units
Unit cost	£0.8	£0.7	£0.6	£0.5

At present the firm sells 30 000 units at a price of £1.20 each.

Consider the significance of the data for Helter Ltd.

Business in focus

Since the 1990s the world steel industry has been reshaping, with numerous companies joining together or buying each other out. The aim is to create fewer, bigger producers with greater economies of scale. For example:

- NKK and Kawasaki joined together to form a new company, JFE Steel
- Arcelor, the world's biggest steelmaker, was formed in 2001, through a combination of three large European companies
- the International Steel Group was formed following the takeover of LTV.

Most steel industry observers expect that the creation of fewer bigger firms will continue.

The industry as whole produces 900m tonnes of the metal in more than 60 countries. The industry's products are used to make anything from skyscrapers to washing machines. Total output of the industry is worth $300bn a year, with the metal available in thousands of different grades that can sell for anything from $200 a tonne to ten or more times this figure. Steel companies have experienced poor profits because they have been unable to increase prices for 20 years. This is because of intense competition by many different steel companies all selling similar undifferentiated types of product, together with the relative maturity of the industry. Another problem for the industry is the extreme capital intensity of steelmaking. The large, capital-intensive plants associated with steelmaking, located on sites that would often require very expensive demolition and clean-up processes before they could be used for anything else, often act as a barrier to steelmakers stopping production, even when there is no economic reason for it to continue. The capital-intensive nature of the sector is one reason why it can take a long time for obsolete steel mills to stop production, during which period they sell products at below cost price, so worsening the trend towards low prices and sparking complaints from other steelmakers. Many US steelmakers reckon that this is what has caused the increase in low-cost imports into the US in recent years, which then led to the Americans imposing a tax on foreign imports.

1 Explain two economies of scale steel firms may achieve by joining with other firms.
2 Examine why firms in the steel industry are eager to achieve economies of scale.

MATHS MOMENT

$1+1=2$

To calculate the average cost (or unit cost) use the following equation:

$$\text{unit cost} = \frac{\text{total cost}}{\text{output}}$$

For example, if total costs are £200 000 and output is 5000 units, the unit cost is £40.

1 If output rises to 10 000 units whilst total costs increase to £380 000, what is the new average or unit cost?
2 If the unit cost is £50 and total costs are £150 000, what is the level of output?

negotiate better deals with suppliers and reduce the price of their components and raw materials. Large firms are also more likely to get discounts when buying advertising space or dealing with distributors. If a firm can become a big customer of a supplier, the supplier will be eager to keep that deal and so is likely to offer better terms and conditions.

Why do economies of scale matter?

Economies of scale can be important because the cost of producing a unit can have a significant impact on a firm's competitiveness. If an organisation can reduce its unit costs, it can either keep its price the same and benefit from higher profit margins, or it can pass the cost saving on to the customer by cutting the price. If it chooses the first option, this may mean higher rewards for the owners or more funds for investment. If, on the other hand, it cuts the price, it may be able to offer better value for money than its competitors.

Diseconomies of scale

Diseconomies of scale occur when a firm expands its output and the cost per unit increases. Diseconomies of scale can occur for several reasons, as listed below.

Communication problems

With more people involved in the business, it can be difficult to make sure messages get to the right people at the right time. Although developments in information technology, such as emails and intranets have helped, it can still be quite difficult to make sure everyone in a large business knows exactly what they are supposed to know when they are supposed to know it.

Coordination and control problems

Just as communicating properly gets more difficult in a large organisation, so does controlling all the different activities and making sure everyone is working towards the same overall goals. As the firm expands and sets up new parts of the business, it is easy for different people to be working in different ways and setting different objectives. It becomes increasingly difficult to monitor what is going on and to make sure everyone is working together.

Motivation

As a firm gets bigger, it can become much harder to make sure everyone feels a part of the organisation. Senior managers are less likely to be able to stay in day-to-day contact with all the employees and so some people may feel less involved. In a small business there is often a good team environment; everyone tends to see everyone else every day and it is easier to feel they are working towards the same goal. Any problems can get sorted quickly face-to-face. As the organisation grows, its employees can feel isolated and have less sense of belonging. As a result, they can become demotivated.

MATHS MOMENT

Calculate the average costs for the following levels of output. What evidence can you find of economies and diseconomies of scale?

Output	Total costs (£)	Unit costs (£)
100	2000	
200	3000	
300	4000	
400	5000	
500	6800	
600	9000	

Table 6.2 *Economies and diseconomies of scale*

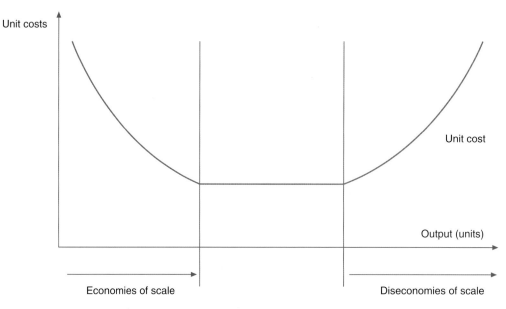

Figure 6.5 *Economies and diseconomies of scale*

Capacity utilisation

The capacity utilisation of a firm measures the amount it is producing compared with the amount it could produce given its existing resources.

To increase its capacity utilisation, a firm could increase the amount it is producing. However, there is no point producing more if it will not be able to sell the goods. A firm may need to boost demand, therefore, so that it can be sure to sell the extra output. It may try to do this in a number of ways:

- Promotion – increasing the promotion of the product makes customers more aware of it and may persuade them to buy the product.
- Marketing mix – changing other elements of the marketing mix, such as the price or the distribution, can stimulate sales.
- Agreeing to produce products for other firms – sometimes producers of well-known brands also produce items for the supermarkets which are sold with the supermarket's name on them (these are called own label items). Although this may seem strange, because it is helping the competition, the manufacturers may actually benefit because they are using their machinery at full capacity and this reduces the cost of each

unit produced. When one firm gets another to produce for it, this is known as sub-contracting.

If a firm is producing below capacity and does not believe that demand will increase again, it may decide to close part of its production process and reduce its capacity. This is known as rationalisation. The banking industry has recently undergone massive changes as firms join together to rationalise their production.

INTERPRETING DATA

Francis Delaney has collected the following information on his business:

Present output	500 units a week
Capacity utilisation	25%
Estimated maximum possible sales	1500 units

Comment on this data with regard to Francis's capacity.

Key terms

Sub-contracting *occurs when one organisation gets another to produce for it.*

Rationalisation *occurs when a firm cuts costs; for example, it may reduce its capacity.*

EXAMINER'S ADVICE

It is important to remember that firms may not be able to suddenly increase their output – it depends whether they have the capacity available or not. The existing capacity of a firm, therefore, acts as a constraint on the firm's decision-making.

Over time, a firm may be able to increase its capacity but this may not be easy to do quickly and the organisation may not be able to afford it. If you do suggest a firm increases its output, try to explore some of the possible problems and implications of this.

Also, remember how significant it can be if a firm is operating below capacity. By producing below full capacity, a firm's unit costs are likely to be higher and this can reduce profit margins. If the firm tries to increase the price to compensate for this, it may lead to even lower sales, creating a vicious circle.

Key issues

Getting the 'right' size of firm is a crucial issue for managers. Firms want to be big enough to have market power and benefit from economies of scale, but not be so big that they suffer from diseconomies of scale. In industries such as brewing and telecommunications many firms have joined together to benefit from economies of scale. At the same time, other firms such as Hanson and ICI have split up into smaller units because of the problems of large size. There is, it seems, no ideal size. It depends on the particular nature of the business, its own culture and communication and the nature of the industry.

APPLICATION IN ACTION

Whether or not firms grow in size depends in part on the existence of economies of scale. In industries such as telecommunications, steel, brewing, pharmaceuticals and car manufacturing the economies of scale are huge, providing a major driving force towards large-scale production. As a result, these industries are dominated by a few big firms. When it comes to sectors such as plumbing, hairdressing, taxis and florists, such economies of scale do not exist so there are lots of small firms competing in different regions.

 QUICK CHECK QUESTIONS

1 The maximum a firm can produce given its resources is called its ....

2 Which of the following statements is true?
a) Economies of scale occur when costs fall as output increases.
b) Economies of scale occur when costs fall as output decreases.
c) Economies of scale occur when unit costs fall as output increases.
d) Economies of scale occur when profits fall as output increases.

3 Which of the following is not an economy of scale?
a) purchasing
b) complexity
c) technical
d) managerial.

4 Unit costs equals
a) revenue − costs
b) total cost × revenue
c) total costs ÷ output
d) total cost × output.

5 If unit costs are £5 and total costs are £20 000, what is the output level?

6 Diseconomies of scale occur when a firm reduces its output. True or false?

7 What is meant by capacity utilisation?
a) the maximum a firm can produce
b) the maximum a firm can sell
c) the existing output of a firm as a percentage of the maximum possible output
d) the existing costs as a percentage of the total costs.

8 If capacity utilisation is low, a firm is likely to
a) reject orders
b) invest in new equipment
c) try to boost demand
d) increase price.

9 To increase capacity a firm could
a) increase demand
b) cut price
c) recruit more employees
d) reduce costs.

10 What is it called when one firm gets another to produce on its behalf ?

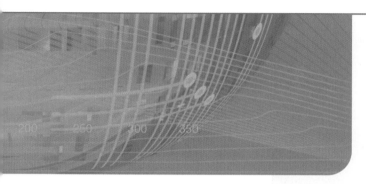

Progress questions

1 If a firm increases its output, its total costs are likely to increase; however its unit costs may fall. Distinguish between total costs and unit costs. *(3 marks)*

2 Some firms benefit from economies of scale when they expand. Explain three types of economy of scale a car manufacturer might experience. *(9 marks)*

3 If a firm gets too large it might suffer from diseconomies of scale. Outline two diseconomies of scale which might occur if a chain of fast-food restaurants expands too much. *(6 marks)*

4 The maximum output a firm can produce is called its capacity. Explain two factors which might increase a manufacturer's capacity. *(6 marks)*

5 Ramdoo Computers Ltd is presently producing at 75% capacity utilisation. What is meant by 'capacity utilisation'? *(2 marks)*

6 Lammy Videos is producing 4000 DVDs a day. Given its present resources it could be producing 6000 DVDs. What is its present level of capacity utilisation? *(2 marks)*

7 Hereford Engineering manufactures parts for the gas industry. The company is operating at 25% capacity. Explain two ways in which the firm might react operating under capacity. *(6 marks)*

8 Livewire Cinemas has been operating at 60% capacity; on average it has 200 people watching a film for each showing. How many people could it fit in the cinema it was operating at full capacity? *(4 marks)*

9 When firms have too much demand they sometimes sub-contract and get other firms to produce for them. Outline two factors a firm might consider before sub-contracting. *(6 marks)*

10 What is meant by 'rationalisation'? *(2 marks)*

Analytical and evaluative questions

11 *Morgan Goodfella runs a factory in northeast America, producing car cleaning products sold under the brand name of Pit Stop. He is now thinking of setting up production in the south of the UK. Examine the factors that might influence the scale of production at the new factory.* *(8 marks)*

12 *Capacity utilisation at Transatlantic Airlines has been low for a few years now. Discuss the ways the firm might react to this underutilisation of capacity.* *(15 marks)*

13 *Hetterfield Ltd owns a chain of three coffee shops in Newcastle called 'Cupacino'. The managers, brother and sister Paul and Holly Golightly, are considering expanding the chain to at least eight shops in the next two years. Discuss the case for and against such expansion.* *(15 marks)*

Case study

25 marks

Holidays.com is an e-commerce travel company. The company is relatively new to the market and at present has a relatively low capacity. Its unit costs are lower than the traditional high street shops but higher than many of its larger competitors. The firm is eager to expand rapidly, believing that it will benefit from economies of scale. However, Georgio Argopolis, the Managing Director, is well aware of the problems that growth can bring.

1 *What is meant by the term 'unit cost'?* *(2 marks)*

2 *Explain two possible benefits to holidays.com of operating on a larger scale.* *(6 marks)*

3 *Analyse two factors that might influence holidays.com's capacity.* *(7 marks)*

4 *To what extent is holidays.com likely to encounter diseconomies of scale if it gets bigger?* *(10 marks)*

>> Stock control

What are stocks?

Stocks are goods which have been produced or are in the process of being produced but which have not been sold yet.

All firms hold different types of stocks. Stocks can take a variety of forms:

- Raw materials and components – these are waiting to be used in the production process.
- Works in progress or unfinished goods – these are stocks of goods in the process of being manufactured.
- Finished goods – as the name suggests, these are goods produced and ready to be sold. In the case of the manufacturer, these are goods waiting to be sold or delivered to the shops, or the final customer. Retailers hold finished goods on their shelves ready to be sold.

Holding stocks is important to firms because they are often needed to maintain production and to meet customers' demand. With stocks available, a business can produce at any time and has goods available for customers.

However, the problem is that holding stocks can be expensive and risky. For example the more stocks a business has:

- the greater the warehousing space needed
- the more money there is tied up in stocks; this means the firm incurs a high opportunity cost (see page 118) because the money that is invested on stocks could be used in other ways
- the higher the security costs to protect the stocks
- the greater the risk; inevitably if a firm holds stocks there is the danger that they will perish or become obsolete.

The decision on how many stocks to hold is, therefore, a trade off between the costs of holding the stocks and the problems which might occur if stocks are not held.

Buffer stocks

The *minimum* amount of stock that a firm wants to hold at any time is known as the buffer stock (or the safety stock). If the level of stocks falls below the buffer level, there may be a risk of running out; this could either halt production or mean that customers have to be turned away because no finished goods are available.

Several factors influence the level of buffer stocks a business holds:

- The rate at which stocks are generally used up – the faster stocks are used up, the more the firm will have to hold at any moment.
- The warehousing space available – the smaller the space the firm has for storage, the lower the level of stocks.
- The nature of the product – if the product is fragile or likely to depreciate, the firm will not want too much stock in case it breaks or loses value rapidly.
- The reliability of suppliers – the more reliable suppliers are, the fewer buffer stocks the firm needs to hold because it knows it can get more as and when required.
- The suppliers' lead time – the lead time is the time it takes for products to arrive from when they are ordered. If the lead time is two days, for example, this means that it takes two days for supplies to arrive once you have ordered them. The shorter the lead time, the smaller the amount of stocks a firm needs to hold. If, however the lead time is long, the firm will need to hold more stocks to last while it waits for a delivery.

Key terms

The **buffer stock** is the minimum stock a firm wants to hold at any moment.
The **lead time** is the time it takes for an item to arrive from the moment it is ordered.

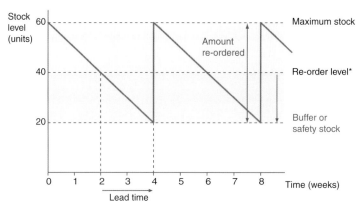

In this example:
- the buffer stock is 20 units
- the firm re-orders when it has 40 units left
- supplies take 2 weeks to arrive (this is the lead time) from the time they are ordered
- each time 40 units are ordered

*In this example items may take 2 weeks to arrive so they have re-ordered before the firm gets to its buffer stock level.

Figure 6.6 *An example of stock control*

The maximum stock that a firm will hold depends on:

- how much space a firm has
- the opportunity cost of having money tied up in them.

Business in focus

The production of malt whisky involves four main stages:

- malting: during which the barley is allowed to germinate
- mashing: involves grinding the malt and mixing it with hot water
- fermentation: involving the addition of yeast
- distillation: involves heating the mixture until the alcohol becomes vapour and is then condensed.

After this the whisky will be stored in casks, often for 12 years or more. Part of the appeal of the product is its age. This type of product cannot be produced in response to an order – the firm must hold high levels of stocks for considerable periods of time.

Famous Scottish malt whiskies include Aberlour, Balvenic, Cardhu, Dalwhinnie, Glenfiddich, Glenlivet, Glenmorangie, Knockando, Laguvulin, Laphoroaig, Macallan, Oban and Talisker.

To be a single malt the whisky must come from one distillery. In 2003 Diageo, which owns Cardhu whisky, started to mix it with whisky from other distilleries to increase supply to meet demand. This move was widely criticised by other producers who felt it could damager the image of Scottish whisky. This highlights how capacity can constrain a firm unless it can find another way to boost supply.

1 Outline the costs involved for whisky producers when holding stocks.
2 What factors might determine how much stock a whisky producer holds at any moment?

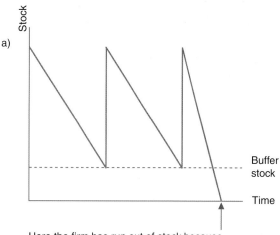

a)

Here the firm has run out of stock because the usage rate has increased due to an increase in demand.

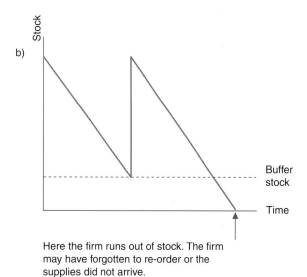

b)

Here the firm runs out of stock. The firm may have forgotten to re-order or the supplies did not arrive.

Figure 6.7 *Charts a) and b) illustrate different reasons for a company running out of stock*

Business in focus

One of Britain's biggest carpet makers, Brintons, is developing a machine that could change the economics of the industry by producing carpet tailor made to individual requirement rather than producing 'off the peg' designs in long production runs.

This move towards Just in Time production could lead to a time when a customer chooses a pattern for their carpet and then instructs a manufacturer to make it, instead of relying on stock. Brinton's was set up in 1783. It is still family owned and is one of the oldest manufacturers in the UK. The made-to-order carpets will first of all be targetted at Brinton's commercial buyers rather than private buyers because they will be willing to pay higher prices; these have included airport terminals but also the Kremlin, Downing Street and the White House. The company has seven worldwide plants. Under the new system the time taken to change the mechanical settings and alter the colours can be reduced from about eight hours in a traditional system to less than an hour.

Source: Adapted from the Financial Times, 20 October 2003

Stock control

Stock control involves **stock rotation**. This is a method of organising stocks so that the oldest supplies are used up first, rather than the newest deliveries. If a supermarket were to put all of its new deliveries at the front of the shelf, this would mean that customers would take the new deliveries whilst the products delivered earlier remain hidden (and probably perish!). To avoid this problem, supermarkets rotate stock so that when the new deliveries arrive, they are put at the back of the shelf. Thus, the older stock is bought first.

Just in Time (JIT)

Just in Time production occurs when firms produce products to order. Instead of producing as much as

they can and building up stocks, firms only produce when they know they can actually sell the items. Similarly, components and supplies are only bought in by a firm as and when they are needed.

EXAMINER'S ADVICE

Controlling stocks is an essential element of operations management. Stock levels can represent an enormous investment for an organisation. Just think how much money is in stock at any moment on a supermarket's shelves. If a firm does have a high level of stocks, it incurs high opportunity costs and is vulnerable to changes in demand. At the same time, a reduction in stock levels may leave the firm vulnerable to sudden increases in demand. The decision on the right level of stocks to hold is, therefore, a very important one with implications for production (will the firm be able to keep the production process going?), marketing (what if the firm runs out of goods and has to keep customers waiting?) and finance (how much does holding stock actually cost the firm?).

The aim of Just in Time production is to reduce a firm's stock levels by as much as possible; in an ideal world there would be no stocks at all. Supplies would arrive and be used to produce items that are sold immediately to the final customer. A Just in Time approach should provide a firm with tremendous flexibility; firms produce what is required, when it is required. In the past, firms have tended to try and estimate what demand would be and produce this amount in advance of actual sales. This system works provided demand has been estimated correctly.

JIT production should also reduce costs. With no stocks, the firm does not have to pay for warehousing or security. The firm also avoids the opportunity cost of having money tied up in stocks.

Just in Time production should help minimise wastage. If goods are produced and left to accumulate as stocks, they are likely to get damaged,

Business in focus

Dell computers only sells its products online – it does not sell via retailers. You visit its site, decide on the different elements of the computer you want (such as screen size and type, graphics and hard drive) and wait for it to be delivered a few days later. The company does not produce in advance – it only produces when it has an order.

In 1994 Dell had only 1.3% of the global PC market; by 2000 its share had grown to 14.5%. In 2001 it became the market leader ahead of Compaq.

Dell's system is well known for being lean. Internally the managers have a saying: 'celebrate for a nanosecond then move on' – the firm is never complacent and is always seeking to improve.

Just in Time production is now spreading rapidly:

- You can customize your own Nike footwear and have them delieverd in weeks.
- At Volvo Construction Equipment's site you can design your own bucket-loader tractor.
- At Lands' End you can custom make your jeans.
- Brooks Brothers is offering custom made suits based on a system that scans 200 000 body points and sends the order direct to the factory.
- Many opticians now produce glasses to order within an hour.

1 Examine the possible advantages to Dell as a result of its Just in Time production approach.

to depreciate, to go out of fashion or be stolen. JIT avoids these issues.

> ### Key terms
>
> *Just in Time* production produces goods to order, thereby minimising stock levels.

However, introducing a Just in Time system is complex and places many demands on a business, as explained below.

Excellent relationships with suppliers

Businesses need to be able to rely on suppliers to deliver goods at precisely the right time. They cannot afford delays as this halts production. Also, the goods must be perfect quality: the manufacturer has no stocks to replace faulty supplies. A firm must be able to trust its suppliers completely.

Reliable employees

Because the business does not have many (if any) stocks at any stage of the process, the firm cannot cope with stoppages. If strikes occur, for example, the whole production process stops. A business cannot supply customers using stocks as none exist. JIT relies upon maintaining a good relationship between employers and employees.

A flexible workforce

To ensure that production can respond to demand, a firm needs a flexible labour force. This means that, if someone is ill, another employee must be able to cover for them or that, if demand is high in one area of the business, people can be moved to that area to help out. Firms using JIT expect employees to be ready to work anywhere, anytime. People must change to meet the demand for different products because JIT is focused entirely on matching supply to customer orders.

Introducing Just in Time production involves:

- investment in machinery which is flexible and can be changed from producing one type of item to another without much delay

People in business

Jeff Bezos set up Amazon.com, the virtual bookstore, which sells books over the Internet, in 1994. After less than ten years, the company is worth several billion pounds. And yet, incredibly, it had never even made a profit until 1999!

Up until 1994, Mr Bezos worked on Wall Street as a senior vice president of a fund management firm called DE Shaw. Having read about the growth of the Internet, he decided to set up a business for himself. He now employs over 2000 people.

Bezos chose Seattle as his location because it has a large pool of people with the necessary technical ability (Microsoft is also based there). It is also near the largest book warehouse in the world. Initially Bezos set up his business in the garage of a house! He then spent a great deal of time and effort building up relationships with suppliers and distributors. These links are the key to his success: it enables the customer to choose from an incredibly large number of titles and have the books delivered efficiently to the door.

Since then, the business has grown at an incredible rate (much faster than its business plan) probably because it had such a unique proposition. On its very first day, it was bigger than any established bookshop offering over 1 million titles. Although the number of Internet users was relatively low at the time, it was growing rapidly. Furthermore, those who were online tended to be people who liked to try new things (they were innovators) and were naturally curious about Amazon.com.

Building on its success in Internet bookselling, Amazon.com has now moved into other areas. In 1998 it started online CD sales and has already become the world's biggest online music seller. The success of Amazon has been matched by an even more astounding increase in its share price. In 1998, for example, Amazon.com's shares grew 966% in value!

The overall aim of Amazon.com is to become an 'electronic commerce destination' where people go to whenever they think of buying something. This is likely to lead to far more brand extensions in the near future.

What is so incredible about Internet 'stores' like Amazon.com is that their levels of stock are low or even non-existent. Whereas a traditional bookstore has to have the products on site for customers to browse, a virtual store can order them direct from producers. They can be delivered to customers without the seller ever actually stocking them. They are able to offer a much wider range of products and services without the stock levels!

(For more information visit www.amazon.com)

Figure 6.8 *Jeff Bezos set up Amazon.com in 1994*

- training of employees so that they have several skills and can do a variety of jobs (multi-skilling)
- negotiation with employees so that their contracts are flexible and allow them to move from one job to another
- building relationships with suppliers who can produce Just in Time as well.

Problems of Just in Time

Although the Just in Time process has many advantages, there are several potential problems or disadvantages as well.

First, the system relies on suppliers providing parts and components at exactly the time they are needed. If this type of flexible and reliable supplier cannot be found, the system breaks down. JIT can also cause problems if the suppliers fail to deliver on time. The manufacturer has no buffer stock and so cannot produce. The system also means that the firm is vulnerable to action taken by employees. Any stoppage can be extremely expensive because production is halted completely.

Switching to Just in Time can also lead to an increase in costs because of the extra reordering. Because parts are ordered much more frequently, the firm may lose bulk discounts and will also have more administration costs.

APPLICATION IN ACTION

- The appropriate level and range of stocks that a firm should hold will vary considerably from industry to industry. In record shops the stocks are continually changing as new bands come into the charts every week. In retailing generally, stocks must be held so customers can see the products in front of them. In the aerospace production industry or shipbuilding there will be huge amounts of stock in the form of works in progress. Internet firms, by comparison, can usually survive with lower levels of stock, producing when the orders come in.
- The need for stocks depends in part on the predictability of demand – think of the problems in retailing of knowing what demand will be on any given day. If you knew exactly what was going to be demanded and when it would be needed you could produce to order.

Benefits of JIT	Problems of JIT
lower warehousing costs	lose bulk discounts
lower security and insurance costs	vulnerable to difficulties with suppliers
lower opportunity costs	vulnerable to industrial action
greater focus on quality	may struggle to meet sudden, major increase in demand

Table 6.3 *Benefits and problems of JIT production*

1   What is the term for the minimum level of stock a firm wants to hold?

2   What is the lead time?

a)   the time it takes to produce a unit

b)   the time it takes between ordering supplies and them arriving

c)   the amount reordered from suppliers

d)   the time customers wait to have the phone answered.

3   Moving stock around to keep it fresh is called………. …………….

4   Money invested in stocks could be invested elsewhere. This means there is an:

a)   opportunity cost

b)   opportunity knock

c)   undefined cost

d)   ultimate cost.

5   Just in Time production involves:

a)   producing items in advance of demand

b)   holding the maximum buffer stock

c)   holding as few stocks as possible

d)   employing as few employees as possible.

6   Just in Time production is usually associated with all of the following except:

a)   purchasing economies of scale

b)   multi-skilling

c)   high levels of training

d)   a close relationship with suppliers.

7   Stocks include finished goods. True or false?

8   Why might a firm increase its stocks of finished goods?

9   Give two reasons why a firm might unexpectedly run out of stocks.

10   Stock levels are likely to be higher in the secondary than in the service sector. True or false? Explain.

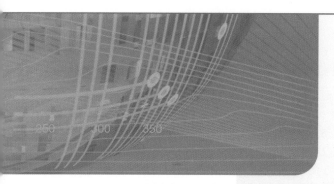

Progress questions

1 Explain two reasons why a manufacturer might hold stocks. *(6 marks)*

2 Holding stocks involves an opportunity cost. What is meant by the term 'opportunity cost'? *(2 marks)*

3 What is meant by 'Just in Time production'? *(3 marks)*

4 Explain the possible benefits of Just in Time techniques to a food retailer. *(7 marks)*

5 Gavin Hamilton is considering introducing Just in Time production techniques into his manufacturing firm. Explain two possible problems he might have when introducing these techniques for the first time. *(6 marks)*

6 Many firms hold buffer stocks. Explain three factors that might influence how much buffer stock a firm holds. *(6 marks)*

7 Outline two factors that may influence the maximum stock a shop would want to hold. *(6 marks)*

8 What is meant by 'stock rotation'? *(2 marks)*

9 Outline two ways in which the workforce might assist the effective introduction of a Just in Time system. *(6 marks)*

10 Not all firms have introduced Just in Time production. Explain two reasons why a firm may not have introduced this type of production process. *(6 marks)*

Analytical and evaluative questions

11 Examine the likely stock control issues facing the manager of a food delicatessen. *(8 marks)*

12 Maureen O'Halloran is the managing director of a chain of several car dealerships. She is considering removing all the cars on show at the dealerships and allowing customers to see videos and computer images of the cars. Customers could discuss their requirements and order their cars from the outlet to be delivered to their home. Discuss the case for and against Maureen's plan. *(15 marks)*

13 Having read about Just in Time production, Alice Merrick, the manager of a family owned pet food manufacturer, wants to introduce this approach into the business. Discuss the issues she could consider before going ahead with the plan. *(15 marks)*

25 marks

Alessandro Oldenburg is the Operations Manager of a company producing washing machines. He is looking at the company's stock control chart for some of its key components (Figure 6.9).

He has recently read a great deal about Just in Time (JIT) production and thinks this production method might be useful for his company. However, he realises that the success of JIT depends a great deal on having the right suppliers and is not sure if these actually exist! He also realises that the contribution of the workforce is essential to the success of JIT. He worries about this as employment relations at the firm have generally been poor.

1 *What is meant by the term 'buffer stock'?*
(1 mark)

2 *What is the 'lead time' for the key components for Oldenburg Ltd?* *(1 mark)*

3 *What is the maximum stock level of the key components held by Oldenburg Ltd?* *(1 mark)*

4 *Explain one factor Alessandro might take into account when choosing a supplier for his firm if he adopts JIT production.* *(4 marks)*

5 *Analyse the ways in which JIT production might benefit Oldenburg Ltd.*
(8 marks)

6 *Discuss the factors that may determine whether or not the introduction of JIT at Oldenburg Ltd is a success or not.* *(10 marks)*

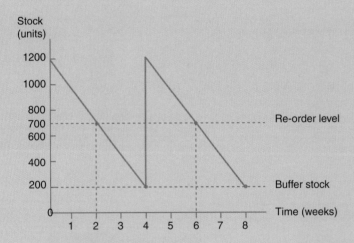

Figure 6.9

>> Productivity

Productivity and operations management

A business's level of output is the total amount it produces. The success of operations management depends not just on the total output but also on the value and quantity of inputs used up in the production process. The aim of operations managers is to use as few resources as possible to produce a given output. At the same time, managers seek to maintain a given level of quality.

A business's productivity measures the output produced in relation to the inputs it has used. There are actually many different measures of productivity, such as:

- output per worker per hour or day or year (labour productivity)
- output per machine per time period (capital productivity).

The most commonly used measure is output per worker.

Labour productivity measures the output of the firm in relation to the number of employees. For example if 10 people produce 50 units in total each week, their productivity is 5 units each. The higher the productivity, the more is produced per person per time period.

Productivity is a crucial concept in operations management because it can have a significant effect on the costs of producing a unit. The higher the productivity, the more units each worker is making and, if wages are unchanged, the labour cost per unit should be cheaper. As a result, managers are constantly seeking ways of improving labour productivity because this means the firm will either make more profit per unit or can reduce the price to become more competitive.

Productivity may be increased by using a variety of techniques.

MATHS MOMENT

1+1=2

To calculate the productivity of the workforce use the equation:

$$\frac{\text{output per time period}}{\text{number of workers}}$$

For example, if 10 workers produce 250 units in total each month, the output per worker is 25 units each.

1 What rate of productivity would be required, if this firm makes one worker redundant but requires 270 units to be produced each month?

Increasing the number of hours worked

If employees work more hours or more days each week, this could increase their output. However this is a not a long-term means of increasing employees' productivity because they are likely to get tired and stressed, and may therefore become less productive in the long term. Also, there is a limit to how many extra hours can be worked.

Training

This is a very important way of increasing productivity. Training can increase employees' output by helping them to gain more skills and to learn new and better ways of doing things.

Investment in equipment and technology

If employees have modern and more efficient machinery, they should be able to make more output. As the Department of Trade and Industry says when commenting on UK productivity compared with that of other countries: 'A worker can be 100% efficient with a shovel but it won't count if his international counterpart is equipped with a JCB!'

POINTS TO PONDER

A In 2002 Nissan's Sunderland car plant was ranked the most productive in Europe for the seventh year running. In the US Nissan has been top of the productivity tables for eight years. According to Nissan's UK managing director its high productivity is mainly due to the skill and adaptability of the workforce.

Rank	Company	Location	Country	Models produced	Workforce	Output	Vehicles per person
1	Nissan	Sunderland	UK	Primera; Almera; Micra	3018	297 719	99
2	Renault	Valladolid	Spain	Clio	3216	287 020	89
3	Toyota	Valenciennes	France	Yaris	1554	136 000	88
4	Ford	Saarlouis	Germany	Focus	4998	433 768	87
5	GM	Antwerp	Belgium	Astra	3598	297 598	83

Table 6.4 *Productivity data for selected European car manufacturers*

Source: WMRC

B Studies have found numerous influences on productivity including:

Coffee – One study found that drinking 350mg of caffeine can cause lapses in concentration and increased stress. The average cup of coffee contains about 100mg of caffeine. Clinical research found that a high caffeine intake causes people to visit the toilet more frequently, which can lead to performance-sapping dehydration. This, coupled with the powerful stimulating effects of caffeine, increases stress and causes failures in concentration.

Stress – Over a fifth of workers view stress as the single biggest negative factor affecting their productivity. Stress has now overtaken the common cold as the biggest cause of staff absence.

1 What other factors in the working environment might affect productivity?

Changing the way the work is done

If the way in which a product is made is changed this can affect the speed and the effectiveness of the production process. Many firms have implemented teamworking in recent years resulting in improved productivity levels.

Motivating employees

If employees can be motivated (perhaps by offering more rewards or by giving people more responsibility) effort and productivity may increase.

Whilst managers might be eager to increase productivity, employees may resist such efforts because:

- they do not want to work longer or harder
- they do not want to learn new skills

Figure 6.10 *How would you measure the productivity of a receptionist?*

- they fear that higher productivity levels may lead to job losses
- they feel it is unfair that they are producing more unless they receive higher rewards.

Productivity versus quality

At times, there may be a conflict within a firm between productivity and quality. In an effort to boost productivity, the firm may demand much greater effort from workers, resulting in lower quality products. In their attempts to increase productivity, employees may make more mistakes or become less careful. There may also be more accidents at work because employees cut corners in their haste.
  Managers must try and achieve productivity gains in a way which is sustainable and which does not lead to a loss in quality.

Measuring productivity

Measuring productivity is fairly easy if there is a physical product. It is easy to calculate the number of mobile telephones produced per employee or the number of pairs of jeans made by each worker. Measuring productivity is more difficult in the service sector – it may not be so obvious what to measure. For example, how might the productivity of a doctor be measured? What about the number of patients treated? If so, there is a real danger in increasing productivity because doctors might just try to see more patients and spend less time with each one. Similar problems exist when trying to measure and increase the productivity of teachers, firefighters or shop assistants.

INTERPRETING DATA

The following data has been produced for the Clayton Car Wash business which 'washes by hand for a better finish'.

	This year	Three years ago
Number of car washes per person per day	16	10
Total number of car washes	80	100

Comment on the significance of the above data.

MATHS MOMENT

$1 + 1 = 2$

Complete the table below. (Assume that employees are paid £200 each per week.)

Number of employees	Weekly wage bill (£)	Output (number of units)	Productivity (output/number of workers)	Labour cost per unit (weekly wage bill/number of units)
100	£20 000	1000	10	£20
100	?	2000	?	?
50	?	1000	?	?
?	?	2000	40	?

Table 6.5 *Calculating productivity*

Key issues

Productivity is a key issue facing the UK at the moment because our levels are generally low compared to our European competitors. Although we do have some outstanding firms, we also have many poorly performing firms. This causes concern because, if productivity is low, the cost of producing a unit is likely to be higher. This means that UK firms will either have to charge more or make lower profit margins. If UK firms want to continue to win orders abroad, and thereby provide jobs and incomes, they may have to significantly improve their productivity in the next decade.

EXAMINER'S ADVICE

Many students misunderstand and misuse certain terms in operations management. Common mistakes include the following:

- *Output versus productivity – if a firm increases its output, this does not necessarily mean it also increases productivity as well. It may be that hiring more workers has increased the total output produced, but the output per worker is the same. Similarly, increasing productivity does not mean that output has also increased. It could be the result of employees being made redundant. The productivity of those left may be higher but the overall output may have fallen.*

- *Output versus sales – there is often a difference between what a firm produces and what a firm sells. Just because a firm produces more does not mean that it necessarily sells more. This depends on demand. If the demand is not there, it will simply end up increasing its stocks.*

APPLICATION IN ACTION

Make sure you use an appropriate measure of productivity for the industry you are examining. Output per worker does not seem appropriate in retailing – sales per employee may be more appropriate. How should productivity be measured in schools? Or libraries? Or cleaning? In the UK, productivity in retailing has been disappointing compared with other countries – this may be due to the size of stores allowed and the amount of investment in technology.

QUICK CHECK QUESTIONS

1 Labour productivity measures
a) total output
b) output per worker
c) cost per sale
d) employees per output.

2 If output is 600 units a week and the number of employees is 30, what is the productivity?

3 What is the difference between output and sales?

4 Can productivity increase if total output falls? Yes or no? Explain.

5 If productivity is 30 units per employee and there are 40 employees, what is the total output?

6 Why might increasing productivity not increase sales? Explain.

7 Some managers believe that paying employees according to their productivity is not desirable. Why might this be?

8 State three possible ways of increasing productivity.

9 What limits the amount of output a firm can produce?

10 How might a firm react if demand is greater than the firm's maximum output?

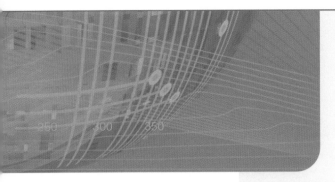

Progress questions

1 Distinguish between 'output' and 'productivity'.

(3 marks)

2 If the output of Shelley's Crisps is 5 million bags a year and it employs 250 employees, what is the productivity of its employees in terms of the number of bags produced?

(3 marks)

3 If the productivity of Castle Ceramics is 80 pots a worker per day and the number of employees at the firm is 5, what is the weekly output at the firm? (assume a 5-day week).

(3 marks)

4 Cake Expectations is a cake factory in Lincoln. It produces 2000 cakes a week and employs 10 people. The average wage is £200 a week. Calculate the labour cost per cake.

(4 marks)

5 Explain how the output of a firm might have fallen but the productivity of its workforce gone up.

(5 marks)

6 Many UK firms are trying to increase the productivity of their workforce. Outline two ways in which they might increase productivity.

(7 marks)

7 Explain why improving productivity might be important to a firm.

(5 marks)

8 Cilla Green is the manager of Green plc, a company producing mobile phones. She believes that the firm can only remain competitive if productivity increases by 5% a year for the next 5 years. However, her employees have resisted any attempts to increase productivity. Outline why her employees might resist her efforts to increase productivity.

(6 marks)

9 Explain how an increase in productivity might lead to a reduction in the quality of a firm's output.

(4 marks)

10 Why might it be difficult to measure productivity in some jobs?

(4 marks)

Analytical and evaluative questions

11 After a recent conference organised by the Smoke Detectors Association, Maureen Obuta has discovered that the productivity at her factory that produces smoke alarms is much lower than most of her competitors'. Examine the possible reasons why this might be.

(8 marks)

12 Ruth Ratisson is the managing director of Carnell Car Insurance. Yesterday she announced that 'given the increasing levels of competitiveness within the industry it is essential for the firm to increase its efficiency'. According to Ruth, this means that productivity at the firm has to increase significantly and she has announced a series of proposals to achieve this. Discuss the reasons why the workforce might resist Ruth's proposals.

(15 marks)

13 To what extent is an increase in productivity at one of its plants desirable for a firm such as Ford?

(15 marks)

30 marks

Hanratty plc is a manufacturing plant that produces bottled water. The firm uses a flow production process. At present its output is 5000 bottles a week. It has a workforce of 60. Compared with its major competitors, this productivity level is very poor and managers are concerned about the implications of this. The managers are hoping to increase productivity by approximately 5% a year for the next few years. However, initial discussions with the workforce have met with tremendous opposition. 'We are working as hard as we can and yet you want us to try and work harder. It's impossible,' said Francis Lee, who had been elected by the production staff to represent their interests.

1 a) *Calculate the productivity of the workforce at Hanratty.* (2 marks)

b) *If the firm does manage to increase productivity by 5% a year, what will the output per worker be in 2 years' time?* (3 marks)

2 *Outline two ways in which the managers of Hanratty might reduce the opposition of the production staff to the plan to increase productivity.* (6 marks)

3 *Analyse the possible implications of low productivity for Hanratty Ltd.* (8 marks)

4 *Discuss the ways in which Hanratty could improve the productivity of its workforce.* (11 marks)

>> Quality

Quality and operations management

An important aspect of operations management is making sure that the goods and services produced are of a suitable quality. This means that the products meet the specifications that the firm has set out and these, in turn, meet customers' needs.

A **quality product** does not have to be expensive – it simply has to meet the requirements of the customers. A pad of paper priced at £1 or a light bulb priced at 75p can be quality products, provided they do what consumers expect them to do. By comparison a £1m house or a £400 suit may be poor quality if they do not meet consumers' expectations. The fact that these products are expensive does not mean they are necessarily good quality.

A **quality product** is 'fit for purpose'. This means it meets customer requirements.

To produce good quality products a firm must identify exactly what customers are looking for; this will involve market research. The firm must then specify exactly what the product has to do and make sure that these specifications are achieved every time.

Business in focus

Mars is a world famous producer of chocolate, making products such as Mars bars, Snickers and Twix. Visit the Mars website *www.mars.com* and you can see the emphasis the company places on quality. According to Mars, quality begins and ends with the customer. After all, the customer is the final judge of whether something is or is not satisfying. Mars believes that quality involves providing products that meet customers' expectations each and every time. To achieve these results the company pays attention to all aspects of its operations. For example, it makes sure it picks the right materials and selects people to work for the company who are interested in achieving quality in their work.

1 What indicators might Mars use to determine whether it is achieving high levels of quality?

EXAMINER'S ADVICE

Remember that your final customers in this subject are the examiners. This means that, to provide a good quality answer, you need to identify exactly what they are looking for. Find out what the examiners want before you start writing! You should try and get hold of past papers and marking schemes, and practise your exam technique.

The traditional approach to improving the quality of a firm's products is to put resources into inspecting the *finished products* to find any faults that exist and remove them. The logic behind this approach is that, if all the products with defects can be found, the customer will only receive perfect products. As a result quality will be improved. This is known as a quality control system and it relies on the inspection of products.

Figure 6.11 *Quality is derived from the customer and market research*

Key terms

A **quality control** process aims to identify any faults or errors in the product or service through inspection.

Quality assurance seeks to guarantee all stages in the production process to ensure high quality final products and satisfied customers.

In recent years many managers have questioned whether quality control is effective. One problem is that quality control assumes defects are inevitable. The task is to make sure they are discovered before the customer receives the product. In effect, this is saying to the production department that it is acceptable for them to make mistakes, because the quality control department will find them later. This may mean that employees do not take care in their work.

The quality assurance approach puts more emphasis on preventing mistakes. If the process can be designed in a way which ensures defects do not happen (and in which employees produce correct work every time) inspection at the end of the production process is unnecessary. This approach to quality focuses more on *prevention,* not just inspection. It stresses the need for employees to get it right first time.

An important part of this new approach is that employees check their own work rather than rely on someone else to check it for them at the end of the process. This is known as 'self-checking'.

Employees also have the right to reject any work of an unacceptable standard, whoever produced it. Previously, employees often accepted poor quality items as they did not feel responsible for the finished product. Faulty products were simply passed along the production line until the quality control department found the mistakes at the end. Under a quality assurance system, employees are held responsible for their own work; if they accept faulty work from other employees or pass on faulty goods they are held responsible. Ensuring that they produce quality work is now seen as a part of everyone's job. At General Motors, for example, employees are told, 'don't accept errors, don't build errors and don't pass them on'.

Quality awards
BS 5750/ISO 9000

ISO 9000 is a quality award available to organisations in the EU. In the UK this used to be known as BS 5750. The government gives these awards to firms which are able to show that they have a system whereby quality is regularly measured and in which action is taken if quality levels fall below the set targets.

To achieve ISO 9000 firms must:

- set quality targets
- examine their production process to ensure that these are achieved
- measure the actual results and take action if what actually happens is different from what the firm wants to happen.

Quality targets might involve:

- the speed with which the firm responds to enquiries
- the delivery time of goods
- customer satisfaction ratings.

ISO 9000 does not, in itself, mean the product or service is good quality. This is because it does not examine the business's actual standards. If the firm sets standards that are easy to achieve, it can still achieve the award provided it has the procedures in place to ensure it meets these targets on an ongoing basis. The award, therefore, rewards *a system of quality*; it does not guarantee that the firm actually provides products that customers want.

> ### Key terms
>
> **BS 5750** is the UK quality standard awarded to firms which have a quality assurance system.
> **ISO 9000** is the European quality standard which is the equivalent of the BS 5750.

The value of the BS 5750 and ISO 9000 awards

Organisations achieving quality awards such as BS 5750 and ISO 9000 are able to use them in their marketing. This might be one way in which they can make themselves look different from their competitors and win more customers. Several leading manufacturers, for example, are more likely to use suppliers who have BS5750.

The award may also improve the whole approach to quality within the firm. Organisations which set out to gain ISO 9000 must develop a whole set of procedures to set and achieve quality targets. This type of process is likely to lead to less wastage and greater focus on customer requirements. This can lead to higher revenues, lower costs and more profits.

> ### EXAMINER'S ADVICE
>
> The word 'quality' is often used to mean 'expensive'. Candidates often suggest that to improve quality the firm needs to use more expensive materials and components. In fact this may reduce the quality of the products if the firm ends up offering things that customers do not want: adding more and more features to a DVD player does not automatically mean better quality if the machine becomes more difficult to operate or more likely to break down. It may be the case that making the machines simpler and easier to use would actually improve quality.
>
> Wherever possible you should consider the concept of quality in the context of customer needs and wants, rather than simply in terms of whether or not an item is expensive.

Approaches to quality
Total Quality Management (TQM)

Total Quality Management (TQM) is an approach to quality involving all the employees in the organisation. This quality assurance system appreciates that everyone within the firm contributes to the overall quality of the product or service.

TQM recognises that, whilst the employees on the factory floor are important but so are the office staff, the cleaners, the maintenance staff and the delivery drivers. The way in which customers are dealt with when they ring up, the accuracy of invoices sent out and the reliability of the vans all have an impact on how customers view the firm. If customers cannot get through to talk to people at the firm, if the delivery van breaks down, if the invoice they are given is wrong they may be dissatisfied with the organisation. It is not just the people who directly make the product who matter.

It is very important that all employees think about the work they do and whether it is of a suitable quality. This means that they need to think

of who *their* customers are. These customers may be the people who actually buy the product, but could be anyone for whom work is produced. Customers are not just external (the people from outside the business who buy the product); they are also internal. Employees need to think of the requirements of all the people they produce work for and ensure they are providing exactly what is required. The secretary produces work for the manager; the manager is, therefore, a customer of the secretary. The warehouse staff have to load materials onto the van for delivery; so the delivery drivers are the customers of the warehouse staff. Under the TQM approach everyone has to think about their customers' needs.

The TQM approach considers that employees should always aim to improve the quality of what they do. It is tempting to assume that what you are doing is good enough and, provided profits are

People in business

Figure 6.12 *W. Edwards Deming*

W. Edwards Deming was one of the first people to stress the importance of quality and the need for organisations to regard improving quality as an absolute priority. Unfortunately, he was ignored in his own country, America, and in Western Europe for most of his life!

Deming gained a doctorate in mathematical physics in 1928 and then became interested in improving quality within manufacturing. However, at the time American firms were more interested in producing high volumes of products than in preventing errors. Few managers were interested in Deming's message.

This was not the case in Japan. Deming was invited there in the late 1940s and regularly lectured to senior managers. He soon became regarded as a national hero and in 1951 The Deming Award for Quality was established in Japan. It was not until the 1980s when American firms lost so much market share to Japanese producers that Western companies began to take a real interest in Deming's work.

'I'm desperate. There's not enough time left,' he said in his last few years when the importance of quality and quality targets were finally beginning to be accepted in America.
(For more information on W. Edwards Deming, visit the W. Edwards Deming Institute website: www.deming.org.)

Key terms

External customers *are buyers from outside of the organisation who purchase the final product or service.*

Internal customers *are people within the organisation for whom work is produced.*

reasonable, it is easy to become complacent. Such complacency is extremely dangerous because markets and conditions can change incredibly rapidly. To succeed, firms must be continually trying to improve what they do to ensure that they actively delight customers. Under TQM, quality is seen as a dynamic process: it is a journey not a destination.

INTERPRETING DATA

The data below shows the sales and number of defects for Morton Ltd – a UK-based company that assembles radio alarm clocks which are then sold by a major supermarket under the supermarket's name.

	This year	Three years ago
Sales (units)	32 000	20 000
Number of defective products	64	20

Comment on the possible significance of the above data for Morton Ltd.

Business in focus

Reckitt Benckiser, producers of a range of cleaning, health personal products, has achieved cost savings of over £30m a year through an approach that seeks to 'look after the pennies'. Its programme, called Squeeze 2-50, has seen Reckitt redesign a handle, or use smaller flaps to save cardboard and change its bottles to use less plastic. Each change makes a tiny saving, but given that the company makes nine million products a day, saving a small amount on each product soon adds up. Another initiative, called X-trim, has looked to make cost savings in the supply chain, for example by using e-auctions to buy materials at savings of 8% to 10%.

Key terms

Total Quality Management *is a management approach which seeks to involve all employees in the process of improving quality.*

Kaizen

This belief that firms can always do better is known as 'kaizen'. Kaizen is a Japanese word meaning continuous improvement. The kaizen approach tries to get employees to improve what they do in some small way every day of every week of every year. If workers improve the quality of their work by 1% every single day, the effect over just one year would be enormous. Too often, businesses seek dramatic changes instead of small, regular changes. If you want to improve your grades in your exams, it is unlikely that there is any one thing you can do which will lead to a sudden improvement in your marks. However, if you begin to change many things over time, your grade is likely to improve gradually.

Key terms

Kaizen *means continuous improvement. The kaizen approach considers that firms should constantly seek to improve their performance.*

Improving quality

The process of improving quality begins with a good understanding of what customers want. This will involve effective market research. The better the market research, the more likely it is that a firm will produce something that meets customers' needs precisely.

The next stage is to design a product to meet customers' requirements and a means of producing the product which enables the firm to make an appropriate amount of profit. The design stage is absolutely critical to the success of a product. Effective planning before production actually begins means the firm will produce something customers want, that it is produced in a simple way and is of high quality. The way the process is laid out, the equipment used, the level of technology involved and the way in which it is organised will all have a

Business in focus

Ambi Rad is a Midlands Engineering company and European market leader in gas-fired, radiant-tube heating systems. The company did well throughout the 1990s but all the new ideas tended to come from the directors. The company tended to focus on the major projects and did not pay much attention to the many small ways in which improvements could be made. Eventually, the firm realised the gains of looking at 'the pennies as well as the pounds'. In 1997, Mike Brookes, the co-founder of the company, started to implement a kaizen approach in which workers lower down the hierarchy were given more control over decisions and encouraged to come up with suggestions for quality and efficiency improvements. The workers at Ambi Rad's main plant have been divided up into relatively small groups which are each responsible for specific aspects of making the company's heaters.

Team leaders encourage new ideas and act as a link between the shop floor and senior managers. Some ideas are very simple but suggestions from employees have saved over £300 000 a year. This has enabled the firm to maintain profits even when other firms in the engineering industry were suffering badly.

(For more information on Ambi Rad, visit www.ambirad.co.uk.)

1 What problems do you think there might be introducing a kaizen approach?

2 Do you think the kaizen approach could work in all organisation?

major impact on the final quality of the goods or services.

Most companies would benefit from investing more at the design stage. If the initial design of the product and process is wrong, it is very expensive to put things right later. Unfortunately, in the rush to put products on the market, firms are willing to accept products and processes that are adequate rather than excellent. This is all part of a very common approach that is often more expensive in the long run. According to the Department of Trade and Industry, 'Many senior managers (in the UK) still consider the design function a necessary evil, a costly and non-productive unit which often delays the introduction of a new product'.

Key issues

Firms are increasingly realising the importance of quality in all areas of their business. Success only comes if a firm meets its customer requirements and if the firm can produce items with zero defects. This involves a whole new approach for many firms: instead of assuming that things will go wrong (and, therefore, having a quality control department to find the mistakes which have occurred) the starting point must be that no faults will be allowed. The objective is to design a process which prevents mistakes occurring.

QUICK CHECK QUESTIONS

1 A quality product:
a) costs more to make
b) is expensive
c) meets customer needs
d) is patented.

2 Quality control involves the inspection of items to find any faulty items. True or false?

3 Quality assurance is:
a) a certificate that guarantees quality to customers
b) an approach to production that seeks to avoid errors
c) a government agency
d) an award from customers.

4 ISO 9000 is an award to show the product is high quality. True or false?

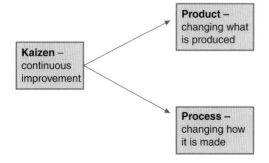

Figure 6.13 *Improvements can be made to the product or the process*

5 Total Quality Management involves all employees taking responsibility for quality. True or false?

6 Kaizen involves:
a) heavy investment in new equipment
b) an authoritarian management approach
c) ongoing efforts to improve quality
d) a switch away from flow production.

7 Improving quality may be a way of making one firm's products stand out from the competition. This is called product
....

8 Better quality is likely to be more important with increasing levels of competition, True or false? Explain.

9 Improving quality can reduce costs. True or false? Explain.

10 Internal customers are:
a) people who buy indoors
b) people within the business for whom work is done
c) managers
d) the people who buy the product.

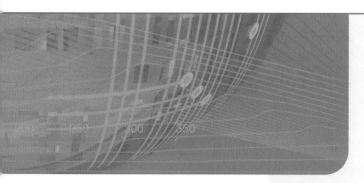

Progress questions

1 Explain two ways in which better quality might benefit a washing machine manufacturer.
(6 marks)

2 What is meant by 'quality control'? *(2 marks)*

3 What is meant by 'quality assurance'? *(2 marks)*

4 People play a crucial part in the quality process. Explain why people are so important in helping a firm achieve high quality. *(5 marks)*

5 Quality assurance places as much emphasis on the internal customer as the external customer. What is meant by the term 'internal customer'?
(2 marks)

6 What is meant by the term 'kaizen'? *(2 marks)*

7 Outline two possible benefits for an organisation of adopting a kaizen approach to production. *(6 marks)*

8 Explain the term 'Total Quality Management'.
(2 marks)

9 What is meant by 'ISO 9000'? *(2 marks)*

10 Explain two possible benefits to a firm of gaining the ISO 9000 award. *(4 marks)*

Analytical and evaluative questions

11 Analyse the possible benefits to a restaurant chain of improving quality. *(8 marks)*

12 Discuss the possible benefits of introducing

Total Quality Management into a business manufacturing white goods such as fridges and freezers. *(15 marks)*

13 Discuss the value of gaining the ISO 9000 award to a manufacturer of components for the computer industry. *(15 marks)*

>> Lean production

What is lean production?

Lean production aims to reduce all forms of waste in the production process. This includes the waste of materials, of time, of energy and of human effort. Lean production streamlines operations so that costs are reduced and efficiency increased. To achieve

this, a number of techniques have been developed (mainly in Japan) aimed at getting things right first time and reducing wastage levels.

The techniques involved include:

- cell production
- time-based management
- benchmarking
- Just in Time production (see page 246)
- Kaizen (see page 262).

Business in focus

Tesco has been one of the greatest success stories in retailing in recent years, and this is partly due to its extremely efficient supply chain and lean production techniques. Predicting demand in retailing is very difficult in this industry, but getting it wrong can be expensive given how perishable many of the goods are. Not knowing when demand was going to peak, Tesco used to anticipate the highest level of demand and made sure it had enough staff to meet this throughout the week – the result was people sitting idle and wasted resources.

The solution involved:

- a detailed examination of demand to identify any patterns on a monthly or weekly basis
- the introduction of a flexible working pattern using an annualised hours system. Staff were given a total number of hours they would be required to work a year, but they could be called on as and when they were needed rather than a fixed 40 hours a week
- working with suppliers to ensure more frequent and more reliable deliveries and a reduced lead time – 98% of deliveries are now within 15 minutes of their scheduled time.

Source: Adapted from www.tesco.com

1 Analyse the ways in which a lean approach to operations could benefit Tesco.
2 What is to prevent other retailers adopting exactly the same techniques as Tesco?

Key terms

Lean production attempts to reduce all forms of waste in the production process.

POINTS TO PONDER

Lean production aims to reduce waste. There are many different causes of waste, including:

- **overproduction**: producing too many items and having to get rid of them because there is no demand
- **stocks**: holding items in stock and spending money storing and maintaining them
- **defects**: wasting money putting right mistakes that have been made
- **waiting:** time wasted while people and machines are idle, waiting for items to get on with production
- **transportation:** wasting time while items are in transit and moving from one part of the business to another.

Techniques of lean production

Cell production

Cell production is a method of organising production around teams. Instead of producing items on a production line, the process is divided into a series of different stages undertaken by teams or cells. Each team is given the responsibility for a stage in the process.

Business in focus

In 1994 BMW took over the Rover group, and as part of the deal acquired the Mini, which is made at its Cowley plant in Oxford. In 2000 the Rover group was split up, with the Rover brand being taken over by MG Rover Group and production of Land Rover moving to Ford. However, BMW held on to the Mini and decided to relaunch the product. This involved a change in working practices and culture. In 2000 the company invested more than £230 million refitting the Oxford plant and introduced a change programme called *The New Oxford Way (Now)*. This focused on:

- upgrading the site and processes to world-class levels
- integrating the different BMW and Rover cultures
- launching a new improved Mini.

The main element of the programme was an approach based on working in groups (WINGS), which involved the creation of 'self steered' teams of between 8 and 15 people. These semi-autonomous teams have the power to fix production problems and allocate jobs within the team. The aim was to empower staff and place continuous improvement in the hands of those doing the work. Every fortnight each of the three shifts has a 45-minute meeting to discuss issues and come up with suggestions. Costs saving schemes have included using reusable rubber protectors to avoid the cars being damaged, as opposed to foam ones which were thrown away – such apparently minor changes can save thousands of pounds. Overall the BMW group plant Oxford has adopted over 8000 ideas from employees which have contributed to cost savings of over £6.3 million a year.

1 Analyse the problems BMW might have had introducing WINGS.

An advantage of this approach is that teams are responsible for a complete unit of work. Instead of each individual working on one simple task and having no real involvement with the final product, working in cells can give employees a sense of team spirit. It can also improve quality because teams have work for which they have overall responsibility and they can clearly see the results of their efforts.

Cell production can be very motivating for employees because they feel they have more control over their own work. The team members can organise amongst themselves when and how items are produced. They can also share their skills and expertise.

Team members are also likely to feel much greater responsibility for their work because the next cell has the right to refuse their work if it is poor quality. Cell production involves self-checking by team members.

Key terms

Cell production *divides the production process into a series of separate stages.*

Time-based production

With the levels of competition in most markets increasing rapidly, firms are always looking for new ways of out-competing their rivals. Many firms have tried to use time as a competitive weapon. If an organisation is able to produce an item in a shorter period of time than its competitors, or deliver it more rapidly to customers, more sales may result. Sony keeps producing new models of its products, for example, so that, by the time the competition has copied the features of the last one, it has already moved on to a new version. Domino's Pizza has competed aggressively in the fast-food market by promising pizza delivery within 30 minutes. Similarly, Dell can produce a computer to a customer's specifications within weeks. Photo developers now promise a one-hour service. Opticians can produce glasses in hours.

As customers become eager for 'instant' service, the ability to supply items as and when they are wanted may be crucial to a business's success. The growth of Internet shopping, 24-hour telephone banking and home delivery by supermarkets all reflect a desire for quick, easy access to products. Firms must try to react by reducing the time it takes to develop products. Also, with new products being launched more frequently and with rapidly changing customer tastes, products do not tend to survive for as long as they used to in the past. Over 80% of new products are likely to fail in the first few years. It may be important, therefore, to develop products very quickly to keep competitive in the market.

To speed up the development of products, firms have adopted simultaneous engineering methods. These involve getting all the engineers and designers who are concerned with a project to work on it at the same time. Instead of having one person look at a product idea, develop it and then pass on to the next person or department, time can be saved if everyone is looking and discussing the work simultaneously. This process has become easier due to the increasing use of information technology.

This enables employees to communicate and share information more easily.

Time-based management also involves building a flexible production system able to respond quickly and effectively to customer demand. This requires employees and equipment that can produce Just in Time so that production reacts to orders. If production can be made to follow demand firms should be able to gain a time advantage over their competitors.

INTERPRETING DATA

Clements plc is a producer of consumer electrical goods such as radios, CD players and DVD players.

	This year	Three years ago
Number of new products launched	77	50
Time from conception to launch (months)	7	14

Comment on the possible significance of the above data for Clements plc.

Business in focus

In the 1980s, Yamaha opened up a new factory which made it the largest motorcycle manufacturer in the world, a position which had previously been held by Honda. Faced with this development Honda fought back with the war cry 'Yamaha wo tsubusu !' (We will crush and slaughter Yamaha!).

In the battle which followed, Honda cut prices, increased its advertising and most importantly, rapidly increased the rate at which it produced new models. At the beginning of the war, Honda had 60 models of motorcycles. Over the next 18 months Honda introduced or replaced 113 models. Yamaha also began the war with 60 models but was only able to manage 37 changes in the same 18 months, The speed with which Honda was able to launch new products devastated Yamaha. In the end Yamaha surrendered, 'We want to end the war. It is our fault. Of course there will be competition in future but it will be based on mutual recognition of our respective positions.'

POINTS TO PONDER

In December 2003 the England rugby team won the World Cup. Five days later two books, *Martin Johnson: The Autobiography* and *Team England Rugby: World Cup 2003* were on the shelves, highlighting the speed with which publishers can now get a book out. The need for speed in this case was to get the books out before Christmas, which was just four weeks after the final. The initial print run for Johnson's autobiography was 60 000, but within hours of the final being won it was increased to 650 000. The final chapter of *Team England Rugby* was delivered on the Saturday of the match and checked on the Sunday, so that it was ready for the printers by 5pm that day.

Benchmarking

Benchmarking occurs when one business measures its performance against other organisation's. Firms benchmark against other organisations that are strong in particular areas. The aim of benchmarking is to learn from the best firms in the world and discover ways of improving operations.

> **Key terms**
>
> The Benchmarking Centre defines **benchmarking** as 'the continuous, systematic search for and implementation of best practices which lead to superior performance'.

POINTS TO PONDER

The UK Government aims to ensure that 50 000 businesses a year, including 10 000 new innovative start-ups, are helped by Business Links to undertake some form of benchmarking or other best practice activity for the first time.

Looking for the ways to improve corporate performance internally assumes that a business's staff know the best way of doing something, or how to improve it. Analysing the actions of other organisations, especially experts in the relevant business area, means a business is more likely to find the best solution. This is particularly true if firms benchmark against the best in the world. Benchmarking may be against other firms in the same industry or even against organisations in a completely different sector.

Typically firms will use benchmarking to assess areas such as:

- reliability of their products
- their ability to send out the correct bills (also called invoices)
- their ability to deliver items on time
- the time it takes to produce a product.

Organisations undertaking benchmarking are those most eager to learn and improve and those which are unafraid to seek outside help.

POINTS TO PONDER

'Knowing the opposition and where it is taking better margins is one of the most crucial bits of information you can get in business,' according to a former Minister for European Trade and Competitiveness. 'Benchmarking is particularly important for small and medium enterprises which often have a smaller knowledge base than big corporations …'

The benchmarking process

1 The firm must **plan** what it wants to benchmark, which firms it wants to benchmark with, how it is going to collect the data, what resources to allocate to the project and who is responsible for the project.
2 The firm must **collect** data from the other firm or firms. This may be through visits to their factories or offices.
3 The firm must **analyse** its findings to identify how it could improve its own process.
4 The firm must **adapt** its findings so it can **implement** the new methods in its own firm given its own circumstances.

The benefits of benchmarking

By undertaking benchmarking a firm should be able to:

- develop a better understanding of customers and competitors
- have fewer complaints and more satisfied customers
- reduce waste and improve quality.

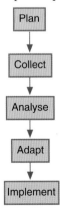

Figure 6.14 *The process of benchmarking*

Benchmarking can be difficult because some firms will naturally be unwilling to share their information. They may want to keep their methods and processes secret and might be reluctant to provide rival businesses with ideas of how to improve. One way of avoiding this problem is to benchmark against firms in different industries.

Firms must also be careful about trying to copy another organisation's methods exactly. Every organisation has its own way of doing things; its own skills and its own circumstances. They may have to *adapt* the other firm's methods for their own use.

POINTS TO PONDER

CenterParcs benchmarks its Sherwood Forest holiday village against 11 European facilities in terms of customer satisfaction and the occupation of chalets. When a European facility shows a significantly better performance, the company considers which features it can adopt.

POINTS TO PONDER

The UK Benchmarking Index gathers data on over 1500 companies. A DTI report based on this Index highlighted startling differences in company performance. The top 25% of companies achieve profit margins five times greater than the bottom 25%. Spending on training is 10 times greater and staff absenteeism rates up to 75% lower than for the bottom 25%.

Business in focus

From the mid-1960s to the mid-1970s, Xerox's profits rose by 20% a year and it had a monopoly on photocopier technology. The company was pleased with its performance. However, as Barry Rand the President of Xerox's US Marketing Group pointed out, 'It's not hard to be the best player when you're the only player.' By 1980 Rank Xerox's market share had halved as aggressive Japanese competitors moved in and beat it on price and quality. By the mid-1980s nearly 80% of copiers in Europe were Japanese.

Xerox's solution was to benchmark competitors. They looked at the cost of each stage of its production, the costs of selling and the quality of the servicing. Whenever Xerox found someone who could do something better than it did, it insisted this level of performance became the new base standard.

Benchmarking became an everyday activity for every department in Xerox and Rank Xerox. The company's philosophy was that, 'anything anyone else can do better, we should aim to do at least equally well'.

(For more information on Xerox, visit www.xerox.com.)

1 How do you think firms decide what to benchmark?
2 How do they identify who to benchmark with?
3 What problems might occur with benchmarking?

Lean production and people

For lean production techniques to work, employees must try constantly to improve the way the business works. This requires a high level of employee involvement and empowerment. In the past, many managers have been rather authoritarian towards their employees. The problem with an authoritarian approach is that it is often demotivating for employees because they are not involved in decision-making. The democratic approach to management considers that the contribution of employees is extremely important to the success of the business and that they should be given more power to make decisions for themselves to assist in improving company performance. This is known as 'people-centred management'.

Firms which introduce lean production techniques will need to make a number of changes in the way they manage their employees:

● Adopting a more listening management style – improvements in the way the work is done are likely to come from the people who actually do the job; employees must be encouraged to come forward with ideas.

● Introducing quality circles – a quality circle is a voluntary group where employees meet to identify ways of improving quality in their particular work area. This can generate new and better ways of doing things.

● Training – this helps employees to develop the skills they need to do the job effectively.

● Multi-skilled employees can undertake several different jobs – this means the firm should be able to meet sudden changes in demand patterns and produce a range of items Just in Time.

● Good relations – developing good relations between management and the workforce rather than a 'them and us' attitude is important. Employees are seen as an essential resource in lean production because they have such a major impact on productivity, costs and quality. 'Lean' firms tend to remove conditions that differentiate the workforce from the managers (separate car parking or eating facilities, for example) because this does not encourage co-operation.

Business in focus

The Property Search Agency conducts local council searches for solicitors. In 1998 it joined the UK Benchmarking Index. Staff productivity was found to be low and the company had underdeveloped systems for seeking and responding to customer feedback. The result was the introduction of quality circles.

Ideas have already paid off. For example, saving computer files into a compressed format before sending them has saved money on phone bills and a new printing and binding process has saved six working hours a day. The company has also invested in a new custom-designed computer system to deliver reference information and reports in a digital format directly to the customer's desktop.

Source: Excerpts from Sunday Times, 5 September 1999

1 What factors are likely to determine whether quality circles are successful?

 ## Key issues

Lean production enables firms to be more flexible and to produce at a lower cost. Lean production techniques are, therefore, vital for a firm's competitiveness. The lean approach also fits with the general desire in society to save resources and avoid wastage. Successful organisations are all striving to reduce the resources required to produce a given level of output and meet given quality targets. These attempts can take many forms, from reorganising the layout of the factory and where tools are kept to introducing Just in Time production techniques.

INTERPRETING DATA

Jackshank Ltd is a printing business that introduced a lean production programme a few years ago. Comment on the significance of the data below.

	This year	Three years ago
Average change-over from one printing job to another	35 minutes	70 minutes
% of items produced that are rejected	2%	4%
Average stock levels as a percentage of sales	6%	12%

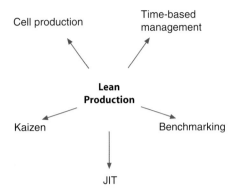

Figure 6.15 *A summary of lean production*

Business in focus

Lean thinking starts by defining customer value rather than thinking that the people and equipment the firm already has have to be kept busy. The company then has to trace every step required to design, order, build, deliver and maintain a product and ask how many of these steps actually create customer value. The shocking answer is very few – usually less than 5% of the steps and time! By examining and changing this process, large amounts of waste can be removed.

Lean thinking is rapidly spreading to every corner of the business world. Porsche survives today because it adopted lean thinking during its crisis in 1992. In aerospace, BAe Systems, Rolls Royce and Westland have followed Pratt and Whitney, GE, Boeing and Lockheed-Martin. Pharmaceutical and chemical producers like Unychem, GlaxoSmithKline and Boots have joined them. Even the NHS is thinking about how lean thinking might be used to improve the flow of patients through hospitals.

Source: Adapted from Lean Thinking Free Press in the UK, James P Womack and Daniel T Jones

1 Think of systems, policies and processes within your college that waste time or resources. Are there procedures the college could change to become leaner?

APPLICATION IN ACTION

- Lean production can be introduced in any business – it simply involves attempts to reduce waste whether this be materials or time. In an office environment time is often wasted finding the information and people you need, just as it is in a factory.
- In some situations, lean production may concentrate on reducing stocks (e.g. in car manufacturing); in others it may look at the way work is processed from one stage to another (e.g. in insurance).

QUICK CHECK QUESTIONS

1 Lean production involves attempts to boost revenue. True or false?
2 Cell production involves
a) working in separate rooms
b) working in teams
c) working on production lines
d) working individually.
3 Learning from others by measuring your performance against theirs is called ....
4 Simultaneous engineering involves:
a) producing two products at once
b) producing more than one product a year
c) undertaking activities at the same time to develop a product more quickly.
5 An approach that seeks to improve continuously is called ....
6 An approach to production that seeks to hold zero stocks is called ....
7 A voluntary group which meets to improve quality is called a 'quality ....'.
8 Lean production is likely to involve:
a) a democratic management style
b) an authoritarian management style

c) an autocratic management style
d) a tell approach.
9 Lean production:
a) boosts revenues
b) cuts costs
c) increases sales

d) reduces efficiency.
10 Time-based management seeks to:
a) manage time as a resource
b) give lots of time to customers
c) make time to listen
d) increase the time taken making a product.

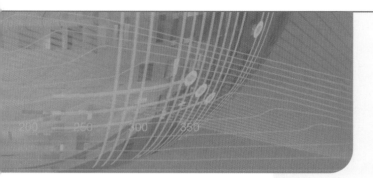

Progress questions

1 What is meant by 'lean production'?   *(2 marks)*

2 Explain two possible benefits of lean production for a firm.   *(6 marks)*

3 Norman Hunter is considering introducing lean production techniques into his firm, but is concerned that this may bring more problems than benefits. Explain two problems a firm might face when introducing lean production techniques.   *(6 marks)*

4 What is meant by 'cell production'?   *(2 marks)*

5 Explain two possible benefits for a firm of cell production.   *(6 marks)*

6 Outline two ways in which training might assist a firm which is implementing lean production techniques.   *(6 marks)*

7 Explain how a firm might be able to use time as a competitive weapon.   *(4 marks)*

8 Angela Lathbury is the Operations Manager of PrintOut, a company making laser printers. She is eager to speed up the time it takes to develop a new model to add to the existing range. Outline how she might reduce the product development time.   *(5 marks)*

9 Explain three ways in which a firm might benefit from benchmarking.   *(6 marks)*

10 Yudai Murata is Managing Director of Farago Insurance plc. Yudai is disappointed with the firm's performance in several areas of the business and believes that a major benchmarking project may prove valuable. Explain the possible problems that may occur when undertaking a benchmarking project.   *(7 marks)*

Analytical and evaluative questions

11 When David Brooklyn recently announced that his chain of health clubs was going to introduce a kaizen approach he had expected support from his staff. Instead, he got a great deal of opposition. Analyse the reasons why David's staff may have opposed his suggestion to introduce kaizen.   *(8 marks)*

12 After years of falling profits, Estelle Dimka is determined that her clothes business introduces lean production techniques. Dimka plc produces fashion clothes and sells them worldwide through over 200 stores. Discuss the possible benefits to Dimka plc of introducing lean techniques.   *(15 marks)*

13 To what extent can improving the time taken to develop a new product and launch it benefit a producer of consumer electronic products?   *(15 marks)*

Harry Carter is the Managing Director of Villa Plastics plc. The company produces plastic parts used in the manufacture of a range of consumer electronics products. Over the past couple of years, Harry has introduced many lean production methods including Just in Time production and kaizen. Harry has also introduced a Total Quality Management approach throughout the organisation. Trained as an engineer and after ten years working in production, Harry is convinced that effective Operations Management lies at the heart of a firm's competitiveness.

1 *What is meant by 'lean production'?*   *(2 marks)*

2 *Explain two possible problems Harry might have faced introducing Total Quality Management into the organisation.*   *(5 marks)*

3 *Analyse the possible benefits of introducing Just in Time production techniques at Villa Plastics plc.*   *(8 marks)*

4 *'Effective Operations Management lies at the heart of a firm's competitiveness.' To what extent do you agree with this statement?*   *(10 marks)*

End of chapter questions

Len Furrow left school at the age of 16 and went to work as an apprentice with Charlbury Furniture Ltd. This was a small family firm, established for over 50 years, which concentrated on making traditional, farmhouse furniture. In the ten years Len spent there, he learnt a great deal about furniture making and became a very skilled craftsman. At the age of 26, he left the company and set up on his own producing hand-made furniture to meet the different requirements of each customer. This job production process means he can target a niche in the market, offering very well-made, individually-designed tables, chairs, cupboards and kitchen furniture. The production process is labour intensive, but Ken loves his work and is extremely proud of everything he produces. His customers regularly praise his attention to detail and his ability to make whatever they want. Even though his prices are relatively high, no one has ever complained about these.

However, although his specialist skills and approach enable him to market his products as 'hand-made' and 'traditional', his output each year is very limited and, increasingly, he feels that he is not generating enough income. He recently got married and is eager to increase his earnings. Some of his friends have suggested that he buys more

modern equipment to work with and hire some assistants. 'What you need to do is invest heavily in equipment, design one or two products that will sell in large numbers and significantly increase the scale of production. Forget about the hand-made approach – no one cares. Just design something pretty basic that you can sell through retail stores and churn them out by the thousand. That way you'll benefit from economies of scale. Large-scale production is always better than small scale.'

1 *What is meant by:*
   a) *'productivity'?*   *(2 marks)*
   b) *'labour-intensive production'?*   *(2 marks)*

2 *Explain two possible benefits to Len of using a job production process.*   *(6 marks)*

3 a) *What is meant by the term 'economies of scale'?*   *(2 marks)*
   b) *Analyse the possible economies of scale that Len's business might benefit from if he significantly increased the output levels.*   *(8 marks)*

4 *'Large-scale production is always better than small scale.' Do you agree with this view? Justify your answer.*   *(10 marks)*

Sandie Harrison was the owner and manager of Wash And Go, a retail outlet in Oxford which specialised in selling washing machines. Washing machines are typically sold in outlets which also stock other electrical goods such as fridges, microwaves and vacuum cleaners. Sandie decided to break the mould by setting up a large shop which only sold washing machines. The company was founded in 1996 and has gone from strength to strength. She carries a range of machines made by almost every producer that exists and claims that she has a wider choice than any other shop in the south-east. She has a staff of 20. Her best selling model this year is the Zantudi Rapido. Although she does not have a very sophisticated stock control system, Sandie tries to make sure she keeps a buffer stock of 50 Rapidos.

Sandie's sister, a management consultant, is impressed with the success of the business so far but believes that the company could do even better financially if it held less stock and opened up more stores around the country. Her sister is also concerned by the way the firm's stock is managed and the fact that there is no form of stock rotation. She also believes the firm could gain a great deal from many Japanese management techniques such as kaizen groups, which she has seen work in many other firms. 'You need to introduce some new ideas into the business and grow it quickly. That way you'll benefit from economies of scale. Just make sure you don't get so big that you incur diseconomies!' she said to Sandie recently.

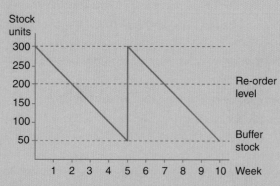

Figure 6.16 *Stock control chart for Zantudi Rapido*

1 *What is meant by 'buffer stock'?* (2 marks)

2 *Explain two ways in which introducing kaizen groups might benefit Wash And Go.* (6 marks)

3 *From the Figure 6.16:*
   a) *What is the re-order level of Zantudi Rapidos?* (1 mark)
   b) *What is the lead time?* (1 mark)
   c) *How many units were used up in week 3?* (1 mark)

4 *Examine the possible diseconomies of scale Wash And Go might experience if the business grows.* (8 marks)

5 *Sandie's sister believes Wash And Go should try and reduce its level of stocks. Discuss the view that Sandie should reduce the level of stocks at Wash And Go.* (11 marks)

Igor Radilov owns a chain of four garages called The Car Doctors in the Birmingham area. Although business has been good for the last few years and the firm has been working at 90% capacity utilisation, Igor is concerned at the increasing number of customer complaints he has been receiving. He recently attended a seminar organised which discussed the merits of the Total Quality Management (TQM) approach. Igor was very impressed by the possible benefits of TQM and returned determined to introduce this within his own business. 'Our aim is to achieve ISO 9000 within a couple of years,' he announced to his employees. 'This will not be easy and will involve change for us all, but I think the benefits could be substantial for us all. We need quality targets, proper systems of measuring what we do and a system of self-checking.'

His employees were not very impressed by what sounded like a lot of extra work and decided it was another of Igor's many ideas which would quickly be forgotten! Igor, however, remained convinced of the value of TQM. 'One of the first things we have to do is benchmark ourselves against other firms – only then can we tell how good we really are. We must also introduce kaizen groups as soon as we can and try to reduce the lead time between us and our suppliers.'

1 *What is meant by:*
  a) *'lead time'?* (2 marks)
  b) *90% capacity utilisation?* (2 marks)

2 *Explain two possible benefits for Igor Radilov's business of achieving the ISO 9000 award.*
(6 marks)

3 a) *What is meant by 'Total Quality Management'?* (2 marks)
  b) *Analyse the possible problems Igor might face when implementing a Total Quality Management approach within his firm. (7 marks)*

4 *To what extent can benchmarking guarantee the success of a firm such as The Car Doctors?*
(11 marks)

In the 1980s DEK, a company which makes machines that apply paste to printed circuit boards, introduced lean production techniques. This involved taking components from suppliers on a Just in Time basis. The introduction of a lean production system require openness and trust. The company now has very little direct supervision; 'People are just encouraged to get on and do things,' says the company's Managing Director, 'if it doesn't work, do something about it, and if it still doesn't work, do something else. But for goodness sake don't do nothing.' 'We have principally moved from a climate where change was only made out of necessity to one where it happens routinely, daily, hourly, and where it is not seen as a threat.'

The same applies to suppliers and customers. The company's mission statement includes a commitment to improve the business of its customers. 'If our machines can't do that, then there is no value to the customer.' There is also the recognition that 'Just in Time' can place a strain on suppliers, so annual and revised weekly forecasts are sent out. Instead of buying individual items from many different suppliers, the company has two-year agreements from a limited number of suppliers.

Production specialists have also designed the production process so that people rarely need to leave their place of work for anything other than their breaks and calls of nature. All the tools they need are in place on mobile trolleys and the components – screws, washers and fastenings – are arranged in compartmentalised trays. A card on the lid indicates the name, size and quantity of parts for each assembly operation. The boxes are filled by the supplier with the set number of parts needed.

A bronze sticker is awarded to an individual who has made parts for a month which are free from errors. If this extends to two months the lettering is silver; three and it is gold. At this point a £50 voucher is awarded.

1 *What is meant by 'Just in Time production'?*
(2 marks)

2 *Explain why the contribution of employees is important to the success of lean production in firms such as DEK.* (5 marks)

3 *Explain why a good relationship with suppliers is essential to the success of lean production techniques at DEK.* (5 marks)

4 *Analyse the possible benefits to DEK of having less direct supervision of staff.* (8 marks)

5 *Discuss the problems a firm such as DEK might have introducing lean production techniques for the first time.* (10 marks)

Figure 6.17 *Relationships between Operations Management and other topics in the AS specification*

External influences

Introduction

- What are the factors outside the organisation that affect how it does business?
- What are the effects of the market, the economy, the business cycle and inflation?
- What are the effects of new laws and government policies?
- How does society put pressure on firms?
- How does technological change affect the operation of businesses?

Markets, competition and the
>> business cycle

Introduction to markets

There are many outside influences which affect businesses, of which the market is just one.

Size of the market

Businesses are heavily influenced by the markets in which they trade. The size of the market influences businesses: whether it is local, national or international will affect the nature of the product they supply, as well as the amount they sell.

Degree of competition

Markets also vary in terms of the degree of competition. It is true to say that improved communications and methods of transportation have made markets more competitive. Many UK businesses now face competition from European and Asian producers, as well as domestic rivals. For example, competition in the UK grocery market has become fiercer following the arrival of foreign supermarket chains such as Aldi. Competition has

become even more intense since the giant American retailer Wal-Mart purchased Asda in 1999 and Safeway was sold in 2004.

What are markets?

A market is a place where buyers and sellers meet to establish prices and to exchange goods and services. Markets can take two main forms:

1 Traditional, geographical markets
2 Non-geographical markets.

Traditional, geographical markets

Consumers can purchase fresh fruit or vegetables at a local street market. Firms wishing to sell these products can take a stall at the market and expect to meet buyers. Thus, the market brings together buyers and sellers. The same is true of a high street in any town or city. Retailers set up stores in these locations and customers know where to find the shops.

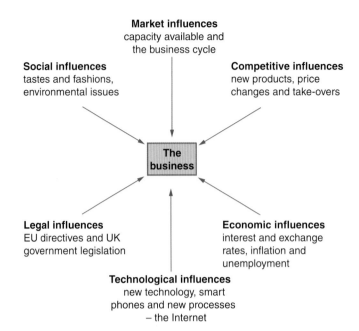

Figure 7.1 *Factors affecting businesses*

Non-geographical markets

An increasing range of products are bought and sold without buyers and sellers ever meeting. It is possible to purchase books, company shares and groceries on the Internet using a credit card. Rail tickets and theatre tickets can be purchased by telephone. Businesses purchase oil and foreign currencies over the telephone. Modern forms of communication have replaced face-to-face communication in traditional markets.

Figure 7.2 *The development of call centres has been a feature of the growth of non-geographical markets*

POINTS TO PONDER

Online spending increased by 1300% between 2000 and 2003. In December 2003, consumers spent over £3 billion shopping on the Internet.

In general, markets do their job efficiently if information on prices and products is available to buyers and sellers.

Classifying markets

Markets can be classified according to the number of firms trading and the degree of competition. This type of categorisation allows the likely effects on the business to be identified and analysed. Three main categories exist:

1 Perfect competition
2 Oligopoly
3 Monopoly.

Perfect competition

Perfectly competitive markets have many small firms producing virtually identical products at very similar prices. Firms can enter and leave such markets freely. Firms operating in such markets do not earn excessive profits and use resources with great efficiency.

It is probable that few markets approximating perfect competition exist in the UK and Europe, though it is a useful model against which to judge the efficiency of other markets. Markets closest to perfect competition might include hairdressing and the selling of stocks and shares. The emphasis on efficient use of resources and price competitiveness draws an interesting comparison with oligopolistic and monopolistic markets.

Oligopoly

A market is said to be oligopolistic when few firms exist and the firms are interdependent in their actions. Oligopolistic firms consider the likely reactions of competitors when considering changing prices or introducing new products. Oligopolistic markets are common and include industries such as chocolate manufacture, television broadcasting and high street banking.

Operating in an oligopolistic market has a number of consequences for businesses.

- Such markets appear to be highly competitive and this is often (but not always) true.
- Oligopolists fear price wars and tend to avoid price competition.
- Non-price competition is frequently used, for example heavy advertising, loyalty cards and special offers.
- Some oligopolistic markets have a high level of take-over activity as firms seek to increase their scale and influence.

There is a risk of firms working together in oligopolistic markets – this is termed 'collusion'. Collusion may result in producers agreeing price levels and, perhaps output levels. If oligopolists have formal agreements about market share and prices they are operating a cartel. Such agreements are illegal in most countries.

POINTS TO PONDER

The merger in 2003 of broadcasting companies Granada and Carlton means the new company will own 11 of the regional companies that make up the ITV network.

Key terms

A **cartel** operates when a group of producers collude to set prices and (sometimes) to share out markets. Cartels are illegal in most countries.

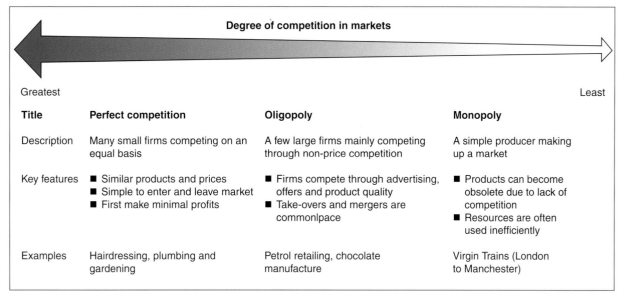

Figure 7.3 *Classifying markets by degree of competition*

Title	Perfect competition	Oligopoly	Monopoly
Description	Many small firms competing on an equal basis	A few large firms mainly competing through non-price competition	A simple producer making up a market
Key features	■ Similar products and prices ■ Simple to enter and leave market ■ First make minimal profits	■ Firms compete through advertising, offers and product quality ■ Take-overs and mergers are commonlpace	■ Products can become obsolete due to lack of competition ■ Resources are often used inefficiently
Examples	Hairdressing, plumbing and gardening	Petrol retailing, chocolate manufacture	Virgin Trains (London to Manchester)

Monopoly

A monopoly exists when only a single producer operates within a market. Examples of UK monopolies might include Virgin Trains (rail services between London and Manchester) and Transco – the company responsible for piping gas.

POINTS TO PONDER

In 2003 there were calls to end the monopoly held by Aurigny Airon flights between the islands of Jersey and Guernsey. Critics said over 31% of existing flights had no empty seats, showing a lack of capacity.

A monopolistic market may have some or all of the following characteristics:

- a single producer able to charge relatively high prices
- infrequent introduction of new products
- inefficient use of the resources available.

True monopolies rarely exist today, particularly since the European Single Market became a reality. However, UK legislation defines any firm having 25% or more of a particular market as a monopoly. Under this interpretation a number of monopolies exist. For example, Birds Eye Walls supplies almost 70% of wrapped ice cream in the UK.

EXAMINER'S ADVICE

It is important to concentrate on the effects of the market structure on the activities of businesses in that market. Thus, what might a monopoly market structure (or an oligopolistic one) mean for the ways in which firms compete and for the consumer? Some candidates write too much on the type of market structure and too little on the implications.

Monopolies in the UK are open to competition from other foreign rivals, and especially from other firms within the European Union. Because monopolies can exploit consumers and may make inefficient use of resources they are subject to strict controls by the UK government and the European Union.

Key terms

Perfectly competitive markets are characterised by many small firms selling identical products at the same price.
Monopoly is a theoretical market situation where a single producer supplies a particular market.
Oligopoly is a market structure with few firms in a market, all of whom consider rivals' reactions before introducing new policies.

Classifying markets in this way is helpful in forecasting the likely behaviour of the firms that compete in those markets.

Capacity utilisation

A major factor affecting the competitiveness of a firm is the extent to which it uses the productive capacity available to it (see page 240). Productive capacity describes the maximum amount an organisation can produce when using fully all its resources. Firms of all sizes and types try to avoid having too much productive capacity lying idle – this is called spare or excess capacity.

Firms can take a number of actions in response to spare or excess capacity within the market. They may seek to sell their products in new markets (possibly overseas). Alternatively, they may use their production capacity to produce other products.

Other solutions to spare capacity include selling factories or offices to eliminate the surplus resources or to stockpile their products in the hope of selling them later. This tactic can only work for a limited period of time.

Capacity and the market

It is not unusual for a market to suffer a shortage of productive capacity. This means that the firms in the market are unable to meet consumers' needs, even when producing at maximum capacity. In these circumstances, the products in question become scarce. This can have a number of implications for firms:

- The market price for the product is likely to rise.
- New producers may be attracted into the market

Business in focus

The Royal Mail is one of Britain's best-known businesses. It owns famous brands such as Royal Mail, Parcelforce Worldwide and Post Office, and has been a public limited company wholly owned by the government since 2001. The Royal Mail's annual turnover is in excess of £8 billion and the company has over 200 000 employees. The Royal Mail operates over 17 500 Post Offices attracting 28 million customers each week. It is a big business by any standards.

Royal Mail plc is passing through troubled times. Financial problems have dogged the business for some time. In 2002 the company made a loss of £1100 million. Although this figure had been reduced to £611 million by May 2003, the company remains in a weak financial position.

The company is subject to close regulation by the watchdog Postcomm. Established in 2000, Postcomm sets tough quality targets for the Royal Mail, restricts the prices it can charge and is in the process of introducing competition into some aspects of the Royal Mail's market. The Royal Mail expects to lose its monopoly over the next few years. It will face tough competition from other businesses in the market for delivering business post between major cities. In November 2003 Royal Mail reached an agreement with one of its rivals, UK Mail, to deliver its letters for an agreed fee. UK Mail will collect the letters and pass them onto its long-established rival for sorting and delivery.

The company has responded to its financial problems by engaging in a tough cost-cutting regime. By July 2003 the company had reduced its workforce by 17 000 people and a further 13 000 jobs are expected to disappear by 2005. Job losses are being accompanied by the closure of small and predominantly loss-making Post Offices.

1 Discuss whether the introduction of competition into the postal market will be in the interest of all of Royal Mail plc's stakeholders.

– or existing producers may invest to increase their output.
● Consumers may seek to purchase supplies from overseas markets.

A shortage of capacity is common in markets where tastes and fashions change quickly or where it takes time for producers to increase their level of output. At times fashionable sportswear manufactured by companies such as Nike and Reebok has been scarce in some parts of the world.

EXAMINER'S ADVICE

This is a common area for questions. It is important to appreciate the implications of excess or insufficient capacity, as well as the actions that a firm can take in response. However, the most important factor is to apply this knowledge to the circumstances of the question. Do not write a purely theoretical answer.

Fair and unfair competition

All British markets are regulated to promote free and fair competition. The UK government and the European Union believe this is in the interests of UK consumers, as well as UK businesses. Fair competition allows businesses to compete on an equal basis and offers consumers the best possible products at the lowest prices. It also encourages the efficient use of resources.

A common form of unfair competition is the creation of a cartel. Cartels normally result in higher prices and less advanced products for consumers as producers share out the market between themselves. This is more likely to occur in oligopolistic markets as the smaller number of producers makes agreement easier to reach. Some collusion in oligopolistic markets may be tacit. That is, firms competing in the market maintain prices at some level without formal agreement, but it is beneficial to all concerned. This type of collusion is extremely difficult for the authorities to identify and prevent.

Both the UK government and the EU Commission have passed legislation outlawing any actions that are deemed to represent unfair competition. We will consider this in detail in a later unit.

Key issues

Markets can be an effective way of using resources. At their best, markets ensure that resources, such as materials and labour, are used with the utmost efficiency.

However, markets do not always operate efficiently. There are two major reasons why markets might fail:

1 Sometimes too little of a product may be produced to meet the needs of consumers.

This is often the case when production is in the hands of a monopoly. By restricting supply, a monopolist can force up prices and enjoy high profits.

2 If businesses do not pay the full cost of producing their goods, then oversupply might result. Thus, a business may release harmful waste products into a nearby river, rather than paying to treat the waste and to dispose of it safely. In these circumstances consumers do not pay the true cost of the product – others, such as local residents, face these costs.

Some argue that the government should intervene in the case of **market failure** to ensure that pollution does not occur and that goods are supplied in sufficient quantities.

The business cycle

All countries suffer fluctuations in the level of activity within their economies. At times spending, output and employment all rise; during other periods the opposite is true. A nation's Gross Domestic Product measures the value of a country's output over a period of time. This figure is

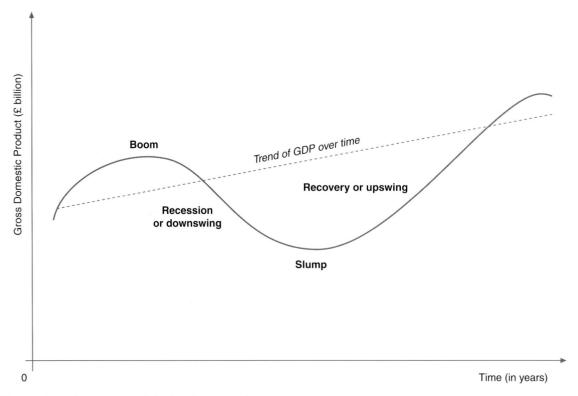

Figure 7.4 *The stages of the business cycle*

dependent upon the level of economic activity. Rising economic activity will cause a higher level of GDP.

The business cycle describes the regular fluctuations in economic activity (and GDP) occurring over time. Figure 7.4 illustrates a typical business cycle.

Trade cycles generally have four stages:

1 Recovery or upswing
2 Boom
3 Downswing
4 Slump.

Recovery or upswing

As the economy recovers from a slump, production and employment both increase. Consumers generally spend more as they are more confident in the security of their employment. Initially, businesses may respond cautiously. No major decisions are required to meet rising demand whilst spare capacity exists: firms simply begin to utilise idle resources. As business confidence increases, firms may invest in further fixed assets (factories and vehicles, for example). Employees find jobs more easily and wages may begin to rise.

Boom

A boom follows with high levels of production and expenditure by firms, consumers and the government. Booms lead to prosperity and confidence in the business community. Investment in fixed assets is likely to increase. However, sectors of the economy experience pressure during booms. Skilled workers may become scarce and firms may offer higher wages. Simultaneously, as the economy approaches maximum production, shortages and bottlenecks occur as insufficient raw materials and

components exist to meet demand. Prices rise. The combination of rising wages and rising prices of raw materials and components creates inflation. Inflation usually leads to the end of a boom.

Downswing

In a downswing incomes and output start to fall. Rising prices of labour and materials increase costs of production. This eats into businesses' profits. In circumstances such as this, the UK government has raised interest rates to avoid inflation. Falling profits and rising interest rates are likely to lead to delays in implementing plans to invest in new factories and offices. The level of production in the economy may stagnate or even fall and the amount of spare capacity rises. Some businesses fail and the level of bankruptcies is also likely to rise.

Slump

A slump often, but not always, follows a downswing. In some circumstances, an economy may enter the upswing stage of the business cycle without moving through a slump period. Governments may take action to encourage this by, for example, increasing their own spending or lowering interest rates. A slump sees production at its lowest, unemployment is high and increasing numbers of firms suffer insolvency (limited companies become insolvent, whilst the term bankruptcy applies to individuals, sole traders and partnerships).

Figure 7.4 illustrates a smooth and regular trade cycle in operation. In reality, the change in Gross Domestic Product is likely to be irregular as economic cycles of different duration and intensity

POINTS TO PONDER

1 These are two important indications of the stages of the business cycle. What other indicators exist?

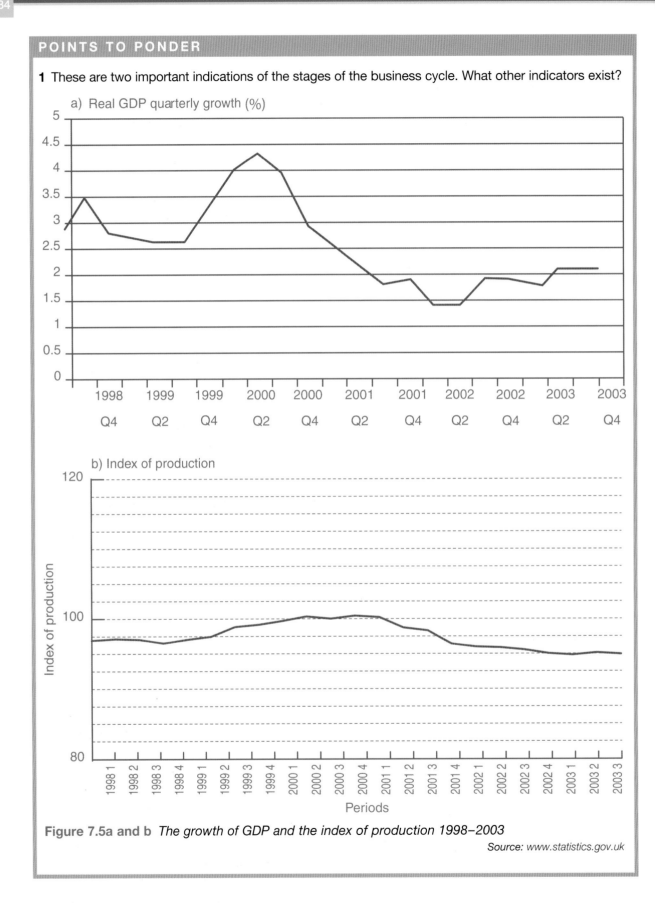

a) Real GDP quarterly growth (%)

b) Index of production

Figure 7.5a and b *The growth of GDP and the index of production 1998–2003*

Source: www.statistics.gov.uk

Stage of Business Cycle	Key features	Likely reactions by businesses
Recovery or upswing	● Increasing consumer expenditure ● Existing spare capacity used ● Production rises ● Business confidence strengthens ● Investment increases	● Opportunity to charge higher prices ● Rising numbers of business start-ups ● Businesses take decisions to invest in fixed assets ● Businesses operate nearer to (or at) full capacity
Boom	● Rate of inflation increases ● Bottlenecks in supply of materials and components ● Some firms unable to satisfy demand ● Profits probably high, but hit by rising costs	● Firms face increasing pressure to increase prices ● Businesses seek alternative methods to increase output ● Wage rises offered to retain or attract skilled labour ● Managers plan for falling levels of demand
Downswing	● Government reduces interest rates ● Firms reduce production as demand falls ● Spare capacity rises ● Business confidence declines and investment is cut ● Profits fall	● Firms seek new markets for products, possibly overseas ● Some products may be stockpiled ● Workeres laid off, or asked to work short-time ● Financially insecure firms may become bankrupt
Slump	● Increasing number of bankruptcies and insolvencies ● Govenment lowers interest rates ● High levels of unemployment ● Low levels of business confidence and consumer spending	● Firms offer basic products at low prices ● Businesses may close factories to reduce capacity ● Large-scale redundancies may occur ● Marketing concentrates on low prices and easy payment deals

Table 7.1 *The trade cycle and business actions*

operate simultaneously. The business cycle is a major influence on the performance of businesses. As the economy moves from one stage of the cycle to another, businesses see substantial changes in their trading conditions.

The impact of the business cycle

Not all businesses are equally affected by the changing trading conditions brought about by the business cycle. Table 7.1 identifies some actions that businesses might take at different times.

Demand and the business cycle

Producers and retailers of basic foodstuffs, public transport and water services may notice little change in demand for their products as the trade cycle moves through its various stages. This is because these are essential items which consumers continue to purchase even when their incomes are falling – demand for them is not sensitive to changes in income.

Demand for other products is more sensitive to changes in income levels and the stages of the business cycle. Examples include foreign holidays, electrical products, such as televisions and CD players, and construction materials, such as bricks.

Firms selling basic foodstuffs might have to take little or no action to survive a downswing. Demand for their products might increase as consumers switch from more expensive alternatives. At the

Figure 7.6 *The UK construction industry is particularly sensitive to the effects of the business cycle. It is normally one of the first industries to be affected by a recession.*

other extreme, businesses supplying materials to the construction industry could be hard hit as firms delay or abandon plans to extend factories and build new offices. Their position might be made worse by a fall in demand for new houses as hard-up consumers abandon schemes to move home.

Government policy and the business cycle

The UK government attempts to offset the worst effects of the business cycle. The government implements counter-cyclical policies to limit the fluctuations in GDP and the consequences of these fluctuations for businesses. Counter-cyclical policies have implications for businesses in the same way that the business cycle does.

In a slump, the government seeks to lessen the impact of falling confidence amongst businesses and falling expenditure by consumers and businesses. By reducing interest rates and cutting the level of taxes paid by individuals and businesses the level of economic activity may remain relatively stable. Recent governments have favoured reducing interest rates in the expectation that they will encourage firms to undertake investment programmes as borrowing becomes cheaper. Similarly, consumers may spend more if credit is less expensive.

A boom may result in governments raising interest rates in an attempt to lower the level of economic activity. Higher interest rates are likely to discourage investment by businesses and spending by consumers. Reducing expenditure in this way can assist in avoiding resources becoming too scarce as firms attempt to produce more than available resources will allow.

Businesses need to take into account the likely effects of counter-cyclical policies when considering their responses to changing trading conditions brought about by the business cycle. Such policies can be beneficial as they avoid the need for firms to prepare for the worst excesses of boom and slump.

APPLICATION IN ACTION

Whether or not the sales of a product are sensitive to income levels as the business cycle moves through its stages can form an important part of an argument in response to an examination question.

Firms supplying these products may be significantly affected by the business cycle	Firms supplying these products are unlikely to be affected to a great extent by the business cycle – in fact demand may rise for some of these products in a recession or slump
• Wine • Sports and leisure goods • Restaurant meals • Jewellery • Household furniture	• Coal • Bread • Cigarettes and tobacco • Petrol • Fresh vegetables

Table 7.2 *Products affected and unaffected by the business cycle*

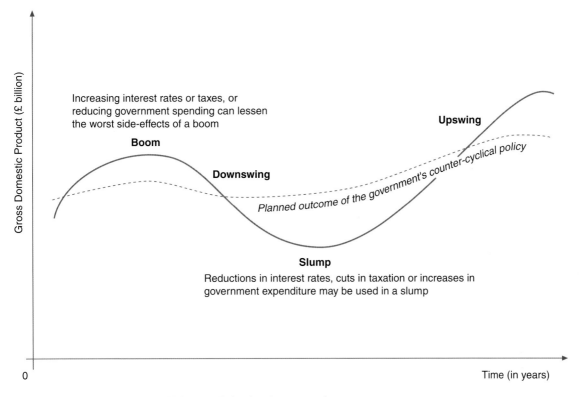

Figure 7.7 *Counter-cyclical policies and the business cycle*

QUICK CHECK QUESTIONS

1 Which of the following is least likely to have made markets more competitive?
a) competition from European rivals
b) fewer, larger businesses in a market
c) improved communications and methods of transportation
d) more informed and knowledgeable consumers.

2 Complete the following sentence by filling in the missing words. 'A .... is a place where buyers and .... meet to establish .... and .... goods and services.'

3 Which type of market is the following sentence describing? 'Few firms operate in the market and those firms are dependent upon each other when deciding prices or introducing new products.'

4 Which of the following is **not** likely to occur in a market made up of a few large firms?
a) price wars
b) competition through the use of loyalty schemes

c) take-overs and mergers
d) extensive use of special offers.

5 Which government organisation has responsibility for creating free and fair competition within UK markets?
a) Customs & Excise
b) The Department of Trade and Industry
c) The Competition Commission
d) The Inland Revenue.

6 Of what is the following a definition? 'A situation in which the firms in a particular market are unable to meet the needs of consumers.'

7 Complete the following sentence by filling in the missing words. '......... competition allows business to compete on an .... basis and offers .... the best possible products at the lowest ....'

8 Which of the following might take place during the upswing or recovery stage of a product life cycle?
a) falling levels of consumer expenditure
b) production increases

c) unemployment increases
d) job vacancies increase.

9   Of what is the following definition? 'A period of time characterised by falling levels of demand and declining levels of output and employment.'

10 Demand for which of the following products is likely to be sensitive to changes in the business cycle?
a) computers
b) coffee
c) petrol
d) tobacco.

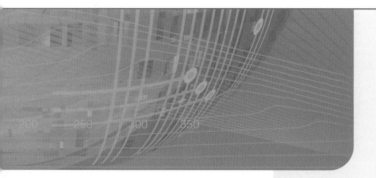

Progress questions

1   What is meant by the term 'market'?   *(3 marks)*

2   Explain two possible benefits that perfectly competitive markets offer to consumers. *(6 marks)*

3   Outline the nature of competition that exists within an oligopolistic market.   *(5 marks)*

4   Explain why cartels are illegal in most European countries.   *(5 marks)*

5   There is substantial excess productive capacity in the world market for motor vehicles. Outline the possible implications of this for a producer of motor vehicles.   *(6 marks)*

6   Consider two ways in which a motor manufacturer might respond to the existence of spare capacity within the industry.   *(6 marks)*

7   An economy is in the recession stage of the business cycle. What are the most common features of this stage of the cycle?   *(5 marks)*

8   Explain why the boom stage of the business cycle may not be good news for a business.   *(6 marks)*

9   Outline two ways in which a company manufacturing digital televisions might be affected by a slump.   *(6 marks)*

10 What are the actions a government might take to offset the worst effects of a boom?   *(7 marks)*

Analytical and evaluative questions

11 Felicity Garments is a small firm that trades in a highly competitive market. The company makes industrial clothing and faces many rivals of equal size. Discuss how the structure of this market might affect the marketing mix used by the company.   *(15 marks)*

12 The UK's supermarket industry is made up of a few large firms, such as Tesco and Asda. Analyse the implications of this for consumers.   *(8 marks)*

13 Broadland Products Ltd manufactures double glazing. It sells its products to the construction industry and to home owners. A recession has been forecast. Evaluate the actions the company might take in these circumstances.   *(15 marks)*

Case study

40 marks

Fran Delaney started her design agency when the economy was booming and had not found it difficult to get orders. Company profits were quite high and managers were willing to spend heavily on design. Fran's strategy had been to focus specifically on website design and there was very little competition. Few other firms had thought this worth bothering with.

Fran brought her creative talents together with the technical wizardry of her partner Jes and this made a winning combination. More and more firms were appreciating the value of having a website. Fran and Jes had to turn away orders because they did not have sufficient capacity.

Encouraged by the high levels of demand, Fran and Jes decided to take the risk and expand. They borrowed to buy new equipment and moved to bigger premises in an exclusive and expensive part of Edinburgh. They also hired two more staff.

Everything was going well until market conditions took a sudden downturn. First, new website design companies seemed to be starting up every few days. In many cases, it was either a traditional design company expanding into the website market or a company which had previously focused on the technical side of computers expanding into the design side. They posed a threat. Increased competition came at a time when the growth in the market was slowing up. To make matters worse, the government increased interest rates and the pound shot up in value. This not only hit Fran and Jes' company: it also hit their clients as well and they began to reduce their own spending.

1 What is meant by 'capacity'? *(2 marks)*

2 Examine the factors that might determine the capacity of Fran and Jes' business. *(8 marks)*

3 Discuss the problems Fran and Jes might have increasing the capacity of their business still further. *(10 marks)*

4 Analyse the ways in which Fran and Jes might respond to the increasing competition in their industry. *(9 marks)*

5 Evaluate the possible implications of the latest changes in the economy for Fran and Jes' firm. *(11 marks)*

>> Interest rates and exchange rates

Introduction

Most textbooks and newspapers refer to the interest rate as if there is only a single rate. In fact, a range of interest rates operates in the UK at any time. However, the UK authorities set the base rate of interest and all other interest rates relate to this.

Interest rates

For many years, the government (or the Chancellor of the Exchequer) took responsibility for setting the base rate of interest. However, in May 1997 the Labour Government gave the Bank of England responsibility for setting interest rates. The Bank of England's Monetary Policy Committee (MPC) meets each month and takes decisions on whether to alter the base rate of interest.

In November 2003, the Bank of England's Monetary Policy Committee decided to increase interest rates. This was the first rise in interest rates for nearly four years. This followed a period during which UK interest rates had been at the lowest level for 50 years.

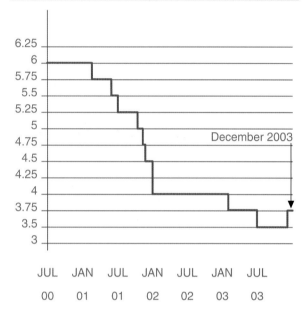

Figure 7.8 *UK interest rates 2000–2003*

Source: Bank of England

Changes in interest rates have significant effects on businesses and the environment in which they operate. Recent UK governments have relied heavily upon interest rates to control the level of economic activity in the economy and to avoid the worst effects of the business cycle.

Key terms

Interest rates are the price paid for borrowed money.

Interest rates and consumer spending

Interest rates affect the level of spending by UK citizens. The level of spending is dependent upon interest rates for a number of reasons:

- Consumers are more likely to take a decision to save when interest rates are rising. The return on their savings is greater and will persuade some consumers to postpone spending decisions. When rates are falling, consumers might save less and spend more.
- Changes in interest rates alter the cost of borrowing. Many goods are purchased on credit: electrical goods, caravans and satellite TV systems, for example. If rates fall, the cost of purchasing these goods on credit will decline, persuading more people to buy the product. Demand for consumer durables is sensitive to interest rates.
- Millions of UK consumers have mortgages. A rise in interest rates will increase the amount paid each month by householders. This reduces the income available for expenditure on other products and demand will fall. A fall in rates will have the opposite effect.
- Britain's population is steadily ageing, meaning that more people are dependent upon pensions and savings. Many pensioners' incomes are dependent upon the rate of interest and thus their expenditure is sensitive to rate changes.

Businesses and changes in interest rates

Changes in interest rates also have significant implications for businesses. A rise in interest rates will result in greater overheads for most businesses, for example, increased interest charges on any loans. When rates rise, firms might limit borrowing (especially short-term borrowing) but may be able to do little about the increased costs of long-term loans. This means that businesses with high proportions of long-term borrowing are likely to be hardest hit by rising interest rates. It is small firms, however, who are often most affected by rising rates due to their smaller financial reserves and greater need to borrow.

The National Federation of Self-Employed and Small Businesses has estimated that every 1% rise in interest rates costs the UK's 1.5 million small firms an extra £200m in interest payments.

Firms may postpone decisions to buy new machinery or to build new factories or offices following a rise in interest rates. Business investment may fall because the cost of borrowing money increases when rates rise. As a result, a previously profitable investment may not be considered worthwhile. Firms may also be put off increasing their productive capacity in this way because they expect consumers to spend less.

If interest rates rise businesses save more, as returns are greater. Postponing investment decisions will reduce the level of economic activity within the economy. The construction and engineering industries may be particularly susceptible to declining order books at such a time. At times of declining interest rates, businesses will increase their investment spending as consumer spending is rising and more productive capacity will probably be required.

Decisions to invest may be postponed or abandoned because of the increasing cost of borrowing. However, much investment is financed from retained profits. Changes in interest rates are likely to have less impact on investment decisions when firms use retained profits.

Firms will be likely to reduce their levels of stocks at a time of rising interest rates. This might entail selling finished goods at reduced prices and reducing orders for raw materials and components. By taking this action, firms reduce the need to borrow to provide working capital and to pay associated interest payments.

Reducing stocks may take place alongside a substantial fall in demand for products and services. This will put businesses under pressure to reduce levels of production. Factories and offices may be closed or put on part-time working. Lay-offs and redundancies might result.

But are all businesses equally affected? The answer is no. Some businesses are particularly susceptible to changes in interest rates:

- Businesses supplying luxury products such as sports cars, jewellery and expensive hotel accommodation. These sorts of products will be amongst the first to be cut from consumers' budgets following a rise in interest rates and become attractive to consumers following a fall in rates.
- Businesses that are heavily involved in overseas trade. Interest rate changes influence exchange rates (see page 292) and directly determine the prices of exports and imports.
- Businesses whose products are frequently purchased on credit. Prices of goods purchased in this way fluctuate directly with the rate of interest. Thus, a rise in rates may lead to a significant fall in sales of fitted kitchens as the increased interest charges mean consumers have to pay more.

Clearly, any business's response to rising rates will depend to some degree on the extent to which its sales are sensitive to changes in interest rates. Suppliers of fuels and basic foodstuffs may take little or no action to maintain sales revenue. Those offering products on credit or luxuries are more likely to respond by use of tactics such as interest-free periods of credit or 'buy now, pay later' deals. These techniques are used extensively by businesses manufacturing and supplying personal computers and domestic furniture. Alternatively, businesses might accept lower prices and reduced profits.

Interest rates and exchange rates

An important link exists between the domestic rate of interest and the value of a nation's currency. This is called an exchange rate and the relationship is summarised in Figure 7.9.

Changes in the UK's rate of interest will lead to an alteration in the exchange value of the pound. Thus following a 1% rise in UK interest rates the following changes could occur:

- the value of £1 rises from $1.50 to $1.60
- the pound is worth €1.54 (rising from €1.45)
- £1 exchanges for 2500 Japanese yen – an increase from 2350 yen.

When interest rates rise, the pound increases in value against most foreign currencies. Similarly, a reduction in interest rates causes a fall in the value of the pound.

As interest rates fall in relation to the rates available in other countries, the UK will become a less attractive target for international investment.

3. Demand for pounds increases raising the price (exchange rates) of pounds.

2. Foreign investors purchase pounds to invest in UK banks and other financial institutions.

1. UK becomes a more attractive location for foreign investors seeking high returns.

Rise
Interest Rates
Fall

1 UK becomes less attractive to foreign investors as UK banks and other financial institutions cut rates.

2. Foreign investors sell pounds to purchase other currencies to enable them to invest overseas.

3. Supply of pounds increases depressing the price (exchange rate).

Figure 7.9 *The relationship between interest rates and the exchange rate of the pound*

Foreigners with money to invest will be tempted by the high returns available from banks in other countries. To take advantage of the relatively higher rates overseas, investors will withdraw funds from UK banks to invest abroad. To do this they will have to exchange their sterling for the currency of the country in which they wish to invest. This means that an increased supply of sterling will be put onto the world's currency markets. As with most products, an increase in the supply tends to lower the price: in this case the exchange rate.

Key terms

*An **exchange rate** is the price of one currency expressed in terms of another. Thus, the pound might be worth €1.5.*

EXAMINER'S ADVICE

A number of businesses actually benefit from a rise in interest rates. For example, supermarkets might see sales of own label products rising as consumers have less money to spend. Similarly, people might decide to save more or open new savings accounts providing banks and other financial institutions with greater custom.

Exchange rates

Exchange rates between most currencies vary regularly according to the balance of supply and demand for each individual currency.

Why do firms purchase foreign currencies?

The main reason businesses purchase foreign currencies is to pay for goods and services bought from overseas. Firms purchasing products from abroad are normally expected to pay using the currency of the exporting country. For example, Sainsbury's purchases wine from Chile. Chilean wine producers would expect to be paid in their local currency – Chilean pesos (Ch$). Thus, traders acting on behalf of Sainsbury's would sell pounds sterling in order to buy pesos. This is illustrated in Figure 7.10.

Demand for foreign currencies may also arise because individuals and businesses wish to invest in enterprises overseas. Thus, a UK citizen wishing to invest in a Belgian business will require Belgian francs to complete the transaction. Sometimes

Business in focus

UK retail sales grew at double the expected rate during October 2003, and were 3.7% higher than in October 2002. Spending grew across nearly all sectors – boosted by bonfire night, Halloween and the start of Christmas shopping. Department stores such as Debenhams enjoyed a 1.6% rise is sales over the month. However, not all retailers benefited from rising sales. Consumer spending on clothing and footwear actually declined by 0.5% during the month.

Consumer spending was one of the main reasons for the Bank of England raising rates to 3.75% in November. Consumer spending is still growing strongly and it looks likely that the UK economy will grow steadily during 2004.

These factors have led to business analysts forecasting that the Bank of England may want to raise interest rates yet again in the near future. They expect interest rates to rise steadily during 2004.

1 Why might a corner shop selling groceries be relatively unaffected if interest rates rise during 2004?
2 Debenhams imports some of the goods it sells from overseas. How might the company view a slow rise in interest rates? How might it respond?

In August 2002 £1 exchanged for €1.60. By January 2004 the pound was worth only €1.42. This meant that the value of the pound had depreciated by over 11% over the period. Alternatively, the value of the euro had increased by the same amount.

Changes in the value of currencies affect the prices of exports and imports as shown in Table 7.3.

The information in Table 7.3 helps to forecast that the fall in the value of the pound against the euro between 2002 and 2004 would have had the following effects:

● Prices of UK exports to Europe (for example Scotch Whisky) would have fallen by approximately 11% unless suppliers decided to increase prices (and profits).
● European imports to the UK would have been up to 11% cheaper. However, the price the European exporters received in euro would not have changed. It is likely, however, that because prices were higher in the UK they would sell smaller quantities of their products.

Small changes in the UK's exchange rate occur all the time as demand for the currency and supplies of it alter; these are of little importance. Of more concern is a sustained rise or fall in the exchange rate – or a sudden and substantial change in the exchange rate.

Significant changes in the exchange rate can create a number of difficulties for businesses:

● Firms find it difficult to forecast earnings from overseas sales in the event of an exchange rate change occurring in between agreeing the price (in the foreign currency) and receiving payment. If the pound rises in value then earnings from export sales can decline.
● Costs of imported raw materials may vary owing to exchange rate fluctuations. Thus, a price quoted to customers might suddenly become

governments buy or sell their own currencies if they wish to influence the price or exchange rate. Government decisions to use reserves of gold or other foreign currencies to purchase their own currency are likely to increase the exchange rate – as long as other people and institutions are not selling huge quantities of the currency. Similarly, selling the currency is likely to depress its exchange value.

The effects of exchange rate changes

Exchange rates can change significantly over time. A rise in the value of a currency is termed appreciation; a decline in its value is a depreciation.

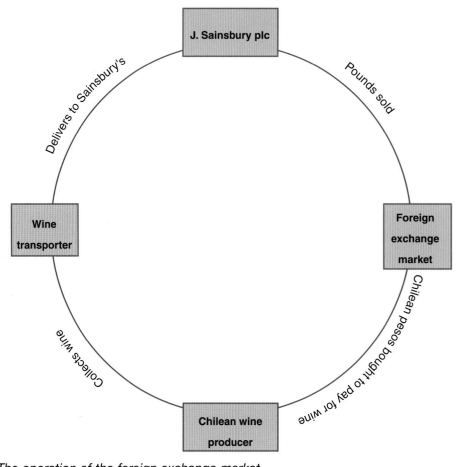

Figure 7.10 *The operation of the foreign exchange market*

unprofitable if the price paid for raw materials from overseas rises.

- Exchange rate fluctuations can change the price charged overseas for a product. A rise in the value of the pound makes it more difficult for exporters, whilst a fall in the value of the pound makes exports more price competitive.

Price elasticity can be an important part of a discussion on the possible effects of exchange rate changes. If overseas demand for a product is price inelastic, then an increase in the exchange rate may not be too harmful. If demand is price elastic exporters might be badly affected by a rise in the exchange rate, but benefit greatly from a fall. This

fall in the value of the pound against the euro might be good news for Scottish whisky distillers.

 **Key issues**

On 1 January 1999 a single European currency – the euro – was introduced into 12 European Union countries. Austria, Belgium, Finland, France, Germany, Greece, Ireland, Italy, Luxembourg, the Netherlands, Portugal and Spain all adopted the new currency. Euro notes and coins became available on 1 January 2002. The 12 countries have locked the foreign exchange values of their national currencies to the euro and share the new currency.

The exchange rate of pounds	Prices of UK exports overseas (in foreign currencies)	Prices of imported goods in the UK (in pounds)
Appreciates (rises)	increase	fall
Depreciates (falls)	fall	increase

Table 7.3 *The effects of changes in the value of sterling*

Business in focus

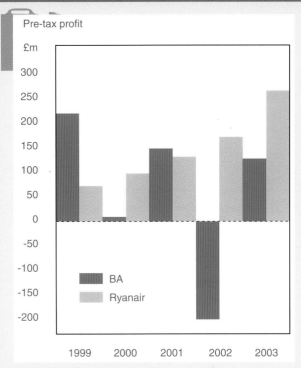

Figure 7.11 *Pre-tax profit for British Airways and Ryanair, 1999– 2003*

Ryanair, the Irish budget airline, has enjoyed a rise of nearly 66% in its net profits over the year to March 2003. At the same time the company has announced plans to cut fares further. The company has just completed the purchase of its low-price rival Buzz; this will enable it to expand its routes and it anticipates flying to 125 destinations by the end of 2003. Ryanair has predicted that it will become Europe's largest scheduled airline by 2006 overtaking established giants such as British Airways and Lufthansa in the process. Passenger numbers are forecast to be 24 million in 2003-4 compared with 15.7 million in 2002-3.

Michael O'Leary, the controversial boss of the airline, recognised that the future would not be untroubled. The high value of the euro could cut the revenue received from each passenger by up to 10% and affect future profits, he warned.

1 Ryanair's success is based on low prices. To what extent might external factors impact on the company's success?

The UK has delayed a decision on when (or if) to join the single currency. UK businesses would benefit from the country adopting the euro. No longer would it be necessary to pay commission to convert one currency into another. Using the single currency would help attract foreign businesses to the UK. The elimination of exchange rates within Europe means that businesses no longer face uncertain earnings owing to changes in currency values. Finally, price comparisons become easier when all goods are quoted in the same currency. Chairman of Ford UK, Roger Putnam, argues that 'any unnecessary delay in adopting the euro is detrimental to UK manufacturing'.

In spite of these advantages, many people in the UK are not keen on joining the euro. In September 1998, research showed 65% of UK businesses in favour of the euro; by 2002 this figure had fallen to 52%. Opposition is based on the high costs of re-equipping to trade in euros. New tills, software and computer systems will need to be bought, as well as investing in staff training. Marks & Spencer has estimated that the changeover would cost £100m, Tesco has forecast £40m. Some UK firms are also nervous about the sharpening of competition that a single currency would bring about.

> **EXAMINER'S ADVICE**
>
> *Remember that products are not sold on the basis on price alone. When considering the likely consequences of a change in exchange rates it is important to note that factors such as quality, reputation, after sales service and meeting delivery dates are important influences on buyers' decisions.*

1   Is this statement true or false? 'If interest rates rise then consumers are likely to increase savings while businesses may postpone or cancel investment plans.'

2   Which of the following is **not** a likely consequence of rising interest rates?
a) reduction in demand for goods and services purchased on credit
b) increased overheads for many businesses
c) increased saving by businesses and individuals
d) increased investment in new factories and machinery.

3   Which of the following businesses is most likely to experience a significant rise in demand for its products following a fall in interest rates?
a) a company building homes for first-time house buyers
b) a dairy selling milk, yogurt and similar products
c) Anglian Water plc (the suppliers of water and drainage services to much of Norfolk and Suffolk)
d) a local corner shop selling newspapers, tobacco and some groceries.

4   Complete the following sentence by filling in the missing words. 'A television manufacturer might respond to a substantial rise in interest rates by .... the level of stocks it holds, it may decide not to expand its .... by extending the factory and it may attempt to reduce short-term ....'

5   Is the following statement true or false? 'A rise in UK interest rates normally results in a fall in the exchange rate of the pound.'

6   Which of the following is the best explanation of why an increase in UK interest rates will affect the exchange rate of the pound?

a) because more UK consumers will buy more home-produced goods
b) because foreign consumers will buy more UK-manufactured goods
c) because some UK investors will invest their money in foreign banks and financial institutions
d) because some foreign investors will decide to invest in UK banks and financial institutions.

7   Of what is the following a definition? 'The price of one currency expressed in terms of another?'

8   Following an appreciation in the exchange rate of the pound, which of the following is most likely to be true?
a) sales of UK exports rise while demand for imports falls
b) sales of UK exports fall while demand for imports rises
c) sales of UK exports fall while demand for imports does not change
d) sales of UK exports fall whilst demand for imports also falls.

9   Is the following statement true or false? 'If the exchange rate of the pound depreciates, the amount in pounds sterling earned by a UK exporter from the sale of a single product will not change as long as the exporter leaves prices unchanged.'

10   Which of the following is an argument for the UK **not** adopting the euro:
a) the most important market for UK businesses is the United States
b) it would no longer be necessary to pay commission to convert currencies on many overseas transactions
c) businesses would be more certain about their earnings from international trade
d) it would help to attract foreign businesses to the UK.

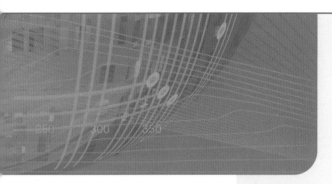

Progress questions

1 Outline two factors that might determine the rate of interest charged on a loan.   *(6 marks)*

2 Explain why sales of consumer durables might be particularly sensitive to changes in interest rates.   *(7 marks)*

3 Explain why firms' investment decisions might be dependent on the rate of interest.   *(6 marks)*

4 Outline two factors that might determine a business's response to a rise in interest rates.   *(6 marks)*

5 Why do firms purchase foreign currencies?   *(4 marks)*

6 Archer and Sons, based in Norwich, purchase raw materials from overseas and sell half their output in foreign markets. Explain the probable effects of a rise in the exchange value of the pound on the company.   *.(7 marks)*

7 Assume the pound has fallen in value against the Danish Kroner from £1 = DK10 to £1 = DK9. Smith plc sells desks to a Danish importer for £500. Explain what would happen to the price in Denmark of the desks (assuming no mark up is added). What would happen to the price (in pounds) received by Smith plc?   *(7 marks)*

8 Explain why price elasticity of demand may partly determine the effects of a change in exchange rates on a business.   *(6 marks)*

9 Outline three factors that might determine the level of export sales apart from the price of the exports.   *(6 marks)*

10 Explain one benefit to UK firms and one drawback to UK firms that may result from the UK joining the European single currency (the euro).   *(6 marks)*

Analytical and evaluative questions

11 John Lewis is one of Britain's leading department stores selling a wide range of clothes, furniture and consumer durables such as fridges and televisions. Analyse the possible effects of a rise in interest rates on this company.   *(8 marks)*

12 Ford UK has urged the British government to adopt the euro in place of the pound. Discuss the advantages and disadvantages the company might experience if the British government followed its advice.   *(15 marks)*

13 Cadbury Schweppes plc is a British manufacturer of confectionery. The company manufactures chocolates and other confectionery in several locations around the world and sells in over 200 countries. Evaluate the possible effects on Cadbury Scheweppes plc of a significant rise in the exchange value of the pound.   *(15 marks)*

>> Inflation and unemployment

What is inflation?

For many businesses a low rate of **inflation** is not a problem. As long as wages are rising at about the same rate, or higher, a low constant rate of price increase simply serves to help maintain demand. Inflation only becomes a major problem for businesses when it is high, rising rapidly or (worst of all) is doing both together.

POINTS TO PONDER

Some countries have experienced amazing rates of inflation. The worst recorded inflation in Europe was that suffered by Hungary: between May and July 1946 prices rose by over 1 million per cent!

Key terms

Inflation *is a persistent rise in the general price level and an associated fall in the value of money.*

How is inflation measured?

The UK government measures the rate of inflation by use of the Retail Price Index (RPI) as well as the Consumer Price Index (CPI). The CPI was introduced in December 2003 and will operate alongside the RPI. The CPI measures the average monthly change in the prices of goods and services purchased by households in the UK, and the government will use this to set targets for inflation in the future. The RPI and the CPI are both calculated using more than 650 separate goods and services for which price changes are measured throughout the country.

The main difference between the CPI and the RPI is that the CPI excludes housing and Council Tax costs. The use of the CPI as the official measure of inflation brings the UK into line with most other European countries. CPI gives a lower rate of inflation. Figure 7.12 illustrates this and also shows that inflation rates have been at a low level in the UK over recent years.

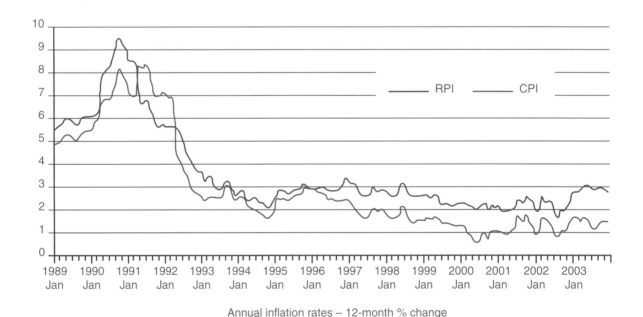

Annual inflation rates – 12-month % change

Figure 7.12 *Inflation in the UK 1989–2003*

Source: www.statistics.gov.uk

POINTS TO PONDER

The CPI shows that the UK's inflation rate has been one of the lowest in the EU since 2000. In October 2003 the UK's rate was 1.4% compared with the EU average of 1.8%.

See Business in Focus below for an explanation of the calculation of the CPI and the RPI.

Business in focus

The CPI and RPI are weighted index numbers. The use of index numbers is very common in business. The CPI and RPI are constructed by determining the pattern of expenditure of an 'average' household in the UK. Thus, assuming that households spend about 11% of their income on food each month, this can be given an 11% weight in the calculation. As the weights in the RPI and CPI actually add up to 1000, the weighting given to food is approximately 110 (11% of 1000).

Once each category of expenditure is given an appropriate weight, inflation can be calculated. For each category the average price change observed is multiplied by the weight. Thus, if an item carrying a heavy weight, such as housing, changes significantly it will have a major impact upon the overall rate of inflation. On the other hand, changes in tobacco (which carry a low weighting), do not have a great effect on inflation.

Finally a base year is decided – currently 2001 for the CPI – and given a figure of 100. This makes it easy to assess at a glance the rate of inflation. By 2003 the CPI had risen to 110.3. Thus, between 2001 and 2003 the prices faced by the average family had risen by 10.3%.

Item in consumer expenditure	Weight
Food and non-alcoholic drinks	108
Alcohol and tobacco	47
Clothing and footwear	62
Water, electricity, gas and other fuels	104
Furniture, household equipment and maintenance of homes	68
Health	23
Transport	144
Communication	25
Recreation	163
Education	20
Restaurant and hotels	135
Miscellaneous	101
TOTAL	**1000**

Table 7.4 *Categories of consumer expenditure and their weights in the CPI index.*

Source: Adapted from www.statistics.gov.uk/pdfdir/cpibrief1203.pdf

The causes of inflation

Economists tend to classify the causes of inflation as caused by demand–pull or cost–push factors.

Demand–pull inflation

Demand–pull inflation occurs when the demand for the country's goods and services exceeds its ability to supply the products. Thus, prices rise generally as a means of restricting demand to the available supply. The underlying cause of this might be the government allowing firms and businesses to have too much money to spend, perhaps as a consequence of cutting taxes or lowering interest rates.

Demand–pull inflation normally occurs at the boom stage of the trade cycle when the economy is at full stretch with most of its resources in use. At this high level of production, shortages and bottlenecks occur in supply. Because resources and labour become relatively scarce, firms offer higher prices and wages, and inflation is the result. Governments are alert for the first signs of demand–pull inflation and raise interest rates to prevent the economy overheating and prices rising.

Cost–push inflation

Cost–push inflation occurs when costs rise due to factors such as rising wages or costs of raw materials

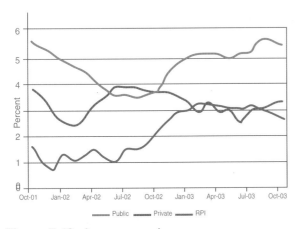

Figure 7.13 *Average earnings*

Source: www.statistics.gov.uk

and components. This type of inflation has several causes.

Wage rises

If trade unions and employees are successful in negotiating pay increases above the rate of inflation, further price rises might result. This becomes more likely if productivity is not increasing, allowing businesses to offset some of the increased wage costs against additional production. Some business analysts became concerned in 2003 that pay rises in the public sector were potentially inflationary. Figure 7.13 illustrates the reasons for this concern.

Imported inflation

One of the hidden causes of inflation is rising import prices. The UK is susceptible to this type of inflation, as it is an 'open' economy importing large quantities of raw materials, components and finished goods. Import prices rise when the exchange rate is falling and more pounds are required to purchase a given amount of a foreign currency.

> ### Key terms
>
> *Cost–push inflation* happens when firms face increasing costs due to rising wages or increasing costs of raw materials and components.
>
> *Demand–pull inflation* occurs when the demand for the country's goods and services exceeds its ability to supply these products.

Expectations and inflation

Expectations are an important part of the process of creating inflation. If managers and businesses anticipate rising inflation, they might take actions which can fuel the inflationary process. If firms expect their suppliers to increase the prices of raw materials and components, they may raise their selling prices in anticipation. The action also provides a windfall profit in that, for a while, firms sell at higher prices whilst their costs have not risen.

Trade unions build in their expectations of inflation into their wage demands for the coming year. If, as in 2004, inflation is forecast to be 2%, this is likely to be the base figure for a negotiated wage rise. In such circumstances, unions will demand a 4 or 5% increase in wages to give their members an increase in their standard of living. Unless productivity rises, inflation may result.

Consumers can also add to inflation. If they expect prices to rise in the near future, they may make major purchases immediately to avoid the price increases. If the economy is near to full capacity, this can add to demand–pull inflation. A large number of consumers deciding to purchase consumer durables may result in price rises as producers are unable to respond to the orders and shortages occur.

Figure 7.14 *The Treasury may have supported the move to using the CPI as it gives a lower figure for inflation in the UK than the RPI and may help to reduce expectations of inflation*

In 2003 pay rises in the private sector averaged 2.3%. The Confederation of British Industry (CBI) said low company profits and intense price competition held down pay increases during the year.

Business in focus

In 2003 inflation in the UK slackened bringing benefits to consumers. In December 2003 inflation in the UK (as measured by the Consumer Price Index) was 1.3%, well below Chancellor Gordon Brown's target of 2%. The Office of National Statistics, announcing the figures, said that the main causes were a slowing of price increases for shoes and women's clothes. These items have benefited from the high exchange value of the pound (and therefore cheaper imports) as many come from overseas. Slow price increases in newspapers and recreation products (such as cinema tickets, games and toys) have also contributed to the slowdown in inflation experienced by UK consumers.

A highly competitive retailing market has also helped to keep price increases sluggish. ASDA has been purchased by the enormous American retailer Wal-Mart and this has helped keep the prices of groceries in the UK down. At the same time increasing foreign competition in the high street (for example clothes retailer Zara) has increased price competition reducing the rate of inflation for many products.

Inflation is expected to increase slightly during 2004 and 2005, but is forecast to remain below 2% throughout this period.

1 What is the difference between a fall in inflation and a fall in prices?
2 Explain why lower than expected rises in the price of recreation products and clothes and groceries might have a significant impact on the rate of inflation in the UK.

Thus, the expectation of inflation can sometimes contribute to its existence.

The impact of inflation on business

Inflation can have a number of effects on businesses:

- Many businesses may suffer falling sales in a period of inflation. Research shows that, during inflationary periods, people save more (perhaps due to uncertainty) and sales for many businesses fall.
- It can be difficult to maintain competitiveness (especially international competitiveness) during bouts of inflation. Rising wages and raw material costs may force firms to raise prices or accept lower profit margins. Overseas firms (with lower rates of inflation) may gain a competitive advantage.

The impact of government anti-inflationary policies

The UK is experiencing a period of low inflation as illustrated in Figure 7.12. In part, this is due to the government's effective control of inflationary pressures.

This has meant that businesses are frequently affected more by anti-inflationary policies than by inflation itself. Over recent years, the UK government has controlled the worst effects of inflation in a number of ways.

Rises in interest rates

Rises in interest rates have been the government's main weapon. Increasing the base rate reduces the possibility of demand–pull inflation occurring. Consumers are discouraged from spending their money by higher savings rates and are less likely to buy on credit as it is more expensive.

Businesses reduce investment as borrowing becomes more expensive. Output and sales decline and the inflationary pressure reduces.

Legislation

Successive governments have introduced legislation designed to restrict the power of trade unions. Acts controlling picketing and making ballots

AS Business Studies

302

compulsory before unions can take industrial action have served to reduce trade union power. This legislation has lessened the chance of wage rises pushing up prices.

Reduced expectations

The government has reduced the expectation of inflation. This has helped businesses to be confident in setting prices and has dissuaded unions from putting in excessive (and inflationary) pay claims. The low rate of inflation enjoyed by the UK has also been one of a number of factors persuading foreign firms to move to Britain.

Inflation can offer some benefits to businesses, however. Some analysts suggest that low and stable rates of inflation may be beneficial. A steady rise in profits can create favourable expectations and encourage investment by businesses.

Low rates of inflation can also encourage long-term borrowing and investment by businesses.

Unemployment

Unemployment is important because it represents a waste of resources if labour is unused – if all available workers were used, the country concerned would be more productive and would enjoy a higher standard of living. The social effects of high and prolonged rates of unemployment can be devastating: poor health and crime are associated with unemployment and poverty.

POINTS TO PONDER

The Department of Social Security estimates that spending on benefits will rise by £400m for every 100 000 people who lose their jobs and join the dole queues.

Types of unemployment

People can be unemployed for a number of reasons. Governments find it useful to distinguish between the various types of unemployment, as each type requires a different remedy.

Although many different types of unemployment exist, we shall focus on three main types.

Structural unemployment

Economies continually change: some industries die and others emerge to replace them. Structural unemployment occurs due to fundamental changes in the economy whereby some industries reach the end of their lives. Structural unemployment occurs for a number of reasons:

- the adoption of new methods of production
- significant and permanent changes in demand
- increasing competition from overseas
- rising income levels meaning demand for some products declines.

The decline of coal mining has contributed significantly to structural unemployment in the UK. Demand for cleaner and more convenient fuels, such as gas and electricity (and the use of gas and oil in generating electricity), has caused the wide-scale loss of jobs in the coal mining industry. In December 1951 over 700 000 people were employed in the UK's coal mining industry; by 2003 this figure had fallen to approximately 5000. Structural change also offers opportunities to businesses. Rising incomes and technological developments have led to the development of the mobile phone industry. This industry employs a large number of people in manufacturing the product, supplying networks and in retail outlets.

Structural unemployment is a difficult problem for governments to solve. Because large numbers of

Industries with structural unemployment	Industries offering increased employment opportunities
- Textiles	- Business consultancy
- Motor vehicle production	- Retailing
- Coal mining	- Leisure
- Steel manufacture	- Mobile telephone services
- Banks and building societies	- Computer production and services

Table 7.5 *All economies undergo structural change. Some industries decline creating structural unemployment, whilst others grow and develop (and can assist in reducing unemployment levels). Here are examples of industries that have caused structural unemployment and those reducing it*

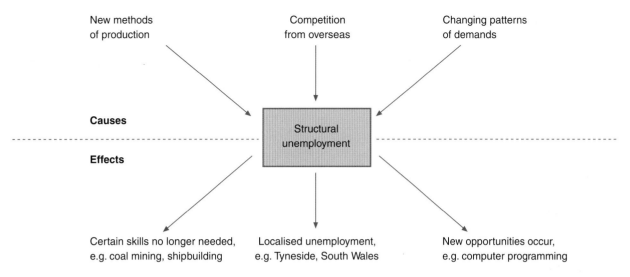

Figure 7.15 *Causes and effects of structural unemployment*

employees may no longer have the skills that employers require, training is an important part of any solution. Other approaches include encouraging foreign producers to establish themselves in the UK to provide employment for those with skills not needed by domestic businesses.

Cyclical unemployment

This type of unemployment arises from the operation of the business cycle. The boom stage of a business cycle will see this type of unemployment minimised as firms increase their production levels. At this stage of the business cycle those who have been unemployed for some time may find work. At the other extreme, much of the unemployment experienced during a slump will be cyclical. Cyclical unemployment was a problem in the mid-1980s and early 1990s. Some firms have helped to protect against cyclical unemployment by the introduction of profit-related pay. Under such schemes, pay falls during a recession along with profits, reducing the need to make workers redundant. Such unemployment is a major target of the government's counter-cyclical policy.

Frictional unemployment

People moving between jobs cause frictional unemployment. If a person leaves one job they may be unable to move into a new position immediately. Whilst they are searching for new employment, they are classified as frictionally unemployed. The government is providing improved information on

job vacancies and this may reduce the level of frictional unemployment. A healthy economy will have some amount of frictional unemployment as people change jobs.

> **Key terms**
>
> *Cyclical unemployment* is caused by the operation of the business cycle rising in slumps and falling in booms.
> *Frictional unemployment* exists because people may be temporarily out of work between leaving one job and starting another.
> *Structural unemployment* occurs due to fundamental changes in the economy whereby some industries reach the end of their lives.

Business and changing unemployment levels

Rises in unemployment can have serious implications for businesses, though the precise impact and likely responses of firms will depend on their circumstances and the type of unemployment.

Cyclical unemployment might result in businesses suffering from falling sales. In the short term, firms may be able to add any surplus production to stocks. Alternatively, businesses may seek new markets – perhaps overseas. Not all businesses will be equally affected by changes in unemployment levels. Businesses selling essential products may be relatively unaffected by cyclical unemployment, whilst suppliers of luxury products could suffer substantial reductions in sales.

Structural unemployment can have a significant effect on businesses because it is often highly localised and very persistent. Thus, high levels of unemployment suffered by former coal mining communities had considerable implications for most businesses in the locality. Unemployment brought about by the decline of an industry also has an impact on associated industries. For example, falling production in the UK's shipbuilding industry contributed to the decline in the country's steel industry.

If there is a need to reduce output, then rationalisation and redundancy might follow and factories and offices may be closed. Research and development plans may be abandoned or postponed as firms seek to reduce their costs to match their (reduced) revenues. The predicted fall in the level of demand may encourage the firm to diversify.

APPLICATION IN ACTION

A business's response to any alteration in the actual or forecast level of unemployment will depend on the type of unemployment. Most businesses would view structural unemployment as a more serious threat.

QUICK CHECK QUESTIONS

1 Is this statement true or false? 'A fall in the rate of inflation means that prices are still rising, but less quickly. If prices were falling this would be termed deflation.'

2 Which of the following is **not** a benefit of using weighted index numbers?
   a) figures are easy to compare as they are based on 100
   b) they make trends easy to identify
   c) they are easy to calculate
   d) using regular base years means that the figures do not become too large.

3 Complete the following sentence by filling in the missing words. 'Demand-pull inflation occurs when the demand for a country's goods and services .... its ability to .... the products.'

4 Is the following statement true or false? 'Businesses always enjoy rising profit margins during periods of inflation because consumers are more willing to pay higher prices.'

5 Which of the following is **not** a method used by the government to reduce the rate of inflation?
   a) increases in interest rates
   b) legislation to restrict the power of trade unions
   c) setting targets for inflation to reduce business's expectations of inflation
   d) reducing taxes such as income tax.

6 Complete the following sentence by filling in the missing words. 'Structural unemployment occurs when changes take place in the economy and some .... reach the end of their .... Cyclical unemployment arises from the operation of the ..../.......................'

7 Which of the following industries is associated with structural unemployment?
   a) retailing
   b) mobile telephone services
   c) restaurants
   d) steel manufacture.

8 Is the following statement true or false? 'As a result of structural unemployment, large numbers of employees may have obsolete skills. For this reason structural unemployment is difficult to reduce.'

9 Of what is the following a definition: 'This exists because people may be temporarily out of work between leaving one job and starting another'?

10 Which of the following statements about the possible effects of structural unemployment is true?
   a) Structural unemployment is a problem for businesses because it is highly localised and very persistent.
   b) Structural unemployment is only a temporary problem as it only occurs during a recession.
   c) Structural unemployment occurs all over the country as people are unemployed when moving between jobs.
   d) Structural unemployment only affects industries that supply consumers with luxury goods.

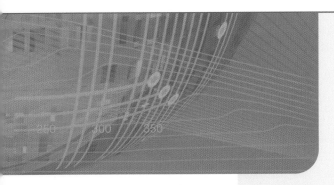

Progress questions

1 Explain why low rates of inflation might not pose problems for the majority of businesses.
(5 marks)

2 Outline why the Retail Prices Index (RPI) might not be a good measure of inflation for many people in the UK.
(6 marks)

3 Explain three possible causes of inflation.
(6 marks)

4 Explain two ways in which inflation might affect a business that is trading overseas.
(6 marks)

5 Outline two ways in which firms selling consumer durables might be affected by the government's counter-cyclical policies.
(6 marks)

6 Distinguish between cyclical and frictional unemployment.
(4 marks)

7 Explain two possible causes of structural unemployment in the UK economy.
(6 marks)

8 Structural changes in the UK economy offer opportunities to businesses. State two examples of the opportunities that might be created.
(2 marks)

9 Explain why the effects of structural unemployment can be particularly severe for businesses.
(7 marks)

10 Outline two actions a manufacturer of consumer durables might take if a period of rising unemployment is forecast.
(6 marks)

Analytical and evaluative questions

11 Redgrave plc is one of the UK's largest manufacturers of household furniture. In 2003 its sales of tables, chairs, sofas, beds and similar items exceeded £780 million. Discuss the possible effects on this company of a substantial rise in unemployment.
(15 marks)

12 Analyse the effects of low and stable inflation for UK businesses that export overseas. *(8 marks)*

13 The Chief Executive of one of the UK's largest hotel chains said recently, 'In the past, the cures for inflation have been worse for this industry than the inflation itself'. To what extent do you agree with this statement?
(15 marks)

Hasker plc is considering making a bid to take over its major competitor Tusk plc. Both firms run a chain of betting shops in the UK and if the deal went ahead it would give Hasker 40% of the market. Hasker is keen to do this deal because it would extend its market: most of its shops are in the southeast whereas Tusk's shops are concentrated in the north. This expansion would allow Hasker's directors to feel more confident about investment and launching new products. The company was keen to develop its own version of the national lottery, for example. At the same time, Hasker was eager to continue its own plans for internal growth by opening more shops. However, its managers were concerned about recent economic indicators and the effect these might have on demand for their services. According to the government, GDP was about to fall whilst unemployment and inflation rates looked set to increase. Another concern was the possible increase in the minimum wage discussed in the media. Hasker's was not known as a generous employer and it was worried about the impact an increase in the minimum wage might have on its costs.

1 *What is meant by the term 'market share'?*
(2 marks)

2 *What is meant by the term 'GDP'?* (2 marks)

3 *Explain two actions the government might take to reduce inflation.* (6 marks)

4 *Examine three ways in which an increase in unemployment might affect Hasker plc.* (8 marks)

5 *Discuss the possible impact of an increase in the minimum wage on Hasker plc.* (15 marks)

6 *Evaluate whether the government should prevent Hasker plc's takeover of its competitor Tusk.* (15 marks)

>> Business and the law

What is law?

The law is a framework of rules governing the way in which our society operates. These rules apply to businesses as well as individuals. The legal framework affects almost all areas of business activity. Marketing, production, employment, relationships with customers and competitors and even the establishment of the business itself are examples of business operations influenced by the law.

The UK law can be classified into two categories as illustrated in Figure 7.16.

Sources of business law

There are three main sources of legislation in the UK:

1 Acts of Parliament
2 Common Law
3 European Law.

Acts of Parliament

Each government passes a series of acts to put into operation the ideas it set out in its election manifesto. Laws passed by Parliament are called statute law. The House of Commons and the House of Lords pass these acts before they are signed by the Queen. Once all these stages are completed an act becomes law. In 2002 the Employment Act became law, granting parents additional rights. Working mothers will be allowed to take up to a year off work to look after their families. Fathers will also receive two weeks' paid paternity leave. The Act came into operation in April 2003.

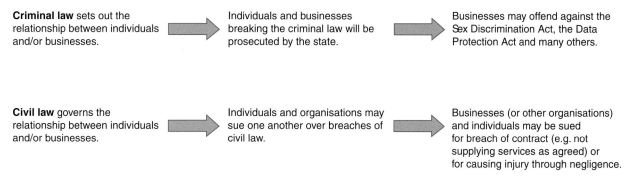

Figure 7.16 *Criminal and civil law*

Common law

Much of the UK's business law is based upon decisions taken by judges. Common law often involves an interpretation of existing legislation, perhaps applying it to new circumstances. Higher courts set Common law. Common law is also called judicial precedent.

European Union law

The EU passes a great deal of legislation relating to UK businesses, called directives. However, it has been proposed that in 2004 they are renamed 'framework laws'. The Working Time Directive, which limits the working hours of many employees, is an example of such a law. EU law covers topics such as free competition between firms, agricultural prices and working conditions. EU law is applicable throughout the UK and overrules any national legislation that may conflict with it.

Additionally, UK businesses operate according to voluntary codes of practice. Voluntary codes are normally an alternative to a new law. These codes are not law and are not enforceable in the courts. They are, however, in widespread use. The chemical industry's *Responsible Care Programme* grew into a voluntary code of practice out of a series of high-profile chemical disasters that eroded public confidence in the industry and raised the threat of tighter government regulation and controls.

Voluntary codes are effective if businesses believe that the government will pass legislation if they do not co-operate.

 ## Key issues

The **Social Chapter** was agreed as part of the **Treaty of Maastricht** in 1991. The Chapter established basic employment rights for employees throughout the EU. The clauses of the Chapter covered various aspects of employment including granting rights to workers to:

- join a trade union
- take industrial action
- have equal treatment for men and women
- have a healthy and safe working environment
- be consulted by employers and participate in business decision-making.

Initially, the UK refused to agree to the implementation of the Social Chapter. It was feared that the Chapter would raise costs of production, making UK businesses less competitive. However, the Labour government, elected in 1997, reversed this decision and the UK has gradually adopted the measures set out in the Chapter.

Competition policy

Competition policy is intended to create free and fair competition within markets in the UK and the European Union. The aim is to provide consumers with quality products at a fair price, allowing producers the opportunity to earn reasonable profits.

Unfair competition can arise in a number of ways:

- The abuse of monopoly power – the lack of competition means that monopolies have the power to exploit consumers by charging high prices and supplying outdated products. In 2003 the Competition Commission forced mobile phone companies to reduce charges when connecting calls from a landline or other mobile networks.

- Mergers and take-overs – these can create monopolies with the power to exploit consumers. In 2003, the Competition Commission rejected the proposed take-over of Safeway by Tesco. The main reason given was that this take-over would give Tesco a market share of over 33%, which would discourage free competition in the market.

- Restrictive practices – these exist when businesses interfere with the free operation of markets. Restrictive practices may take the form of producers making agreements to share out a particular market between them or forcing retailers to stock all of a firm's products by threatening to withdraw all supplies.

The UK's approach to competition policy is described as 'pragmatic'. This means that the authorities do not believe automatically that monopolies or mergers are damaging and anti-competitive. Each case is investigated and a decision

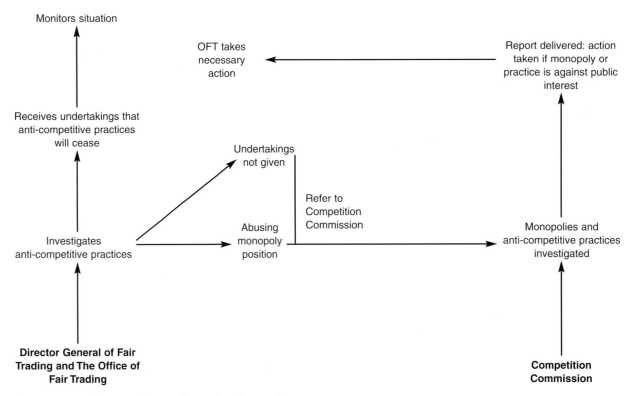

Figure 7.17 *Competition policy: who does what*

is taken on whether a particular monopoly or mergers is 'against the public interest'. Restrictive practices are viewed differently: they are considered to be against the public interest unless the firms concerned can prove otherwise.

Institutions and competition policy

The Competition Commission

The Competition Act of 1998 established the Competition Commission. It inherited many of the responsibilities previously carried out by the Monopolies and Mergers Commission. The Commission conducts investigations into monopoly and mergers situations at the request of the Director-General of Fair Trading. Any business

Business in focus

In 2002 the Office of Fair Trading (OFT) requested that the Competition Commission investigate the market for extended warranties offered by many retailers and propose reforms. These reforms provide customers with a longer period of support than the guarantees given by manufacturers and may grant greater benefits.

The Competition Commission has revealed the outcome of its investigation into the market for extended warranties. It said a 'complex monopoly' was operating in the market and it was not in the public interest. As a result of this investigation consumers will be given more details on the benefits of the warranties and a longer period during which they can change their mind about extended guarantees and still receive a full refund.

The OFT will conduct a review of the market in 2006 to determine whether the reforms are effective.

having more than 25% of a particular market is defined as a monopoly.

The Office of Fair Trading (OFT)

The Fair Trading Act of 1973 established the Office of Fair Trading. It is responsible for the production of consumer information and media relations in the field of consumer affairs and competition policy. The OFT:

- provides legal advice on the application and enforcement of relevant legislation
- protects consumers and promotes their interests
- is responsible for monitoring any possible anti-competitive actions by businesses.

'Watchdog' organisations

A number of monopolies operate as public limited companies within the UK economy. Firms such as British Telecom, the water boards (e.g. Anglian Water) are all monopolies in the sense that they control more than 25% of a particular market. To protect consumers from high prices or poor service at the hands of these businesses, bodies such as OFTEL and OFWAT have been established.

Key competition legislation

Since 1948, the UK government has passed a series of acts intended to promote free and fair competition in markets. A number of these have been vital in creating the UK's competition policy framework.

EXAMINER'S ADVICE

It is not important to have detailed knowledge of the various acts covered by the AS specification you are following. The key points are to have some general knowledge of the scope of the legislation and an understanding of the likely effects of the legislation on businesses.

The Fair Trading Act, 1973

This Act established the Office of Fair Trading, giving the organisation responsibility for providing ministers with advice on legislation and action with regard to monopolies, mergers and restrictive practices. It also created the post of Director-General of Fair Trading. The OFT has the authority to supervise all aspects of competition policy, including the monitoring of changes in the structure of markets and the referral of mergers or monopolies for investigation by the Competition Commission.

Restrictive Practices Acts, 1956, 1968 and 1976

The UK government has passed a series of restrictive practices acts to eliminate behaviour preventing the free and fair operation of markets. Restrictive practices are against the consumers' interest as they normally result in higher prices and products of inferior quality. The Acts established the Restrictive Practices Court to investigate complaints. Unusually, the Court judges practices to be restrictive, and therefore illegal, unless it can be proved this is not the case.

POINTS TO PONDER

In 2003 the OFT conducted an investigation into an alleged cartel among some of Britain's major fee paying schools. The investigation was prompted by public and independent schools across the country increasing fees by an average of 9% – over four times the rate of inflation.

The Competition Acts, 1980 and 1998

These Acts reinforced the UK's anti-competitive regulations. They extended the scope of existing legislation to include refusing to supply products without good reason and strengthened the rules against the operation of cartels. The 1998 Act also increased the penalties for firms who abuse their monopoly position.

The EU's competition policy

UK businesses are subject to the EU's competition legislation. The principal elements of the EU's competition policy include the following:

- There are laws preventing any activities by businesses restricting free competition within the EU markets.
- Legislation prohibits any firm from abusing a dominant position in any EU market.
- The EU will control any merger creating a new firm with a turnover in excess of £4.2 billion.

Some differences exist between EU and UK competition laws. For example, the UK bans certain restrictive practices irrespective of its effect on consumers, whilst EU legislation only operates if consumers are harmed by the practice. In the case of any conflict between the two policies, EU legislation overrules that of the UK.

Consumer protection

Consumer protection is a term used to describe a series of acts designed to safeguard consumers against:

- businesses charging excessively high prices or rates of interest
- unfair trading practices, for example selling quantities less than those advertised
- unsafe products, such as children's toys with sharp objects or toxic paint
- having insufficient information on which to take purchasing decisions.

Since 1973 the Office of Fair Trading has overseen consumer protection in the UK. The OFT's Consumer Affairs Division seeks to improve the position of consumers by giving consumers information to allow them to make better decisions when purchasing goods and services. It also protects consumers by prosecuting offenders against consumer legislation and negotiating voluntary codes of practice with producers.

Consumers in the UK have become more informed and less accepting of poor products or unfair trading practices by businesses. Consumers often conduct research (aided by organisations such as *Which?*) before making major purchases. This trend is known as **consumerism**.

Key issue

Consumerism is an organised movement that has developed steadily in the UK since the 1970s. Its objective is to persuade businesses to behave in more socially responsible ways and to consider the interests of consumers.

The consumer movement developed in response to a number of factors:

- the increasing technical complexity of products
- a better educated and informed general public
- the increasing market power of large businesses
- publicity given to unethical and socially irresponsible behaviour by companies, for example causing pollution.

The champion of the consumer movement is the **Consumers' Association**. This organisation publishes *Which?* magazine giving reports of product testing and comparisons between brands. The pressures of consumerism have resulted in firms supplying aerosols without CFCs, foodstuffs free from genetically modified products and the adoption of more ethical trading policies.

Key terms

Consumerism is an approach that places the interests of the consumer at the heart of discussions about business decisions or activities.

Consumer protection legislation

There is a considerable quantity of consumer protection legislation in the UK. The acts listed below represent some of the highlights.

Sale of Goods Act, 1979

The basic requirement of this Act is that the goods sold should be:

- of merchantable quality – must be unbroken and work properly
- fit for the purpose
- as described by the manufacturer.

Consumer Protection Act, 1987

This makes producers liable for any harm to consumers caused by their products.

The Weights and Measures Act, 1986

This states that weights and measures used in trading must be guaranteed in terms of accuracy.

The Consumer Credit Act, 1974

This lays down that consumer credit can only be given by licensed organisations. It also sets out the terms under which credit may be given. In 2004 the government plans to expand the safeguards offered to consumers under this law.

The control of advertising

Control is necessary to protect the public from improper use of advertising. It involves a combination of legal controls and self-regulation.

- The Trade Descriptions Act, 1968 makes misleading descriptions of goods and services an offence.
- The Advertising Standards Authority – this body supervises the operation of this code of practice. It is an independent body that protects the public and deals with complaints from the public.

The impact of consumer protection legislation

Increases in the scope of consumer protection have had a number of implications for businesses. Meeting the requirements of consumer credit regulations, for example, means extra processes and personnel and higher costs. Under consumer legislation, firms are expected to supply products that are safe and are of high quality. Processes used in production should minimise pollution and raw materials should be from sustainable sources. All of these expectations mean that production costs are greater, partly owing to additional costs of materials and employing extra workers to carry out the necessary checks.

Consumerism has resulted in higher expectations on the part of consumers, in areas not necessarily covered by legislation. They require firms to provide advice and technical support, an effective after-sales service and to behave in a socially responsible manner.

POINTS TO PONDER

Businesses in the UK are predicted to face costs in excess of £1 billion to implement European laws designed to allow individuals greater access to files held on them by firms. Companies are also bracing themselves for an annual bill of £700 million to operate computer systems and to complete paperwork required under the Act.

Employment Protection

Employment protection is a body of legislation relating to industrial relations, trade unions and employment. The aim of this legislation is to protect the rights of workers and to avoid exploitation by unscrupulous employers.

Key terms

Industrial relations describe the relationship that exists between employers on the one hand and trade unions and employees on the other.
A *trade union* is an association of workers formed with the objective of improving pay, working conditions and job security.

Individual employment law

The amount of legislation covering the rights of individual workers has grown considerably since the 1960s. Some of the major pieces of legislation include the following.

The Sex Discrimination Acts, 1975 and 1986

These outlaw discrimination on grounds of gender in employment and education. The Employment Act of 1989 reinforced this legislation.

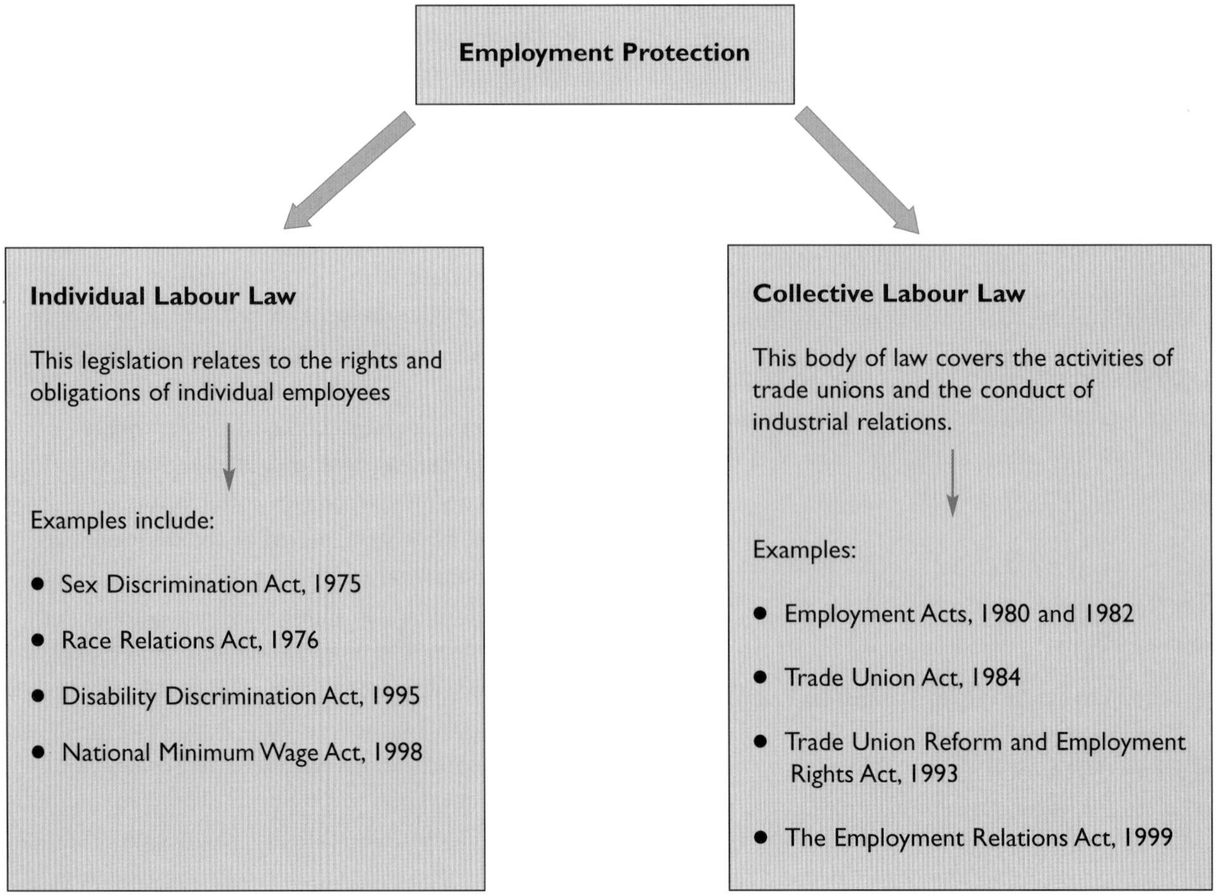

Employment Protection

Individual Labour Law

This legislation relates to the rights and obligations of individual employees

Examples include:

- Sex Discrimination Act, 1975
- Race Relations Act, 1976
- Disability Discrimination Act, 1995
- National Minimum Wage Act, 1998

Collective Labour Law

This body of law covers the activities of trade unions and the conduct of industrial relations.

Examples:

- Employment Acts, 1980 and 1982
- Trade Union Act, 1984
- Trade Union Reform and Employment Rights Act, 1993
- The Employment Relations Act, 1999

Figure 7.18 *Employment protection*

Rachel Anderson, who is the only female football agent in Britain, won a sex discrimination case against the Professional Footballers' Association in 1999. Ms Anderson was told she was not allowed to attend the Association's annual dinner in spite of having been invited by her client, West Ham footballer, Julian Dicks.

The Race Relations Act of 1976

This Act makes it unlawful to discriminate, in relation to employment, against men or women on the grounds of colour, race ethnic or national origin. This legislation applies to the recruitment of employees as well as to their employment.

The Disability Discrimination Act, 1995

This legislation makes it illegal for an employer to treat a disabled person less favourably than others. It also requires employers to make 'reasonable adjustments' to the working environment to allow the employment of disabled people.

The National Minimum Wage Act, 1998

This highly publicised Act came into force on 1 April 1999. The key features of the new legislation were:

- a general minimum wage of £3.60 per hour (£4.50 from October 2003)
- a minimum level of £3.00 an hour for 18- to 21-year-olds (£3.80 an hour from October 2003)
- all part-time and temporary workers must be paid the minimum wage.

In December 2003 it became illegal to discriminate against workers on the grounds of religion or sexual orientation.

Collective labour law

Over the last 20 years the law has played a more prominent role in relationships between employers and trade unions. Some of the important pieces of legislation are described next.

Employment Acts, 1980 and 1982

These Acts reduced the power of trade unions in the workplace:

- They allowed employers to refuse to negotiate with unions.
- Employees were only allowed to picket their *own* place of work.
- Unions could be liable for damages caused by industrial action.

The Trade Union Act, 1984

This Act required unions to conduct secret ballots amongst employees before taking industrial action.

The Trade Union Reform and Employment Rights Act, 1993

These abolished the Wages Councils which were responsible for imposing minimum wages (replaced by the minimum wage in 1999). It also required unions to give employers 7 days' notice of industrial action – in effect providing a 'cooling off' period, making industrial action less likely.

The Employment Relations Act, 1999

The main elements of this Act include the following:

- It established legal guidelines for union recognition by employers in businesses with over 21 employees.
- It advocated simplification and extension of the use of secret ballots before taking industrial action.
- It gave rules to force firms to re-employ immediately people who they have unfairly dismissed.
- It grants up to three months parental leave to mothers and fathers.

In 2002 Belfast City Council's employees took an average of 13.3 days off – almost double the figure for the whole of Northern Ireland. A Council spokesperson said he was 'not shocked, but disappointed' by the figures.

Health and safety legislation

Health and safety legislation has been enacted to discourage dangerous practices by businesses and to protect the workforce. The legislation is designed to prevent accidents in the workplace, and has developed steadily over the last 30 years.

The main act in the UK is the Health and Safety Act of 1974. This is an example of delegated legislation whereby Parliament gives responsibility to government departments to update the scope of the legislation and avoids the legislation taking up too much of Parliament's time.

The Health and Safety at Work Act gives employers a legal obligation 'to ensure that they safeguard all their employees' health, safety and welfare at work'. The Act covers a range of business activities:

- The installation and maintenance of safety equipment and clothing.
- The maintenance of workplace temperatures.
- Rules for working with and protecting against dangerous substances.

Businesses are required to protect the health and safety of their employees 'as far as it is reasonably practicable'. This means that businesses must have provided protection *appropriate to the risks*.

The Act also requires employees to follow all health and safety procedures and to take care of their own and others' safety. The Health and Safety Executive (HSE) oversees the operation of the Act and carries out inspections of businesses' premises.

The effects of employment protection and health and safety legislation

It is simple to view employment protection as a cause of higher production costs for many firms. Of course this is true. Most employment legislation has forced up labour costs. Equally, implementing health and safety legislation can be expensive with the greatest burden falling on manufacturing industry. Meeting the requirements of health and safety legislation may call for additional equipment, more expensive methods of production and extra non-productive personnel such as safety officers. Costs increase and this may damage competitiveness.

However, there are also benefits to businesses from such legislation. Well-paid and secure employees are likely to be better motivated and more productive. This can offset some of the rise in costs. It may also result in firms having a lower rate of labour turnover, and a better public image.

The impact of collective labour law is difficult to assess. Employment acts have regulated working conditions and offered some security of employment. However, legislation in the 1980s and 1990s reduced the influence of trade unions and their ability to protect their members' interests. The aim of this legislation was to make employment more flexible, to reduce labour costs to employers and to reduce the number of industrial disputes. UK businesses have gained competitive advantages from the changes in trade union legislation; the benefits to employees are less obvious.

1   Of what is this a definition: 'A framework of rules governing the way in which society operates'?

2   Is this statement true or false? 'Civil law sets out the relationship between individuals, businesses and the state.'

3   Which of the following is an alternative to a new law and is not enforceable in the courts?
a) a directive
b) a voluntary code of practice
c) judicial precedent
d) an Act of Parliament.

4   Complete the following sentence by filling in the missing words. 'A ....
practice exists when businesses interfere with the .... operation of ....'

5   Which of the following organisations carries out investigations into monopolies and mergers potentially acting against the public interest?
a) the Office of Fair Trading
b) the Department of Trade and Industry
c) OFTEL
d) the Competition Commission.

6   Which of the following is not a responsibility of the Office of Fair Trading?
a) the supervision of all aspects of competition policy
b) providing the government with advice on legislation relating to monopolies, mergers and restrictive practices
c) investigating complaints regarding restrictive practices
d) the referral of monopolies or mergers for investigation by the Competition Commission.

7   Is this statement true or false? 'In the event of any conflict between EU competition legislation and UK competition laws, the EU legislation will overrule that of the UK.'

8   Of what is the following a definition: 'A group of Acts of Parliament relating to industrial relations, trade unions and employment'?

9   Complete the following sentence by filling in the missing words.
'...................................... is an organised movement whose objective is to persuade businesses to behave in more socially .... ways and to consider the interest of ....'

10 Is this statement true or false? 'Health and safety legislation does not offer any benefits to businesses – it only increases the costs of production.'

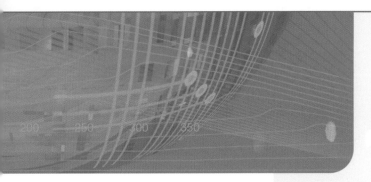

Progress questions

1 Explain the difference between 'statute law' and 'common law'. *(5 marks)*

2 Outline two aspects of employment covered by the Social Chapter. *(4 marks)*

3 Examine the ways in which the operation of restrictive practices may disadvantage consumers. *(7 marks)*

4 Outline two benefits businesses in the UK might receive from legislation intended to create free and fair competition in markets. *(6 marks)*

5 The UK is described as having a 'pragmatic' approach to monopolies and their possible abuse of market power. Explain what this means. *(4 marks)*

6 Outline two possible objectives of the UK's consumer legislation. *(6 marks)*

7 Explain the effects that the rise of consumerism may have had on the activities of businesses in the UK. *(7 marks)*

8 What is meant by the term 'delegated legislation'. *(3 marks)*

9 Distinguish between 'individual' and 'collective labour law'. *(5 marks)*

10 Explain the benefits employers might receive as a result of providing a healthy and safe working environment. *(6 marks)*

Analytical and evaluative questions

11 Discuss whether the banning of all monopolies in the UK would be in the interest of consumers. *(15 marks)*

12 Analyse two ways in which Marks & Spencer plc might be affected by the Employment Act 2002, which granted mothers the right to take up to a year off work to look after their families. *(8 marks)*

13 'Consumer protection legislation is sufficient,' said the Chief Executive of one of the UK's largest banks. 'Today's consumer is better informed and further legislation is not needed.' To what extent do you agree with this view? *(15 marks)*

>> Ethics and social responsibility

Ethics may be defined as a code of behaviour which is considered morally correct. A business's social responsibilities are the duties it has to employees, customers, society and the environment, as well as to its shareholders. These two concepts are becoming linked in modern businesses. Any business taking a morally-correct decision is likely to be taking other groups in society into account.

For example, Shell has been criticised for causing pollution as a side effect of its oil drilling activities in Nigeria and for failing to lobby the Nigerian government to improve its record on human rights. Shell's Chairman has acknowledged that the company needs to become 'a better corporate citizen in Nigeria'. Socially-responsible actions by Shell in these circumstances would also be ethical ones.

Social responsibility

Any firm meeting its social responsibilities will manage its affairs by taking into account the interests of society in general and of those groups and individuals with a direct interest in the business. Thus, a socially responsible business attempts to fulfil the duties that it has towards its employees, customers, suppliers and other interested groups. Collectively these individuals and groups are termed a business's stakeholders.

Stakeholders and business

Businesses have become much more aware of the varying expectations of stakeholder groups. Previously, managers operated businesses largely in the interests of the shareholders. A growing awareness of business activities and the rise of consumerism has complicated the task of the management team. Today's managers have to attempt to meet the conflicting demands of a number of stakeholder groups.

The terms 'stakeholders' and 'social responsibility' are interrelated. Social responsibility is a philosophy proposing that firms should behave as good citizens. Socially-responsible businesses should not only operate within the law, but should

avoid pollution, the reckless use of limited resources or the mistreatment of employees or consumers. Some businesses willingly accept these responsibilities partly because their managers want to do so, partly because they fear a negative public image.

EXAMINER'S ADVICE

Figure 7.19 shows the primary stakeholders for most businesses – a number of others exist. When writing on stakeholders it is important to develop answers fully. This is impossible if you attempt to cover too many stakeholder groups – just concentrate on a few.

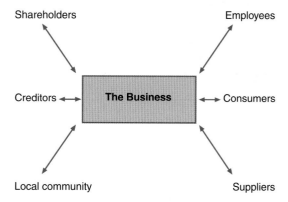

Figure 7.19 *A business's stakeholders*

Stakeholder and shareholder concepts

Many businesses have accepted that they should manage their businesses in a socially-responsible manner and not merely concentrate on profits and legal requirements. Multinational businesses, such as British Telecom, are recognising that reputation is an important competitive weapon. Reputation depends upon how society views the business. There are important commercial reasons why businesses should be, and be seen to be, socially responsible.

The stakeholder approach can lead to many benefits for organisations and may, if successful, improve the image and long-term profitability of the business.

Stakeholder Concept	Shareholder Concept
Under this concept the business attempts to satisfy the needs of all groups and individuals associated with the business.	This view makes managers solely responsible to the owners of the organisation – the shareholders in the case of a company.
Advantages:	Advantages:
■ If successful, the business may enjoy higher long-term profit	■ It avoids conflicting objectives – managers simply take decisions in the interests of the shareholders
■ It is likely to improve a business's public image as it receives favourable coverage in the media	■ This approach may improve short-term profitability as funds are not used for community projects, etc.
■ The business may attract investors seeking a socially responsible and ethical investment	

Figure 7.20 *The stakeholder concept versus the shareholder concept*

Stakeholder group	Possible nature of stakeholder's interest
Shareholders	● Expectation of regular dividends ● Rising share prices ● Preferential treatment as customers – for example lower prices
Employees	● Steady and regular income ● Healthy and safe working conditions ● Job security ● Promotion and higher incomes
Customers	● Certain and reliable supply of goods ● Stable prices ● Safe products ● After sales service and technical support
Suppliers	● Frequent and regular orders ● A sole supplier agreement ● Fair prices
Creditors	● Repayment of money owed at agreed date ● High returns on investments ● Minimal risk of failure to repay money owed
The local community	● Steady employment ● Minimal pollution and noise ● Provision of facilities (e.g. scholarships, arts centres or reclaimed areas) for local community

Table 7.6 *Stakeholders' interests. It is difficult to meet the demands of all these stakeholders simultaneously. For example, paying employees higher wages may reduce the dividend paid to shareholders*

Business in focus

Thames Water is the world's third largest water and sanitation company; it supplies more than 70 million customers in 21 countries. The company endorses the principle that 'access to clean water is a fundamental human right and should not be denied to those unable to afford it'. The company attempts to put this principle into practice throughout its operations.

Thames Water assists community initiatives in less developed countries to bring clean water to the world's poorest people. It offers its employees' financial and engineering skills to assist in completing projects. Thames Water also refuses to issue bills and collect payment from some very poor communities. A company spokesperson said, 'You would not have the world's poorest people paying money to one of the world's richest companies'. The company has supported a scheme in Chile where the government pays for water supply to the poorest citizens by charging wealthy groups higher rates. The company published a 62-page report in 2003 detailing its policies and activities in respect of social responsibility.

However, critics have said that companies such as Thames Water only offer support when governments agree to privatise their water industries, offering potentially lucrative opportunities. Thames Water has acknowledged that it could become more socially responsible. The company has been fined several times for causing pollution in the UK. In 2002 the High Court ruled that allowing water from its sewers regularly to flood homes in London infringed the human rights of the householders. Thames Water has appealed against this decision.

Source: Adapted from The Guardian, 17 November 2003

1 Do you think that Thames Water is genuinely concerned about the welfare of the world's poorest people, or hopes to improve its profits by appearing socially responsible to its customers in the West?

In spite of the growing popularity amongst managers for projecting their business as socially responsible, there are opponents to the philosophy. Milton Friedman, the famous economist, has argued that a business can best meet its social responsibilities by making the largest possible profit and then using its resources as efficiently as possible whilst operating within the law. Friedman is arguing for the continuation of the shareholder concept.

Meeting social responsibilities

POINTS TO PONDER

'In the future, the successful company will not be judged solely in terms of the financial bottom line. Some would argue that this is already the case. Responsibilities to the environment, to the health, safety and welfare of our staff, and to wider society will form an integral part of the way in which we do business.'

Dr Chris Fay, Shell UK Chairman and Chief Executive

Meeting social responsibilities inevitably has a cost for a business but may also bring benefits – financial and otherwise.

Providing information

Providing consumers with detailed information about the product is just one way in which businesses fulfil their responsibilities to consumers. Firms are also keen to be seen to meet the demands of consumers. Since 2000, businesses have been under increasing pressure to become more socially accountable, providing information on their actions.

Working for the community

Firms can gain considerable benefits from behaving responsibly with regard to the wider community. Some companies, for example, the bank Northern Rock, concentrate on meeting responsibilities to communities within the UK.

The Newcastle-based Northern Rock set up a special foundation in 1997, when it converted from a building society to a bank. The company pledged to donate 5% of its annual earnings to charitable organisations. The company announced that in

2003, 40 organisations would receive a share of £2.29m distributed by the Northern Rock Foundation. In 2003 the company had given nearly £12m to charitable causes. The money has been used to support people with mental health problems and to offer training to young people who have left school with no qualifications.

Voluntary work

Meeting their responsibilities to employees can be costly but also has the potential to offer considerable benefits to businesses. Firms can fulfil these responsibilities by providing job security, good working conditions and training to develop their skills and interests. Barclays Mortgages, a division of the high street bank, has pioneered an 'hour for hour' voluntary work scheme. For each hour of leisure time an employee gives up to work in the community, the bank grants a matching hour off work. Over 40% of the company's staff has taken part in the scheme.

Working for the environment

Environmental responsibilities are high on the agenda for most companies and governments. The UK government has acknowledged the importance of social responsibility in this area by planning to produce 'green league tables' to step up the pressure on companies which are not taking environmental issues seriously. UK businesses have responded to demands for a 'greener' business community in a number of ways. Tetra Pak, the Swedish packaging company, has invested heavily in campaigns to promote the use of recyclable and sustainable packaging materials.

Key issues

There has been a large rise in the number of businesses carrying out **social and environmental audits** to assess the impact their activities have on the environment and society. The results of these audits are normally made available to the general public as environmental and social reports.

It is not surprising that companies with enormous potential to pollute (BP and Shell, for example) should attempt to reassure stakeholders with social and environmental reports. Other businesses leading the way in social reporting are BT, the Co-operative Bank and Body Shop. In 2003, the mining group Rio Tinto Zinc, which has the potential to cause enormous environmental damage, produced an extensive report following a social and environmental audit. By 2000 the majority of the UK's largest 350 companies produced some form of social report.

Reports may provide information on many factors including pollution, noise, working conditions, contributions to local communities and use of scarce resources.

Key terms

A **social audit** is an independent investigation into a firm's activities and its impact on society. These audits encompass pollution, waste and workforce health and safety.

There are advantages and disadvantages to businesses arising from meeting social responsibilities. Firms may benefit in terms of an enhanced corporate image. This may result in increased sales, attracting more higher calibre employees and greater profitability. Such a positive outcome is not inevitable, however. Behaving in a socially responsible manner can be expensive. Firms may have to spend more on training employees, fitting devices designed to minimise pollution, maintaining uneconomic plants to protect employment and contributing to community projects. These increased costs may be sufficiently large to offset any increase in sales revenue. If they are, profits may fall.

Perhaps the major factor influencing whether firms behave in a socially responsible way, is the actions of their competitors. A potential exists for a competitive advantage in terms of socially responsible behaviour. BP has stated that reputation is a competitive weapon and expects that social and environmental performance will determine future success in the oil industry.

Business ethics
What are ethics?

Business ethics can provide moral guidelines for decision-making by organisations. An ethical decision means doing what is morally right; it is not a matter of merely calculating the costs and benefits associated with a decision. Individuals' ethical values vary. Ethic values are shaped by a number of factors, including the values and norms of parents or guardians, those of religion, and the values of the society in which a person lives and works. Most actions and activities in the business world have an ethical dimension.

> ### Key terms
>
> An **ethical code of practice** states how a business believes its employees should respond to situations that might challenge the values of the business.
>
> An **ethical stance** refers to a business that has introduced an ethical policy.

Ethics and decision-making

Companies can encounter ethical issues in many activities. UK supermarkets have been criticised for setting prices unnecessarily high and exploiting consumers. Companies have come under fire for closing closing call centres and moving jobs to India, creating unemployment as a result. In such circumstances, decisions on employment have been taken with a view to maintaining or improving profitability. Critics would argue, however, that putting profits before living standards and jobs is morally wrong.

Ethical behaviour requires businesses to operate within certain moral guidelines and to do 'the right thing' when taking decisions. What exactly is ethical behaviour? This is a tricky question. An ethical decision would take into account the moral dimension, but not everyone would agree on what is ethical. Some may argue that it is not ethically wrong for supermarkets to charge high prices for basic foodstuffs; others would disagree. Differing moral values mean ethical decision-making is tricky.

> ### POINTS TO PONDER
>
> A survey of 5000 job seekers in 2003 revealed that 43% of them would not work for a business lacking ethical and enviromental policies, even for an extra £10 000 a year.

Ethical codes of practice

As a response to consumer expectations and, in many cases, competitive pressures, businesses have introduced ethical codes of practice. By 2000 over 65% of the UK's major businesses operated an ethical code of practice. They are intended to improve the behaviour and image of a business. Common themes in ethical codes of practice may include:

- promoting products with integrity and honesty
- minimising possible damage to the environment

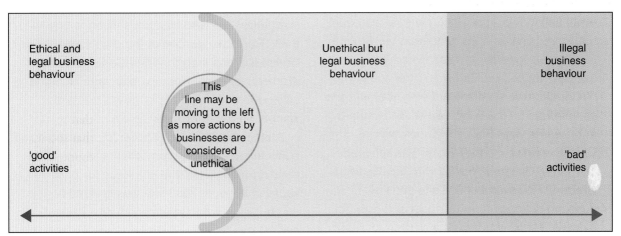

Business activities

Figure 7.21 *Legal and ethical behaviour*

by, for example, using sustainable sources of raw materials

- competing fairly and avoiding collusion or other anti-competitive practices
- taking into account the needs of the business's stakeholders.

POINTS TO PONDER

Even some of Britain's best-known companies have been heavily criticized for what some people judge to be unethical behaviour. In 2003, the insurer Norwich Union transferred some of its call centre work to India, resulting in the loss of 2000 jobs in the UK.

Ethics and profits

Some people believe that, if a business behaves ethically, its profits will suffer. Any of the following ethical actions is likely to increase costs of production and possibly reduce profits:

- using more expensive resources (perhaps recycled or from sustainable sources)
- training employees to behave in an ethical manner
- treating animals with respect
- implementing safety systems beyond the legal requirements.

However, the argument is not so simple as it might appear at first.

The Co-operative Bank is an example of a business that uses its ethical stance as a central part of its marketing strategy. The Bank's ethical position is unique within the UK's financial sector and has resulted in an improved performance by the

People in business

The daughter of Italian immigrants, Anita Roddick travelled the world and worked as a teacher before opening the first Body Shop in 1976.

'If you do things well, do them better. Be daring, be first, be different, be just.'
                                          Anita Roddick

There are now 1200 Body Shop stores in 45 countries. Two people make a purchase from a Body Shop store, somewhere in the world every second! In April 1984, the business went public and shares were quoted on the Stock Exchange. However, in 1998 Body Shop hit troubled waters, profits fell and the company decided to give up manufacturing cosmetics to concentrate on the retail side of the business. In the same year, Roddick stood down as Chief Executive of Body Shop. She retained the role of Chairman (jointly with her husband, Gordon). However, in 2002 she and her husband resigned from this post and now act as consultants to the company.

Part of the reason for the Body Shop's

success is that it anticipated the rise of environmentally-concerned consumers. Roddick made sure the company was always caring about the consequences of its own actions. In May 1992, the Body Shop became the first company to issue an environmental statement (*The Green Book*) based on a full audit of its operations.

The former Chief Executive and founder of the Body Shop is not content with building up her brand of environmentally-friendly cosmetics: she also wants to influence how we think. Roddick was one of the organisers of the United Nations' Fourth World Conference on Women in Beijing. Her next plan is to launch a college to ensure that tomorrow's business leaders are more ethically aware.

Anita Roddick is well known for challenging conventional business practices and for creating a business that is a force for positive social change. In 2003 she was created a dame for her work on environmental issues and human rights.

business. In 2002, the Bank turned down business that would have been worth £4.4 million as it did not meet its ethical and environmental standards. However, the Bank announced that its ethical stance had helped it to gain more than £30 million in new business, more than off-setting the losses.

This example highlights that there are marketing advantages from being seen to behave ethically. Businesses may attract new customers with more money to spend. A reputation for ethical behaviour can provide a business with a Unique Selling Point. This can be particularly valuable when products provided by rivals are similar and may explain some of the success of the Co-operative Bank's approach. A positive corporate image may also assist businesses by allowing them to charge higher prices and enjoy increased profits.

Benefits also exist in terms of recruiting the best employees. A business that is successful and has a good reputation is attractive to potential employees. High-calibre employees may to be recruited in these circumstances and valuable employees will be less likely to leave.

However, a high profile, ethical stance is not a guarantee of profits. Littlewoods dropped its ethical stance in 2003, following several years during which the company had struggled financially. The company's approach ensured that its suppliers operated ethically, but meant that higher costs were incurred in purchasing from reputable suppliers.

Businesses introducing ethical practices for the first time may face other costs leading to reduced profits. Training is an obvious cost – for a company to be ethical, all employees must carry out their everyday activities in the right ways. Firms may also need to spend heavily, adapting production processes to reduce the possibility of pollution. These factors make it probable that profits will be lower, at least in the short run.

Unethical actions by businesses are likely to be covered in the media and to influence the public's view of a business. Such stories are increasingly newsworthy at a time when consumers' expectations of business behaviour are increasing. This is placing great pressure on businesses to be seen to be ethical and socially responsible.

One important development in modern businesses is that ethical accountability has become an issue for top managers. Thus, senior managers within firms are playing a leading role in shaping ethical business behaviour. This trend suggests that social responsibility and ethical behaviour is not merely a fad but may be part of a move towards a more caring and responsible attitude amongst the business community.

EXAMINER'S ADVICE

Ethics and social responsibility are topics that are continuously developing. The actions of Thames Water (see page 319) would have been highly unlikely a few years ago. It is important to keep up to date with events in this area and to use examples in support of theory.

QUICK CHECK QUESTIONS

1   Is this statement true or false? 'Any company meeting its shareholders' needs can be said to be socially responsible.'

2   Complete the following sentence by filling in the missing words. 'Any business that is socially responsible will take into account the interests of .... in general and will fulfil its responsibilities to the business's ....,'

3   Which of the following may not be a benefit of meeting social responsibilities?
a)   improved corporate image
b)   ability to charge higher prices for products
c)   paying premium prices for supplies
d)   ability to attract better qualified and more highly motivated employees.

4   Is the following statement true or false? 'Meeting social responsibilities is almost certain to mean that a business incurs higher costs.'

5   Of what is the following a definition: 'An independent investigation into a business's activities and its impact on society. This investigation may encompass pollution and waste, as well as the health and safety of the workforce'?

6   Which of the following might many people regard as an unethical decision:
a)   a decision to pay senior managers a large pay increase while not offering any pay rise to more junior employees

b) a decision by a supermarket to increase prices following an increase in costs

c) a decision to reduce payments to charities after a fall in profits

d) a decision to close a factory following a long period during which sales and profits have declined.

7 Of what is the following a definition: 'A statement of how a business believes its employees should respond to situations that might challenge the values of a business.'

8 Is the following statement true or false? 'A business that adopts an ethical stance will inevitably suffer from lower profits in the short run, but will be more profitable in the long run.'

9 Which of the following is unlikely to explain why a business adopting an ethical stance might suffer a fall in profits?

a) the business is able to charge premium prices

b) suppliers charge higher prices

c) some potentially profitable orders are rejected

d) competitors increase prices in response.

10 Complete the following sentence by filling in the missing words. 'One of the major benefits to a business of adopting an ethical .... is that the business can base its .... campaigns on its ethics and thereby improve its .... image.'

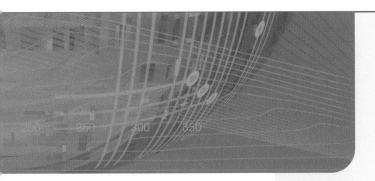

Progress questions

1 Explain the term 'social responsibility'. *(3 marks)*

2 Identify two business stakeholders and the interests that they might have in a business. *(6 marks)*

3 Distinguish between the 'shareholder concept' and the 'stakeholder concept'. *(6 marks)*

4 Outline three ways in which businesses might meet their social responsibilities. *(6 marks)*

5 What is a 'social audit'? *(3 marks)*

6 Explain the arguments in favour of a major high street bank fulfilling its social responsibilities. *(7 marks)*

7 Give two examples of business actions that might be considered unethical by some people. *(2 marks)*

8 What is an ethical code of practice? *(3 marks)*

9 Outline two arguments why a business might suffer reduced profits as a result of introducing an ethical policy. *(6 marks)*

10 Explain the arguments in favour of a multinational business implementing an ethical policy. *(7 marks)*

Analytical and evaluative questions

11 Analyse the responsibilities that a coal mining company might have to its employees. *(8 marks)*

12 One of Britain's leading insurance companies recently implemented an ethical policy amid much publicity. Discuss the case for and against this decision. *(15 marks)*

13 'For multinational firms to be successful in the twenty-first century, it is essential that they meet their social responsibilities.' To what extent do you agree with this statement?

(15 marks)

>> Technological change

Modern advances

The last two decades have seen a number of technological advances having significant implications for businesses. Some of these developments included:

- personal computers
- CDs and mini discs
- facsimile machines (faxes)
- the Internet, intranets and extranets
- mobile telephones.

These and other developments in technology have enormous implications for businesses throughout the world.

POINTS TO PONDER

Sales of mobile phone handsets boomed in India during 2003. The number of phone owners rose from 10 million to 20.7 million. However, India still lags behind China, which has 200 million mobile phone users.

Technological advances have created new markets for new products. In 1990, few people had mobile telephones. At the start of 2003 there were an estimated 42 million mobile phones in use in the UK. Companies such as Orange have grown as a consequence of the developments in communications technology. Similarly, one of the world's largest businesses – the Microsoft Corporation – has developed alongside the technological revolution in computing. But technological change can be threatening, as well as providing opportunities for businesses. Figure 7.22 illustrates that electronic mail, whilst offering opportunities for companies providing Internet services, can pose a threat to more established businesses such as the Post Office. Sales of CDs in the UK were 4% lower in 2003 than in 2002. Part of the reason for this was the downloading of music from the Internet. Some of this was illegal and some legal. In the United States, over 65% of consumers download their favourite music, compared with 35% who purchase CDs.

Technological advances also affect the ways in which businesses operate. Communications within businesses have been transformed by technology. Businesses can communicate simply, cheaply and (most importantly) quickly across the globe. Developments such as the fax have allowed detailed documents to be sent immediately to anywhere in the world. Similarly, email allows employees and organisations to communicate immediately and messages can be sent to many recipients at the same time.

The development of extranets has created closer links between businesses, helping to improve

Postal Market Share
100%
80
60
40
20
0
1995
2005
Hybrid mail
Email
Telephone
Fax
Physical mail

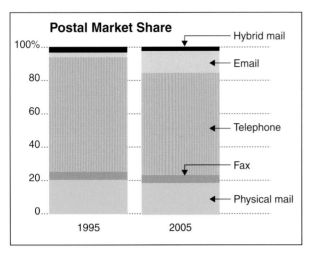

Figure 7.22 *Postal market share. Electronic communications threaten the Post Office's paper-based postal services. Research by the Universal Postal Union shows that physical mail (letters) will decline to about 15% of communications by 2005*

Source: Adapted from The Observer, 4 July 1999

efficiency. Companies like the giant American retailer Wal-Mart share sales data through an extranet with suppliers such as Proctor and Gamble, to enable production and deliveries to match demand in the stores. Wal-Mart estimates that this improved its stock control enormously in 1997 saving $2 billion in costs.

POINTS TO PONDER

Recent research by accountants KPMG has discovered that directors of UK companies spend an average of 11% of their working lives sending and responding to email.

The technological revolution has extended beyond communications. The process of manufacturing has been transformed by automation whereby machines replace people. The most dramatic aspect of this has

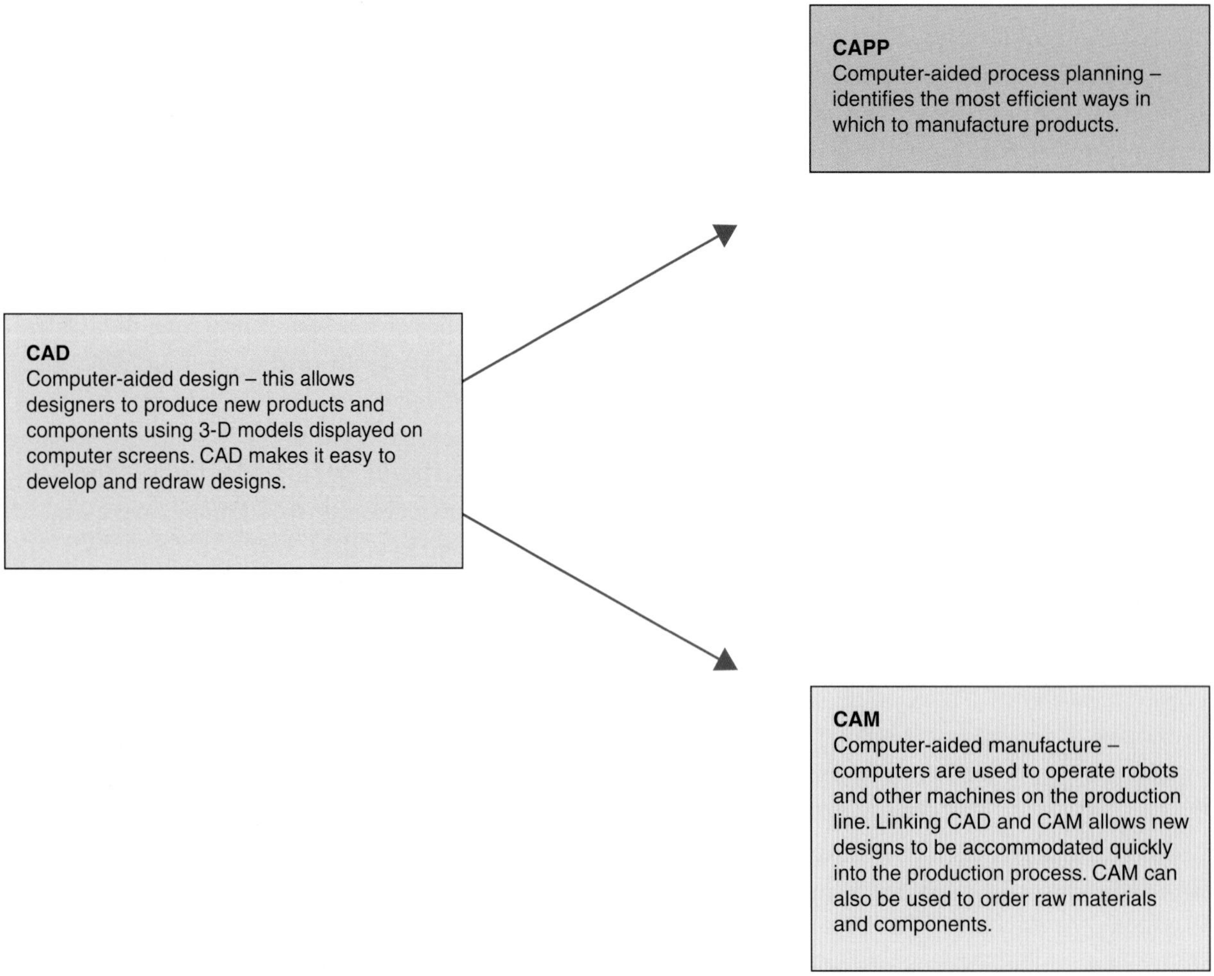

CAPP
Computer-aided process planning – identifies the most efficient ways in which to manufacture products.
CAD
Computer-aided design – this allows designers to produce new products and components using 3-D models displayed on computer screens. CAD makes it easy to develop and redraw designs.
CAM
Computer-aided manufacture – computers are used to operate robots and other machines on the production line. Linking CAD and CAM allows new designs to be accommodated quickly into the production process. CAM can also be used to order raw materials and components.

Figure 7.23 *Computer-aided design, computer-aided manufacture and computer-aided process planning*

been the use of computer-controlled technology on the production line. This has assisted in improving productivity levels helping to reduce costs and to enhance productivity.

Business in focus

The data created by computer-aided design can be passed onto other computers to continue the process of product development. Designers at the American aeroplane manufacturer, Boeing, created a virtual aeroplane to test and check their ideas before commencing production.

Figure 7.24 *'The virtual becomes reality – a Boeing 777.'*

The American designers assembled an entire virtual Boeing 777 to check that the several hundred thousand parts that make up the airliner fitted together. Any that did not were redesigned to overcome problems. The benefits of this approach were seen when the first 777 was built: the model was assembled with few of the normal difficulties occurring. The costs of this process were also much cheaper than the traditional technique of actually constructing a prototype airliner to discover the potential problems.

The benefits of technological change

Arguably, the major advantage of technology to businesses is to allow the development of new methods of production resulting in lower costs and higher profits on each sale. However, in an increasingly competitive global market firms seek to improve their market position by offering high quality and sophisticated products at low prices. Using ever more sophisticated technology in planning and producing products is one way of achieving lower costs.

Key terms

Computer-aided design and **computer-aided manufacture** *use computer programmes to design new products and to control production. Used together they can create a highly efficient method of production.*
Extranets *link the computers of a business to those of suppliers and retailers allowing the effective exchange of information between key commercial partners.*
Intranets *link computers within an individual business allowing employees to use email and access to a range of online services.*

POINTS TO PONDER

An Israeli company, Tecnomatix Technologies, has created software that can simulate an entire factory. Using this software, manufacturing techniques can be tested in a virtual factory to discover the most efficient (and cheapest) methods of production.

Using technology in the products themselves, rather than in their production also offers great advantages to businesses. Firms possessing technological leads over rival producers are frequently able to charge a high price for their products. This technique of price skimming (see page 94) is likely to boost profits – until the competition catches up! Possessing a technological edge may attract new customers to a business. Tesco has outperformed its rival Sainsbury in the UK grocery market since offering customers the opportunity to purchase their goods over the Internet. This has proved an attractive offer to consumers leading busy lives.

New technology can open up new markets for businesses. Markets for personal stereos and mobile telephones were created as a consequence of technological advances. Today they are multi-billion pound markets selling products to millions of consumers. Smaller businesses have also developed. Dinesh Dhamija established Ebookers as an online travel group in 1999. By 2003, the company had achieved turnover of nearly £20 million. This was achieved despite the holiday market being hit by the Iraq conflict and on-going concerns about terrorism. The company has, however, been boosted by the increasing popularity of online booking.

Key issues

The Internet links computers across the world allowing communication and commercial activities to be conducted electronically. It originated on 30 October, 1969 when a small team of researchers at the University of California transmitted the first message between networked computers. By the year 2003, the Internet brought together an estimated 625 million computer users.

The development of the World Wide Web, enabling navigation of Internet sites, expanded dramatically during the 1990s to become the most important component of the Internet.

The commercial possibilities of the Internet are attracting enormous attention. E-tailing (selling products on the Internet) is the most obvious commercial possibility offering relatively small businesses the opportunity to sell their products internationally. Consumers spent over £12 billion on the Internet in 2003 and the figure is expected to rise further in the future.

The disadvantages of technological change

The disadvantages of rapidly changing technology are considerable. Firms in high technology markets face demands to research new products and to

implement more efficient methods of production. Thus, commercial pressures may exist to improve technology used in products and processes.

New technology, in whatever form, can be a major drain on an organisation's financial resources. Installing new technology on the production line will involve a heavy capital outlay and disruption to production while the work is completed. Thus, a business may lose sales revenue at the time its expenditure rises significantly. Costs of research and development can be huge and many years may pass before any return is received on them. The share price of GlaxoSmithKline, the pharmaceutical company, fell in 2003 despite the company having 20 new drugs in various stages of the research and development process. However, the company's record in producing drugs that are approved for use by the NHS has disappointed some shareholders. If the drugs are certified for use, the company is unlikely to receive major financial returns until 2007.

Businesses operating in markets experiencing rapidly changing technology can be left behind – or find it too expensive to keep up. Small firms can be particularly vulnerable, even if they are well managed. This may lead to mergers and take-overs in markets supplying high technology products. The series of mergers and take-overs in the European mobile telephone market has been brought about, in part, by the high costs of developing new products and networks.

New production methods do not always work effectively from the start: some teething problems are almost inevitable. Workers take time to adapt to what is required of them and the technology may not work effectively. This may result in lower levels of productivity and profits.

EXAMINER'S ADVICE

Technology and the implications of technology are an increasingly important element of Business Studies syllabuses. Questions on the effects of technological change require an integrated response. Technology affects all the functions of business – marketing, finance, human resource management, and so on. Answers to questions should reflect this.

Technology and human relations

Humans within businesses are always affected by technological change. Technological developments can result in enormous changes for a business's workforce. For some, it may be redundancy: replaced by technology as part of the process of automation. At the end of 2003, sweet manufacturer Nestlé Rowntree made 150 workers redundant as they were replaced by production-line technology. This followed a further 220 job losses earlier in the year. Other employees may be required to undertake duties dramatically different from those with which they are familiar.

Employees' reactions to technological change can be equally diverse. For some employees, it may represent an opportunity. They may have a chance to acquire new skills, to make their jobs more secure and enjoy higher wages or salaries. The new working practices may offer great benefits. Technology can allow employees greater control over their working lives leading to increased responsibility and the possibility of achievement.

POINTS TO PONDER

Technological advances have their down sides too. A survey by the University of Nottingham in 2003 revealed that British workers spend an hour a day clearing their inboxes of junk emails.

Source: news.bbc.co.uk, 28 December 2003

Technological change increases job insecurity, especially for people with few skills, carrying out tasks that may be easily automated. Fear of unemployment may lead to industrial action as workers seek to protect their jobs. In such circumstances, the introduction of new technology may be awkward and expensive. Redundancy payments may be expensive and corporate images may suffer.

So, new technology-based products create jobs and unemployment at the same time. For example, automated telephone switchboards have resulted in a loss of jobs for telephonists. Direct dial numbers and electronic answering systems have made telephonists obsolete in many firms. Simultaneously, employment has been created in industries manufacturing and maintaining the automatic telephone systems.

 QUICK CHECK QUESTIONS

1   Is the following statement true or false? 'Developments in technology have enormous implications for businesses throughout the world.'

2   The growth of which of the businesses listed below is **not** primarily due to technological developments?

a)   Dyson (vacuum cleaners and washing machines)

b)   Amazon (online retailing)

c)   Body Shop (socially responsible cosmetics)

d)   Vodafone (mobile telephone services).

3   Complete the following sentence by filling in the missing words. 'Technological developments have transformed business

.... by allowing it to take place more cheaply, more simply and (above all) more ....'

4   Of what is the following a definition: 'A means of linking the computers of a specific business to those of suppliers and retailers, allowing the effective exchange of information between key commercial partners.'

5   Which of the following may be a disadvantage to businesses of technological change?

a)   increased levels of productivity

b)   lower costs of production per unit of output

c)   substantial capital outlays

d)   the development of new markets.

6   Is the following statement true or false? 'Developments in technology create unemployment and jobs at the same time.'

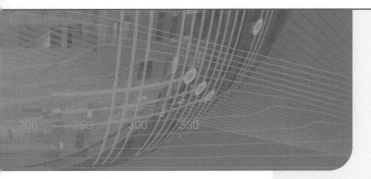

Progress questions

1 Outline two major technological changes that have affected businesses. *(6 marks)*

2 Explain the ways in which technological change can result in opportunities for businesses. *(7 marks)*

3 Technological change can affect products and processes. Carefully distinguish between these two types of technological change. *(5 marks)*

4 Outline the ways in which technology has changed the ways in which businesses operate. *(7 marks)*

5 Explain the advantages a business might gain from introducing computer-aided design and manufacturing systems. *(6 marks)*

6 Outline whether or not the development of the Internet is likely to create employment in the UK. *(7 marks)*

7 Explain the difficulties a business might face if trading in a market subject to rapid changes in technology. *(6 marks)*

8 Distinguish between an 'extranet' and an 'intranet'. *(4 marks)*

9 Explain why unskilled employees might fear technological change. *(7 marks)*

10 Outline the ways in which adopting new production technology might affect the public image of a company. *(7 marks)*

Analytical and evaluative questions

11 To what extent might changes in technology benefit the owners of a small, private limited company manufacturing electronic components for the computer industry? *(15 marks)*

12 Analyse the factors a small, family-run corner shop might consider before purchasing new technology to manage its stock control. *(8 marks)*

13 Discuss whether the Internet represents a threat or an opportunity for a company that transports letters and parcels throughout the UK. *(15 marks)*

Franklin and Malvern Ltd is a firm of estate agents based in the southeast. The Managing Director, Tom Godfrey, is eager to use the Internet. He would like to develop a website where visitors can enter their requirements and be shown suitable properties that the firm has available. Ultimately, he would like to be able to show people around the properties online and to use IT to link his ten different branches. However, this requires a huge investment. Competitors are beginning to offer this sort of service, but Tom is worried about the risk and the cost.

Tom is also increasingly concerned about the number of complaints he is receiving from clients about the service they have received. Recently Mrs Matahari expressed her disgust at the fact that problems with a property they purchased through Franklin and Malvern had not been brought to their attention by the agents.

Tom telephoned the sales representative concerned and had been surprised by her answer. 'You tell us to sell, sell, sell and that's what I did. I sold the property. I did not lie at any stage; had they asked me if I knew that the fields opposite were soon going to have a nightclub built on them I would have told them. They didn't ask. Who cares what the buyer thinks? If you wanted us to think about the ethics of what we do we would never sell anything. Ethics do not matter in business. Anyway, ultimately our responsibilities are to our shareholders, no one else. If you don't want us to sell properties don't have a performance-related pay scheme which links our rewards to sales.' Tom was concerned by this conversation and wondered whether his employees should be taking into account more of their stakeholders, including customers.

He was also worried about the state of the economy and the possible effect this might have on his business. Recent economic forecasts had been unfavourable and Tom was not sure what he would do if market conditions got worse.

1 *What is meant by 'performance related pay'?*
(2 marks)

2 *What is meant by the term 'stakeholders'?*
(2 marks)

3 *Discuss the factors Tom should consider before investing in Internet technology.* *(15 marks)*

4 *Examine two ways in which increasing competition in the market might affect Franklin and Malvern.* *(10 marks)*

5 *What is meant by 'business ethics'?* *(2 marks)*

6 *To what extent should a firm such as Franklin and Malvern be concerned about the ethics of its actions?* *(15 marks)*

7 *Discuss the ways in which changes in the economy could affect Franklin and Malvern.*
(15 marks)

8 *What is meant by the term 'shareholder'?*
(2 marks)

9 *'Ultimately our responsibilities are to our shareholders, no one else.' To what extent would you agree with this view?* *(15 marks)*

End of chapter questions

Case study   **32 marks**

The announcement by the postal regulator, Postcomm, that Royal Mail is to lose its monopoly to deliver letters, has resulted in the entry of a rival into the market. UK Mail, a subsidiary of the Business Post Group, has reached an agreement with Royal Mail over the operation of its new postal service. Under this agreement, UK Mail will have access to Royal Mail's sorting and delivery facilities.

Although some consumer groups welcome the development of competition in the postal markets, many analysts fear that Royal Mail's rivals will only compete in the lucrative inter-city markets, focussing on delivering mail for business customers. It is forecast that a two-tier postal service may develop, with rural areas receiving a poorer quality service.

Earlier in 2003, Royal Mail had clashed with Postcomm over its decision to open up the letter market to competition. The company claimed that it would cost the company £650 million in lost profits over a three-year period. The company has sought to eliminate excess capacity and has reduced its 180 000 strong workforce by 17 000 during 2003, and a further 13 000 job losses are forecast. It has further sought to strengthen its financial position by raising the price of a first-class stamp by a penny.

Source: Adapted from The Guardian, 16 July 2003

1 Explain the meaning of the term excess capacity.
(2 marks)

2 Explain how technology might change the market for business mail.
(6 marks)

3 Analyse two other methods that the government might have used to control the possible abuse of Royal Mail's monopoly power, other than by allowing competition.
(9 marks)

4 To what extent might consumers benefit from the introduction of competition into the UK postal market?
(15 marks)

Case study

32 marks

A large number of UK businesses that are opposed to the adoption of the euro have applauded Gordon Brown's decision to defer a decision on the single currency. They argued that the UK economy is incompatible with those of the twelve countries that have replaced their currencies with the euro. The Institute of Directors has pointed out that UK businesses have benefited from sterling and also from a well managed economy with low inflation, steady growth and falling unemployment. Opponents of the euro predict that embracing the single currency would result in the European Central Bank (ECB) imposing interest rates that are not appropriate for UK businesses. Many retailers have also welcomed the decision. They fear the cost of conversion to using the euro, not least changing tills and software.

However, supporters of the single currency have criticised the decision. They have highlighted a number of disadvantages including:

■ The UK is an attractive destination for foreign businesses. Foreign businesses employ nearly 1.5 million people in this country. Major employers such as Toyota have said they will review future investment decisions if the UK does not adopt the euro.
■ Manufacturers suffer greatly from fluctuations in the value of sterling. As Europe is a major

market, using the euro would reduce the risk involved in trading with the Continent.
■ Tourism – over 60% of visitors to the UK are Europeans. The retention of the pound means that European tourists have the trouble and expense of changing euros into pounds.

Businesses cannot agree on whether to adopt the euro – they appear to be split evenly on the issue. Although the falling value of the pound over recent months has helped manufacturers, this may prove to only be a short-term trend and not a substitute for adopting the single currency.

1 *What is meant by the term 'low inflation'?*
(2 marks)

2 *Outline why UK businesses might support the idea of 'permanently lower interest rates.'*
(6 marks)

3 *Analyse two possible implications for British car manufacturers of 'a falling value of the pound.'*
(9 marks)

4 *British business leaders disagree as to whether the UK should replace the pound with the euro. Discuss the possible reasons for this disagreement.*
(15 marks)

A distressing number of well-known companies are continuing to cause pollution despite the name and shame policy of the Environment Agency, Barbara Young, its chief executive, said yesterday.

The agency's policy of producing a league table of the most fined polluters in England and Wales has deterred many, but some firms continue year after year to repeat offences. There are still far too many serious pollution incidents, according to Lady Young, indicating that businesses continue to fail to meet their social responsibilities.

In a foreword to the agency's Spotlight on Business report for 2002, she wrote: 'It seems extraordinary that multi-million pound businesses are still prepared to risk their reputations with careless, avoidable neglect of environmental responsibility.'

Among the worst repeat offenders are the water companies Thames, Severn Trent, Southern, South West, Anglian, Wessex Water, Yorkshire Water and United Utilities. Other high-street names include Tesco, BP Oil, and TotalFinaElf.

The waste sector has continued to be responsible for the largest number of pollution incidents; and 3.5% of all landfill sites are said to 'still pose an unacceptable risk to the environment'. A spokesperson for the water industry said that water firms were responsible for a tiny proportion of offences, but that lessons would be learned and that production methods would be altered and employees would be required to change the way in which they worked.

Source: Adapted from The Guardian, 31 July 2003

1 What is meant by the term 'social responsibility'?
(2 marks)

2 Explain **one** other way in which the government could enforce rules regarding the protection of the environment. (6 marks)

3 Examine the possible reaction of employees in the water industry to significant changes in working methods. (9 marks)

4 Evaluate the arguments for and against a large multinational company, such as Tesco, meeting its social responsibilities. (15 marks)

Case study

44 marks

Jon Canwell started Pan Hellenic Holidays in 1980. The company was established to fill a niche market: it provides luxury holidays for tourists wishing to spend their summers sailing amongst the beautiful Greek islands. Jon's business struggled in the early days; hit by a deep recession soon after the launch. However, working long hours for low returns and only employing casual workers meant that the company survived the economic downturn. The more prosperous periods of the late 1980s and early 1990s allowed the company to become firmly established and to build up a list of regular customers impressed by Pan Hellenic Holidays' attention to detail and high quality service. In spite of the success of the company it faces fierce competition.

Economic factors have helped and hindered Jon in establishing his business. In the latter part of the 1980s the government has attempted to control inflation through the use of interest rates. This has meant that UK interest rates have been high in comparison to those of the rest of Europe. 'This has, of course, meant that the value of the pound has been strong against the euro (and the drachma before it),' Jon remarked. 'This has not been a critical factor because demand for the holidays I sell is more sensitive to the business cycle than to the price at which I sell them.'

Pan Hellenic Holidays is a small firm selling in a market dominated by much larger firms. Jon decided from the outset that he would have to differentiate his products from that of his competitors. His competitive position has become more difficult over the last few years because of the increasing number of competitors entering the market for luxury Mediterranean holidays, as well as the increasing threat of terrorism. 'The market has too many firms,' Jon observed. 'I fear that we have the capacity to supply more holidays than customers require. Because of this excess capacity, I fear that some of the newer firms might drive the price down to levels at which I cannot compete. I have some loyal customers, but their loyalty may not extend to paying 10% or 20% more for their holidays, just to travel with me.'

One of the interesting aspects of Pan Hellenic Holidays, is the speed with which the company

appreciated the potential of the Internet to a business selling holidays at high prices to a wealthy section of the community. Jon is a great believer in the value of the Internet to the business community. 'I have saved a substantial amount of money through my website. Within a couple of years, this will become the major means by which I sell holidays.'

Year	Revenue £000s
1995	121.8
1996	134.6
1997	141.9
1998	142.2
1999	150.6
2000	161.7
2001	150.4
2002	141.9
2003	158.7
2004	166.6 (forecast)

Table 7.7 – *Pan Hellenic Holidays sales revenue 1995–2004*

1 *Outline three factors that might influence the level of demand for luxury holidays in the Greek islands.* (6 marks)

2 *Analyse the relationship between a country's interest rate and the exchange rate of its currency.* (8 marks)

3 *Discuss why Jon believes that '... demand for the holidays I sell is more sensitive to the business cycle than to the price at which I sell them.'* (15 marks)

4 *What does Jon mean when he refers to 'excess capacity' in the market for sailing holidays amongst the Greek Islands?* (6 marks)

5 *Evaluate the advantages and disadvantages of the Internet to a company such as Pan Hellenic Holidays selling luxury products.* (15 marks)

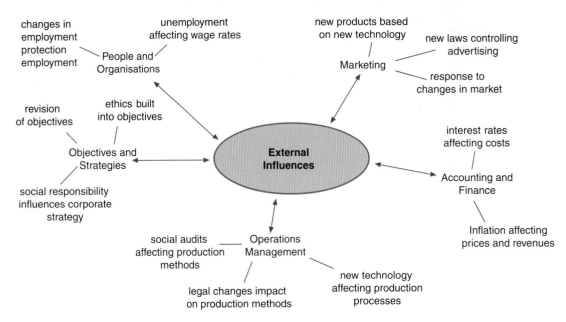

Figure 7.25 *Relationships between External Influences and other topics in the AS specification*

Index

Note: page numbers in **bold** refer to Key items, page numbers in *italics* refer to information presented in tables or diagrams.

accountability 169
accountants 23
accounting and finance 114–68
  break-even analysis 121–30
  budgets 149–58
  cash flow forecasting and management 131–40
  cost centres 158–64
  costs 114–18
  profit 114, 118–19
  profit centres 158–64
  revenue 114, 118
  sources of finance 141–9
accounts, company 23
Acts of Parliament 306
advertising **98**, *100*, 311
Advertising Standards Authority 311
age, market segmentation by 70
aims *see* business aims
Alldaypa 15
Amazon.com 101, 248
Ambi Rad 263
analytic skills 2, 3
Anderson, Rachel 313
Annual General Meetings (AGMs) 27, 28, 144
Annual Reports 27
Ansoff's matrix 76–7, *76*
Anywayup Cup 12
AOL 7
Apple 86
appraisal schemes (employee) 194
appreciation (currency) 293, **293**

Asda 45, 95, 188, 277, 301
assessment centres 207–8
asset-led marketing 59, *59*, **59**, 72
assets **143**
Aston Martin 232
auditors 23
authoritarian/autocratic leadership 212–13, *212*, 215, 269
authority **169**, 173, 197

baby products market 71
BAE systems 199
Balon, Adam 9
Bamford family 27
Bank of England 289–90, 293
bank loans 14, 22, 121, 131–2, 143, 290
  see also overdrafts
bankruptcy 283
banks
  use of break-even analysis 121
  use of business plans 16
  use of cash flow forecasting 132
base rate 289
Batt, Mike 13
Bayliss, Trevor 11
Ben and Jerry's Ice Cream 42
benchmarking 268–9, *269*, **269**
Bezos, Jeff 101, 248
BHP Billiton 213
Bilimoria, Karan 47
BMW 266
Board of Directors 27
Body Shop 322
Boeing 327
Bollywood 123
booms, economic 283, **283**, *285*, 286, 299, 303
Boots the Chemist 45
Boston Matrix 86–8, *86*, **86**

brands 48
  brand loyalty 48, 96
  and price elasticity of demand 106
  v product 106
Branson, Richard 26, 135, 239
break-even analysis 121–30
  advantages/disadvantages 128
  break-even charts 123–8, *124*, 125, 126, 127
  break-even output 121, 122, 123, 127
  break-even point 122–4, 123
  and contribution 121–2
  and market research 128
  uses 121
break-even charts 123–8
  drawing-up 123–6, *124*, 125, 126
  margin of safety 128
  reading 126–8, 127
break-even output 121, 122, 123, 127
break-even point 122–4, *123*
Brin, Sergey 25
Brintons 246
British Airways 45, 50, 161
Bryant Homes 93
BS 5750 260, **260**
budget-holders 150, **150**
budgets 117, 148–59, *154*
  advantages/disadvantages 153–4
  creation 150, *150*
  definition 149, 149
  delegated budgets 150, **150**, 153, 161
  and fund allocation 154
  for marketing 99

monitoring (variance analysis) 152–3, *152*, **152**, *153*
production/expenditure budgets 149, 150, 151
sales budgets 150, 151
setting 150–1, *151*
short-term v long-term planning 154
uses 150
buffer stocks 244, **244**
Burger King 11
business aims 30–2
business cycles 282–7, *282*, *284*, 290
booms 283, **283**, *285*, 286, 299, 303
and demand 285–6, *286*
downswings 283, **283**, 285–6, *285*
and government policy 286, *287*
impact 285, *285*
recoveries/upswings 283, *285*
slumps 283, **283**, *285*, 286
business goals 30
business ideas 8–13, *13*
protection 12–13
business objectives 16, 30–8
and business strategy 44–5, *45*
definition 32
long-term 35–6
and management 211, 215–17, *216*
and organisational structure 176–7
and price 92
purpose 36, *36*
short-term 35–6
SMART objectives 32, 33
and teamworking 217
business planning 105
business plans 15–16
business sectors 6, 293
business strategy 44–56
and business objectives 44–5, *45*
definition 44, **44**

devising 45
influences on 46–7, *46*
and organisational structure 176–7
SWOT analysis 47–50, **48**
types of 46–7
businesses
see also start-up
definition 5–7
impact of inflation on 301–2
and interest rates 290–1
and the law 306–16
and stakeholders 39–44
strengths 46, 47, 48, 49, 50, 78
types 6, 21–30
and unemployment 303–4
weaknesses 46, 47, 48, 49, 50

CAD *see* Computer Aided Design
Cadbury Schweppes 7, 171, 194
Cage, John 13
Calderwood Zoo 141
Caledonian McBride 194
CAM *see* Computer Aided Manufacture
capacity 83–4, **84**, 236, **236**, 241
shortages 280–1
capacity utilisation 83–4, **84**, 240, 280–1, 282
capital
share/equity 144–5
working 137
capital intensive processes **233**, 238
car industry 49, 70, *71*, 72
carpet industry 246
Carphone Warehouse 75
carterls **279**, 281
'cash cows' 87, 88
cash flow 15
definition 131, **131**
graphs *132*
management 131–40
methods of improving 137–8
and product life cycle 84

and profit 131
and sources of finance 141, 143
cash flow forecasting 131–40, **131**
case study 133–7, *135*, *137*
cash in 133
cash out 133
causes of cash flow problems 136
construction 133–7, *133*, *134*, *135*, *137*
monitoring cash flow 136
net monthly cash flow 133, 134
uses 131–2
cash sales 133, 134
cell production 265–6, **266**
CenterParcs 269
centralisation 172, 173
chain of command 170, **170**
chocolate confectionery market 70
Christmas Day (Trading) Act 2004 307
civil law *307*
Co-Operative Bank 42, 322–3
coal mining 302
Cobra beer 47
Coca Cola 86, 87, 106
collateral 14, 143, 144
collective bargaining **195**
collusion 279, 281
Common Law 306, 307
communication 234
and diseconomies of scale 239
skills 213
communications technologies 325–6
communities 39, 40, 41, 319–20
companies 22–8, **22**
see also private limited companies; public limited companies
advantages of being *23*
disadvantages of being *23*
ownership 22, *22*, 23, 26, 27–8

Companies House 22
company accounts 23
company orientation 58–9, *59*
competition 277, 278–81
    and business strategy 47
    and capacity utilisation 280–1
    classification 278–80, *279*
    fair 281–2
    and inflation 301
    and market size 68
    and marketing strategy 78
    monopolies 280, **280**
    and niche marketing 75
    oligopolies 279, **280**
    and operations management
        227–8, *228*
    perfect 278–9, **280**
    policy 308–10, *308*
    and price 92, 94
    and production 234
    and social responsibility 320
    threat of new 49
    unfair 281–2, 308
Competition Acts (1980, 1998)
    310
Competition Commission 282,
    308, 309, 310
competitive advantage 146, 301,
    314
competitive pricing 94
components 243
Computer Aided Design (CAD)
    234, *326*, **327**
Computer Aided Manufacture
    (CAM) 234, *326*, **327**
Computer Aided Process
    Planning *326*
confidence level 64, **64**
construction industry 286, *286*
consultation 218, **218**
Consumer Credit Act (1974)
    311
consumer goods 97
consumer movement 311
Consumer Price Index (CPI)
    298–9, *298, 299*, **299**
consumer protection 310–12

Consumer Protection Act (1987)
    311
consumer spending, and interest
    rates 290, 291, 293, 301
consumerism 311–12, **311**
consumers
    characteristics 71
    difference from the customer
        102
    and inflation 300
    motivations 71–2
Consumers' Association 311
contribution 121–2, *122*, **122**
contribution pricing 95
control
    and diseconomies of scale 239
    and distribution 97
    divorce between ownership
        and 27–8
    span of 170, **170**, 171, *171*,
        172
convenience items 97, 102, 106
coordination problems, and
        diseconomies of scale 239
copyright **12**, 13
corporate image 26, 181, 317,
    320
Corus 195
cost centres 158–64, *158*, **158**
cost plus pricing 94, 95, 117
cost-push inflation 299–300,
    300
costs 8, 114–18
    associated 158
    and budgets 149, 150, 151,
        152, 153
    and capacity 236
    and cost centres 158, 159,
        161
    definition 114
    direct 117
    and diseconomies of scale 239
    and distribution 97
    and economies of scale 237,
        239
    fixed 95, 114–15, **114**, *115*,
        116–17, *117*, 121–4,
        124, 126, 127

high 48
    indirect (overheads) 117, 290
    opportunity 117, 244
    and organisational structure
        170
    and price elasticity of demand
        106
    and profit centres 158, 162
    reasons for calculating 117–18
    semi-variable 116
    of social responsibility 320
    of technological change 328
    total **114**, 116, 117, *117*, 124,
        125, 127, *127*, 239
    unexpected 136
    unit 84, 92, 93, 226–7, *227*,
        237, 239, 241, 253
    variable 95, 114–17, **114**,
        115, 117, 121–4, *124*,
        126, *126, 127*, 128
counter-cyclical policies 286,
    287, 303
credit 290, 291
credit control 136
credit sales 133, 136, 137, 141,
    142
criminal law *307*
culture of the organisation 176,
    200
currency
    appreciation 293, **293**
    depreciation 293, **293**
    foreign 292–3
customer service 181
customers
    ability to delight 57
    difference from the consumer
        102
    external 261, **262**
    internal 60, 261, **262**
    loyalty 15
    needs 8–10, 16, 57, 58, 60
    of niche markets 75
    wants 8–10

debentures 145
debt factoring *137*, 138, 142–3
decentralisation 172–3

delayering 171–2, *172*
delegated budgets 150, **150**, 153, 161
delegated legislation **314**
delegation 161, **173**, 213, 218, *218*
Dell 160, 247, 266
Dell, Michael 160
demand 8, 10, 11
   see also elasticity of demand
   and the business cycle 285–6, *286*
   and interest rates 291
   prediction 265
   and price 92
   and share price 24
   and stock control 249
demand-pull inflation 299, 300, **300**, 301
Deming, W. Edwards 261
democratic/participative leadership 213–14, 215, 218, 269–70
Department for Education and Employment (DfEE) 207
depreciation (currency) 293, **293**
design
   see also Computer Aided Design
   product 99, *100*, 262–3
desk research *see* secondary research
determinism 85
direct mail 99, *100*
directors 27–8
Disability Discrimination Act (1995) 313
diseconomies of scale **237**, 239, *240*, 241
distribution 96–8
distribution channels 96–7, *96*, 98
   one level channels 96, *96*
   two level channels 96, *96*
   zero level channels 96, *96*
distribution networks 48
distribution targets 98
diversification **44**, 45, 77

dividends 27, 28, 118, 119, 145
   definition 23, **23**
   fixed 144
   and profit reinvestment 144
division of labour 181–2, **181**
Doc Martens 82
'dogs' 87–8
down time 232
downswings, economic 283, **283**, 285–6, 285
Drucker, Peter 215, 216–17
Dunstone, Charles 75
Dyson, James 17

e-commerce 48, 51, 101, 248, 278, 325, 328
Ebookers 160
economic activity 283, **283**, 290
economic change 48–9
economies of scale 237–9, **237**, *240*, 241
   purchasing economies 237–8
   and specialisation 237
   technical 237
EGM *see* Extraordinary General Meeting
elasticity of demand 104–10
   calculation 105, 107
   income elastic 104, 105, 107, 108
   price elastic 104, 105–6, *105*, 107–8
   problems with 108
email 325, 326, 329
employees 48
   appraisal schemes 194
   empowerment 198–9, **199**
   and Just in Time production 247–9
   and lean production 269–70
   motivation 153, 154, 181, 254–5, 266
   multi-skilled 270
   needs 184, 185–6, 186, 187–8, *188*, 199–200
   and responsibly 161
   as stakeholders 39, 40, 41
   welfare 32, 34

employers, and employee motivation 181
employment, and technological change 329
Employment Acts
   (1980) 313
   (1982) 313
   (1989) 312
   (2002) 306
employment agencies 207
employment protection 312–13, *312*, 314
   collective *312*, 313, 314
   individual 312–13, *312*
Employment Relations Act (1999) 313
empowerment, employee 198–9, **199**
Enterprise Grants 145
Enterprise Zones 145
entrepreneurial structures 175, *175*
entrepreneurs 26
environmental audits 320
environmental issues 40, 41, 49, 320, 322
equity capital 144–5
ethical codes of practice 321–2, **321**
ethical stance **321**
ethics *312*, 317, 321–3
   and decision-making 321
   and profits 322–3
euro 51, 106, 293, 294–5
European Single Market 280
European Structural Funds 145
European Union (EU) 51, 115, 145, 146, 202, 260, 280, 281–2, 299, 308, 310
   directives (framework laws) 306, 307, **308**
evaluation skills 2, 3
examinations 2–4
   marks schemes 2–4
   preparation 4
   reading the question 4
   timing 4

exchange rates 48–9, 291–5, **292**, *294*
  and interest rates 291–2, *292*
expenditure/production budgets 149, 150, 151
experiments 64
exports 293
extended warranties 309
extension strategies 82, *83*, **83**
external influences 16–7, 48–9, 277–336
  business cycles 282–7
  competition 277, 278–81
  ethics 317, 321–3
  exchange rates 291–5
  inflation 298–302
  interest rates 289–92
  legal issues 306–16
  markets 277–81
  social responsibility 317–30
  unemployment 302–6
extractive industries 6
extranets 325–6, **327**
Extraordinary General Meeting (EGM) 27–8

Fair Trading Act (1973) 309, 310
Farmer, Sir Tom 41
Fay, Chris 319
field research *see* primary research
finance
see also accounting and finance
  long-term 143–6
  medium-term 143
  short-term 141–3
  sources of 13–14, *14*, 21–2, 141–9, **146**
  start-up 13–14, 14, 21–2
financial control 153
financial planning 150
finished goods 243
fixed costs 95, 117, *117*
  and break-even analysis 122, 123, 124, *124, 126, 127*
  and contribution 121–2
  definition 114–15, **114**, *115*
  and prices 116

flat organisations 170–1, *171*, 175
flotation 25, **25**, 26, 27
Ford 234
foreign currency 292–3
Friedman, Milton 319
fringe benefits (perks) 193, **193**
fund allocation 154

games consoles market 81, *81*
Gates, Bill 214
GDP *see* Gross Domestic Product
gender, market segmentation by 70
General Electric (GE) 49
Gilbertson, Brian 213
Gillette 69
Glasgow Zoo 141
globalisation 45
goods **5**, 11
see also stocks
  consumer goods 97
  convenience items 97, 102, 106
  finished goods 243
  industrial goods 97
  inferior goods 107
  and price elasticity of demand 106
  shopping goods 95, 102, 106
  works in progress (unfinished goods) 243
Google 25
government 40
  and the business cycle 286, *287*
  grants 145, *145*
  and inflation 301
  and new businesses 16
  organisations owned by 33
  publications 65
  support for training 208, 218
grants 145, *145*
greeting card market 71
Gross Domestic Product (GDP) 282–5, **283**, *284*, 286
growth 32, 33, 35

Guardian newspaper 10

Haberman, Mandy 12
Hawthorne effect 184
headhunting 205–7
Health and Safety at Work Act (1974) 314
Health and Safety Executive (HSE) 314
health and safety legislation 314
Hellewell, Rick 8
Herzberg, Frederick 185, 186–8, *187, 188*, 191, *192*, 195, 197, 199, 215, *216*
hierarchies, formal/traditional 173, *174*
holiday policies 198
home working 185
Honda 267
human resource management (HRM) 202–11
  definition 202–3, **202**
  developing the workforce 204–8, *204*
  and operations management 228–9
  planning the workforce 203, *204*
hygiene (maintenance) factors 186–7, *187*, 199

IBM 195
Ibuka, Masuru 77
ideas, business 8–13, *13*
image
  corporate 26, 181, 317, 320
  product 82
imported inflation 300
imports 293
income, market segmentation by 70
income elasticity of demand 104, 105, 107, 108
incorporation 22
induction training 208
industrial goods 97
industrial relations 312, **312**
inferior goods 107

inflation 283, 298–302, *298*
    cost-push 299–300, **300**
    definition 298, **298**
    demand-pull 299, 300, **300**,
        301
    and expectations 300–1, 302
    impact on businesses 301–2
    imported 300
    and interest rates 283, 301
    measurement 298–9
informal organisational structures
    175–6, *176*, 177
information technology 65
innocent drinks 9
inputs 5, 6, 7, 253
insolvency 16, 283
integration 229
Intel 86
interest rates 14, 145, 289–92,
    290
    base rate 289
    and businesses 290–1
    and consumer spending 290,
        291, 293
    and demand 291
    and exchange rates 291–2,
        292
    fixed 143
    and inflation 283, 301
    reductions 286
    rises 286
    variable 143
internal customers 60
internal environment 16–7, 48
Internet 101, 325, 328
    see also e-commerce
    and competitive pricing 94
    and distribution 98
    and piecework pay 192
    and the price elasticity of
        demand 106
    and secondary research 65
intranets **327**
Invest UK 146
investment 14, 291
    and interest rates 301
    international 291–2
investors 40

Investors in People scheme 208
ISO 9000 260, **260**

J Sainsbury plc 31, 32
`Japanese approach to
    production' 199
Japanese business techniques 48,
    199, 217
    business objectives 33, 35
    human resource management
        202, 204
    lean production 265
    quality management 262
JCB 27
job advertisements 206
job centres 207
job descriptions 204–5, **205**
job design 197, **197**
job enlargement (horizontal
    loading) 198, *198*, **198**
job enrichment (vertical loading)
    197, **197**
job insecurity 329
job interviews 207, 208
job rotation 198
John Lewis Partnership 40, 42,
    94, 119, 184, 199
Just in Time (JIT) production
    246–9, **247**, *249*, 267

kaizen **217**, 262, 263
Kwik Fit 41

labour
    see also human resource
        management
    costs 117
    flexibility 247–9
labour intensive processes **233**
labour market, failure of 209
labour turnover **205**, 213
Lands' End 97
lead time 244, **244**
leadership 211–20, **211**
    authoritarian/autocratic
        212–13, *212*, 215, 269
    and consultation 218
    and delegation 218

democratic/participative
    213–14, 215, 218,
    269–70
duties 211
paternalistic 213, 218
qualities 211–12
single status 217, **218**
styles 200, 212–14, *212*
team-based 217
Theory X and Y leaders
    214–15, *215, 216*
lean production 171, 247,
    265–3, *271*
    benchmarking 268–9, *269*,
        269
    cell production 265–6, **266**
    definition 265, 265
    and people 269–70
    team-based production 266–7
leasing 143
legislation 49, 306–16
    competition policy 308–10
    consumer protection 310–12
    defining the law 306
    delegated **314**
    employment protection
        312–13, 314
    health and safety 314
    and inflation 301–2
    sources of law 306–7
Lego 31, 50
levels of hierarchy 170–1, **170**,
    171
liability
    limited 23
    unlimited 22, **22**
limited companies *see* private
        limited companies; public
        limited companies
limited liability 23
Lloyd Weber, Andrew 26
Lloyds TSB 178
loans
    see also debentures; overdrafts
    and cash flow forecasting
        131–2
    from banks 14, 22, 121,
        131–2, 143, 290

from family and friends
13–14, 22
large 48
local business
and cost/profit centres 161
as stakeholders 39
local communities 39, 40, 41,
319–20
location of business 14, 91, 96–8
loss leaders 95
loyalty cards 65
luxury products 291

McDonald's 31
McGregor, Douglas 214–15
machinery, and productivity 253
magazines 65
mailshots 99
management 6, 7, 7, 27–8,
211–20
and authority 169
use of budgets 151, 153, 154
and business aims 31
and business objectives 35, 36
and capacity levels 236
and consultation 218
use of cost centres 159, 160
and decentralisation 173
definition 211, **211**
and delayering 171
duties 211
and ethical behaviour 323
and lean production systems
269–70
and motivation 181–2, 185,
186, 187–8, 200
and organisational structure
173
people-centred 269
use of the product life cycle
model 85
use of profit centres 162
and public limited companies
26
qualities of 211–12
and responsibility 169
and short-term objectives 35
single status 217, **218**

and social responsibility 317,
319
and the span of control 171
and stakeholders v
shareholders 41
styles 212–14, *212*, 269–70
use of SWOT analysis 49, 50
Theory X and Y leaders
214–15, *215, 216*
management by objectives
(MBO) 215–17, *216*
management teams 199
manufacturing 6, 234, 326–7
margin of safety 128, **128**
market analysis 57, 68–73, **69**
market capitalisation **24**
market coverage 97
market development 76, 77
market failure 282
market orientation 58, *59*, **59**
market penetration 76, 76
market research 8–10, **10**, 16,
57, 62–7, **62**
and break-even analysis 128
definition 62–4
primary research **10**, 63–5,
63, **63**, *64*
and quality 258, *259*, 262
secondary research **10**, 63–4,
63, **63**, 65
types 63–5, *63*
usefulness 66
uses 62–3, *63*
market segments 68–72, **69**
market share 33, 68
calculation 69
relative 87–8
market size 68, **69**, 277
marketing 57–113
budgets 99
and company orientation
58–9, *59*
definition 57–62, *58*, **58**
and elasticity of demand
104–10
market analysis 68–73
market research 62–7

and operations management
228
and portfolio analysis 80,
86–8, **86**
process 57–8, *58*
and product life cycle 80–6,
80, 88
and value added 59–60
marketing mix 57, 91–104, *92*,
240
7 Ps 101–2, *101*
definition 91, **91**
integration 100–2, *101*
people 101
physical environment 101–2
place 91, 96–8
price 91, 92–6, 101
process 102
product 91, 99–100
promotion 91, 98–9, *99, 100*
marketing objectives 74, *74*, **74**,
78
marketing strategies 57, 74–80,
74, **74**
influences on 78, *78*
types 74–7
marketing tactics 74, *74*, **74**
markets 277–81
and business strategy 47
and capacity utilisation
280–1, 282
classification 278–80, *279*
definition 58, 277
new 48
non-geographical 278
traditional, geographical 277
Marks & Spencer 7, 48, 119,
184, 194, 197
Mars 24, 26, 259
Maslow, Abraham 185–6,
187–8, *188, 192*, 195,
199–200, 215, *216*
mass markets
marketing 46, 74, 76
production techniques 181–2,
183
strategies 46

matrix structures 173–5, *174,* *175,* 177
Mayo, Elton 184–5
MBO *see* management by objectives
mergers 279, 308–9
Microsoft 6, 7, 31, 48, 60, 86, 144, 214
Millennium Dome 66
minimum wage 192–3, *193,* 313
Miss Attitude 15
mission statements 30–1, **30,** 32
mobile phones 325, 328
Monetary Policy Committee (MPC) 289–90
money, as motivator 182, 183, 191–7, 214
monopolies 280, **280,** 282, 308–9, 310
Monopolies and Mergers Commission 309
Morgan Motor Company *236,* 237
Morita, Akio 77
mortgages 144, 290
motivation 214–15
  benefits 180, 181
  and budgets 153, 154
  and business objectives 36
  and cell production 266
  consumer 71–2
  and cost/profit centres 160, 161
  definition 180–1, **180**
  and diseconomies of scale 239
  employee 153, 154, 181, 254–5, 266
  Human Relations School *181,* 184–5
  monetary forms 191–7
  most effective motivators 200
  Neo-human Relations School of Management *181,* 185–8
  non-monetary forms 197–200
  in practice 191–102
  and productivity 180, *180,* 183, 184, 227, 254–5

School of Scientific Management 181–4, *181*
  theories of 180–91, *181*
Mouncey Engineering 162
music industry 325

NASA 31
National Health Service (NHS) 6, 205, 207
National Minimum Wage Act (1998) 313
needs
  basic 186
  customer 8–10, 16, 57, 58, 60
  employee 184, 185–6, *186,* 187–8, *188,* 199–200
  hierarchy of 185–6, *186,* 187–8, *188*
  social 184
New Deal 207, 208
newspapers 65
niche markets 46, 74, 75
Nike 31
Nissan 254
non-profit making organisations 33, 119, *146*
Northern Rock 319–20
nuts and bolts market 228

objectives *see* business objectives; marketing objectives
observation 64
off-shoring 178
off-the-job training 208
Office of Fair Trading (OFT) 309, **309,** 310
Office of National Statistics (ONS) 10, 301
OFTEL 309
OFWAT 309
oligopolies 279, **280**
on-the-job training 208
ONS *see* Office of National Statistics
operations management 226–76
  competitiveness 227–8, *228*
  definition 226–31

human resources 228–9
  integration 229
  lean production 265–3
  marketing 228
  production 229
  productivity 226–7, 253–8
  quality 258–64
  scale of production 236–43
  stock control 243–52
  types of production 231–6, *231*
operations managers 253
opportunities 47, 48, 50, 78
opportunity costs 117, 244
oral hygiene market 70, 71
organisational charts 169, *169,* **170**
organisational culture 176, 200
organisational structure 169–80
  and cost/profit centres 159–60
  definition 169
  influences on 176–7
  key issues 170–3
  and management 211
  types 174–6
output *5,* 6, 7, 236–7, 241
  per machine 253
  per worker 253, 256
  and productivity 253, 255
  and sales 255
Ovenu 8
overdrafts **133,** 135, 138, 141–2, *142*
overheads 117, 290
overproduction 265
overseas trade 291
overtime 192
overtrading 136
Owen, Robert 184
owners, and business aims 31
ownership, company 22, *22,* 23, 26
  divorce from control 27–8
Oxfam 31, 35

Page, Larry 25
partnerships *146*

patents **12**, 13, 94
Patents Office 12, 13
paternalistic leadership 213, 218
penetration pricing 93–4
pensions 290
people (part of marketing mix) 101
people-centred management 269
percentages 107
perfect competition 278–9, **280**
performance 160
performance-related pay (PRP) 193–5, **193**, *194*
perks 193, **193**
person specifications (job specifications) 204–5, **205**
personal selling 98, *100*
personnel departments 184
personnel management 202, **202**
Philidas 228
Philip Electronics Group 194
physical environment 101–2
piecework pay 183, 191–2, *192*, **193**
Pilkington's 78
Pirelli 233
place 14, 91, 96–8
poaching 209
pollution 282
population, ageing 290
portfolio analysis 80, 86–8, **86**
Post Office 281, 325, *326*
Postcomm 281
pound, value of 291–2, *292*, 293, 294, *294*
predator pricing 94
price 10, 91, 92–6, 101
    and break-even analysis 122
    and cost 116, 117–18
    and economies of scale 239
    influences on 92–3, *93*
    pricing methods 94–5
    pricing strategies 93–4, *94*
    pricing tactics 95
    and profit margins 118
    reductions 82
    and the rest of the marketing mix 93, 95

and revenue 118
setting 159
shares 24, 26, 28
price discrimination 95
price elasticity of demand 104, 105–6, *105*, 118, 294
    calculation 105, 107–8
    influences on 106
    price elastic demand 105, 106
    price inelastic demand 105, 106, 108
    and profit 106
    and revenue 106
price leadership 94
price skimming 94, 327
price taking 94
price wars 45
primary research 63–5, *63*, **63**, 64, 66
primary sector businesses 6
private limited companies 21, **24**, 24, 26, 28
    sources of finance *146*
'problem children' ('question marks') 87, 88
process (part of marketing mix) 102
product **5**, 8, 10, 11, 91, 99–100
    availability 106
    design 99, *100*, 262–3
    development *76*, 77
    failure 86
    lack of new 48
    and organisational structure 176
    and price elasticity of demand 106
    promotion 99
    v brand 106
product differentiation **76**
product image 82
product launch 83–4
product life cycle 80–6, *80*, 88
    capacity utilisation 83–4, **84**
    cash flow 84
    criticisms of 85–6
    decline 81–2
    extension strategies 82, *83*, **83**

growth 81, 85
introduction 80–1
maturity/saturation 81, 84, 85, 92
and price 92
product launch 83–4
and the promotional mix 99
research and development 80
value 85
product orientation 58–9, *59*, **59**
production
    see also lean production
    batch production 231, 232, *233*, 234
    and competitiveness 234
    flow production 231, 232–3, *233*, 234
    future of 234
    job production 231, *233*, 234
    and operations management 229
    scale of 236–43
    types of 231–6, *231*, *233*
production budgets 149, 150, 151
production teams 199
productivity **180**, 218, 226–7, 253–8
    measurement of 253, 255
    and motivation 180, *180*, 183, 184
    v output 255
    v quality 255
Professional Researcher 177
profit 8, **30**, 114, 118–19
    and break-even analysis 121, 123, 127–8
    as business aim 30
    as business objective 32, 33, *33*, 35
    calculation 118
    and cash flow 131
    definition **106**
    distributed 118–19
    and ethics 322–3
    importance 119
    and price elasticity of demand 106

reinvestment 143–4
  undistributed 118
profit centres 158–64, *158*, **158**, *159*
profit margins 118
profit sharing 195–6
promotion 91, 98–9, *99, 100*, 240
  informative 98
  persuasive 98
promotional mix 99, *99*
promotional offers 82
Property Search Agency 270
PRP see performance-related pay
psychological pricing 95
psychometric tests 207, 208
public limited companies 21, 24, **24**, 25–8
  advantages of 25–6, *26*
  becoming 25–6
  disadvantages of 26, *26*
  ownership and control 27–8
  sources of finance 145, *146*
public relations (PR) 98, *100*
purchase occasions, market segmentation by 71
purchasing economies 237–8

qualitative research 65
quality 258–64, **258**, *259*
  and employee motivation 181
  v productivity 255
quality assurance 259–60, **259**
quality awards 260
quality circles 199, **217**, 270
quality control 259–60, **259**
quality targets 260
quantitative research 65
'question marks' ('problem children') 87, 88

Race Relations Act (1976) 313
radio 75
rationalisation 240, **241**
raw materials 243, 293–4
Reckitt Benckiser 262
recoveries/upswings, economic 283, *285*

recruitment agencies 207
recruitment and selection 40, 203, 204–8, *204*, **205**
  external recruitment 205–8, **205**
  internal recruitment 205, **205**
  training **205**, 208–9, *209*
redeployment **203**
redundancy **203**, 329
Reed, Richard 9
remortgages 144
reputations, corporate 317
research, advice for students 2
research and development 80, 99, 328
resources 6
responsibility 161, 169, **169**, 197, 266
restrictive practices 308, 309, **309**, 310
Restrictive Practices Acts (1956, 1968, 1976) 310
Retail Price Index (RPI) 298–9, *298*
retail sector 39, 96, 293
revenue **106**, 114, **114**, 118
  and break-even analysis 123–4, 125–6, *125, 126*, 127, *127*
  and budgets 149, 151, 152, 153, 154
  calculation 11, 118
  and contribution 121
  and cost centres 158
  and price 118
  and price elasticity of demand 106
  and profit centres 158
risk 244
Roddck, Anita 322
role-playing 208
Rover 266
Royal College of Nursing (RCN) 207
Royal Mail 281
royalties 13
Ryanair 6, 295

salaries 192
Sale of Goods Act (1979) 311
sale and leaseback 138
sales
  increasing as marketing objective 74
  v output 255
  volume/amount of 118
sales budgets 150, 151
sales credit 133, 136, 137, 141, 142
sales promotions 98, *100*
sales revenue *see* revenue
sampling 64, **64**
  quota 64, **65**
  random 64, **65**
  savings 290
Schick 69
schools of thought 181–8, **182**
seasonal markets 83, 88
secondary research 63–4, *63*, **63**, 65
secondary sector businesses 6
Selective Regional Assistance 145
self-checking 259
service economies **5**, 6, 8, 11, 229
Sex Discrimination Acts (1975, 1986) 312
share capital 144–5
share ownership 196, *197*
shareholder concept 317, *318*
shareholders 22–3, **23**, 24, 27–8, 144–5
  and profit 118–19, 144
  and short-term objectives 35
  v stakeholders 41–2
  voting rights 23
shares 22, 22, 23, 24, 25–6, 145
  definition 144
  flotation 25, 26
  ordinary 144, **144**
  preference 144
  price 24, 26, 28
Shell 39, 317, 319
shop-floor employees 169
shopping goods 95, 102, 106
simulations 208

Singh, Reuben 15
single currency 51, 294–5
single status 217, **218**
size of the business 6, 176, 241
skilled workers 176
skills audits 203
slumps, economic 283, **283**, *285*, 286
small firms 290
Smart cars 100, 125
SMART objectives 32, *33*, 74
social audits 320, **320**
Social Chapter 307, **308**
social considerations 32, 34
social needs, employee 184
social responsibility 317–30
    communities 319–20
    environmental work 320
    information provision 319
    voluntary work 320
socio-economic group, market segmentation by 70
sole traders 21–2
    advantages of being 21, *22*
    disadvantages of being 21–2, *22*
    qualities 21
    sources of finance *146*
Somerfield 45
Sony 77, 81, 86, 96, 203, 227
span of control 170, **170**, 171, *172*
    broad 171, *171*
    narrow 171, *171*
specialisation 237
spreadsheets 136
stakeholder concept 317, *317*, *318*
stakeholders 39–44, *41*
    and business success 39–41, *39*
    definition 39
    interests 317, *318*
    v shareholders 41–2
Starbucks *161*
'stars' 87, 88
start-up 5–20
    business ideas 8–13, *13*

business plans 15–16, **16**
    finances 13–14, *14*, 21–2
    first few years 15
    siting a business 14
    sole traders 21
    survival rates 16
statute law 306
steel industry 238
StemCell Technologies Inc 206
stock control 243–52, *244*
Stock Exchange 24, 25, 145
stock rotation 246
stocks 243–4
    buffer stocks 244, **244**
    and interest rates 291
    and lean production 265
    maximum stock 245
    running out of *245*
store cards 65
strategies *see* business strategy; marketing strategies
strengths of a business 46, 47, 48, 49, 50, 78
sub-contracting 240, **241**
Sunny Delight 85
suppliers
    and Just in Time production 247, 249
    and lead time 244
    reliability 244
    as stakeholders 39, 40, 41
surveys 64
SWOT analysis 47–50, **48**

takeovers **24**, 308
tall organisations 170, *171*, 173
Taylor, Frederick Winslow 182–4, *192*, 195, 212
Taylorism 182–4, *183*
team-based leadership 217
team-based production 266–7
teamworking 184, 185, 199–200
    see also cell production
technical economies of scale 237
technological development 48, 65, 203, 234, 253, 325–31
tertiary sector businesses 6, 293

Tesco 6, 31, 45, 46, 96, 196, 265, 308, 327–8
Thames Water 319
Theory X and Y leaders 214–15, *215, 216*
threats 47, 48, 50
time, and price elasticity of demand 106
time and motion studies (work studies) *181*, **182**
Tomkins 169
toothpaste market 70
total costs **114**, 116, 117, *117*, 239
    and break-even analysis 124, *125*, 127, *127*
total quality management (TQM) 260–2, **262**
trade credit 133, 136, 137, 141, 142
Trade Descriptions Act (1968) 311
Trade Union Act (1984) 313
Trade Union Reform and Employment Rights Act (1993) 313
trade unions 188, 300, 301–2, **312**, 312, 314
trademarks 13, 94
training **205**, 207, 208–9, *209*, 218
    for budget management 154
    government support for 208, 218
    induction training 208
    for Just in Time production 249
    for lean production systems 270
    off-the-job training 208
    on-the-job training 208
    and productivity 253
trait theory 211
transformation process 5, *5*, 6, 7
transportation 265
Treaty of Maastricht 307
trust breaks 198
turnover *see* revenue

TV guide market 93–4
two-factor theory of motivation
    186–8, *187, 188*
types of business 6, 21–30

UK Mail 281
unemployment 302–6
    and businesses 303–4
    cyclical 303–4, **303**
    frictional 303, **303**
    structural 302–3, *302, 303,*
        303, 304
    and technological change 329
Unilever 30, 45
unique selling proposition/point
    (USP) 11, 16, 76, 100,
    231, 323
unit cost 84, 226–7, *227*, **237**,
    239, 241
    and price 92, 93
    and productivity 253
unlimited liability 22, **22**
usage rate, market segmentation
    by 70–1

value **59**
value added 5, 6, 59–60
values 321
variable costs 95, 117, *117*

and break-even analysis 122,
    123, 124, *124*, 126, *126,*
    127, 128
and contribution 121
definition 114, **114**, 115–16,
    115
variable pay 194–5, **195**
variance analysis 152–3, *152,*
    152
    adverse variances *152,* 153
    favourable variances *152,* 153
Vauxhall Motors 199
Vegetarian Shoes 76
Virgin 45, 135, 239
voluntary codes of practice 307,
    308
voluntary work 320
voting rights 23

Wage Councils 313
wages 192–3, *193,* 313
    rises 300, *300,* 301
Wal-Mart 49, 188, 277, 301,
    326
Walkers 78
Walton, Gregory 159
warehousing space 244
warranties, extended 309
washing powder market 70

watchdog organisations 309
weaknesses of a business 46, 47,
    48, 49, 50
Webb, Robin 76
Weights and Measures Act
    (1986) 311
Welch, Jack 49
Which? magazine 310, 311
Whirlpool 234
whisky 245
wholesalers 96
WHSmith's 33
working capital 137
working environment 186–7
working hours
    flexible 185
    and productivity 253
works in progress (unfinished
    goods) 243
World Wide Web 328
Wright, Jonathan 9
Wrigley Company 88, 227

Xerox 31, 50, 269

Yamaha 267

zero budgets 151, **151**
zero-allocation policy 198